THE PRINCE

THE TURBULENT REIGN OF
JUSTIN TRUDEAU

STEPHEN MAHER

PUBLISHED BY SIMON & SCHUSTER CANADA

New York   London   Toronto   Sydney   New Delhi

A Division of Simon & Schuster, LLC
166 King Street East, Suite 300
Toronto, Ontario M5A 1J3

This Simon & Schuster Canada edition May 2024

SIMON & SCHUSTER CANADA and colophon are registered trademarks of Simon & Schuster, LLC

Simon & Schuster: Celebrating 100 Years of Publishing in 2024

For information about special discounts for bulk purchases, please contact Simon & Schuster Special Sales at 1-800-268-3216 or CustomerService@simonandschuster.ca.

Interior design by Wendy Blum

Manufactured in the United States of America

1   3   5   7   9   10   8   6   4   2

Library and Archives Canada Cataloguing in Publication

Title: The prince : the turbulent reign of Justin Trudeau / by Stephen Maher.
Names: Maher, Stephen, 1965- author.
Description: Includes bibliographical references and index.
Identifiers: Canadiana (print) 20230583865 | Canadiana (ebook) 2023058389X |
ISBN 9781668024492 (hardcover) | ISBN 9781668024515 (EPUB)
Subjects: LCSH: Trudeau, Justin. | LCSH: Prime ministers—Canada—Biography. |
LCSH: Canada—Politics and government—21st century. |
CSH: Canada—Politics and government—2015-
Classification: LCC FC655 .M36 2024 | DDC 971.07/4—dc23

ISBN 978-1-6680-2449-2
ISBN 978-1-6680-2451-5 (ebook)

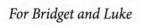
For Bridget and Luke

Nor do I wish it to be thought presumptuous that a man of low and humble condition like myself should presume to map out and direct the government of princes. But just as a cartographer will descend into the plains in order to study the nature of the mountains, and will then climb the highest peaks in order to study the low-lying land, so, too, only an exalted prince can grasp the nature of the people, and only a lesser man can perceive the nature of a prince.

Niccolò Machiavelli, *The Prince*

CONTENTS

BECAUSE IT'S 2015

On the morning of November 4, 2015, Canadian prime minister Justin Trudeau met with his senior staff in the Centre Block of Parliament Hill, the wood-panelled office he'd first visited when his father was the occupant. The scene was captured by the CBC's Peter Mansbridge and his crew, who had behind-the-scenes access for the big day.

Trudeau, ebullient and anxious to get started, sat in an armchair. Gerald Butts, his principal secretary, was on his right, and Katie Telford, his chief of staff, on the couch to his left. Beside her was Michael McNair, Trudeau's key policy advisor, with pen and notepad. They had been discussing the big event later that day: the swearing-in of Trudeau's first Cabinet.

"You've got a lot to talk about," Telford said. "Gender parity. You've got some historic . . . in terms of breaking ceilings and things, ministers and things. There's no statement earlier, so that is your opportunity to talk about that."

Kate Purchase, communications director, stood beside Butts. "That's one of the things I was going to raise about the scrum," she said. "Gender parity."

"Ah, that just frustrates me so much," said Trudeau, shaking his head. "Do people think they can still get away with the arguments they're making now against this?"

"Yeah," said Butts. "I think just calling people's attention to the year is all you need to say."

They had discussed this point before. Everyone agreed. They had a plan.

Trudeau delivered the line a few hours later, with a diverse and accomplished group of thirty people standing behind him in rows on the front steps of Rideau Hall. It was his new Cabinet, and it included fifteen women.

A gaggle of journalists was waiting behind a rope in the driveway. The first question was from Laurie Graham of the CBC: "Your Cabinet, you said, looks a lot like Canada. I understand one of the priorities for you was to have a Cabinet that was gender balanced. Why was that so important for you?"

Trudeau smiled and let loose the prepared response: "Because it's 2015."

It was perfect. The line made Trudeau a feminist darling around the world. He received global media coverage, all of it positive. Even Britain's stodgy conservative broadsheet the *Telegraph* ran an upbeat story, and progressives on the internet positively swooned. Jezebel tweeted: "The sexiest thing about Canadian PM Justin Trudeau is his Cabinet's gender parity." Actor Emma Watson was captivated: "Why a gender-balanced 50:50 government? 'Because it's 2015!' Coolest thing I've seen in a while. ♥ U Canada."

The new government felt like a breath of fresh air after years of Stephen Harper's grim warnings. Trudeau brought his beautiful young family to the ceremony and mingled with the crowd afterward for celebratory high fives and selfies. Trudeau was on the cusp of global stardom—a handsome, smiling prince, ready to lead Canadians away from the divisions of the Harper years toward a progressive future.

It is hard now, after all the difficulties Trudeau has faced in the years since—many of them brought on by his own mistakes—to recall the feeling of hope and optimism that he embodied at that moment. It was like the ending of a fairy tale. But this is the beginning, not the end, of the story, and not everything went as planned.

PART ONE

SON OF CANADA

2012–2016

There are fewer difficulties in holding hereditary states, and those long accustomed to the family of their prince, than new ones; for it is sufficient only not to transgress the customs of his ancestors, and to deal prudently with circumstances as they arise.

Niccolò Machiavelli, *The Prince*

1

FIGHTER

I didn't fully understand the Justin Trudeau phenomenon when I arrived in the Montreal riding of Papineau on October 2, 2012, to cover the launch of his campaign for the leadership of the Liberal Party of Canada for the *National Post*.

I knew Trudeau was a celebrity who attracted attention wherever he went, but I was skeptical about his political future. It was hard to take him entirely seriously in those days. He had great hair, a famous name, and a friendly, open way with people, but he had no particular accomplishments for the job. He made jokes that weren't funny, and when he talked about policy he often seemed like a poser, with convictions based on his own inclinations rather than a deep understanding of the issues. He looked like a charismatic lightweight, one of those characters who show up on the Hill, strut and fret for a season or two, and then wander off to a less demanding career. Politics, Max Weber wrote, is the "slow boring of hard boards." Trudeau didn't look like a slow borer of hard boards, unlike the other men he would face in Parliament if he won the leadership.

Stephen Harper, the incumbent Conservative prime minister, was an economist who had engineered the merger of the Canadian Alliance and the Progressive Conservatives. Through patience, ruthlessness, and guile, he had won three elections in a row—two minorities, in 2006 and 2008, and finally a majority in 2011. By the autumn of 2012, his government was fading in the polls, but he was *serious*. So was his chief tormentor, New Democratic Party leader Thomas Mulcair, a lawyer and former Quebec Liberal Cabinet minister who had been elected leader after the death of the popular Jack Layton. The interim leader of the Liberals, lawyer Bob Rae, the former NDP premier of Ontario and a talented off-the-cuff speaker with a deep understanding of Canadian politics, was of similar stature.

Trudeau, in contrast, was a former high-school teacher. He had never served as a minister and had made little impression in his four years sitting on the backbench amid the third party in the House of Commons. But there was more to him than his weak resumé. He was famous. In a Parliament of drudges, full of former mayors, car dealers, and immigration lawyers, Trudeau stood out like a red rose on a grey suit lapel. He was young and handsome. He wore flip-flops and skateboarded to the Hill. When he entered a room, people said, "Hey! There's Justin!"

I first met him in Darcy McGee's, an Irish pub on the corner of Sparks and Elgin Streets, before he was elected to Parliament in 2008. I was then Ottawa bureau chief for the Halifax *Chronicle Herald* and often went to Darcy's, a gathering place for political staffers, journalists, and lobbyists. Trudeau, who was known only as the flamboyant son of our former prime minister Pierre Trudeau, came in with his friend Gerry Butts, a hulking, bearded Cape Bretoner. I knew Trudeau was a quasi celebrity, and already there was speculation that he might one day run for office. A network of highly placed people associated with Trudeau *père* were rumoured to be waiting for the day when another Trudeau was ready to seek office.

I struck up a conversation with Justin and, at some point, mentioned his father in passing. "That's weird," I said. "I just realized I'm talking about your dad."

He looked at me, squaring his shoulders. "Oh," he said, "I never forget I'm a Trudeau." He looked confident, poised, his eyes fixed. *Huh*, I thought. *He's like a prince.*

Over the next couple of years, I had a few beers with him. He was friendly and chatty and, without making the slightest effort, was always the centre of attention. Almost everyone found it exciting to be around him. He has been famous since birth, the first child of Prime Minister Pierre Trudeau and the beautiful Margaret Sinclair. That was the X factor that made his candidacy remotely plausible, that made him a wild card entering the deck on that October day in 2012 when he took the stage in Papineau.

The speech he gave that night in Papineau did little to explain why he wanted to lead the party or why the party should lead the country. He praised Canada, the Liberal Party, progress, national unity, diversity, the environment, youth, and First Nations, and promised to work for the middle class. In the *Globe and Mail*, Daniel Leblanc described the speech as laying out an "ambitious but vague agenda." The only substantial point was his personal relationship to Canadians. "Think about it for a moment: when was the last time you had a leader you actually trusted? And not just the nebulous 'trust to govern competently' but . . . the way you trust a friend to pick up your kids from school, or a neighbour to keep your extra front door key? That's a respect that has to be earned, step by step." Trudeau argued that Canadians knew him. "I feel so privileged to have had the relationship I've had, all my life, with this country, with its land, and with its people," he said. "We've travelled many miles together, my friends. You have always been there for me."

Later I spoke with Butts, expressing mild skepticism about Trudeau. He laughed and assured me Trudeau's name recognition was likely "the highest for a leadership candidate in the history of the country." What I didn't know, but he did, was that Canadians wanted Trudeau to be prime minister. "The positive vibe that people have about him shows they're not satisfied with what they have in leadership and they're hoping for something more. In that sense, it has nothing to do with him and his personal attributes other than a kind of positive feeling they attribute to him. And our job, and his job, is to work our collective arses off to show people that he can be about something more."

Butts had already been working his arse off on the project. "The Trudeau organization starts with one person, Gerald Butts," says David Herle, a pollster and strategist Butts had recruited to the cause. Another insider called Butts the "mastermind" behind it all: "The thing that impressed me most about him was just his Rolodex. I've literally never seen anybody who was so good at accumulating friends and contacts, internationally, across the country, in this town, wherever. There's just one guy. He's got some kind of supernatural skill, finding powerful people and getting close with them."

"Gerry is my best friend," Trudeau told Leblanc in 2013. "He and I have been talking about the possibility and the potential of politics all my life."

Butts is the son of a coal miner and a nurse from Glace Bay, a gritty working-class town near Sydney, Nova Scotia. When he was eight, the coal mine blew up, killing ten men and throwing everyone else out of work. The steel industry in nearby Sydney was slowly dying, and the moratorium on cod fishing was undercutting the fish-processing industry. There were too many people and not enough jobs. Politically, the area has always been left wing, influenced by the Antigonish Movement—a Catholic social justice movement that encouraged poor workers to organize co-operatives and credit unions. It was a place of strident unionism, patronage politics, hard drinking, Export A cigarettes, Celtic music, and working-class solidarity. Rather than following his classmates to St. Francis Xavier University, in nearby Antigonish, Butts, a promising student, went to McGill to study physics. He changed gears eventually and studied literature, doing his thesis on James Joyce's *Ulysses*. In the debating club, he met Trudeau, who was then leery of introducing himself by his real name. He called himself Jason Tremblay and revealed his true identity only after he formed a favourable judgment of Butts. They bonded on the debating circuit, became fast friends.

After university, Butts cut his teeth working for Allan J. MacEachen, the Celtic Sphinx, a legendary Cape Breton political mastermind who helped engineer Pierre Trudeau's 1980 election victory. He did research for MacEachen's memoirs, which gave him insight into the history of the party. Angered by the Progressive Conservative government of Mike Harris in Ontario, Butts went to work for the provincial Liberals, eventually becoming principal secretary to Premier Dalton McGuinty, helping to engineer two election victories for him and developing a reputation for political acumen.

Butts and Trudeau had an unusually close relationship. "They didn't work together," says Herle. "They *were* together. They were friends, as thick as thieves, vacationed together, planned this project together."

———

JUSTIN PIERRE JAMES TRUDEAU was born on Christmas Day in 1971, less than a year after his father, Prime Minister Pierre Elliott Trudeau, married Margaret Sinclair, a "flower child" twenty-nine years his junior.* Although Justin grew up in the lap of luxury, with chauffeurs, servants, and global travel, his childhood was traumatic.

The Trudeaus lived at 24 Sussex Drive, the prime ministerial residence overlooking the Ottawa River. In 1973, Margaret gave birth to Alexandre "Sacha" Trudeau—another son born on Christmas Day—and in 1975 to Michel, who died tragically in an avalanche in British Columbia in 1998. The artistic and adventurous Margaret was then unaware she was suffering from bipolar disorder, a psychological condition that leads to manic episodes followed by paralyzing depression. She found life at the residence oppressive, and the marriage broke down in spectacular fashion in 1977.

On the night of her sixth wedding anniversary, Margaret showed up at

---

* John Diefenbaker remarked that Trudeau had two choices: to marry her or adopt her.

the legendary Toronto rock club El Mocambo with Ron Wood and Mick Jagger, where the Rolling Stones were about to take the stage for a two-night stand. Her appearance caused a sensation. The Stones were then long-haired bad boys, famous for their dedication to sex, drugs, and rock and roll. "I wouldn't want my wife associating with us," drummer Charlie Watts joked at the time. Tabloids feasted on the scandal, linking Margaret romantically to both Wood and Jagger, and she followed them to New York when they left town. At home in Canada, her husband stoically declined to comment.

The marriage ended within months, and the boys continued to live with Pierre. Margaret became a regular at New York disco Studio 54, dating Hollywood actors and self-medicating with alcohol and drugs, as she later recounted in three memoirs. She and Trudeau had terrible rows, particularly over money. Once when he refused to give her enough, she confronted him at home. After she threw herself at him and tried to scratch out his eyes, he pinned her to the ground, where she screamed and struggled until their young sons broke up the fight.

This kind of thing was terrible for the boys. In his memoir, *Common Ground*, released in 2014, Trudeau writes that he felt "a diminished sense of self-worth" because of his parents' split. He missed his mother terribly and would try to make special events of her visits. He prepared for one by cueing up a song his mother liked—"Open Arms" by Journey—on the tinny record player in his room. As she opened the front door, he cranked up the volume and shouted from the top of the stairs, "Listen, Mom, it's our song!" But she couldn't hear it, and his treat fell flat.

This sad anecdote is what sticks with the ghostwriter who put the story on paper, Toronto journalist Jonathan Kay. In the *Walrus* years later, Kay wrote that he was struck by Trudeau's childhood suffering, the extremity of which was still palpable years later as he interviewed him for the book. Trudeau is defined by "a need to deal with maternal rejection," which colours the views of those around him, who are aware of his traumatic childhood. "What good is the glitz of being a prime minister's son when you're living a childhood parched of mother's milk?"

Along with the trauma of his difficult childhood, his intimates think his role as a big brother is also significant. He was a leader in the family, trying to look after his younger brothers—and several stepsiblings—amid a complicated family life.

"Justin, 6, is a prince—a very good little boy," his mother said in an interview in 1977. "Sasha, born Christmas Day, 1973, is a bit of a revolutionary, very determined and strong-willed. Miche is a happy, well-adjusted child, who combined the best traits of both brothers."

In an interview in early 2024, Trudeau told me that his role within the family led him, ultimately, to politics. "When I was busy being big brother, eldest of a composite family, it was much more around making sure everyone played well or everyone had fun. That was my focus, and it was very much in the moment." He believes this focus helped him develop skills "around responsibility, conflict resolution, reading people, figuring out what they need as opposed to what they want." And in turn, those skills took him into the classroom. "Being the eldest led me to becoming a teacher, and that was the path I was on. This, for me, feels like a detour from teaching or a continuation of teaching . . . I'll always be a teacher. I just happen to be, like so many teachers, doing something different right now, but I'm still a teacher."

After Pierre left office in 1984, he moved with his sons to Montreal, to the stunning art deco Cormier House on Mont Royal. He enrolled Justin in Collège Jean-de-Brébeuf, the elite Jesuit school he himself had attended— as have most men who later became prominent Quebec politicians. Justin quickly developed a network of friends, mostly anglos, but he was tested by other students. In his memoir, he writes about one incident when a boy confronted him with an upskirt photograph of his mother, taken at Studio 54 and printed by an American pornographic magazine. He kept his cool, refusing the bully any satisfaction. "I learned at Brébeuf not to give people the emotional response they are looking for when they attack me person- ally. Needless to say, that skill has served me well over the years."

Justin fit in socially but did not excel academically. When he flunked a psychology class, his father showed him his own report cards from Brébeuf in the 1930s—"a straight line of As stretching from top to bottom." The exchange convinced Justin that he should follow his own path. If he worked hard, he decided, it would be for something important to him, not just a grade on a report card. He doesn't mention it in the book, but in a speech he once admitted to what he called a "slight learning disability"—dyscalculia, an inability to do mathematics in his head. Whatever the reason for his academic struggles, Justin did not do well. Everyone who has spent time with him remarks on his keen intelligence, although not everyone agrees that he has a focused, disciplined mind.

After Brébeuf, Justin graduated from McGill with a bachelor's degree in literature and from the University of British Columbia with a degree in education. Then he went backpacking in Africa and Asia, worked as a snowboard instructor and a bouncer, and eventually became a high-school teacher at a private school in Vancouver. He must have been seeking a different career path, however, because he started and abandoned two advanced degrees in the early 2000s.

Until he entered politics, Justin Trudeau had not distinguished himself except in ways connected to his family's celebrity. In 2000, when his father died, he delivered a nationally televised eulogy at the funeral, concluding in tears with the line "Je t'aime, Papa." Canadians found the eulogy touching, although critics in the media called it overwrought and sentimental—a pattern that has continued with Trudeau—with pundits sniffing at his emotional tone even as many voters find it sincere and affecting. In 2003, he was invited to be chair of the board of Katimavik, a national youth program started by his father. He promoted avalanche safety as a way of honouring the memory of his brother, acted in the TV movie *The Great War*, did some radio commentary, and drew big crowds on the speaking circuit. All along, he seems to have known he might end up in politics. "When it happens it will be in my own time," he informed Jonathon Gatehouse of *Maclean's* in 2002.

Years later, he told David Herle that politics was like an open door, waiting for him. "He said, so matter of factly . . . 'David, I've always known my whole life that this would be available to me if I want.'"

The remark is typical of Trudeau. He is aware of his privilege and open to discussing himself frankly. His father always presented a carefully composed mask to the world, maintaining an artful mystique that served him well in politics, never giving the public access to his inner life. Justin is better-looking than his father was but does not have his reserve. He also wears a mask, but it is simpler, projecting affability, empathy. Those emotions may be real, but his persona is a construction, something he has worked hard to develop. Early in life, he was forced to become hardened to the public gaze and has developed skin like a crocodile. He doesn't let haters get to him. He can guard his private feelings from the world, presenting a cheerful public face without revealing his inner life.

"I think Justin Trudeau is deeply unknowable," says one person who knows him and has studied him for years. "I think from a very early age he kind of sensed that anybody who wanted to get close to him was wanting to use him because of his name, and therefore he wears a mask. I think his affability is a mask. I think that he is a deeply guarded person who opens himself up to nobody. And I think that's why he likes to keep the same people around him."

People who socialized with Trudeau in his youth remember him as a playboy, a moderate drinker, a celebrity who was popular with women and caused scenes whenever he entered night clubs on boulevard Saint-Laurent in Montreal or Queen Street West in Toronto. He seems to have changed after he fell in love with the glamorous society reporter and personal shopper Sophie Grégoire, a vivacious and gracious person with a spiritual side. Grégoire had been one of Michel's childhood friends, with happy memories of pool parties at Trudeau's Montreal home. She charmed Trudeau when they co-hosted the 2003 Mercedes-Benz Grand Prix ball in Montreal, but when she emailed later to say hello, he didn't reply because he was in a "very socially active phase," he later told *Maclean's* Lianne George. At the end of that active summer, he ran into her on the street. He chased her down and asked her out. Their first date, at Khyber Pass, on Avenue Duluth, ended with an intensely emotional exchange of devotion. As Grégoire told *Vogue* later: "At the end of dinner he said, 'I'm 31 years old, and I've been waiting for you for 31 years.' And we both cried like babies." "I call him my prince," she told *Maclean's*, "because he treats me like a princess." They married in 2005. Several men who would later play an important role in his government served as groomsmen: Gerry Butts, Tom Pitfield, Marc Miller, and Seamus O'Regan.

In 2006, Tom Axworthy, who had been a key advisor to Trudeau's father, asked him to serve on a party renewal committee, which led him to mix for the first time with Liberals across the country. At the leadership convention that year to replace Paul Martin, Trudeau showed up in the entourage of Gerard Kennedy, a young and dashing former Ontario education minister. Trudeau gave the speech nominating him and thoroughly enjoyed himself. Butts had "never heard him this jazzed at anything" before, and he got the feeling "this guy's going to run for office." At the convention, however, Kennedy eventually threw his support behind Stéphane Dion, the donnish professor Jean Chrétien had raised to prominence in the aftermath of the 1995 Quebec referendum. With Chrétien's support, Dion pushed through the Clarity Act to establish rules for a sovereigntist referendum. Dion was a strong minister, but he had poor political instincts, as the party would learn before long.

Trudeau, raised at the heart of Canadian politics, knowledgeable about the country, desirous of public attention, with a hide as thick as a rhinoceros's, and no other appealing career prospects, was ready to enter the fray. He started by calling Dion to ask if he could run in the coming by-election in Outremont, one of the most desirable seats in Montreal for a star candidate. Dion hesitated, knowing that Trudeau was unpopular with Quebec Liberals. Among francophone nationalists, Pierre Trudeau is remembered as a despised centralizer, the icy figure who thwarted the ambitions of René Lévesque. "The entire Quebec wing of the party was against him," a senior Quebec Liberal told me later. "Nobody wanted the Trudeau name."

Instead of giving the opportunity to former astronaut Marc Garneau, a high-profile Liberal who had run unsuccessfully in Montreal in 2006, Dion gave the nomination to his friend Jocelyn Coulon, a University of Montreal professor without political experience. NDP leader Jack Layton, seeing an opportunity, sweet-talked Tom Mulcair, who had recently left Liberal premier Jean Charest's Cabinet in a snit, to stand. Mulcair agreed to become a New Democrat and won the by-election, giving the NDP its first real foothold in Quebec—and Dion an enormous black eye.

So, instead of being handed an easy seat, Trudeau had to fight to win Papineau, a densely populated and diverse working-class riding in the heart of the city. It was then held by Bloc Québécois MP Vivian Barbot, a well-regarded women's activist. Born in Haiti, Barbot fled that country with her family to escape political violence. The first woman from a visible minority to serve as president of the Quebec Women's Federation and a former vice-president of the Bloc Québécois, she was a formidable opponent, but the riding was winnable for the right Liberal. Barbot had managed to squeak past Liberal incumbent Pierre Pettigrew by only 990 votes in 2006 at the height of the Liberal sponsorship scandal.

Before Trudeau could run against her, he had to win the nomination, and two local figures—municipal councillor Mary Deros and Italian newspaper publisher Basilio Giordano—stood in his way. Veteran Liberal organizer Reine Hébert, who knew Trudeau *père* and had run Chrétien's Quebec Liberal leadership campaign, offered to help Trudeau. With his future on the line, he threw himself into the work. Even Sophie joined in, selling Liberal memberships in a grocery store parking lot. Italians, Greeks, Haitians, and South Asians in the riding—who credit his father with opening immigration to their families—were receptive to his pitch, and he won on the first ballot on the night of April 29, 2007. That was the easy part. To beat Barbot and win the seat, he would have to do a lot more.

FOR THE ELECTION AHEAD, Trudeau was advised to ask for help from Louis-Alexandre Lanthier, a seasoned political professional with good judgment and experience working for Ken Dryden and other Liberal politicians. He invited Lanthier for lunch in Ottawa, but their initial conversation was difficult. Lanthier wasn't sure he wanted the job. In previous encounters, he had found Trudeau standoffish and aloof. He told him candidly: "I met you twice before and I was not impressed." They sorted out their differences and started talking about how they could run a campaign. "If you want somebody to be getting you interviews with *La Presse* and the *Toronto Star* and whatever, I'm not your guy. If you want somebody to make you go door to door, bring you to clean parks . . . I can do that." Trudeau replied that he intended to work at ground level, and he wanted Lanthier to help him.

He could not have had a better assistant. Lanthier grew up in the party. His mother, Jacline, had worked for Pierre Laporte, the Liberal deputy premier of Quebec, who was kidnapped and murdered by the Front de libération du Québec in 1970 during what came to be known as the October Crisis. Then just twenty-two, she had been with his family while they waited for news and learned of his murder. Raised in a household where the struggle with sovereigntists was an existential matter, Lanthier was a seasoned professional, with experience, patience, and judgment. He first campaigned for a Liberal candidate at the age of seven, delivering pamphlets on his bike.

Lanthier soon found he had a raw but hard-working candidate on his hands. Trudeau was willing to do the tough street-level tasks that candidates often try to avoid—participating in park cleanups, knocking on doors, handing out literature in malls and the metro. Lanthier trained Trudeau in the ways of politicking, teaching the tricks that veteran politicians learn along the way—how to greet people on the street and engage with them on their doorsteps.

Papineau is a dense, urban riding divided, like the rest of the city, by boulevard Saint-Laurent. On the west side is Parc Extension, an immigrant neighbourhood once dominated by Italians and Greeks and now, increasingly, by immigrants from the Middle East, South Asia, and the Caribbean—a quartier of shawarma shops, curry houses, mosques, and temples. It is a natural constituency for the Liberals, whom many immigrant voters favour. On the east side is Villeray, an old working-class francophone neighbourhood, where the Bloc Québécois is strong.

"People, at the first few times we went door knocking, they would yell at us," Lanthier recalls. "They would slam the door. They would say he was the son of the devil." Trudeau engaged cheerfully with them all, pointing to areas where they agreed. Lanthier has a picture of him sitting in the living room of one home and drinking beer with a group of young francophone sovereigntists who began as personally hostile.

Trudeau took Lanthier's lead on how to sell himself to voters but not on policy. During a visit to one important mosque in the riding, for instance, Lanthier cautioned him to avoid discussing same-sex marriage. "I said, 'Maybe we don't raise this issue today when we meet with this group.' And the first thing he does is he talks about gay marriage and the liberty of women." When Lanthier chided him later, Trudeau replied: "No. You said it, but I thought it was important that they knew where I came from."

———

TRUDEAU WON THE RIDING in the election of October 2008, besting Barbot by just 1,189 votes. It was an impressive victory because, under Dion's leadership, the Liberals had lost eighteen seats. Dion had proposed a complicated environmental proposal—the Green Shift—that would have imposed a carbon tax to reduce emissions and distributed the money through progressive tax rebates. It was a thoughtful policy, but voters found it confusing. The Conservatives portrayed it as a zany Liberal cash grab promoted by a wacky professor. Before the election, an abortive coalition attempt—featuring Dion, Layton, and Bloc Québécois leader Gilles Duceppe—helped Stephen Harper portray his opponents as reckless. Dion, whose English was shaky, never connected on the campaign trail.

Trudeau got himself an apartment in Ottawa and set about learning the ropes, bringing his natural exuberance to the staid parliamentary precinct. There was a significant amount of eye-rolling in his early days on the Hill. It started during his Papineau campaign when he posted a treacly, overly earnest video on his campaign website in which he alternated rapidly from French to English, overacted, and seemed extremely pleased with himself. "You have no doubt noticed *que ce video est un mélange* of English and *français*. Although everything written on this site *est disponible en anglais* and in French, my personal videos *seront bilingues*." A Quebec comedy troupe quickly produced a spoof video of a deranged-looking Trudeau switching back and forth between languages. That spelled the end of Trudeau's mixed-language videos.

Pierre Trudeau had insisted that his children grow up at ease in both languages. The effortlessly bilingual Justin had a hard time accepting that not everyone is so lucky. In 2007, during a speech to elementary school teachers in Saint John, New Brunswick, he said it might be better to do away with French-language schools in the province. "The segregation of French and English in schools is something to be looked at seriously," he suggested. "It is dividing people and affixing labels to people." His comments reflected a surprising naïveté about New Brunswick language politics. The province's Acadians, long treated as second-class citizens, had pushed hard to establish French-language schools and saw a separate system as the only way to prevent assimilation. They were willing to go into the streets when necessary to protect their language. In 1997, RCMP used tear gas and police dogs to attack Acadian parents protesting school closures. As an anglophone from neighbouring Nova Scotia, I found Trudeau's gaffe astonishing. If I was aware of the long and difficult Acadian struggle for linguistic equality in New Brunswick, how could he not be?

The Société des Acadiens et Acadiennes du Nouveau-Brunswick issued a statement asking him to "mind his own business." Trudeau apologized, and Dion asked voters to be indulgent. "He is new. He will likely have to explain his thoughts further."

Trudeau's exuberance and confidence, his princely certainty in the importance of his ideas, have often led him to make comments he has later had to disavow. It is part and parcel of the certainty that led him to speak forcefully about his support for gay marriage in a mosque—an admirable belief in presenting his views forthrightly and bravely. The problem is that he had a similar certainty about matters where he didn't know what he was talking about. It reflected the immaturity of an academic dilettante, someone whose opinions were always greeted with interest because of his charisma and family name but who lacked the intellectual discipline for which his father was famous.

Once in Ottawa, Trudeau proved to be a loner rather than a team player. Liberal MPs found him a bit much, as he continued to arrive on the Hill riding a skateboard. They resented the way reporters sought him out, ignoring his more experienced, harder-working colleagues, and found him uninterested in policy work. "When he showed up, I mean he used to sit in the corner of the caucus room, when Bob Rae was leading caucus, on his iPad—iPads were brand new then—and then he'd get up an hour early and leave," one MP told me. His caucus colleagues may have been irked by his gaffes and flamboyance, but they were also keen to have him headline fundraisers in their ridings, where he was guaranteed to pack a hall. Some MPs complained, though, that he insisted on taking a cut, having them pay his riding association for the honour of his presence, which was not the way other MPs operated. He was eventually called on the carpet by the party and told he could not bill them so much for his appearances.

Trudeau's legislative track record was unimpressive. He sat in the back-bench and served as his party's associate critic for human resources and skills development (youth). In his first session, miraculously, he won the lottery that MPs hold to determine who gets to table a private member's bill. Instead of finding an issue around which he could build support across party lines—the only way to advance a private member's bill—he wasted the opportunity by presenting a bill to promote youth volunteer service, which the other parties swiftly killed.

None of it mattered, though, because Canadians remained fixated on him. He was *interesting*. There were admiring profiles in magazines, invitations to high-profile events. Strangers regularly stopped him on the street to wish him well. He split his time between Ottawa and Montreal, where he spent weekends with Sophie and Xavier, their son, who was born four days after the election. There was already speculation he might take over from Dion, but he shrugged it off.

Others were thinking about it though. In 2009, during a fact-finding trip to Israel sponsored by the Canada-Israel Committee, Trudeau got to know Bruce Young, a Vancouver Liberal who had been involved in politics since he volunteered for John Turner in 1984. Young had met Trudeau in 2006 when they were both involved with Gerard Kennedy's campaign, but they really bonded as they toured around Israel.

After dinner one night, they ended up drinking scotch with kibbutzniks until the small hours in a Jerusalem pub. Young woke up the next morning in his hotel room with a dry mouth, a terrible headache, and a ringing phone. Trudeau was calling from the lobby. "Hey dude, we leave in five minutes and everyone's here and you're not." Young splashed water on his face and rushed downstairs to join the tour. The first stop was a meeting with an Israeli foreign affairs official, who briefed the Canadians on the assassination of a Hamas leader in Syria the night before. Trudeau quizzed the official at length, showing a detailed knowledge of Iranian, Israeli, and Syrian politics. "Meanwhile, all I'm trying to do is, you know, keep down the five aspirin I've had for breakfast," Young recalls. He was so impressed by Trudeau's stamina that he called his wife later and told her: "He's going to be the prime minister of Canada, and I'm going to help him."

———

ON THE NIGHT OF May 2, 2011, Trudeau again won his riding of Papineau, this time by a margin of 4,327 votes. Barbot ran against him, but this time she came in third, behind a New Democrat. The NDP won fifty-nine of Quebec's seventy-five seats in a historic shift that nobody saw coming until it happened. The party, never previously a force in Quebec politics, took off under the leadership of Jack Layton, who grew up in the Montreal suburb of Hudson but represented a Toronto riding. Beginning at a policy convention in Quebec in 2006, Layton had succeeded in changing NDP policies to appeal to left-wing nationalists who typically voted for the Bloc. A key piece of the puzzle was the Sherbrooke Declaration, which sought to nullify Dion's Clarity Act, asserting that an NDP government would recognize a sovereignty referendum if the sovereigntists won 50 percent of the vote. For "soft nationalists," it was a crucial policy, recognizing Quebec's right to self-determination.

Many Quebecers wanted to get rid of Stephen Harper, who by that point had been governing the country for five years. They knew the Bloc could not replace the Conservatives and had not warmed to Liberal leader Michael Ignatieff. When Layton went on the popular Quebec Sunday night talk show *Tout le monde en parle*, he charmed the host, Guy Lepage, who called him a "bon jack," a good guy. Quebecers agreed, and they elected dozens of previously unknown candidates, nicknamed *poteaux orange*—traffic cones—because they were orange and stationary. The most celebrated was Ruth Ellen Brosseau, an Ottawa barmaid who was elected in rural Berthier–Maskinongé even after it was revealed she took a mid-election vacation to Las Vegas.

In the rest of the country, the NDP did better, but not well enough to stop Harper from winning a majority. Ontarians, with painful memories of Bob Rae's NDP government, did not follow Quebec's lead, and at the last minute a small but decisive group of voters switched from the Liberals to the Tories to prevent an NDP government, delivering vote splits in close ridings that devastated the Liberals. Harper had focused on a powerful economic message while his party pummelled Ignatieff with attack ads. A Harvard professor with a celebrated career as a global intellectual, Ignatieff, who entered politics at sixty, never learned the political discipline necessary in modern politics and often seemed to be lecturing voters rather than listening to them. The Conservatives framed him effectively in a wave of TV ads that declared, "He didn't come back for you."

Layton helped deliver the *coup de grâce* in a debate when he attacked Ignatieff for missing votes in the House. An indignant Ignatieff sputtered that he wouldn't take lessons from Layton. "Most Canadians, if they don't show up for work, they don't get a promotion," Layton replied, delivering the most effective knockout blow in a Canadian election debate since Mulroney mauled Turner in the 1984 election over patronage appointments to Pierre Trudeau loyalists. When the dust settled, Ignatieff and Bloc leader Gilles Duceppe were gone, the NDP was in opposition, and the Liberals were in third place with just thirty-four seats—a record low.

It was a wrenching loss. The party that thought of itself as the natural governing party had overnight lost its dominant position. The Liberal Party of Canada was one of the most successful political parties in the world, governing Canada for seventy years in the twentieth century. Now it had been brought low, a victim, largely, of infighting. The internal battles between Jean Chrétien and Paul Martin were so toxic, so personal and virulent that many senior figures were pleased to see their opponents, rather than internal rivals, succeed. Liberals were out of touch and complacent, with aging MPs in (supposedly) safe ridings focused on their own careers, not the hard work of knocking on doors, raising money, and attending events.

At the time, it looked like a structural change—a permanent realignment along more ideological lines. The Liberal Party was a brokerage party, dispensing patronage and influence, managing regional, linguistic, and religious electoral blocs, moving forward with progressive policies when possible, insofar as it didn't disrupt the delicate business of managing a fractious, regionally disparate country. The party more closely resembled Japan's LDP, India's Congress, or Mexico's PRI than Labour in the United Kingdom or the Democrats in the United States, governing by straddling the middle, veering back and forth, assembling coalitions across ideological lines. As politics globally became more polarized in the twenty-first century, the big brokerage parties everywhere were losing their grip. Why should Canada be any different? It was the long-held ambition of some less progressive Conservatives—including Ernest (Preston's father) Manning and Harper—to reorder the system so that the Conservatives and the NDP would take turns in governing. They wanted to break the cycle where they were too often on the outside looking in while a massive, unmovable Liberal blob ran the country, rewarding their friends in the Laurentian Elite and appointing one another to the Order of Canada. After the electoral wipeout of 2011, it looked as though they might finally get their wish.

We will never know what would have happened if Layton had not succumbed to cancer in August 2011, four months after he led his party to the opposition benches. He was an unusually good politician, a hard-working glad-hander with the common touch, a disciplined communicator who refused to be knocked off his talking points, and a patient and calculating strategist. If he had survived and faced Harper in the House, opposition to the Conservatives might have coalesced around him, giving the NDP the opportunity to behave like a government in waiting. And Trudeau might have found a different line of work.

In the aftermath of the Harper majority, Trudeau had been thinking about giving up politics, maybe leaving the country. "He thought he was going to leave politics in the summer of 2011, and he went out to Ucluelet and had a surfing holiday," recalls Butts. "And Jack Layton died when he was out there." That changed everything.

Trudeau says he was struggling with his role after Harper's victory. "There was a moment in there where I was wondering if the drive to have an impact and change things and make a difference was not mistimed." And yet, he was under pressure to run for the leadership. "Everyone said, 'Okay, we tried two smart intellectuals in Stéphane [Dion] and Michael

[Ignatieff], let's go with the kid with the big name who we don't know how smart he is. Maybe that's the Hail Mary we need.'"

Trudeau was afraid of being seen that way because he "knew how much work there was to do." It wasn't that with Layton gone the path was clear for a Liberal victory. "I really thought about family and the country and what I could contribute to it. A good man like that giving his everything to his last days in service to country—it just inspired me."

———

WHEN HARPER WON A majority in 2011, he took a more combative tone than in his minority years. Progressives were shocked and dismayed to find supposedly liberal Canada led by an Albertan intent on shrinking government and creating the kind of country where pipelines could get built without much red tape. Dismayed and freaked out by Harper, lefty Canadians were casting about for champions. Trudeau answered the call.

In December, Conservative environment minister Peter Kent, a normally gentlemanly and thoughtful former CTV reporter, took a low blow at NDP MP Megan Leslie while she was questioning him about the government's decision to withdraw from the Kyoto climate accord in a meeting in Durban, South Africa. The Conservatives had gone to Durban determined to undercut the climate deal and had declined to provide accreditation to opposition critics, like Leslie, presumably to prevent them from providing negative commentary to the journalists covering the event. Under pressure from Leslie, instead of defending his government's position, Kent attacked her for not going to Durban.

"Mr. Speaker, if my honourable colleague had been in Durban, she would have seen that Canada was among the leaders in the . . ."

Before he could finish, he was shouted down by enraged opposition MPs, including Trudeau, who was then sporting long hair, a moustache, and a d'Artagnan soul patch. His words were rendered decorously in

Hansard as "Some hon. members: Oh, oh!" But he didn't say "Oh, oh." He yelled at Kent, "Oh, you piece of shit," which led to mayhem in the House. Kent insisted on an apology, which Trudeau delivered. Much ink was spilled.

Early in the new year, he was again making headlines. In a French-language Radio-Canada interview, he mused that if Harper kept running the country, "maybe I would consider wanting to make Quebec a separate country," an awkward way of trying to undercut the sovereigntist argument. When he took heat on February 14, he went to the lobby of the House to respond, against the advice of party communications staffers Kevin Bosch and Daniel Lauzon, who thought it might go badly.

"The question is not why does Justin Trudeau suddenly not love his country, because the question is ridiculous," Trudeau said emphatically, as if his patriotism should be beyond question. "I feel this country in my bones with every breath I take, and I'm not going to stand here and defend that I actually do love Canada, because we know I love Canada. The question is, What's happening to our country?"

Trudeau's performance was so over the top that the reporters standing around him were fighting not to giggle. He knew it had gone badly. "That didn't go very well, did it?" he said to Bosch and Lauzon when he returned to the lobby. "You used to be a drama teacher," Bosch said. "Not a very good one," Trudeau replied.

Politicians don't typically speak of themselves in the third person, and they don't declare that they feel the country in their bones with every breath they take. But this kind of thing may not bother voters as much as it does jaded reporters. And perhaps Trudeau does feel Canada in his bones, or believes he does. When Jonathan Kay spent time with him researching *Common Ground*, he was struck by Trudeau's knowledge of the country, which he has been travelling since he was a child.

Kay watched Trudeau do a speaking event at Algonquin College in Ottawa. "He was talking to a bunch of like, seventeen- and eighteen-year-olds, people barely out of high school. And somebody said, 'Hey, what's your favourite Canadian band?' And honestly, if you're like me, I'd say, um, Loverboy, Arcade Fire. And then the list runs out, right? He listed like ten bands in French, ten bands in English, named some of his favourite songs. And the whole room was just eating out of his hands. But I talked to him after, and he knew these bands. It wasn't just like someone gave him a cue card, like names of Canadian bands."

During this period, Trudeau decided he did want to lead the Liberal Party, beat Harper, and become prime minister. "He said, 'I think I really want to do this,'" Butts recalls. "'And I think if I don't do it now, it's never going to happen.'"

———

A MONTH BEFORE TRUDEAU'S theatrical interview, Prime Minister Stephen Harper appointed thirty-four-year-old Patrick Brazeau to the Senate, the youngest senator in the chamber. An Algonquin from the Kitigan Zibi Anishinabeg First Nation, up the Gatineau River from Ottawa, Brazeau was national chief of the Congress of Aboriginal Peoples, a group representing Indigenous people who lived off-reserve and tended to be more open to Harper's pitches than those influenced by the Assembly of First Nations chiefs. Brazeau's appointment angered many Indigenous people because they saw him as a suck-up to a government hostile to their interests. He also had a reputation as a hothead, with a record of behaving in a non-senatorial manner.

In 2012, Trudeau, with his eye on the leadership of his party, decided to fight in a charity boxing match. He had been training for years in a Montreal gym, and he and his trainer thought he was good enough. He first challenged Conservative MPs Peter MacKay and Rob Anders, but they wisely declined. Brazeau, who had a black belt in karate, jumped at the chance. Trudeau was delighted. He later told *Rolling Stone*: "I wanted someone who would be a good foil, and we stumbled upon the scrappy tough-guy senator from an Indigenous community. He fit the bill and it was a very nice counterpoint. I saw it as the right kind of narrative, the right story to tell."*

Before the fight, Trudeau and Butts decided that Katie Telford, who had worked with Trudeau on the Kennedy campaign, was the organizer they needed to build a team. Telford grew up in Toronto, the daughter of public servants. As a young woman, she went to work for Gerard Kennedy when he was minister of education in Ontario and ended up, at twenty-five, as his chief of staff. She impressed many Liberals when she ran his vigorous though ultimately unsuccessful campaign for the Liberal leadership before moving to Ottawa to work for Dion.

She didn't think the fight was a good idea. When she went out to dinner with Butts and Trudeau to talk about playing a role on his campaign, she tried to talk him out of it. She imagined him getting bloodied, which would look bad. "You let me worry about that," Trudeau said. "You guys start thinking about the leadership."

Ahead of the fight, the smart money was on the heavily muscled Brazeau, who looks like a tougher guy than Trudeau. Trudeau, who had been boxing regularly for twenty-five years, says he knew he could beat him, showing the profound confidence that is part of his character. "He's got a black belt in karate, but we're not doing a karate fight," Trudeau told me. He was so sure he would win that he let his stepfather wager on him. "I ran into him at one point, [and he said], 'You sure about this?' 'Yeah. I got this.' He's like, 'Okay.' And he turned around and made a handful of bets with his buddies at some great odds and made a lot of money off them because he knew that when I think I've got something, it's because I've thought it through."

Brazeau came out strong in the first round and hit Trudeau harder than he'd ever been hit before. But Trudeau was able to wait until Brazeau

---

* When the story came out, Indigenous activists complained that Trudeau's comment was insensitive. He apologized.

was out of wind and, by the third round, he was mauling him at will. He bloodied the senator's nose.

The match was broadcast live on Sun TV, a short-lived right-wing network, with ringside commentary from Ezra Levant, who kept calling Trudeau "Shiny Pony." Levant was forced to keep up his comments as Trudeau slowly beat the stuffing out of Brazeau. Tories, expecting that Trudeau would take a shellacking, were there in large numbers and quickly vacated after he triumphed.

The match was crucial to reframing Trudeau's image, says Nik Nanos, CTV's pollster of record. "The boxing match refuted every single claim that the Conservatives made. It refuted the fact that he was weak. It refuted the fact that he was not tough. One of the traps that the Conservatives fell into is that they created expectations for Trudeau that were so low that he realistically just stepped over that."

The ink-stained wretches of the press gallery had a primal spectacle to write about and, tired of being kicked around by the Harper government, leapt at the chance to celebrate the new progressive champion. "Should Justin Trudeau stop playing coy, put family life on hold and leap into the Liberal leadership race, thereby saving the party of Laurier and Pearson, and perhaps the country, from certain doom?" wrote Michael Den Tandt in the Postmedia papers. "Since the big fight at the end of March—let's face it, that was the turning point—disparaging references to Trudeau as 'the Dauphin' have been rare indeed."

Teresa-Elise Maiolino, a Toronto sociologist, wrote in a 2017 paper that "media coverage of the boxing match provided Trudeau with the opportunity to transition from precariously masculine to sufficiently masculine."

———

AFTER HIS PUGILISTIC TRIUMPH, Trudeau started to build a leadership team. Telford brought on Michael McNair. He had done the heavy policy lifting on Dion's ill-fated Green Shift and stayed on to work for the even less successful Ignatieff. McNair, a wonk with master's degrees from Columbia University and the London School of Economics, had left for a job on Bay Street. He agreed to come back as policy advisor, and, in the early days, was a jack of all trades, carrying Trudeau's bags when necessary.

The first step, the team decided, was to gather a group of supporters to kick around ideas. They invited about thirty people, a mix of Trudeau's friends and hard-nosed political operatives, for a weekend of discussion sessions at Mont-Tremblant, the most beautiful resort in Quebec—a village built in the style of Old Quebec at the base of a world-class ski hill. Tom Pitfield, whose father had been clerk of the Privy Council under Pierre Trudeau, handled the logistics, renting a chalet.

Pitfield, who is six years younger than Trudeau, was close to Michel Trudeau as a child. When his mother, Nancy, and Justin's father died in the same year, the two young men were drawn together in their grief. They have remained close ever since, with Pitfield offering advice from outside the Ottawa bubble about politics and personal matters. His wife, Anna Gainey, was a former Liberal political staffer, and would eventually become party president. But back then, Pitfield, who has a master's degree in political philosophy from the London School of Economics, was handling logistics. He was interested in policy, but Trudeau suggested he focus instead on digital strategy for the leadership campaign, and Butts convinced him to do it. At the time of the Tremblant meeting, he was already building the digital operation that would be at the heart of the Trudeau political machine for the next decade.

As the weekend started, Butts drove Telford to the Trudeaus' chalet in the hills nearby to meet and have lunch with Margaret. Alexandre, known widely as Sacha, was there too—and he joined them as part of the team when the sessions began.

The participants gathered in a chalet, where Trudeau, Telford, and Butts led most of the discussions. Lanthier, now Trudeau's executive assistant, was there, part of a significant Quebec contingent, as was Bruce Young from British Columbia, and former Mississauga MPs Navdeep Bains and Omar Alghabra, who would later serve as ministers. Many, including western organizer Richard Maksymetz, were veterans of the Kennedy campaign.

As they sat around a fire pit, participants discussed the way forward. Should they start a new party? Should the Liberals merge with the NDP? The idea was then being promoted by Chrétien and former NDP leader Ed Broadbent, who reasoned that vote-splitting on the left was allowing the Conservatives to divide and conquer progressive voters. The Quebecers were interested because the fundamental cleavage in that province was typically around the national question, whether Quebec should secede or not, so it seemed counterproductive for the federalist vote to be divided between two parties. But Liberals from English Canada were vehemently opposed. Maksymetz, Butts, and Telford were certain that whatever votes they might win on the left they would lose on the right. Advocates for a merger were convinced to give up the idea.

Butts had convinced David Herle to sign up, despite his misgivings about Trudeau, whom Herle thought of as a lightweight. Herle agreed to help, but he was occupied with the Kathleen Wynne government in Ontario at the time and suggested that Butts hire Frank Graves, president of EKOS Research Associates, to do the polling. Though non-partisan, Graves felt, with some evidence, that he had been persecuted by Harper's people and wanted to see a change in Ottawa. He gave a presentation to the group at Mont-Tremblant, first running through slides that showed the country might be ready to switch governments. He found a mood of discontent in the land, the feeling that the country was going the wrong way. Three-quarters of the population, for example, said that the Canadian dream was getting out of reach. The numbers were not great for the Liberals either. The Conservatives and NDP were tied for first place with a percentage in the mid-30s, with the Liberals a distant third, below 20 percent. But there was reason to think the Liberals had room to grow:

45 percent of Canadians considered themselves "small-l liberals." And Trudeau's numbers were good: 38 percent of Canadians had a favourable view of him, compared with just 27 percent who were unfavourable. Thomas Mulcair's numbers were better—42 percent to 26—but he was Opposition leader. Harper's numbers were bleak: only 32 percent approved of him, and 56 percent disapproved.

As to the leadership race, which had yet to be called, Trudeau could expect to enter with a commanding lead, with the support of 26 percent. Former astronaut Marc Garneau, former finance minister Ralph Goodale, Quebec MP Denis Coderre, Nova Scotia MP Scott Brison, New Brunswick MP Dominic LeBlanc, and former MP Martha Hall Findlay were all basically tied for a distant second. Trudeau scored badly with Conservative supporters but performed well with Liberals, New Democrats, and Greens. Compared with Harper, he was seen as weak on the economy but had a strong advantage on social issues and the environment.

Graves told the group that Trudeau would probably have an "insurmountable lead" in the race. He was "a strongly recognized national figure who is seen in much more favourable terms than [Harper], or any of the plausible contenders for Liberal Party leadership." But beating Harper in a general election would be a "much more elusive and uncertain goal." Although Trudeau was viewed as having charisma, empathy, and love of country, Harper was seen as tougher. Mulcair, who was strong in Quebec, was regarded as the "most plausible option to depose the Harper government." Yet Mulcair was anything but a sure thing: while the top-line numbers showed NDP strength, centre-left voters were persuadable: "There is a lot of churning and shifting and low levels of emotional engagement," said Graves, who advised Trudeau to be "positive and future-oriented, decisive about real dominant progressive values," and to emphasize "jobs and growth, economic progress and fairness."

McNair, who had been researching the messages that were succeeding for Democrats in the United States, gave a presentation on the "economic context of Trudeau as a politician." "It was at Tremblant where we settled on our economic stories that we're here to help strengthen and grow the middle class," he says. In retrospect, that message seems obvious, but at the time it was anything but. "That's language that Liberals had often been uncomfortable with because just the language of class is not something that people were used to, even though most Canadians do self-identify as middle class."

Butts left Tremblant convinced that the Liberals needed to be liberal again. From his perch in Queen's Park, home to Ontario's Legislative Assembly, he had observed a federal party that seemed to have lost its way, offering timid, neo-conservative economic policies. And after Dion's defeat in 2008, the party concluded it was a mistake to offer ambitious environmental policies. "The takeaway from the weekend was that the problem with the Liberal Party was that it wasn't very liberal, and it had obvious screaming telltale signs to voters who were liberal that it wasn't liberal," he says. From this conviction would follow—eventually—decisively progressive policies, on abortion, same-sex marriage, marijuana legalization, and the economy, but all of that would wait. Trudeau, the clear frontrunner of a race that hadn't yet started, had no reason to roll out policies that his opponents could use to pin him down.

Before the coalescing Trudeau team could get to work, though, they had to sort out the Sacha factor. Trudeau's younger brother was a key part of Team Justin at the time of the Mont-Tremblant meeting. People who attended expected him to keep on being part of the team, but it was not to be. While Justin resembles his mother, in his openness and creativity, Sacha is more like his father, more private. He is as guarded as Justin is open. "I was very close to my father and remain very close," Sacha told Shannon Proudfoot in *Maclean's* in 2016. "I live in his home, I'm the guardian of his private spirit." He is a documentarian and has travelled to war zones around the world, including Liberia, Afghanistan, Iraq, and Darfur. When Liberals gathered at Mont-Tremblant, some thought he would be Bobby Kennedy to Justin's JFK, seek a seat, and become foreign minister. People who were present, however, came away with different views of how realistic that idea was in practice.

Sacha had close connections to older Liberals across the country. He also had strong opinions about foreign affairs and had been critical of Israel's human rights record, which, the professionals feared, would open a political vulnerability on an issue they didn't need. But he was politically astute, with sharp observations, for instance, about Chrétien's political machine in Quebec.

"The thing I remember most was how impressive Sacha was," says Herle. "He seemed like a very sharp, practical tactician, hardball political operator. He was astute." But the campaign already had a chief strategist, and it wasn't Sacha. As such, "he didn't look like a guy to me who was going to fall in line with whatever Gerry's view were."

The unstable dynamic continued until after Justin declared his candidacy for the Liberal leadership. Sacha was there to film the announcement, but his working relationship with Justin was becoming increasingly strained. They argued repeatedly over the French in his launch speech, having "epic dust-ups" past the point, professionals thought, that it made sense to be discussing it.

Soon afterward, Sacha was in Ottawa for a dinner with senior Liberals at Mamma Teresa, the old-fashioned Italian restaurant where for decades the people who run the country have been conspiring over linguine alle vongole. Dominic LeBlanc, whose father, Roméo, had been Pierre Trudeau's governor general and who had babysat both boys, was telling people that Liberals were about to pick "the wrong Trudeau," pointing out that Pierre had made Sacha, not Justin, executor of his estate. Word of LeBlanc's warning got back to Butts, who called him to ask him to stop saying that, which he did.

The two Trudeaus could not get along, and, in the end, Justin had to proceed without Sacha. "I think it put a substantial amount of strain on the brothers, as you would expect, and I think they agreed it wasn't worth it," says a friend. "Justin needed a brother more than he needed another advisor."

Sacha was grumpy about the split. He mostly stays out of the news but is reputed to be critical of the government in private conversations. In his 2016 interview with Proudfoot, he said he couldn't do what his brother is doing. "To a certain extent, I was ashamed of being a prince, and he's embraced it, used it. The person I chose to be is the one who's hitchhiking in the rain in January in Israel, trying to get work on a farm. It's so much realer to me." He offered a surprisingly grim take on his brother's political success: "I'm not sure I agree with this turn in politics, but it certainly is the mainstay one—the movie-star politician is a formidable force in this kind of world. Maybe a dangerous one, in the long run."

Justin never speaks about what must have been a painful family episode. He had found the ruthlessness necessary to proceed toward his goal. He was going to run for the leadership, and Sacha was not going to be part of the team.

2

SMART MOVES
AND APOLOGIES

On April 14, 2013, surprising no one, Justin Trudeau won the leadership of the Liberal Party of Canada, taking nearly 80 percent of the vote on the first ballot. His most competitive rival, former astronaut Marc Garneau, had dropped out a month earlier after looking at the numbers. "I cannot mathematically win," he said. "Numbers don't lie."

Garneau, whose resumé was vastly superior to Justin's, had chided Trudeau for running an idea-free campaign. "I believe that Canadians want to see substance," he said in one debate. "They don't want empty words. They want direct answers to direct questions. I believe that is what Liberals are looking for." He was wrong: Liberals were not looking for substance. They were looking for Justin Trudeau to lead the party, substance or not.

Secure in the knowledge they had the leadership sewed up, with absolutely no requirement to lay out policies during the campaign, Team Trudeau began to plan for what came next. They were aware, for instance, that there would inevitably be questions about Trudeau's inherited wealth and his public-speaking business, so Butts asked Trudeau's law firm to prepare a report for eventual public release. Soon after, the *Ottawa Cit-*

izen's Glen McGregor sent a question about Trudeau's inheritance, suspecting it might raise questions about the team's promise to work for the middle class. The family had money—Pierre's father, Charles-Émile Trudeau, had built a successful chain of gas stations in Montreal in the 1920s—but the public did not know how much. To McGregor's surprise, he soon received a detailed breakdown of Justin Trudeau's personal financial history—and an interview with Trudeau.

At that time, reporters were being treated disdainfully by the Harper government, which reacted to many media inquiries with silence or boilerplate talking points. Trudeau's proactive transparency was a welcome change, reflecting the view that the public had a right to know a certain amount about a would-be leader.

The report showed that Trudeau had inherited from his father shares in a corporation that were worth about $1.2 million by 2012, paying dividends of about $20,000 a year. Trudeau used the money to travel and supplement his teacher's pay until he got into the lucrative speaking business, which paid him $462,000 in 2007. He was not as rich as people expected, and in his interview with McGregor he struck the right tone. "Whatever we wanted to do, we had enough to live a modest but decent life. And that was incredibly lucky."

The Trudeau team had a lot of work to do to make their candidate ready for prime time. They started to hone his debating skills: "We took a lot of time . . . because he's going to face Steven Harper and Tom Mulcair and he needs to be good at it," said Robert Asselin, a University of Ottawa professor who helped with the preparation. Dominic LeBlanc and David McGuinty stood in for his opponents.

Trudeau was willing to be drilled. "He got serious and he got better," says Asselin. "He worked hard. We worked really hard. Five of us would drill him until he was ready. Me, McNair, Cyrus [Reporter], Suzanne Cowan, and Gerry and Katie."

The staffers also worked on Trudeau's speaking skills. Ironically, given how well he did in the public-speaking business, his speeches needed a lot of work. When Lanthier was assisting him, he would stand at the back of the room. If Trudeau began racing through his words, Lanthier would walk toward the stage until Trudeau spotted him and slowed down. Left to his own devices, Trudeau was also too breathy and delivered lines with excessive emotion, sounding like a ham actor. The staffers brought in consultants to help, but also showed him videos and critiqued him. Trudeau endured it without complaint. "He sees the value in it," says one staffer. "He accepts it, doesn't take it as a criticism." The process continues into the present because his bad habits will return if he doesn't keep working at it.

He is scrupulous about his media appearances, carefully considering lighting, camera angles. "I think he literally thinks of every day as a scene," says a politician who has worked closely with him for years. "He is his own stage manager. Sometimes that's brilliant and sometimes it's not, but it is always him. That's why if you walked up to him, he would grab the phone in your hand to take the selfie himself. He wouldn't let you do it."

After winning the leadership, Trudeau and his family moved to Ottawa and set about integrating his team with the staff he inherited from Bob Rae. Kate Purchase stayed on and became Trudeau's director of communications. Her family network lay at the heart of Canadian politics, and she had deep insight into how the game is played. Cyrus Reporter, a calm, disciplined lawyer who had been chief of staff to Justice Minister Allan Rock in Jean Chrétien's government, came aboard. Reporter in turn brought in Marlene Floyd, an energetic Nova Scotian, to handle operations.

When Butts was in McGuinty's office, he got to know Daniel Gagnier, then chief of staff to Jean Charest in Quebec and, previously, to Ontario premier David Peterson. Gagnier, semi-retired and working as a consultant, was reluctant to sign on, but when Trudeau, Butts, and Telford drove up to sweet-talk him, he agreed to come in as a volunteer on condition he could continue his consulting business, including work for the Energy East pipeline. His experience proved invaluable for the energetic and talented young people around Trudeau. "When Dan talked, the entire room just went quiet and listened to him," Purchase recalls. Gagnier was similarly impressed by their enthusiasm and capacities and rated them the best people he worked with during his career: "I had a very good team in Quebec and good teams in Ontario, but this one leading up to the first Trudeau government was exceptional."

At that time, the Trudeau-Butts-Telford triumvirate was extraordinarily effective because they trusted each other implicitly. Jonathan Kay remembers their close connection. As one person left the room, he says, "the other would kind of finish the other one's sentences."

Things were looking good. The public was open to Trudeau, and he had a lead in the national polls beginning two weeks before he won the leadership.

The Conservatives were aware of the threat. In a memo to Harper and his senior political staff on March 13, Alykhan Velshi, responsible for strategic planning in the Prime Minister's Office (PMO), laid out a plan for a barrage of attack ads against the "fresh and appealing" Trudeau: "Unfortunately," he wrote, "we believe that trying to persuade Canadians to dislike or even resent Trudeau is unlikely to be successful with swing voters. Our recommended approach, instead, is to focus on persuading voters already predisposed to liking Trudeau that, because of his poor judgment and inexperience, he's in way over his head."

Velshi proposed using a video of Trudeau taking off his shirt during a charity event where he raised money for the Canadian Liver Foundation. The party took his advice and rolled out an attack ad using the striptease footage to contrast Trudeau's slight resumé with Harper's record of economic stewardship. The ad flopped. The party looked bad for using footage from a charity event. "Canadians were rooting for him," recalls Fred DeLorey, Harper's director of political operations. "He was the son of a prime minister who was born on Christmas Day. He grew up on the front pages of Canadian newspapers. He's always been this person that was there, and he did that amazing eulogy that everyone adored at his father's funeral. The guy grew up in front of us, so if we didn't know him, we felt like we knew him. He was the son of Canada. That's tough to go against."

These were not good days for the Conservatives. A month after Trudeau won the leadership, Harper's chief of staff, Nigel Wright, resigned. Wright, a wealthy Bay Street wizard who ran a half marathon every morning before work, had decided to try to settle a minor scandal over the expenses of Senator Mike Duffy, a former CTV journalist, by quietly reimbursing him for the disputed expenses using $90,000 of his own money.* The only problem was that someone told CTV's Robert Fife, and Fife told the world. The whole thing looked unbelievably seedy.

Harper's PMO was full of long-time loyalists who had not had notable careers before they started working for the boss. MPs called them the "boys in short pants." With Wright gone, so was the most mature voice in the PMO. It was the beginning of the end for the Harper outfit. For the rest of his time in office, details from the Senate expense saga continued to dribble out. Several senators were charged with criminal offences, which led to court documents becoming public. The revelations pierced the secrecy of the Harper operation, undercutting the prime minister's hard-won reputation for financial rectitude, exposing some senators as expense cheats, and revealing insiders as back-biting schemers jockeying for advantage as the operation slid into the ditch.

When Auditor General Michael Ferguson began an audit of every senator's expenses, Team Trudeau decided they had better do something to distance themselves from the mess, particularly if Ferguson found that some Liberal senators had also had their hands in the cookie jar, as eventually turned out to be the case. The Liberals had to get out of the way of the dumpster fire headed their way.

Butts, Telford, Gagnier, Reporter, and national Liberal director Jeremy

---

* Duffy was later charged with thirty-one counts, including fraud, connected with Senate expenses. He was acquitted on all counts and served in the Senate until he retired at age seventy-five.

Broadhurst got their heads together and came up with a plan. Trudeau insisted that whatever they did, it should be something concrete, not an election promise, and that it not involve reopening the constitution, as Harper's idea of electing senators would do. The brain trust decided to expel all Liberal senators from the caucus and promise a new, non-partisan appointment process if the Liberals took power.

The big problem was that the thirty-two Liberal senators would not like this solution. There was no point in negotiating with them. The decision was made, and the team acted on the morning of January 29, 2014.

It was crucial to keep the matter quiet until the announcement, but that made the rollout difficult internally. The Liberal House leader in the Senate was Halifax lawyer Jim Cowan, who was out of town to give a speech. Cyrus Reporter called him and told him to return to Ottawa: "I can't tell you why, but it's something that's going to become public, and you'll want to be here." Cowan's flight was delayed, so he arrived too late for the meeting. He had wrecked his trip to arrive back to find that he and his colleagues were out of the caucus.

Although the senators didn't enjoy being exiled, the reaction outside the Red Chamber was positive. Trudeau had acted decisively, setting up an appealing contrast with Harper. Despite his criticism of previous prime ministers for partisan appointments, Harper was worse, appointing Conservative donors, fundraisers, and failed candidates. Trudeau rid himself of the whole mess. Conservatives and New Democrats cried foul, claiming that Trudeau hadn't really done anything, that Liberal-appointed senators would continue to be Liberal, but that did not turn out to be the case. The Senate, post-reform, is a less partisan place, and no longer a dumping ground for bagmen and politicians rejected by voters.

The public approved. An Angus Reid poll found 52 percent of Canadians supported Trudeau's reform, and only 16 percent were opposed. The Trudeau honeymoon continued.

ON OCTOBER 22, 2014, a Montreal drug addict with mental health issues named Michael Zehaf-Bibeau drove to Ottawa in his Toyota Corolla. When he got to town, he sat in the front seat of his car and recorded a video on his cellphone declaring holy war on Canada because its soldiers were in Afghanistan. He then fatally shot Corporal Nathan Cirillo, a reservist from Hamilton who was standing sentinel in front of the Tomb of the Unknown Soldier.

Zehaf-Bibeau went on to the Parliament Buildings, where he forced his way in through the doors at the bottom of the Peace Tower, shooting House of Commons security officer Samearn Son in the leg. He ran down the marble floor of the Hall of Honour, bent on murder, until he was gunned down by Mounties and Sergeant-at-Arms Kevin Vickers, who put thirty-one bullets in him. NDP and Conservative MPs barricaded themselves in the caucus rooms on either side of the hallway while the bullets flew. Harper's staff rushed him into a utility closet.

Two weeks later, thousands of people in the big-hearted city of Hamilton turned out to lay their fallen soldier to rest. I was there to cover the sombre event. So many bouquets lay in front of the armoury where Cirillo trained that the street smelled of flowers.

MPs came from Ottawa on buses to pay their respects. On the way back, a young NDP MP from Quebec, overcome by the emotion of the day, confronted Trudeau, telling him that another young female NDP MP had been harassed by Liberal Newfoundland MP Scott Andrews. "If you don't believe me," she said, "ask Scott Simms."

Simms, then the Liberal member for Coast of Bays–Central–Notre Dame, on the north coast of Newfoundland, was at home in his riding. He got a call from the whip's office asking what he knew about the matter. Simms was friends with the victim, who had sought his advice for how to deal with Andrews. She didn't want to make a complaint, fearing the impact it might have on her career.

When the MP who had spoken to Trudeau met with the Liberal and NDP whips to discuss the situation, she alleged that she, too, had been mistreated in March, by Montreal Liberal MP Massimo Pacetti. She eventually told the *Huffington Post* that after a sports night, Pacetti invited her to his room, where they had "sex without explicit consent."

Trudeau and his team were afraid that the NDP leadership might, to embarrass the Liberals, make the allegations public. The fact that the parties would soon be facing each other in Quebec ridings made it impossible for them to tackle the situation together. Moreover, there was no mechanism to handle the matter. Because of parliamentary privilege, Ontario provincial labour law does not apply on Parliament Hill, and at the time there was no good way to deal with sexual wrongdoing. For this situation—an accusation directed to a party leader about alleged misconduct by and against MPs—there was no playbook.

Telford, Butts, and Trudeau took legal advice and huddled. In Purchase's words, "it was like a twenty-four- maybe forty-eight-hour period of everything. Everybody was on the same page." They quickly decided that Pacetti and Andrews would have to be suspended from caucus until an investigation could be conducted. Trudeau announced it less than a week after the MP had approached him, telling reporters he had a "duty to act." "It's 2014, it's time this workplace, like other workplaces across the country, had a process whereby these issues can be aired and dealt with," he said.

The story made national headlines. Pacetti and Andrews—both family men—claimed innocence. After receiving an investigation report from a law firm, in March 2015, Trudeau expelled both MPs permanently, ending their political careers. The report has never been made public. (Neither Andrews nor Pacetti were ever charged in relation to the complaints.)

It was a difficult situation in a place where for decades such incidents had been quietly swept under the rug. For generations, in a workplace where partisan loyalty trumped all other considerations, where people regularly gathered with alcohol after hours and young staffers were expected to defer to the lordly men who run the country, women often had to put up with abuse. When the #MeToo movement finally hit, and women started sharing their stories publicly, the culture changed. MPs brought in a new sexual harassment policy in the wake of the Pacetti-Andrews affair. Trudeau's decisive action helped bring the policy on the Hill into something more like what employees can expect in other workplaces.

Diamond Isinger, a young staffer from British Columbia who came to Ottawa to work for Trudeau, later went public to deal with harassment after an incident during a leadership race in BC. She believes the training and structure the Liberals set up made the Hill a safer place to work. "It was very interesting comparing and contrasting my experience at that time. They had no preventative measures in place as to how to deal with this stuff. That's opposite of my experience here in Ottawa, where when you reported stuff, it was taken seriously."

In the short term, the incident was another success for the Trudeau team. It didn't give them a bump in the polls, but as with the Senate expulsions, they had demonstrated that they could manage a difficult situation and come out of it with the reputation of the leader improved.

———

WHEN POLITICIANS WIN A party leadership, they normally get a post-convention boost from the media coverage. Trudeau, with his special connection to Canadians, got a bigger boost than normal, and it lasted a lot longer. But he was not immune to the effects of gravity. In the months after winning, as he went around the country giving speeches and doing interviews, he repeatedly had to apologize or explain away comments he made, especially in matters relating to foreign affairs, the military, and national security.

During the leadership campaign, in a "ladies night" meet-and-greet with Liberal women in Toronto, he praised the Communist government of China: "There's a level of admiration I have for China. Their basic dictatorship is actually allowing them to turn their economy around on a dime." Chinese Canadians were appalled at his lighthearted comments about a country responsible for terrible human rights abuses.

On the day after he won the leadership, in an interview with the CBC's Peter Mansbridge, Trudeau was asked about the Boston Marathon bombing, a terrorist attack that took three lives. He said it was necessary to "look at root causes." "We don't know if it was terrorism, or a single crazy, or a domestic issue or a foreign issue . . . But there is no question that this happened because of someone who feels completely excluded, someone who feels completely at war with innocence, at war with society." Harper, who was in London for the funeral of Margaret Thatcher, pounced on Trudeau's squishy comments and asked the CBC for the chance to respond. He declared that the right response was to "condemn it categorically, and to the extent you can, deal with the perpetrators as harshly as possible." The next day, Trudeau clarified his remarks.

In February 2014, in an appearance on *Tout le monde en parle*, Trudeau was asked about the deaths of more than a hundred Ukrainian protesters in Maidan square. "It's very worrying, especially because Russia lost in hockey, they'll be in a bad mood," he said. Host Guy Lepage looked shocked that Trudeau could be so flippant. After the Ukrainian Canadian Congress and the Ukrainian ambassador complained, Trudeau apologized.

In May, Trudeau announced that the Liberals, like the NDP, would start whipping caucus votes on abortion, meaning that pro-life MPs could no longer vote to restrict abortion rights. Social conservatives and religious leaders denounced him as dictatorial, and he made this new position more painful by not properly explaining the policy, promising that "existing MPs . . . have been grandfathered in to a certain extent." Lawrence MacAulay, a veteran MP from Prince Edward Island, told the hometown *Guardian* that he would be able to continue to vote as he always had done. Behind the scenes, Trudeau's team made it clear he couldn't make this exception. Trudeau was still clarifying his policy weeks later, dragging out the controversy.

Later in October, in a speech to Canada 2020, the think tank run by his friend Tom Pitfield, Trudeau was asked about the Liberal position on the war against the homicidal maniacs in ISIS. The Liberal position was that other countries should fight ISIS. "Why aren't we talking more about the kind of humanitarian aid that Canada can and must be engaged in, rather than trying to whip out our CF-18s and show them how big they are?" Trudeau said. Pollster Frank Graves, who had spoken just before him, couldn't believe his ears. "I just fucking pained over putting together this sort of policy architecture framing and he comes up and makes a dick joke?"

Throughout this period, Mulcair was delivering excellent performances in the House of Commons. He did not inspire the same kind of adulation that Trudeau effortlessly attracted, but as the election drew nearer, he was starting to look like the alternative to Harper. He was strong on policy, with an analytical mind, and he rarely made dumb jokes.

Then on May 5, 2015, NDP leader Rachel Notley was elected in Alberta. It was a political earthquake. Alberta had been a one-party state since Peter Lougheed led the Progressive Conservatives to victory in 1971. Jim Prentice,* one of Harper's most impressive ministers, became premier in September 2014 and, given his record and intellectual abilities, was expected to keep governing. But Notley, an unusually good communicator, humbled him in the election debates and won a majority.

This unexpected victory breathed fresh life into Mulcair's federal leadership. According to Nanos's tracking poll, the NDP went from third place to first in voter intention overnight. At the time, voters on the left were desperate to get rid of Harper, and they were not particularly fussy about who could accomplish this task. Frank Graves called them "promiscuous progressives." A poll in May found that about 40 percent of both Liberal and NDP supporters identified the other party as their second choice, but only 13 percent of Liberal supporters and 8 percent of NDP supporters

---

* Prentice died tragically in a small plane crash in British Columbia on October 13, 2016.

would consider voting Conservative, and 58 percent of Canadians would not consider voting Conservative under any circumstances. Canadians looked to be ready to move on from Harper, but they were open to either Trudeau or Mulcair as the agent. After Notley's shocking victory, they seemed to settle on Mulcair.

———

EVEN WHEN THE NDP moved ahead, Trudeau kept doing rallies, drawing big crowds across the country. With his boundless confidence and high energy, he is a master of retail politics. On the road, he would go to bed early, get up while his staff was sleeping, work out for an hour, and then campaign hard all day, glad-handing and speechifying. "I've never seen anything like it," says McNair, who staffed him on the road in the early days. "I've been on campaigns where you do a certain number of events a day, and Justin could double or triple what a normal politician could do in a day."

In 2015, the party decided to mark the fiftieth anniversary of the adoption of the Canadian flag. The Harper government, which had run big campaigns for the two-hundredth anniversary of the War of 1812 and the two-hundredth birthday of Sir John A. Macdonald, was planning little to mark the occasion. The maple leaf flag had been a Liberal project, initiated by Lester Pearson and bitterly opposed by John Diefenbaker, and Harper seemed to be downplaying it.

The Liberals decided on a rally in Mississauga. They convinced Jean Chrétien, who as a young MP had taken part in the parliamentary debate around the flag, to give a speech along with Trudeau. "We had no money, no staff," says Marlene Floyd, who stayed up half the night steaming flags she found in a storage room. They hung the flags, put a riser in the middle of the room, promoted the event on social media, and hoped for the best. "We didn't know how it was going to go. We didn't know how many people were going to show up."

Some twenty-five hundred people attended the celebration. "It was beautiful," Floyd remembers. "The diversity, the excitement, the pride. It was Trudeau at his best. Chrétien came in like it was a taste of the past. It was so good. And that was when I knew something was happening, the crowds we were attracting and the excitement we were attracting."

They used the same technique in rallies across the country, and the crowds kept on coming. Trudeau could pack them in.

———

IN FEBRUARY 2015, WITH eight months to go until the election, Eve Adams, the Conservative MP for Mississauga–Brampton South, was looking at the end of her career as an MP. Because of a redistribution and an ugly riding-level nomination battle, she was not going to be able to run as a Conservative in the next election. She decided to defect. Butts negotiated the details with her and her partner, Dimitri Soudas, who had been resigned from his job as executive director of the Conservative Party of Canada after interfering in her nomination battle.

Trudeau and Adams appeared together in the National Press Theatre in Ottawa to deliver their mini-bombshell. "I can no longer support mean-spirited leadership that divides people instead of bringing them together," she said. "We need a kind, generous and strong leadership that champions a shared vision for how to make Canada work for everyone."

Trudeau's director of communications, Kate Purchase, tweeted: "Can I just say, in my job, it's highly gratifying to hear the entire gallery go 'whoa' when we start a press conference."

Over at Conservative Party headquarters, the reaction was lighthearted. "We were all in our offices laughing," says Fred DeLorey. "Like, we're not gasping for the reason you think. It's not a prize." Jenni Byrne, Harper's campaign manager, was angered by what she saw as Soudas's betrayal of the tight-knit group around her boss but was pleased to be rid of this pair. She sent Butts a bouquet to thank him for taking them off her hands.

There was something sordid about the whole thing. The Liberals were behaving as though they had scored a coup, and the defection looked good on TV, but nobody who knew the details thought the Liberals had done something clever. Columnist Andrew Coyne wrote that Trudeau had delivered a "crawlingly demeaning performance."

At the time, the anticipated high-stakes conflict between Liberals and Conservatives in the election had led to speculation about parties looking for what insiders call "oppo"—opposition research that could be dropped during a campaign. There was gossip about the private lives of both leaders, rumours of explosive stories that could damage either of them. In that context, the defection of Adams, and, with her, Soudas, who had been a key part of the Harper operation, set off speculation that he, not Adams, was the real prize because of the oppo he could provide. Butts admits he was hoping to rattle the Tories. "I kind of thought it was a good idea . . . that it would play with their team's head because they assumed with Dimitri would come intelligence. 'Cause that's the way they thought of it. They were very Nixonian." In retrospect, he doesn't think it was a good idea. "It was unbelievably stupid."

The Liberals did try to get oppo out of it. A campaign staffer went to the Adams/Soudas residence and Soudas showed them what he had, but it didn't amount to much. Kevin Bosch, the research director for the Liberal Research Bureau, shopped the content to Bob Fife, but Fife didn't see anything newsworthy.

The Conservatives were never that uneasy about Soudas handing over dirty laundry. "I didn't think there was any," said DeLorey. "And if there was, there's nothing he was aware of."

After crossing the floor, Adams had to win a Liberal nomination. The party encouraged her to run in Milton, but she wanted the riding of Eglinton–Lawrence. Conservative Joe Oliver had won it in 2011, but it was likely to flip back to the Liberals. Standing in her way was Marco Mendicino, a mob-fighting prosecutor and a son of the influential Italian community in the riding.

I was there that day at the polling place, watching Soudas and Adams ushering new Canadians in to vote for her, mostly Somali and South Asians, while Mendicino's people, mostly Italians, streamed in. Mendicino was ahead all along and eventually won the nomination and the election. He went on to become an important minister for Trudeau, until he was eventually dropped from Cabinet. The Liberals had let Adams run, but they didn't help her enough to win. "There were no candidates we really wanted who lost," said one senior member of Team Trudeau.

———

BY JULY 2015, AS the Adams business came to its shabby denouement and summer gave way to fall, the Liberals were no longer looking great. The week before Zehaf-Bibeau's attack on Parliament Hill, they announced they would oppose the Canadian mission in Iraq. Liberals supported the fight against ISIS but wanted other countries to do the fighting. After the murder of Nathan Cirillo, however, Harper increasingly focused on the threat of Islamist terrorism and brought in Bill C-51, legislation to give new powers to CSIS, the Canadian Security Intelligence Service. The NDP, convinced by civil libertarian arguments that the government was overreaching, opposed the bill. The Liberals reluctantly agreed to support it, promising to amend it after they formed the government. One Liberal MP told me that the party felt cornered: "The feeling was we can't do this again, therefore we better support C-51, otherwise they'll use soft on national security, soft on terror against us."

Harper, who surely knew that his re-election was a long shot, was delivering harsh rhetoric, by Canadian standards, on national security. That appeared to strike a chord with some voters, giving the Conservatives a boost in the polls, while the NDP's opposition to the same measures found favour among their supporters. The Liberals, in the mushy middle, were nowhere. MPs from big cities were hearing about the security bill from their constituents and complaining to the people around Trudeau. It was one more thing that raised questions about his seriousness.

The young prince was looking like a lightweight. To respond, the Liberals rolled out two big policy positions to get ready for the election. The first, delivered in May on the day before Notley's victory, was the central plank of the party's campaign—a tax cut for the middle class. The Liberals made the announcement at a diner in Aylmer, across the river from Ottawa. Trudeau announced he would cut income taxes on those who made between $44,701 and $89,401 a year. He would pay for it by creating a new, higher tax bracket for those who made more than $200,000. He also promised to combine two programs—the Canada Child Tax Benefit and the National Child Benefit Supplement—into a single larger benefit that would give families up to $6,400 annually for every child under the age of six, and up to $5,400 for children between six and seventeen.

The promise was based on the discussion at Mont-Tremblant—the decision to propose policies that would benefit the middle class. "We can do more for the people who need it, by doing less for the people who don't," Trudeau said.

It was difficult, outside a campaign, to get the public to pay attention, but Trudeau was laying out the argument that Liberals would be taking into the election: "Canada has always done well when most Canadians are doing well—when we have a strong and successful middle class. The fact is, over the past 10 years, Mr. Harper's plan has failed. We are not getting the economic growth, and we're not getting fairness and success for the middle class."

The second big rollout, at the Château Laurier in June, was a democratic reform package, a thirty-two-point plan to breathe new life into the democracy, which many voters believed had been damaged by the Conservatives. "Harper has turned Ottawa into a partisan swamp, promoting partisan interests at the expense of public trust." Trudeau promised gender parity in decision-making roles, improved government transparency, and a parliamentary committee to study alternatives to the first-past-the-post system, including ranked ballots and proportional representation. "We are committed to ensuring that the 2015 election will be the last federal election using first-past-the-post," he said, a promise he was to repeat daily during the coming election.

I was there for the announcement that day, and I was impressed by Trudeau's upbeat, confident, energetic performance. He was widely considered to be failing, but his boundless self-confidence was buoying him and the people around him. He didn't seem bothered.

I was not impressed by the promise to consider proportional representation because I didn't believe it was real. I have long thought it would be good for Canadian democracy, given that the first-past-the-post system often provides winning parties with an unfair election-day seat bonus while wasting the votes of people who vote for the NDP and the Greens. It exaggerates the impact of swings, rewards regional parties, and guarantees blocks of safe seats—the Conservatives in Saskatchewan, for example, and the Liberals in Toronto—meaning that hundreds of thousands of voters have no voice in the House of Commons.

Opponents of proportional representation—including Liberal and Conservative electoral strategists—point to the danger of elevating radical voices and the benefits of stability. I thought Trudeau was hypocritically dangling the carrot of proportional representation to appeal to New Democrat and Green voters, while the people who ran Liberal election campaigns would be crystal clear behind closed doors that no change should be made under any circumstances.

Suspicious, I asked Trudeau why we should believe he was opening the door to proportional representation when he had always opposed coalition governments, knowing they would be the inevitable outcome. "I start from a position of trust of Canadians," he said. "I'm confident that Canadians will make the right choices at the ballot box. I don't believe in limiting their choices or reducing the options at the ballot box that they get to make. The fact of the matter is we need electoral reform. We need to move beyond the first-past-the-post system that doesn't ensure Canadian voices and votes are valued and valid."

I reported his comments, but I did not believe him—and, as things turned out, I was right not to believe him.

———

STANDING BEHIND TRUDEAU THAT day at the Château, clapping obediently on the applause lines, stood an impressive group of candidates, including Lieutenant-General Andrew Leslie, the former commander of the Canadian Army; Kent Hehr, a disability activist, lawyer, and former MLA from Alberta; Maryam Monsef, a refugee with Afghan roots; Bill Blair, the former Toronto police chief; and Amarjeet Sohi, a former Edmonton city councillor.

The Liberals were struggling in the polls, but they had signed up high-profile candidates for the 2015 election. Harjit Singh Sajjan, from Vancouver, had served with distinction in the Canadian Armed Forces in Afghanistan and in the Vancouver Police Department. Jane Philpott, a doctor from Markham, had an admirable track record doing health advocacy in Canada and medical development work in Africa. Jody Wilson-Raybould, a Kwakwaka'wakw prosecutor from Vancouver, had broken through glass ceilings in First Nations politics. Jim Carr, from Winnipeg, had experience as a journalist and a provincial Cabinet minister. Ahmed Hussen, from Toronto, had been president of the Canadian Somali Congress. Bill Morneau, from Toronto, the chairman of the pension firm Morneau Shepell and the C.D. Howe Institute, also played an active role on charitable boards. Mélanie Joly, a Montreal lawyer, had run a surprisingly effective (though unsuccessful) mayoral campaign against Denis Coderre.

Chrystia Freeland, of Toronto, was the most important recruit. She grew up on a farm in Peace River, Alberta, had family roots in Ukraine, and had studied Russian history and literature at Harvard University before getting a master's degree at Oxford. Then, in 1988 and 1989, when the Soviet Union was collapsing, she moved to Kyiv, where she worked as a fixer for foreign journalists, helping, for instance, the *New York Times* expose Soviet responsibility for a historic massacre at Bykovnya. Her work brought her to the attention of the KGB, who in internal reports called her "a remarkable individual" with "an analytical mindset." They saw her as a threat—"erudite, sociable, persistent, and inventive in achieving her goals"—and eventually expelled her.

Freeland went on to build a successful career as a journalist in Toronto and New York and published the bestselling and well-reviewed *Plutocrats: The Rise of the New Global Super-Rich and the Fall of Everyone Else*. When she invited Trudeau and Butts to the book's Toronto launch, they showed up to woo her. "I think Chrystia wanted to run," says Butts, though "she was genuinely hot and cold on the idea." Early in 2013, when Bob Rae announced he was going to give up his seat in Toronto Centre, Trudeau asked Freeland to run there. She said no, but the Trudeau team were tenacious, and in June she agreed.

There were other candidates who could not be persuaded—Vancouver mayor Gregor Robertson and future Manitoba premier Wab Kinew. Butts had booked a breakfast meeting with Jian Ghomeshi, but the night before, a friend warned him not to proceed with his invitation—thereby avoiding what would have been a disastrous connection for the Liberals.

Trudeau's people put a lot of effort into finding potential candidates, and former prime minister Paul Martin acted as a talent spotter. The result was an impressive lineup. "Because we were up in the polls," Butts says, "we had the opportunity to attract a kind of candidate that we wouldn't otherwise." Regardless, as everyone got ready for the 2015 election, Trudeau was not looking like a winner.

The one political ally who stuck with Trudeau during that period was Ontario premier Kathleen Wynne, who was fresh from winning a majority government in 2014. Harper had refused to help her improve retirement benefits for Ontario after she had campaigned on doing so, treating her like an opponent rather than a premier. She pushed back harder than is traditional. When Trudeau looked like a dud, she stuck with him, and as the election loomed, her team arranged to have dozens of ministerial staffers go to work for Trudeau. They ran campaigns at the riding level across the province, and several key operators joined the central campaign, including the especially useful Brian Clow and Zita Astravas. As Andrew Bevan, Wynne's chief of staff, puts it: "We wanted to give him the best possible chances by having the best people at his disposal to do it. So we were happy."

Against the odds, Trudeau and his people had built a formidable political machine around the son of Canada. He was accident-prone but hard-working, resilient, and confident, and Canadians felt they knew him. He had good instincts, had gathered a team of talented people around him, and, crucially, was listening to them, working on his skills, applying himself, getting better. He was ready for an election and looking forward to proving himself.

3

READY OR NOT

O n August 2, 2015, Stephen Harper went to Rideau Hall to call an
election for October 19. Canadians were in for an unusually long
campaign. "This is no time for risky plans that could harm our future," he
said. "It is time to stay the course and stick to our plan." Harper and his
minister for democratic reform, Pierre Poilievre, had brought in changes
to the Elections Act that added $5 million to the spending cap for each
additional week of the campaign. This meant that the Conservatives,
who had by far the biggest war chest, were poised to outspend the other
parties. Jean-Pierre Kingsley, the former head of Elections Canada, went
on CBC Radio's *The House* to cry foul: "What it does is completely distort
everything we've ever fought for, everything we've established as rules."

By this point, Harper had annoyed so many people that he was facing
stiff headwinds in his quest for a fourth mandate. He was using stark
language, warning of an "uncertain and unstable" economy and the threat
of a "violent global jihadist movement."

The national security argument was new, but the economic argument
had been a central part of the Harper formula all along. For nine years,
he had been presiding over the Canadian economy, smoothing the way

for natural resource projects and emphasizing the value of tax cuts, particularly by taking two percentage points off the Goods and Services Tax. Finance Minister Joe Oliver had delivered a balanced budget, but it was not then clear whether revenues would be high enough to leave the government in the black.

Harper got good marks from Canadians for guiding Canada through the 2008 financial crisis, which in this country did nothing like the damage it did elsewhere, and he had signed dozens of trade agreements. But the polls showed that Canadians were nervous about a recession. There was a growing sense that economic benefits were not being shared equally, and uncertainty about whether Harper would help the middle class if there were hard times ahead.

As the campaign began, the smart money was on a Conservative-NDP contest. Both the CBC and the *Globe and Mail* headlined seat projections that put the Liberals a distant third. The opening day matched those expectations. After Harper announced the election, Mulcair launched his campaign from Gatineau, with Parliament Hill in the background, while Trudeau was on a plane for British Columbia, which meant he missed the crucial first news cycle of the day.

Expectations for Trudeau were low. Before the first debate, the typically astute Conservative campaign spokesman Kory Teneycke foolishly said that Trudeau would do badly. "I think that if he comes on stage with his pants on, he will probably exceed expectations," he joked. But Trudeau was on top of his files, and although most of the immediate coverage focused on the exchanges between Mulcair and Harper, Trudeau held his own, which gave him a boost.

In the Conservative war room, the campaign staff were disappointed. "I remember people being like 'Oh no, he didn't mess up,'" recalls one staffer. "That's not good. 'Cause everyone kind of was hoping that he would."

Throughout the debate, Mulcair was wearing a frozen grin, the result of media coaching designed to downplay his image as a nasty character. It came off as weird, particularly when he was delivering his typically peevish lines. Like Teneycke, Mulcair seemed to have underestimated Trudeau.

The NDP leader's big miscalculation was on the Clarity Act. During the Liberal leadership race, Trudeau had told a forum at McGill that he thought a sovereignty referendum would require a 66 percent mandate to break up Canada, a comment he had been forced to retract. Mulcair would never make such a mistake, and he sought to barbecue Trudeau for it, pressing him repeatedly on what number he thought would be necessary.

"Mr. Trudeau has an obligation . . . to come clean with Canadians. What's his number? What is your number, Mr. Trudeau?"

Trudeau sputtered, looked lost, and then sprung the trap. "You want a number, Mr. Mulcair?"

"Yeah," Mulcair said, looking like he expected Trudeau to say something dumb. "Give us a number."

Trudeau pounced: "I'll give you a number. Nine. My number is nine. Nine Supreme Court justices said one vote is not enough to break up this country, and yet that is Mr. Mulcair's position. He wants to be prime minister of this country, and he's choosing to side with the separatist movement in Quebec and not with the Supreme Court of Canada."

The Liberal war room packaged the clip and quickly pushed it out as a paid advertisement on social media. They were able to get the exchange in front of voters and framed it as Trudeau besting the NDP leader. To David Herle, "It was the most telegraphed punch in political history. Mulcair had been saying for a week that's what he was going to ask. 'When I get in front of you, I'm going to launch a right upper cut to the left side of your jaw.' You have a week to think about that. It was crazy. Trudeau was completely prepared. They knew it was a winner, and they were ready to do the ads when he did it."

And Mulcair had a big problem—people didn't know who he was. He had been leading the party since 2012, regularly appearing on TV screens, but even voters who did recognize him thought his name was Mulclair. In

Herle's focus groups, people shown his picture struggled to identify him. Sometimes more people recognized Herle from his TV appearances than Mulcair. For some reason, Canadians "just weren't interested in the guy."

The early days of the campaign were also tough for Harper. Mike Duffy was on trial, facing thirty-one counts, including fraud, connected with Senate expenses. (He was later acquitted on all counts and served in the Senate until he retired at age seventy-five.) In the second week of the campaign, emails were released in court that showed some of Harper's closest aides squabbling and dissembling as they bickered about how to contain the scandal.

Following Trudeau's strong debate performance, the Liberals began to creep up in the polls, making it a three-way race. Then, on August 25, speaking in Hamilton, Mulcair made a key election pledge: "Our first budget will be a balanced budget."

Frank Graves, who was polling the electorate—sharing the costs among unions, the Liberals, and a media client—says Mulcair's promise was the most tone-deaf move he had seen in a career around politics. Nobody who might vote for the NDP wanted balanced budgets. The people Graves calls promiscuous progressives—left-leaning voters who wanted a progressive government but didn't care what colour it was—rejected austerity. "Nobody who's going to vote for you gives a fuck about the balanced budget," he says. "They see you're making yourself somewhat less objectionable to people that aren't going to vote for you. It's really dumb."

The NDP announcement gave the Liberals an opening, and they pounced, immediately attacking Mulcair for making a promise that would lead to economic pain. "Why does he want to take billions of dollars out of the economy in a recession, and what public investments will he be cutting to do that?" Trudeau asked, with former prime minister Paul Martin by his side. "Let me tell you this, the choice in this election is clear. It's between jobs and growth or austerity and cuts—and Tom Mulcair just made the wrong choice."

Two days later, in Oakville, in the heart of the political battleground in the Toronto suburbs, Trudeau announced his financial plan. He promised

$125 billion in infrastructure spending, double what the Conservatives planned, to be financed with "a modest short-term deficit" for three years. Thereafter, he would balance the budget.

Butts was thinking of the first part of the campaign as the "progressive primary," in which voters would figure out who was on their side. "It became kind of the ballot question on whether they were real progressives," he says. "Our willingness to slay that sacred cow and their timidity, I guess is the right word, clearly differentiated us for progressives."

Harper made fun of Trudeau's promise. "He now says he'll run a modest deficit, a tiny deficit, so small you can hardly see it," he said, holding his fingers barely apart. "Friends, we've gone through this before. Look at the mess in Ontario with a modest deficit from a Liberal government."

Harper was right to cast doubt on Trudeau's promises. Since 2015, the government has never balanced a budget—and never will. The forecast deficit for 2023/24 is $40 billion. The national debt is approaching $1.2 trillion, about double what it was when Trudeau took office. At the time, however, Canadians were anxious about the economy and wanted their government to invest in infrastructure. Trudeau's campaign was the only one promising to do so.

"I've probably done more polling on fiscal policy than anybody in Canada has," says Herle, who did a lot of work for Paul Martin when he was tackling the deficit in the 1990s. "And I knew that people had only cared about the deficit for a very brief period . . . Essentially, people wanted the government to be doing more than it was doing, and they were not very fussed about whether or not that created deficits. I knew it was going to be well received by the public, and I knew it was essential to the strategy of the campaign."

———

ON SEPTEMBER 2, ABDULLAH and Rehanna Kurdi, refugees who had fled the war in Syria, got in an inflatable boat in Bodrum, Turkey, to make the crossing to Kos, Greece, a few kilometres away, with their two sons, Alan, three, and Ghalib, five. The boat sank five minutes after leaving the coast, and Alan, Ghalib, and Rehanna drowned. When the remains of little Alan washed up on a Turkish beach, a photographer took a picture of him face down at the water's edge. The horrifying image went viral.

The day after the photos landed, Alan's aunt gave a tearful news conference from British Columbia in which she told Canadians that the family had tried and failed to get approval to come to Canada. She blamed the government for the tragedy. Harper responded that the deaths were "heartbreaking" but defended Canada's refugee policy. He looked defiant rather than heartbroken. Many voters, however, believed the opposition attacks, that the Conservatives were to blame. Fred DeLorey, who was trying unsuccessfully to win Peter MacKay's old riding in Nova Scotia, started hearing about it on doorsteps from voters who believed the government was responsible. "We got it everywhere. It became one of the hot issues."

Trudeau faulted the government for being insufficiently compassionate and promised to take in twenty-five thousand Syrian refugees, fifteen thousand more than Harper planned to welcome. It was another bad media day for the government and a good day for Trudeau.

———

IN 2012, THE CBC'S *Marketplace* set up a hidden camera to secretly record appliance repairmen who they suspected of running scams on Toronto homeowners. When host Tom Harrington reviewed the tape of one appliance repairman, Jerry Bance (who did a good job repairing a dishwasher), he was shocked to see him pick up a cup, urinate in it, and dump the pee in the sink. *Marketplace* aired the clip but did not realize that the man was not only a candidate but had run for the Conservatives in Scarborough–Rouge Park once before. Local Liberals noticed, and they told Liberal researcher Kevin Bosch, who found the *Marketplace* clip on-line and quickly confirmed it was the same guy. His people fed the story to the CBC. It led the national news that night. Bosch and his colleagues were at a wedding, watching with delight as the story broke and #Peegate started trending on Twitter.

The story was bad news for Jenni Byrne, Harper's campaign manager. Her team was responsible for vetting candidates to avoid this kind of embarrassment. It was not that Byrne hadn't tackled the job with suffi-cient zeal. In July she had blacklisted the candidacy of Newfoundland candidate Ches Crosbie, son of John, a legendary Cabinet minister in Brian Mulroney's government. Ches had appeared in a *Macbeth* parody, gently poking fun at Harper to raise money for a St. John's theatre. That was enough for Byrne to redline him, which I thought betrayed an insuf-ficient appreciation for the bard, among other things.

Byrne couldn't have been expected to know that her candidate had urinated in a cup on camera, but the campaign was going badly and, in the war room, tension was developing between her and both Ray Novak and Guy Giorno, national campaign chair. Novak, who had taken over as chief of staff after Nigel Wright resigned, was personally close to the prime minister. When Harper became Opposition leader, and Novak and he were constantly on the road, Novak briefly stayed rent-free above the garage at Stornaway, the official residence. Giorno, a former chief of staff to Ontario premier Mike Harris, had been Harper's chief of staff before Wright. As the campaign struggled, staffers sensed that these two men were disappointed in Byrne's performance. That tension boiled over after the repairman story broke.

At 10:30 p.m. on September 6, Giorno emailed a copy of the CBC story to Byrne and Novak, adding, "Is there any reason not to recom-mend to the PM that he be dumped?"

Byrne responded by pointing out that a Conservative MP was the subject of a sex assault complaint: "As much as this is disgusting and em-barrassing—Jerry is not the biggest candidate concern we have."

Byrne was referring to Rick Dykstra, the MP for St. Catharines, who had been the subject of a sexual assault complaint by a young Conservative staffer in 2014. The woman had gone to the Ottawa police, who opened an investigation, but she was fearful of the implications for her career and had asked police not to proceed with charges. She eventually moved home to her family. Byrne was unhappy with the way it had transpired.

Novak replied to Byrne and Giorno early the next morning: "I will just note, on the assumption this exchange is likely to come to light in a discovery process should the matter go to court, that I have no such knowledge. I am aware of allegations, I have never met the complainant, and I am assured that those who did interact with her at the time urged her to take the matter to authorities."

"This is correct," replied Giorno. "I am aware of no evidence either. However, I do think there is a case for [Conservative Party lawyer] Arthur [Hamilton] or other counsel to be asked to review and report on the matter."

Byrne shot back moments later: "Great—you guys are protected legally. That makes everything better. Sleep well at night."

Two days after the tense exchange, Byrne was off the campaign tour and back in campaign headquarters in Ottawa. Insiders leaked to both CTV and the CBC that she had been sent away because Harper was unhappy with her. For the overworked staffers in the war room, it was tense and unpleasant. They knew they were losing, and the talented woman leading them had been undercut.

———

BY EARLY SEPTEMBER, IN contrast, the Liberals were feeling great. The team had gelled, they were sticking to their plan, and the polls were going up. Already the election was a close three-way race. Trudeau, with his boundless confidence, was sure he was going to win but was frustrated that he wasn't already in front.

"I had known since 2012 that I was going to get a majority, and everyone told me I was wrong. Everyone. I said, 'No, no, no. The country is ready to swing,' and it was certainly ready by 2015. But at that moment, there wasn't any math that justified it. I remember through the first stretch of that campaign I'd say, 'Okay, Katie, Gerry, you tell me the way to win an election campaign is go out and win every day. Well, I'm going out and I'm winning every day. And yet the numbers aren't moving. The polls aren't moving.' Everyone goes, 'Yeah, but you feel it on the ground.' 'Yeah, I feel it on the ground. It's just nobody's noticing.' And they're like, 'No, no, no. It'll happen. Just keep connecting. Just keep doing the work. The polls will eventually shift.'"

Trudeau was waiting for the shift to show up. He said it was like watching a TV program. "Oh my God, there's five minutes left in the show and, as Seinfeld said, 'Timmy's still stuck in the cave.' How are they gonna get him out?"

On September 5, the day before the pee-in-a-cup story broke, Forum Research released a poll showing that 47 percent of Canadians believed Trudeau was not ready to be prime minister. A slick Conservative attack ad had convinced Canadians to be skeptical of the young man. The ad showed a panel of managers considering Trudeau's resumé and concluding that he was not yet ready to make the tough decisions Canada needed. "I'm not saying no forever, but not now," said a woman as they prepared to reject his application. "Nice hair, though," said an older South Asian man. A female narrator drove home the point: "Justin Trudeau. He's just not ready."

The Tories sought to convince Canadians to discount Trudeau, and they were somewhat successful, but many Canadians who felt they knew him hesitated to go along. In focus groups, Butts noticed that people accepted the Conservative message only reluctantly. "The body language of people was like, 'Yeah, I guess that's right.' They were kind of disappointed to be convinced by it. And that was when we got the idea that if we could answer that decisively, people would forget it ever happened . . . So we let [the Conservatives] spend and spend and our numbers were going down and down and down. And a lot of people in the party were like, 'You've got to respond to this . . .' We were like, 'We're going to get one chance to respond to this. And it's not now.'"

The moment came during the first English debate, when Trudeau showed he could go toe to toe with Harper and Mulcair. That day, the Liberals released an upbeat ad, filmed in Major's Hill Park behind the Château Laurier, with the Parliament Buildings in the background. Trudeau, looking fit and comfortable in an open-necked dress shirt, walked toward the camera, talking. "Stephen Harper says I'm not ready. I'll tell you what I'm not ready for—I'm not ready to stand by as our economy slides into recession, not ready to watch hard-working Canadians lose jobs and fall further behind."

Herle had brought in advertising guru David Rosenberg, of Toronto's Bensimon Byrne, who had worked with him on Paul Martin and Kathleen Wynne campaigns. Rosenberg had a breakfast meeting with his partner Jack Bensimon, Trudeau, and Butts at Pearson International Airport. Rosenberg was impressed by Trudeau's physical energy. "He's got a lot of charisma. The word I use for it is vigour. You can see it coming out of every pore. He projected a huge amount of self-confidence." The ad made the most of that physical presence, but it was a gamble. One of the rules of political communication is not to repeat an opponent's message about you. Herle felt the campaign had no choice but to confront it. "It was the conventional wisdom now that he wasn't ready. It wasn't just something Conservatives were saying; it was something people would say if you talk to them. So it had to be addressed. But he totally turned it around with his campaign performance, which was flawless."

Trudeau was gradually convincing Canadians that he was ready for the job. Internal polling showed that in the Greater Toronto Area (GTA), opinion on the question shifted as the campaign went on. On August 5, only 38 percent of voters thought he was ready. By the end of October, 66 percent believed he was up to the job.

In September, the Liberals rolled out a second ad, the escalator spot, which featured Trudeau walking up a down escalator looking poised in a shirt and tie, talking to the camera. "This is what's happening to millions of Canadians for ten years under Stephen Harper. His idea—to give benefits to the wealthy but make cuts to everything else—has made it harder for most people to get ahead. And Mulcair promises more cuts." The ad ends with the escalator reversing, and Trudeau talking positively about Liberal plans as he ascends. It was clever and effective, and it spread virally online, with three million views on YouTube.

The Liberals were doing a good job, but what they were trying to do—go from third to first in a single election—was without precedent. To accomplish it, they would have to be both good and lucky. "To win a majority government when you are in third place in the polls, you need the frontrunner to mess up and you need the person in second to mess up," says Nik Nanos. "The probability of those two things happening at the same time, it is very rare. In 2015, they benefited from that piece of luck."

———

IN 2013, WHEN ZUNERA Ishaq, a Pakistani woman resident in Ontario, received approval to become a Canadian citizen, she was informed she would have to remove her face-covering niqab to take the oath, as departmental policy required. Ishaq sued and won, securing the right for veiled women to take the oath. Immigration Minister Jason Kenney appealed the decision to the Federal Court of Appeal, which issued its ruling on September 15, in the middle of the campaign. Ishaq won again.

Campaigning in Victoriaville, Quebec, Harper said Ottawa would appeal: "I believe, and I think most Canadians believe, that it is offensive that someone would hide their identity at the very moment where they are committing to join the Canadian family."

Trudeau attacked Harper: "Canada defends the rights of minorities; we respect people's rights. That's what we will always do."

Mulcair took the same position: "I see that Muslims are often scape-goats for political debate, and that, I find it heartbreaking."

After the 2011 election, the NDP held fifty-nine of Quebec's seventy-five seats. The Liberals, Conservatives, and Bloc Québécois all wanted badly to take them, and on the niqab issue, the Bloc and the Tories had positions that lined up with the view of most Quebecers, unlike the NDP. Mulcair was in a bind, and the Bloc and Conservatives sought to profit from the disconnection between Mulcair's position and public opinion in the province. Denis Lebel, Harper's Quebec lieutenant, attacked Mulcair's position as he toured the province by bus. The Bloc Québécois ran an attack ad on the issue, with oil from an animated pipeline spill forming a niqab. The Quebec media zeroed in on the NDP weakness—and it started to hurt them.

Mulcair's campaign staff tried to convince him to soften his position, but rather than back down, Mulcair doubled down, giving a speech dedicated to the issue in Montreal on September 23, the eve of a French-language debate, declaring it a matter of human rights. To Mulcair, this issue is non-negotiable; his wife, Catherine Pinhas, is the child of Holocaust survivors. Senior NDP staffers Karl Bélanger and Anne McGrath tried to persuade him to find a way to neutralize the issue. "I said, 'I can't.'"

The Liberals did not have the same kind of problem. Bélanger, after a career spent working for the lefty underdogs, was watching a once-in-a-lifetime chance at victory fade away. Early in the campaign, he spoke to a senior Conservative campaign official who acknowledged the Tories were expecting a hard slog. "If we're going to lose, we'd rather lose to the NDP," he told Bélanger. "We'd rather lose to you guys."

When the niqab attacks began damaging the Mulcair campaign, Bélanger talked to the CPC staffer again.

"You're killing us."

"Your numbers are holding," said the Conservative.

"They're not holding. We're tanking. You're going to elect Trudeau."

The Tories kept up the attack. "He did not believe me," says Bélanger.

He should have. During the French-language debate, Gilles Duceppe and Harper hammered Mulcair on the niqab. The NDP slide continued in Quebec.

Inside the Conservative campaign, the controversy seemed to offer a glimmer of hope. Byrne told her troops that they needed to make the most of the issue.

"We were losing," says a campaign staffer. "Early on in the campaign, obviously we were losing, and she was one of the only senior people who accepted it. A lot of people were in denial. But she basically said that we needed a cultural issue like that to be in the news to turn out our base because we were losing on everything else, like the economy. It was like, our base is racist, and we need them to vote because nobody else is going to vote for us."

The problem for the Conservatives was that the niqab issue was only getting airtime in Quebec. So, on October 2, Immigration Minister Chris Alexander and Labour Minister Kellie Leitch held an event in Ottawa to announce that a re-elected Conservative government would introduce a police snitch line to encourage Canadians to report "barbaric cultural practices"—forced marriages, for example.

The promise backfired. While the Conservatives were likely looking at polls showing Canadians were concerned about barbaric cultural practices, the proposed snitch line looked transparently opportunistic, and new Canadians—not just Muslims—felt scapegoated. If the Tories were going after Muslims, what would stop them from going after some other group?

It was a desperate move by a losing campaign, and it has left a scar on the party, undoing a decade's work in building bridges to immigrant communities.

Alexander, who had an admirable career as a diplomat before he entered politics, told journalist Evan Solomon in 2016 that he regretted the whole thing. "I regret very much several issues that we blew up to a scale they should never have reached in the last campaign. It's why we lost. It was a terrible campaign."

TOWARD THE END OF September, as the campaign neared its peak, it was becoming clear that the Liberals were going to win—including in places where they had not been expected to be competitive. The three-way race was over as the NDP dropped daily in the polls. The "progressive primary" that Butts foresaw had settled on the agent of change, and it wasn't Mulcair. It was a two-way race, and Trudeau had the momentum.

On October 4, Trudeau held a rally in a Brampton rink, and seven thousand people turned up. They cheered every attack he made on Harper, especially when he accused the prime minister of encouraging "the politics of fear and division." "Stephen Harper isn't afraid of me, my friends," Trudeau said. "He's afraid of you. And he should be."

Trudeau promised hope and hard work, and the crowd in the rink loved it, loved him, cheered and applauded on cue. Rosenberg had a crew there, with three cameras focused on Trudeau, and two on the crowd. They quickly turned out an advertisement to capture the energy and emotion of the night. "We had to plan it before we had polling numbers to back it up," says Butts. "We took a big risk in putting that rally together, being convinced we would need a momentum ad to conclude the campaign. So it was a huge undertaking . . . Justin just hit it out of the park."

The parties' internal numbers are always better and more detailed than publicly available polls. By a week out, the Liberals were finding it hard to believe their results. "Katie [Telford] just showed me our internals," says Marlene Floyd. "And I just looked at her and I was like, 'Shut the fuck up' . . . When the wave came, it came hard." The party had assigned every riding in the country a designation, from platinum (the safest ridings) to bronze (those they might pick up if they were bound for a majority) to wood (those impossible to win). "On election night, I was like, who are these people winning? I had no idea. Bronze was what we needed for a majority, and the bronzes just kept winning."

A Liberal landslide was on the way. The Liberals were going to win everywhere. "We had two objectives going into 2015," recalls Butts. "One was that we obviously wanted to win a majority government, but the other was that we wanted to win seats in every province, and those are not as compatible objectives as they look. And we spent a lot of time in places where our time would've been better spent elsewhere."

It was coming together, everywhere at once. On October 7, *La Presse*, Montreal's most important newspaper, endorsed Trudeau, pointing to his particular qualities: "He avoids personal attacks," the editors wrote. "He likes people, and they like him back. He has a bit of Laurier in him . . . He is ready." On the campaign bus in Ontario, when Trudeau read the crucial editorial, he burst into tears. The Quebec media establishment, which had always been skeptical of him, had shifted. "In the polls, things were coming together, and then we had that endorsement," says Robert Asselin, who helped soften the ground for Trudeau at *La Presse*. "Quebec was the last piece."

Trudeau's eyes got wet again when I asked him about that moment during an interview in his Ottawa office in 2024. "I'm getting choked up just thinking about it right now. I am such a proud Quebecer, always have been. And I am so proud of what my dad did for Quebec and for this country, but . . . the collective wisdom out there, through my entry into politics . . . particularly the chattering classes in Quebec, was a Trudeau won't fly in Quebec. And I hadn't realized how much that weighed on me. I was confident . . . because I had so many conversations with great, real, salt-of-the-earth Quebecers who responded positively to me." The endorsement showed that he had convinced Quebecers that he was not as portrayed by the nationalist media elite. "My people saw me."

Trudeau had campaigned hard in British Columbia, where his maternal grandfather—Jimmy Sinclair—had been a popular Cabinet minister in Lester Pearson's government. He had taught high school in Vancouver and emphasized his ties to the province. In September, the campaign released a BC ad showing him hiking the Grouse Grind Trail, in which he promised to be a "prime minister who doesn't just talk BC but has it in the blood." The province was opening to him. On October 18, the last day of the campaign, he had a huge rally in North Vancouver, where Bruce Young led a contingent of people holding Jimmy Sinclair campaign signs.

Earlier that day, Trudeau held a rally for a thousand people in Calgary. David Frum, who had left Canada to work for the younger President Bush, was sure he was wasting his time: "Like George W. Bush campaigning hopelessly in California last weekend 2000, Justin Trudeau was in Calgary to create a false image of momentum," he tweeted. But Frum was wrong—the momentum was real. "It was pure magic," says Butts. "The last week of that campaign was the closest thing I've ever experienced to pure magic."

The one last roadblock was Dan Gagnier, the campaign's greybeard, who had guided Team Trudeau and helped to manage delicate questions. On October 14, just five days before the election, the Canadian Press ran a story based on an email Gagnier had sent to TransCanada executives. The company was then trying to build the Energy East pipeline to move Alberta oil to the Atlantic through Quebec, where the proposal was unpopular. Gagnier advised TransCanada to act quickly to lobby a new government, whether it would be NDP or Liberal, if it wanted to influence energy policy. "An energy strategy for Canada is on the radar and we need a spear carrier for those in the industry who are part of the solution going forward rather than refusing to grasp the implications of a changing global reality," he wrote.

Someone on the recipient list—it included the family member of a Harper Cabinet minister—saw that Gagnier's pitch would look bad if it became public. Gagnier, an unpaid volunteer, had told the Trudeau team when he signed up that he was working for Energy East. Although the campaign put out a release defending him, they needed the story to go away and found a way to let him know.

"They were looking at me and saying, 'Well, you know, what do you think you should do?'" Gagnier says. He resigned and returned to his retirement, somewhat bruised. "Politics being what it is, you basically get thrown under the wheels of the bus," he notes. "You have a lot of people saying, 'He's a great guy. He helped us a lot. Thank you very much.' But as they speed away, you know, there's not much you can do."

Mulcair and Harper both attacked, calling the Liberals hypocrites. Trudeau responded to Harper's attack by pointing out that the prime minister looked bad for having attended a Saturday night rally with former Toronto mayor Rob Ford. Harper campaigned on tough-on-crime policies, issuing dire warnings about Trudeau's plan to legalize marijuana, but with his back to the wall, he was seeking help from Ford, who had been filmed smoking crack. The man who took the video was later shot over it, according to a police report obtained by the *Toronto Star*. Harper was not tough on all criminals. In the *National Post*, Chris Selley described it as "a brand new low."

While Harper was embracing Rob Ford, the Liberals were in better company in the Greater Toronto Area. They had rolled out a new ad featuring "Hurricane" Hazel McCallion, the ninety-four-year-old former mayor of Mississauga, a beloved political heavyweight west of Toronto. Harper and his ministers had repeatedly accused both the Liberals and the New Democrats of planning to end pension income splitting, a measure that allows seniors to shift income for taxation purposes from one partner to another, reducing their overall tax burden. Neither party planned to do any such thing. The Canadian Press had fact-checked the assertion and labelled it "full of baloney," but the Conservative message was sticking.

Butts emailed Rosenberg on October 10 to propose pushing back with an ad featuring McCallion, who had agreed to help. Harper's dishonesty on the question reminded Rosenberg of the way scammers would deceive seniors: "It really just pissed me off." In less than an hour he wrote a script hammering Harper. In the ad, McCallion speaks directly to the camera. "Stephen Harper's not telling the truth saying Justin Trudeau will cancel income splitting for seniors. It's like one of those phone scams seniors get, because Harper thinks we're scared . . . Stephen, do I look scared to you?"

The Liberals hurriedly pushed the ad out through social media, where it took off, getting millions of views. It shifted vote intention among seniors by nineteen points in the last week of the campaign, according to EKOS polling. It was the closing argument the Liberals needed.

———

EARLY ON ELECTION NIGHT, when the numbers started coming in from Atlantic Canada, it was clear that Trudeau would get a majority. The Liberals swept that region, and then went on to win forty seats in Quebec, eighty seats in Ontario, seven in Manitoba, one in Saskatchewan, four in Alberta, and seventeen in British Columbia.

At the Queen Elizabeth hotel in Montreal, Trudeau gave a joyful speech. He started in French, his voice hoarse: "Canadians have chosen change, real change." He switched to English: "Sunny ways, my friends. Sunny ways. We beat fear with hope. We beat cynicism with hard work. We beat negative, divisive politics with a positive vision that brings Canadians together. Most of all, we defeated the idea that Canadians should be satisfied with less, that good enough is good enough and that better just isn't possible. Well, my friends, this is Canada, and in Canada better is always possible."

———

TRUDEAU BORROWED THE PHRASE "sunny ways" from Wilfrid Laurier's 1895 election campaign. Laurier got it from Aesop's fable of "The North Wind and the Sun," in which the wind and the sun compete to see who can make a man remove his coat. The north wind gives up after his gusts make the man clutch his coat even tighter. Then the sun shines, and the man gladly removes it. It was a promise to be positive, to resolve conflict with warmth rather than through force, a promise to approach government in a kinder way. It was a promise Trudeau would keep . . . for a while.

4

LONG HONEYMOON

Justin Trudeau's first Cabinet came from central casting, reflecting the diversity and breadth of Canada. Among the newly elected MPs, Bill Morneau, presented as a Bay Street whiz, was appointed finance minister. Harjit Singh Sajjan, a decorated combat veteran from Afghanistan and a Sikh (one of four in the Cabinet), was defence minister. Jody Wilson-Raybould, a lawyer from British Columbia and daughter of Bill Wilson, who had crossed swords with Trudeau *père* in the constitutional battles, became justice minister—by far the most prominent Cabinet role in Canadian history for an Indigenous person. Hunter Tootoo from Nunavut got Fisheries. Chrystia Freeland, who had mixed with international captains of industry, would handle International Trade. Navdeep Bains, a Sikh businessman from Brampton, would lead innovation and economic development. Maryam Monsef, the daughter of Afghan refugees, became minister of democratic institutions. Catherine McKenna, a lawyer and former diplomat who won an upset victory over the NDP's Paul Dewar in Ottawa, was appointed minister of environment and climate change. Jane Philpott, a physician with a stellar record, became minister of health.

There was also room for Liberal veterans. The previous leader, Stéphane Dion, got Foreign Affairs, a portfolio that often goes to former leaders. Marc Garneau got Transport; Ralph Goodale, Public Safety; John McCallum, Immigration; and Scott Brison became Treasury Board president. Dominic LeBlanc became House leader.

Crucially, the Cabinet was gender balanced, which gave Trudeau good headlines around the world. Not *everyone* was enthusiastic, however. Andrew Coyne, writing in the *National Post*, pointed out that because Trudeau was drawing from a less-than-balanced caucus, it was unlikely he selected the best candidates. "Women make up just over a quarter of the Liberal caucus, yet they will make up precisely half of cabinet. Your chances of getting into cabinet as a woman are as such roughly three times that of a man: 30 per cent, in a 28-member cabinet, versus 10 per cent."

Nobody, including Coyne, felt bad for the unfairly snubbed male politicians: "The issue here, God knows, is not fairness to male MPs. They knew what they were getting into when they signed up." But there were bitterly disappointed politicians, talented loyal soldiers who had slugged it out in election after election, men and women alike who had suddenly been eclipsed by Liberals elected on the Trudeau wave.

It was an impressive Cabinet, diverse and accomplished. Only later, after many unhappy exits and recriminations, would it seem that mistakes were made in the selections. As one senior former Liberal staffer told me later: "The Cabinet in 2015, that slate of candidates was incredible, and I think it showcased the best of Canada. The recruiting effort and the professionalization that people like Gerry and Katie brought in was amazing. They brought in a master narrative of what this government is and wants to be. And then they cast the Cabinet: 'Wouldn't it be great if an astronaut was transport minister? Wouldn't it be great if we had a Quebecer in charge of official languages and heritage? Wouldn't it be great if we had a rich guy taxing the rich? Wouldn't it be great if there was an Indigenous justice minister?' And they were able to do that because they recruited an unbelievable amount of talent, right? But then at a certain point, that master narrative confronted reality to a certain extent in the sense that these people weren't just a cast, actors. They were decision makers and elected officials."

Many of the ministers had little or no experience in politics, an unforgiving business in which inexperience soon makes itself clear. The same was true of staff. A huge number were brought over from the Liberal operation in Queen's Park, but there still weren't enough experienced staffers to fill all the jobs in ministerial offices. But in November 2015, few people in Ottawa were thinking about that. The city felt more like a pageant ground than the scene of grim partisan struggle.

Two days after Trudeau's new Cabinet was sworn in, the CBC's Julie Van Dusen heard there was to be an orientation for new ministers at Fort Pearson—the Lester B. Pearson Building at 125 Sussex Drive, home of Global Affairs Canada. She headed over with a crew to try to get a story. Accustomed to the hard-edged media management approach of the Harperites, they were surprised to be allowed into the building. They set up their cameras and shot footage of Trudeau being mobbed and cheered by hundreds of civil servants as he tried to leave the building.

For Conservatives convinced the bureaucracy was out to get them—Canada's version of the "deep state"—it was a discouraging scene, with supposedly non-partisan civil servants actually cheering for the Liberals.

And it was not just that way with civil servants. Tyler Meredith, a policy wonk who came to the new PMO as a policy advisor, says everyone was happy to see the new government in those days. "I would sometimes go to meetings with stakeholders or with the prime minister and it would feel like the good people have arrived."

Even Conservatives had to recognize the spirit of the moment. At the Press Gallery dinner in 2016, interim Conservative leader Rona Ambrose jokingly proposed a new slogan: "The Conservative Party of Canada. It's okay. The bad man's gone away."

That is how Ottawa felt then, like a Camelot on the Rideau, with a handsome prince leading the restoration of progressive Canada. The polls reflected the mood. The Liberals won 39 percent of the vote but had the support of 44 percent in Nanos's poll of November 4—meaning that some people who didn't vote for Trudeau changed their minds after seeing him win. International media outlets wrote cheerful and chatty profiles of him. In December, Justin and Sophie were featured in *Vogue* looking splendidly fashionable. He was quoted as saying: "My whole life has been about figuring out the balance between knowing who I am and being who I am, and accepting that people will come to me with all sorts of preconceptions."

On the opposition benches, the Conservatives would have to come to grips with the end of their government and a fairly thorough rejection of their message. After losing sixty seats, they were down to ninety-nine, the same number they had won in 2004. On election night, Harper resigned as leader of the party he had created, which left it without much sense of itself. The NDP lost fifty-one seats, down to forty-four, and was back in third place in the House under a leader who came from outside the movement and whom members had selected in the hope of victory.

Amid all the gushing, the cheers, and the admiring profiles, Trudeau and his people got down to work. Early on, they chalked up easy wins by reversing decisions of the previous government. Bains immediately stated that the mandatory long-form census would be revived, five years after the Conservatives killed it, leaving a huge hole in Statistics Canada data sets. In November, Trudeau confirmed he would, as promised, withdraw Canada's CF-18s from the battle against ISIS. In December, Indigenous Affairs Minister Carolyn Bennett announced that the government would stop enforcing the First Nations Financial Transparency Act, which required 581 Indigenous governments across Canada to post detailed financial disclosures or jeopardize their funding from the federal government. Indigenous voters, urged on by Perry Bellegarde, national chief of the Assembly of First Nations, had come out to vote in record numbers. The Liberals would no longer press them as hard for financial reporting, a setback for accountability in Indigenous communities but a step toward a more productive working relationship with the chiefs.

After the government delivered on its commitment to Indigenous people, it did the same for the labour movement, which had rallied behind Trudeau in the campaign. The Liberals moved to get rid of Bill C-377, a Conservative initiative that would have imposed onerous transparency requirements on Canadian unions through the Canada Revenue Agency. Described as an unconstitutional nightmare by bar associations, unions, and even Conservative senator Hugh Segal, who fought it for years, it had been introduced as a private member's bill, which critics saw as an underhanded technique to avoid the scrutiny that accompanies government bills. Labour unions, which had worked frantically behind the scenes to elect Trudeau, heaved a sigh of relief when they were spared its union-busting provisions.

Philpott, the new health minister, quickly took action on opioid overdoses, which had caused about two thousand deaths in 2015. The Harper government had opposed harm-reduction policies such as safe injection sites. Philpott ordered naloxone, the drug used to save lives during overdoses: "I literally signed off on the regulatory change to make naloxone available without prescription," she says, and that alone has "probably single-handedly saved thousands of lives." The government also approved safe-supply programs and supervised consumption sites, evidence-based policies that help front-line workers prevent overdose deaths. (Tragically, the situation has not improved, and accidental overdoses have continued to increase.)

On December 11, Trudeau was at Toronto Pearson International Airport to greet the first planeload of Syrian refugees, posing for photos with relieved families. He said Canada was "showing the world how to open our hearts." The *Toronto Star* ran a huge banner headline in English and Arabic the next day: "Welcome to Canada."

The Liberals had promised during the campaign to settle twenty-five thousand Syrians in Canada, and it was not clear if that would be possible. Immigration Minister John McCallum was under pressure from what the *Star* called "angry crowds of do-gooders" who were moved by the suffering in Syria and wanted personally to sponsor refugees. Behind the scenes were bureaucratic barriers. Senior advisor Cyrus Reporter took the lead in the PMO, working with a Cabinet committee including McCallum and Philpott to figure out how and where to do security screenings. "I think the fear was less than the reality," says Philpott. "We had to do everything possible to avoid that and also to allay people's anxieties about it."

The committee set up screening facilities in the region, authorized special flights, and got people moving. By May 27, twenty-five thousand Syrian refugees had arrived in Canada, and polling showed that support for the initiative increased over time. Although Germany, under the leadership of Chancellor Angela Merkel, far surpassed Canada in the number of Syrians welcomed, photogenic Trudeau was credited in the global media, which helped to build his brand around the world.

———

THE LIBERALS HAD WON the election by promising to make life better for the middle class "and those working hard to join it," and during the first year, they did most of what they had promised, taking big steps toward a more equal Canada. The centrepiece of the agenda was the Canada Child Benefit, a new income support program for parents. The idea was the brainchild of economists Sherri Torjman and Ken Battle, who had spent much of their careers studying child benefit systems. The Trudeau team invited them to sit on an economic advisory committee that helped to devise policy before the 2015 election. They decided on one simple plan that increased benefits considerably and clawed back those from better-off families.

Trudeau enjoyed working with Torjman and McNair on the design, playing policy wonk. "We had a huge conversation. Should it be means tested? Where should the cut-off be? And I was there with Mike McNair, with rulers, talking about the slope. Where it would start. Where it would be. How much would be there."

Overall, low-income parents received more than previously, as much as $6,400 a year for parents of kids under five. "Good social policy is good economic policy, because when you have good economic policy, you provide incentives to work, you're giving people purchasing power, you're stabilizing your economy," Torjman says.

The big rollout would have to wait for the budget in the spring, but the government could enact the tax changes immediately. In November, Morneau cut taxes for those making $45,282 to $90,563 and increased taxes on those making more than $200,000. The Liberals had promised the change would be revenue neutral, but once they were in office and ran their numbers past the officials in the Finance Department, they learned that their projections had been optimistic by about $1 billion. Trudeau backed away from his proposed fiscal framework, which meant that the deficit would be larger than promised. It was the first example of what would become a familiar pattern with the Trudeau government, with rosy projections quietly explained away, leading to larger-than-expected borrowing.

As the Liberals set to work on the budget, it became clear that the government could not keep its promises unless it went deeper into debt than promised. To make matters worse, commodity prices had dropped, meaning that federal royalties took a hit, and the government was facing an inherited deficit before it could implement any of the items it had campaigned on. Morneau, a rookie politician, did not want to go deep into the red on his first budget. He was working with Tyler Meredith from the PMO, but he could not convince people there to spend less. In Meredith's words: "For the folks in the PMO, who had just come out of a campaign where they had gone from third to first . . . the reaction was 'No. That's the opposite of what we should do. We should do all the things we said we were going to do.' And so it created this tension from the very beginning about what is the key objective that we're trying to manage." Reluctantly, Morneau increased the income tax rate on high-income taxpayers but later regretted it because it "made it difficult to have a constructive dialogue with the people prepared to invest in research and development to benefit the country."

Although Morneau and Trudeau were presenting a common public front, behind the scenes the new finance minister was struggling with the agenda. He opposed the promise made late in the campaign to undo the Harper plan to delay Old Age Security for two years. The number of Canadians aged sixty-five and over was projected to double from 4.7 million to 9.4 million by 2030, and, to support the benefits for these retirees, the economy needed people to work until they were sixty-seven. Morneau wrote later that he had to "deliver economically illiterate political promises." He lost that battle and the policy was put in the budget. He does not seem to have won many battles.

Early on, in a get-acquainted meeting with Liberal MPs on the finance committee, one member advised Morneau to announce fiscal targets that the government would be obliged to honour. "If not, you're going to be a victim," he warned. "There'll always be another 10 billion." Morneau did not introduce fiscal targets, and as a result, wasn't ever able to push back on the agenda from the PMO. He never seemed to be a good fit for politics. Married to French-fry heir Nancy McCain and generous in philanthropy, he was more comfortable in corporate boardrooms than in political confrontations. He was accustomed to polite and sincere expressions of appreciation for his good works, not withering critiques from the likes of Pierre Poilievre, who regularly implied, without evidence, that he was trying to line his own pockets.

When Morneau tabled his budget in March 2016, it projected a $29.4 billion deficit, $20 billion higher than the party had promised in the election campaign. Although in December Trudeau had told the Canadian Press that the commitment to balance the books after two years of modest deficits was "very" cast in stone, by spring the government had quietly dropped this promise. The budget—with billions for infrastructure spending and a significant increase in funding for Indigenous services—made real progress on delivering on the Liberals' election promises, but it did so at the expense of fiscal restraint. It was the beginning of a pattern that has continued throughout the Trudeau era. Unable politically to raise taxes on all but the very rich, and unwilling to say no to constituencies that are crucial to the government, the Liberals have relied on borrowing.

Aside from that, the budget was a political success, making significant progress in the cause of strengthening the middle class. The income-tax changes shifted the tax burden upward, and the Canada Child Benefit did end up lifting 782,000 children out of poverty by 2020, which, in a utilitarian sense, might be the most important thing any Canadian government has done in decades. It also helped many more people, especially young people in big cities who were struggling to raise a family, easing their economic anxiety, giving them security when they were dealing with the challenges of parenthood. As Mike McNair put it in an interview later, "For the millions of families that were the lower middle class, this provides an anchor in their economic security to keep them in the middle class as opposed to potentially falling into poverty."

In June, Morneau scored a significant win when he convinced the provinces to sign on to an expansion of the Canada Pension Plan, the first significant change to the program since it was launched in 1965. The idea was to increase premiums paid by both workers and employers so that payments to retiring Canadians could increase. This would be good news for the provinces, relieving them of providing social services to seniors whose retirement incomes were too low, but some premiers were nervous about the economic impact of increasing premiums on lower-income workers. Kathleen Wynne, in Ontario, was onside, and the Atlantic premiers were all Liberals, but those in Saskatchewan and Quebec were skeptical. Morneau, who had spent decades working on private-sector pensions and had a calm negotiating style, was perfect for the job. He listened to objections from Saskatchewan's Conservative government and agreed to boost the federal Working Income Tax Benefit to ease the burden. All the provinces eventually signed on.

"All the premiers were eating out of his hand," says one of Morneau's aides. "If we ever hit an impasse in the room, he'd be like, 'All right, let's take thirty. And he'd go talk to people individually. Of all the politicians I worked for in twenty years, he was better at that stuff than anyone."

———

THERE WAS A SELF-CONGRATULATORY tone to the long honeymoon of 2015/16—and no shortage of people singing Trudeau's praises. In April 2016, *Marie Claire*, the British women's magazine, ran an article under the headline "Justin Trudeau: Full-Time Canadian Prime Minister, Part-Time Lover," celebrating him as a "total Mr Hotsticks" as a politician, father, husband, boxer, and feminist.

Before he was sworn in, Trudeau announced at a rally in Ottawa that Canada was back. "Many of you have worried that Canada has lost its compassionate and constructive voice in the world over the past ten years. Well, I have a simple message for you: on behalf of 35 million Canadians, we're back." He was not the first leader to deliver the line, but he repeated it several times in the early months of his premiership—in Malta at a meeting of Commonwealth leaders, where he announced billions in aid for developing countries coping with climate change, and in Paris at a climate change conference. Climate activists were delighted with the new Canadian leader, and so were other people who simply found him young and attractive. In Japan, female fans swooned. In China, he was greeted warmly and nicknamed "Little Potato," a Mandarin pun. For months he strode onto the world stage with the kind of runway poise that few politicians can manage, and his social-media-savvy team promoted him adeptly.

The high-flying operation came a little closer to earth in May 2016, when Trudeau lost his temper in the House of Commons and charged onto the floor to tussle with New Democratic Party MPs who were delaying a vote by preventing Conservative whip Gord Brown from returning to his seat. Rather than waiting patiently for the shenanigans to play out, Trudeau shouted at parliamentarians to "get the fuck out of the way," grabbed Brown by the arm, and elbowed Ruth Ellen Brosseau in the chest. Enraged, Tom Mulcair shouted, "What kind of man elbows a woman? You're pathetic."

It was a bizarre and unprecedented display of anger by a prime minister, and opposition MPs made the most of it. They called him a bully, accused him of assault and violence against women, and derailed the business of the legislature for a day. Privately, Trudeau was rueful. "How could I be so stupid?" Butts recalls him saying.

Trudeau apologized effectively, repeatedly, and unreservedly, but his handlers had to watch as his carefully developed celebrity began to turn against him. *People* magazine and the *Jakarta Post* carried the news and, as it spread, it pierced his carefully constructed international image as a feminist Mr. Hotsticks, boosted the morale of his opponents, and raised questions about his state of mind. Trudeau had carelessly damaged his brand.

At home, though, he stayed high in the polls. Trudeau was someone Canadians knew: he had done something that seemed out of character and had promptly apologized. If they thought about it at all, they registered it as an oddity.

———

IN QUESTION PERIOD THAT same day in May, interim Conservative leader Rona Ambrose grilled Trudeau about his recent appointment of a committee to study electoral reform. The Conservatives opposed any change, and she pressed him to agree to hold a referendum on any new system. Trudeau declined to make such a promise but renewed his commitment that the 2015 election would be "the last one in our country under first-past-the-post." The previous week, Democratic Institutions Minister Maryam Monsef had announced that a parliamentary committee would study alternatives to the first-past-the-post system and that the government would hold public meetings in every riding in Canada. They were "determined" to meet the reform commitment.

Monsef organized workshops, which featured breakout sessions where small groups discussed the mechanics of proportional voting and ranked ballots. In September, when Monsef held a session in a Gatineau hotel ballroom, across the river from Ottawa, I went over to observe. Her enthusiasm and good cheer made the event intermittently pleasant. Dozens of democracy nerds turned up. It was a praiseworthy exercise in participatory democracy, the kind of thing we should have more of—except that it was all a hollow sham, as we learned a month later when Trudeau indicated he was less enthusiastic about the idea.

In an interview with Marie Vastel of *Le Devoir*, Trudeau stepped away from the promise. "Under Stephen Harper, there were so many people unhappy with the government and their approach that people were saying, 'It will take electoral reform to no longer have a government we don't like.' But under the current system, they now have a government they're more satisfied with and the motivation to change the electoral system is less compelling."

The committee continued to wrangle until December. The Conservatives refused to accept any change without a referendum. The NDP and the Greens favoured proportional representation, but many Liberals reacted with horror because they were often the beneficiaries of first-past-the-post elections.

The Liberals had done nothing for six months, wasting precious time that Elections Canada would need if they were to roll out a new electoral system before the next election. The appointment of Monsef, a thirty-year-old rookie with no parliamentary experience, sent a clear signal. "Looking at how Trudeau has stacked the electoral reform deck, a cynic could conclude that his bid to move to a different voting system is programmed to fail," wrote Chantal Hébert in the *Toronto Star*.

Trudeau told me in 2024 that he regrets not being clearer when he introduced the policy. "I wish I had been as firm against PR [proportional representation] publicly as I am personally. I think it would be bad for Canada, and I will continue to say that, but I thought maybe we could bring them along and convince them of ranked ballots—and that ended up not working."

The PMO had given Monsef an impossible assignment, and then wouldn't back her up. They gave her a rookie chief of staff, and she couldn't get a meeting with Trudeau to figure out how to proceed. "We were basically set adrift to try to figure out how to do this, and she didn't get any time with him for months and months," says an official who worked with her then. When Monsef finally did get marching orders, they were direct: Do not proceed with any outcome that would lead to proportional representation. "How are we supposed to run a consultation with the result predetermined?" the official continued. "If you really do support women, and you want them in your Cabinet and you want to have women in positions of power, then you've got to put in the things that will help them be a success. You can't just drop them in and walk away, which is exactly what he did with her." Monsef had reached a cul-de-sac. Trudeau had decided to break his promise. She had been wasting her time, and the time of a lot of other people. He eventually moved her out of the democratic reform job and made her minister for the status of women. She lost her riding in 2019 and now works as a public speaker.

Trudeau's abandonment of electoral reform revealed him as a leader of limited ambitions, a transactional rather than a transformational leader. Like every other Canadian politician who had ever campaigned on a promise to change our electoral system, once he was elected and confronted with the reality that keeping his promise would make it impossible for him to ever win another false majority, he backed away from it. In this, he was no different from premiers in PEI, New Brunswick,

Quebec, and BC, who had all played the same greasy trick but usually had an administrative reason for giving up—blaming a failed referendum or unclear public opinion.

But Trudeau's rationale was special. He had promised hundreds of times that he would deliver a change to the electoral system, leaving the door open to proportional representation and luring in voters who wanted change. After he won, he became so enraptured with his own success that he dropped the idea. He encouraged Canadians to travel to hotel meeting rooms and church halls to discuss the matter, and then threw away their input because he had already replaced Stephen Harper, and Canadians were so delighted to have him in office.

It looked like princely vanity. He had restored the political coalition first assembled by his father, based on the same principles of multiculturalism, bilingualism, and progressive social policies that were edging Canada toward a society more like a Northern European social welfare state than the United States. He had undone the retrograde policies of the Harper era, ended the attack on science, created job-boosting growth in infrastructure, initiated the most significant reduction in child poverty in a generation, made progress on climate and reconciliation, and assembled a team that reflected the diversity of Canada. He had seen for himself the joy the people took in the glorious Trudeau restoration, not just in Canada but around the world. When the people were so happy, so pleased with his accomplishments, it would be foolish to change the system that had made that joyous event possible. It seems narcissistic.

Several people who have worked closely with Trudeau describe him that way, if they are assured they won't be quoted by name.

"I think he's narcissistic," says one of his former ministers. "I think he truly believes that he is needed by Canada, has done great things to save Canada."

"He really does believe he operates above that sort of mortal existence," says another former minister. "I mean, he has a combination of superpowers, and to a certain extent what he's been able to achieve is a function of believing he can do anything. And if all of us had that, we would probably achieve a lot more."

Trudeau has "gotten to a place now where he actually believes what he's doing is good for the country, irrespective of anything else, which I think is hugely scary and problematic," says another former minister.

He thinks "that he is the only subject and everybody else isn't," says a former senior staffer. "That's, I think, a key to his personality and to understanding how there can be so many pissed-off people out there."

The quality they are describing seems to match the Mayo Clinic's definition of narcissistic personality disorder: "A mental health condition in which people have an unreasonably high sense of their own importance. They need and seek too much attention and want people to admire them. People with this disorder may lack the ability to understand or care about the feelings of others."

A close friend of Trudeau says he may be a narcissist, but we should expect that. "You know any prime minister who wasn't a narcissist? I mean, how do you win? How do you ever decide you should be prime minister?"

Despite Trudeau's attention seeking, there is a more charitable interpretation. He does think he "is needed by Canada [and] has done great things to save Canada," but he is not alone in that. When he said he feels Canada in his bones with every breath, that is true. "It serves as his overwhelming preoccupation every day," says his friend and former staffer Cyrus Reporter. "I know that sounds like a simple thing. But that's where his head is at every day." Even behind closed doors with trusted aides, he speaks about politics in an earnest way, not cynically, and is often thoughtful and caring to members of his team.

In late 2023, with dire opinion polls, he was humble with staff, frankly admitting the political difficulties he faces. But during his long honeymoon with voters, he was seeing joy not just in the faces of the throngs of adoring people who yearned to connect with him but also in the faces of the great and the good in the halls of power. He was surrounded by positive reinforcement in Canada and abroad. It is not surprising, in retrospect, that it went to his head for a time.

———

TRUDEAU WAS STILL POLLING well, but the cracks in the edifice were starting to appear as the first year of his government came to a close and political gravity returned to Ottawa. At that point, Robert Fife, the *Globe and Mail*'s Ottawa bureau chief, landed his first significant scoop of the Trudeau era. Previously at CTV, he had broken the story of Nigel Wright's payment to Mike Duffy, which hastened the end of the Harper era. Now he focused on getting behind the scenes in the Trudeau government. He had the backing of the *Globe*'s new editor-in-chief, David Walmsley. Both men have made their name on the strength of their work, not as members of the establishment, and they brought a new rigour to political coverage. The *Globe* worked to keep the government accountable in ways it had not during the Harper years.

In September, Fife revealed why Fisheries Minister Hunter Tootoo had left the Cabinet in May. Tootoo, the MP for the vast northern riding of Nunavut, the largest in Canada, had been struggling to keep his drinking in control and was having an affair with both a young staffer in his office and the staffer's mother. When he informed the young woman that he was breaking off his affair with her to take up a serious relationship with her mother, she went on a rampage in his Parliament Hill office. A few days later, he went to see Trudeau and let him know he had to resign because of a "consensual but inappropriate relationship." "I knew I had to go in there and let him know my decision and what happened," Tootoo later told the CBC. "I was going in knowing that I had let him down. He gave me a hug. He's an amazing individual."

Later in September, the *Globe* had a major story that posed a challenge to the new government. It reported that Trudeau's closest aides, Gerald Butts and Katie Telford, had been reimbursed more than $200,000 for moving their families to Ottawa from Toronto, part of $1.1 million spent in moving forty-seven political staffers to town. Butts had received $126,669, Telford $80,382, including tens of thousands in cash for miscellaneous moving expenses. The payments followed the National Joint Council Relocation Directive, the same set of rules used to cover payments to senior public servants, so there was no suggestion that Butts or Telford had broken any rules. But the amounts were large, and the government looked bad. The Conservatives attacked in the House: "There are no ifs, ands, or buts about these expenses. They are wrong," Conservative MP Blaine Calkins said.

The Conservatives had imposed a $30,000 cap on moves by staffers, part of a penny-pinching culture that Harper brought to the job. The Liberals, in their scramble to take over the government, had decided that ministerial office budgets had to stay below what the Conservatives had been spending, but nobody thought much about the moving expenses until the *Globe* called. Neither Butts nor Telford were aware of how much they were getting before the story broke. They huddled and decided to pay back some of the money, a total of $65,000. "As this process relates to us, we were eligible to be reimbursed for a bunch of costs that we don't feel comfortable about," they said in a joint statement.

Internally, the news caused morale issues. One young staffer who paid for his own move was surprised to learn that others were getting gold-plated treatment. "All of us were consciously told, yeah, you're going to have to pay some stuff out of pocket. There's some tax credits that you can use that'll help you. But it is what it is because you're coming to work for the prime minister of Canada, and we all just kind of accepted that."

There was also grumbling about who was in and who was out. Older Liberals, long established in Ottawa, felt nudged out of the way by the stylish younger set close to Trudeau, many of them fresh from Toronto. Such discontent is a normal part of every court, but after a year, the strains that had earlier been subsumed by the euphoria of the honeymoon were harder to ignore.

The expense story was an embarrassing headache for Butts and Telford, but nothing like what was to come from Fife and his team.

PART TWO

WALKING INTO THE RAKE

2016–2019

A prince is despised if he is considered changeable, foolish, weak, mean, and uncertain. A prince should avoid these characteristics. In his actions he should try to show greatness, courage, seriousness, and strength. In his private dealings with his subjects he should show that his judgments must be followed, and he should maintain himself with such a reputation that no one can hope either to deceive him or to get round him.

Niccolò Machiavelli, *The Prince*

5

FREQUENT FLIER

On March 15, 2016, Artur Wilczynski, Canada's ambassador to Norway, was instructed by his bosses in Ottawa to go to the Norwegian Ministry of Foreign Affairs in Oslo and let them know that the next day, Justin Trudeau would announce that Canada was seeking a seat on the United Nations Security Council for 2020. Winning would give Canada a more prominent role on the world stage, a chance to rub elbows for two years with the five permanent members—the United States, Russia, China, the United Kingdom, and France—and greater influence in international decision-making. The problem was that Norway and Ireland had already declared their candidacies for the two seats open to Western nations, and both, as small powers that support multilateralism and the rule of law, had similar messages to Canada's. Objectively, they were better candidates than Canada, with thoughtful campaigns they had kicked off earlier. Canada seemed to be betting that other countries would be keen to see more of its glamorous new prime minister. "I could have told them back then—they didn't bother to ask me—that it was a bad idea," says Wilczynski.

Canada's forlorn, time-wasting hunt for a Security Council seat brought Trudeau to New York in September to address the General Assembly. Gerry Butts and Katie Telford accompanied him and had dinner with John Podesta, who had been Bill Clinton's chief of staff. He had also advised the Trudeau campaign during the 2015 election and was now chair of Hillary Clinton's presidential campaign. The first debate was coming up, and Clinton was polling well ahead of Donald Trump. Podesta told Butts, though, that he was afraid Trump would win. "I remember him saying, 'Ohio's gone. It's tough out there.'"

Podesta said Clinton's campaign was struggling because of Trump's bizarre behaviour: she would do a policy-focused event in the morning, outlining a children's dental program, for instance, then Trump would say someone should murder her. "Guess who carries the news cycle?" Butts took the warning seriously. The Trudeau operation had deep links to Clinton World but knew nobody in the Trump camp. They had no idea what a Trump presidency might bring, but, clearly, his election would have implications for the vital trade relationship.

In the presidential debate, when Trump denounced the North American Free Trade Agreement, Clinton replied that the trade deal had "increased global exports 40 percent" while she was secretary of state. Trump replied: "You go to New England, Ohio, Pennsylvania, you go anywhere you want, Secretary Clinton, and you will see devastation where manufacturing is down 30, 40, sometimes 50 percent. NAFTA is the worst trade deal maybe ever."

As it turned out, that line was Trump's winning message in the Rust Belt on election night. Trump won Pennsylvania, Michigan, and Ohio, which gave him the presidency. The news landed in Ottawa like a punch in the guts. Nobody expected it; few welcomed it. Even most Conservatives had at best ambiguous feelings about the president-elect.

In the basement at Rideau Cottage, Trudeau was watching the results come in with Butts, Telford, Mike McNair, Kate Purchase, and Jeremy Broadhurst. They were having a few beers, expecting Clinton to win. They got quieter as the night went on and Trump took the lead. "I remember around nine fifteen looking around the room and realizing nobody'd actually said anything for four minutes and we were all having the same thoughts," recalls Butts. Around 10 p.m., when the Florida results came in, putting Trump over the top, Trudeau got up and said it was time for bed. "We're all going to have a lot of work to do," he warned.

Chrystia Freeland, as minister of international trade, had been working closely with Steve Verheul, the civil service's top trade negotiator, on a free trade deal with the Europeans. The two worked well together, salvaging the deal by overcoming the objections of the regional government of Wallonia in Belgium. Freeland had staged an emotional walkout, bringing the intransigent Walloons around.

In the early hours of the morning after Trump won, Freeland called Verheul. "The discussion was about, what do we do now?" he recalled later. "We'd obviously been giving some thinking to it and laid out some plans . . . but having them actually [win], it kind of brought a sharper focus to it all. So very quickly, we started to prepare a lot of analysis about what we can do."

———

TRUDEAU TALKED WITH ADVISORS the next day to plan his congratulatory call to Trump. The civil servants listed the trade items he needed to mention—softwood and dairy—but Butts and Telford wanted him to be more strategic. "Katie and I stayed on the phone with him after [the advisors] got off and we were like, 'You know, you've got to make a personal connection with him. That's the only thing that matters,'" Butts recalls. "Our advice was, the thing you can connect on is you both won. You both just won big election victories that nobody expected you to win. So just congratulate him . . . Don't blow smoke up his ass. Just try and find some kind of truthful, authentic common ground."

Trudeau also commiserated with Trump about "being knocked around by the media," he told his friend Terry DiMonte in an interview later. "That's the experience that I've had for years, of people just slamming me and saying, you'll never become prime minister. So there was a little bit of common ground."

The call went well. Trump told Trudeau he had once met his father.

Later, Trudeau was upbeat about the news when he spoke to a boisterous crowd of young people at a WE Day "youth empowerment" event in suburban Ottawa. "We're going to keep working with people right around the world," he told them. "We're going to work with our neighbours, and I'm going to work with president-elect Trump's administration, as we move forward in a positive way for, not just Canadians and Americans, but the whole world."

Trump's election posed a dramatic challenge to Trudeau because of the importance of the trade relationship, with more than $2 billion worth of goods and services crossing the border every day, all governed by the provisions of NAFTA. Any significant interruption threatened millions of Canadian jobs.

Trudeau's team had carefully avoided attacking Trump, staying silent during the campaign and resisting the temptation to score political points with Canadians by dunking on him. In March, Trudeau had appointed David MacNaughton, a businessman and political strategist, as Canada's ambassador to Washington. MacNaughton was close to Butts, who had worked for him in Dalton McGuinty's office, and also to Telford, who had worked with his wife, Leslie Noble, at StrategyCorp in Toronto.

In August, MacNaughton had met with Trudeau's Cabinet, warning them not to count on a Clinton victory and to be diplomatic. "I said, everybody thinks that Hillary's going to win," he told me in an interview later. "Maybe, but . . . keep your mouth shut. And they did. And I think the prime minister sort of internalized all of this."

Rather than sit back and wait for Trump to set the agenda, Trudeau's people were proactive. They asked MacNaughton to tell reporters that Canada was open to renegotiating NAFTA. "If they want to have a discussion about improving NAFTA, we're ready to come to the table to try and put before the new administration anything that will benefit both Canada and the United States and obviously Mexico also."

Conservatives derided this approach. "Canada is now in a weaker position, and all this has done is create more uncertainty," said Rona Ambrose in the House. "Why is the prime minister jumping the gun to open up NAFTA with the Americans?" In the *National Post*, John Ivison wrote that it was a case of a "sovereign government disintegrating like cheap toilet paper."

Verheul, a veteran of many high-level trade negotiations, encouraged the Trudeau people. "One way or another, we're going to get a negotiation. I think a big part of the reason why that message was put out was because we did see how a negotiation could be held where we essentially modernize elements of the agreement, and then declare victory."

The pattern established by the Trudeau team in the first twenty-four hours after the US election was to continue through the Trump presidency. They were disciplined: they were thinking strategically about how to maximize their advantage in the relationship and trying to make personal connections, not just with Trump but with the people around him.

It was not an easy job. "Our basic strategy was to find every Canadian who was close to Donald Trump and his network," says Butts. Brian Mulroney "was by far the most valuable person in that period." Mulroney agrees with that view: "The Liberals had put all their eggs in the Hillary Clinton basket," he told me in an interview later. "When the election was over and Donald Trump won, [Trudeau] didn't know a single leading Republican in Washington anywhere. That's when the prime minister called."

Mulroney had known Trump since the 1980s. He and Mila often dined at Mar-a-Lago, Trump's opulent waterfront resort in West Palm Beach, not far from the Mulroney's winter getaway. Mila and Melania were friendly and could converse in Serbo-Croatian. In February 2017, after Mulroney sang "When Irish Eyes Are Smiling" on stage at Mar-a-Lago, Trump and Melania led a standing ovation. Trump came to Mulroney's table and said: "You know, Brian, you were right about Justin. I was told he's a good guy, and he is. I think we can do good business together." Mulroney had long-standing connections in Trump World. "I know them all, almost the whole Cabinet," he says. "They all worked for Ronald Reagan and George Bush, at one point in time, all these Republicans . . . So I was able to help [the Liberals] out in various ways."

It did not all fall on Mulroney's shoulders. Freeland already knew Blackstone CEO Stephen Schwarzman, an economic advisor to Trump. She had New York friends who knew Ivanka Trump and her husband, Jared Kushner, who both played a key role in the Trump campaign. In early December, she and Telford flew down to meet them in their opulent Fifth Avenue penthouse. They were impressed by the savvy Canadians. Telford "basically offered Jared and Ivanka, 'I'll teach you how to do politics,' and became super tight with them right away," says one insider.

Telford had seen Ivanka speak during the campaign and had been impressed by her message about women in business. They had a lot in common—were the same age, were both having to balance motherhood with politics. They clicked, and Telford had an important communications channel to her and her husband throughout the Trump presidency.

Members of Trudeau's team had all been assigned a counterpart to focus on, and they soon got to work. Mulroney had heard that Trump would make Robert Lighthizer the trade representative, so Butts started to research him. Freeland, Butts, and Telford repeatedly travelled to the States to meet the oddballs and extremists who would soon play key roles in the Trump White House, including populist firebrand Steve Bannon and China-despising Peter Navarro. "It was hard to get a sense of who was driving the bus for the Americans on this stuff," said one of the Canadians.

As they wound down for the holidays, the Trudeau team had a new, singular focus—how to handle Trump and keep the trade relationship intact. But first, it was time for a holiday after an incredibly hectic year. Trudeau needed a getaway with family and friends.

ON DECEMBER 31, 2016, the eve of Canada's 150th anniversary celebrations, Governor General David Johnston tweeted: "Where better to kick off #Canada150 than on Parliament Hill?"

Comedian Rick Mercer hosted the New Year's Day event featuring Carly Rae Jepsen and other musical acts for the crowd huddled against the cold in front of the Centre Block. Heritage Minister Mélanie Joly was there to represent the government. Trudeau issued a statement talking up "spectacular events" to celebrate Canada's 150th birthday "from coast to coast to coast"—but he didn't appear himself.

National Post reporter David Akin, watching the show on television from his suburban Ottawa home, wondered where Trudeau was. "I thought it was a big deal turning a hundred and fifty, and maybe the prime minister might want to show up at that particular party." Akin is a persistent journalist with a long attention span and an almost frantic desire to dig up news. He contacted the Prime Minister's Office and asked where Trudeau was. The office wouldn't say. So he did a little story, headlined "As Canada Begins Celebrating 'Once-in-a-lifetime' Anniversary, Trudeau Is in Some Other Country on Holiday." This secrecy seemed silly to *Post* columnist Chris Selley, who wrote a lighthearted column complaining about the official silence around the prime minister's travel plans. "Were the Trudeaus cruising the West Indies on a disreputable Russian oligarch's yacht? Odds are they were having a regular rich-people vacation in an uncontroversial location." After the column was published, someone contacted Selley to ask if he was being coy. "No," he said. "I really don't know." The informant told him that Trudeau and his family were on an island in the Bahamas, hosted by the Aga Khan, the hereditary leader of the world's fifteen million Ismaili Muslims.

Selley called Akin. "Am I the only person who doesn't know where they are, and you just can't report it, or has this really just landed in my lap?"

"No," Akin said. "That is a scoop."

They put together a story. In the afternoon of January 6, Akin tweeted: "Justin Trudeau was the guest of the Aga Khan at the Aga Khan's private $100 million island in the Bahamas."

The Trudeaus had flown down to Nassau on Boxing Day on a Royal Canadian Air Force CC-144 Challenger to bring in the new year with the Aga Khan and his family and friends on Bells Cay, a 394-acre tropical island in the Exumas.

A few days later, Akin had a follow-up revealing that the Trudeaus were accompanied to the island by Seamus O'Regan, MP for St. John's South–Mount Pearl and former host of *Canada AM*, his husband Stelios (Steve) Doussis, and Liberal Party president Anna Gainey and her husband, Tom Pitfield. Akin reached O'Regan on the phone and learned that the other guests flew commercially to Nassau. They all flew to the island on a helicopter belonging to the Aga Khan.

The optics were terrible. Trudeau not only skipped an important party on the Hill but was basking in the sun on a billionaire's private island with political allies—and he took a private aircraft to get there.

When Akin contacted the PMO and let them know he was going with a story, neither Gerry Butts nor Katie Telford wanted to call Trudeau to talk to him about it, so the awkward conversation fell to Kate Purchase. "Everyone was like, 'This is a disaster. Like, why are we just walking into the rake?'"

Back in Canada, Trudeau told reporters it was no big deal. "The fact is the Aga Khan has been a long-time family friend. He was a pallbearer at my father's funeral. He has known me since I was a toddler, and this was our family vacation."

Conservative MP Blain Calkins wrote to Ethics Commissioner Mary Dawson, pointing out that the Conflict of Interest Act states that no minister or family member "shall accept travel on non-commercial chartered or private aircraft for any purpose unless required in his or her capacity as a public office holder or in exceptional circumstances or with the prior approval of the commissioner." He also noted that Akin had pointed out in his story that the Aga Khan Foundation Canada had received $55 million in foreign aid money from the Canadian government in the previous year and was registered to lobby the government. If Trudeau and the Aga Khan are actually friends, Calkins wrote, Trudeau would need a conflict-of-interest screen to manage any dealings with him. Dawson agreed to investigate.

The trip, which raised difficult ethical and optical questions for the one-year-old government, came as a surprise to Canadians—and to many on the prime minister's own staff. "It was very guarded internally as to where the Prime Minister was going for Christmas," said one senior staffer who learned about the journey from media reports. "Most people in the office did not know where he was going."

Those who did know—Telford, Butts, and Purchase, for instance— had advised him that it was a bad idea. If he was going to go, he should let Canadians know ahead of time. "He was the most famous Canadian on earth," said one senior staffer. "It's Christmas. Canadians are everywhere. Some of them are not favorably predisposed to him. There's no way it's not going to get out." They told him that maybe they could try to spin it, but only if they announced it first. "If you're really going to do this, we've got to talk about it ahead of time and tell people you're doing it and try and turn it into . . . this man's views are sought after by one of the Muslim leaders of the world." Trudeau did not listen. "There was nobody who was stopping Justin Trudeau from going on that fucking trip."

The incident dragged on in headlines for months as Trudeau travelled the country on a listening tour. He welcomed questions and said he was happy to work with the ethics commissioner on the matter. The opposition accused him of poor judgment, and on January 11 Rona Ambrose tweeted a link to Calkins's letter. The next day, she sharpened her attack: "Justin Trudeau knew what he did was against the law. All he had to do was say no, but he couldn't resist the billionaire lifestyle."

I was working at iPolitics, an Ottawa political website, at the time. We got a tip that we should look into Ambrose's whereabouts when she made the attack on Trudeau.

Reporter B.J. Siekierski and I poked around. Eventually, I tracked down someone who had spent the holiday on Saint Martin, part of the Leeward Islands chain. On the way back to Canada, the Canadian ended up sharing a taxi with someone who had just come off a superyacht that had been cruising to nearby St. Barts. "Oh," he said, "there was a Canadian politician on the boat." He didn't recall the name, but he described her, and the Canadian figured it had to be Ambrose. The superyacht belonged to billionaire Calgary Flames co-owner Murray Edwards.

I contacted Ambrose's office to ask whether she'd really attacked Trudeau for enjoying the "billionaire lifestyle" from the deck of a billionaire's yacht. A staffer asked for time to check. After several tense hours they confirmed that it was true. Ambrose had not let her staff know where she was going, and they had assumed she was spending the holiday skiing in Alberta.

A spokesperson pointed out that Ambrose had violated no rules in taking her trip and had written to the ethics commissioner to make sure it was okay. But the letter to Mary Dawson was dated January 12, the same day she criticized Trudeau on Twitter. I imagined her waking up on the superyacht, having some coffee in the sun, gazing at beautiful St. Barts, and eventually checking her phone, only to discover a staffer had tweeted a critique of Trudeau that, given her location, might seem hypocritical, and then retiring to a cabin to see about getting a letter sent to Dawson.

The absurd Ambrose story took some of the sting out of opposition attacks on Trudeau, but it didn't get him off the hook. When Dawson's report came out in December, a year after the trip in question, his lapse of political judgment could not be denied. She found that Trudeau had violated four sections of the Conflict of Interest Act, the first prime minister to do so.

There is no reason to think there was some greasy quid pro quo—that Trudeau negotiated a private room for Seamus O'Regan, for example, in exchange for a larger grant for the Global Centre for Pluralism—but prime ministers are supposed to arrange their affairs so we don't have to

wonder about that kind of thing. Harper was always scrupulously careful about such conflicts. Trudeau had not recused himself from business
matters related to a registered lobbyist, as would have been proper.

In 2014, after Trudeau became leader of the Liberal Party, he and
Sophie, her parents, and the kids were invited to the Aga Khan's island over
the holiday period. In 2016, Sophie arranged another visit with a friend
following the splendid state dinner the Obamas hosted for the Trudeaus
at the White House. "On March 9, 2016, two days before Ms. Grégoire
Trudeau went on her trip, a representative of the Aga Khan requested that
a formal bilateral meeting be held between the Aga Khan and Mr. Trudeau
as Prime Minister," Dawson noted in her report. "The meeting took place in
May 2016 and a number of issues were raised at the meeting, including the
$15-million grant and the riverfront project." The Aga Khan was seeking
Trudeau's support for a $200 million riverfront development in Ottawa and
wanted to make sure that a $15 million grant that Harper approved would
be paid as promised.

There is no reason to give anyone the benefit of the doubt. Ministers
are allowed to accept hospitality from friends, but Dawson found that
relationship did not apply because "there were no private interactions between Mr. Trudeau and the Aga Khan until Mr. Trudeau became Leader
of the Liberal Party of Canada." Money was also at stake: "The evidence
clearly shows that there was ongoing official business between the government of Canada and the Aga Khan at the time each invitation to visit
the island was accepted and that Mr. Trudeau, as prime minister, was in
a position to be able to advance some of the matters of interest to the Aga
Khan, whether he did so or not. This leads to the conclusion that the gifts
could reasonably be seen to have been given to influence Mr. Trudeau in
the exercise of an official power, duty or function."

Tom Pitfield, who was on the island on the time, disagrees with the
ethics commissioner's conclusion that Trudeau and the Aga Khan were
not friends. "I witnessed, much better than the commissioner could witness, a very sincere and authentic friendship between him and the Aga

Khan. They spent lots of time talking about the burdens of leadership and getting advice on how to be a good leader. It was a very father-figure-type conversation. I'm sure that's lost on people." Pitfield thinks Trudeau needed a break, time to build sandcastles with his kids. "He was burned out. His family hadn't had meaningful time together for years because it was a multi-year project to get to where he was. He needed to spend time with his family."

Then there was the question of the helicopter ride, something Trudeau or his staff ought to have known was off limits. In the last days of the Chrétien government, a number of Liberal politicians—Allan Rock, Jane Stewart, and Dominic LeBlanc—were embarrassed after it was revealed they had taken free flights to a salmon camp on New Brunswick's Restigouche River that belonged to the wealthy and powerful Irving family. Paul Martin had similarly been humiliated after he took free flights from friends. He tightened the rules, and Harper then gave them the force of law when he was elected. The PMO should have known that history.

Trudeau's lawyers gamely tried to convince Dawson she should give him a pass on that point, arguing that the French section of the act refers to "avions," meaning airplanes. Obviously Trudeau, a francophone, couldn't have been expected to know that helicopters were forbidden! Dawson was not persuaded.

"Here's the problem with these fucking processes, with these commissioners," says Butts. "It's like taking a lawyer to an argument with your mother. You can take one, but it's not going to help you. And if anything, it's probably going to piss off your mother."

Some of Trudeau's friends think Justin got a rough ride for what was, at its root, a failure of staffing. Even though he had rejected the advice of his team, who told him not to go, they failed to protect him from himself by making sure he checked with the ethics commissioner and avoided private helicopter rides. "I can't speak to what the office did in terms of its due diligence," says one friend, "but obviously the prime minister doesn't arrange his own vacation."

IN JANUARY 2024, I sailed around the Aga Khan's island and had a look at it from the water. It's in one of the most beautiful places in the world, inside the Exuma Cays Land and Sea Park, a national park in a pristine archipelago of palm-topped limestone islands rimmed with white sand beaches. Below the astonishingly clear turquoise water are vibrant coral reefs teeming with colourful fish. Johnny Depp, David Copperfield, and Faith Hill and Tim McGraw own islands nearby.

The Aga Khan, or a company that is controlled by him, bought the 349-acre island in 2009 for US$100 million. It is beautifully landscaped, with several secluded coves where the water laps at the sand beaches, and beach catamarans lie in wait next to palm-frond palapas. In one cove, there is a large two-storey warehouse surrounded by forklifts and golf carts, and the constant thrum of a diesel generator can be heard from the water. The island has its own cellphone tower and helipad, five kilometres of roads, and about a dozen buildings in clusters, like a series of mini private resorts. Trudeau and his friends and family seem to have had a lovely break there. One day, US Secretary of State John Kerry, who was staying elsewhere on the island as a guest of the Aga Khan, came by to talk politics informally with Trudeau and his people. At the historic nearby Staniel Cay Yacht Club—a favourite hangout for the late singer Jimmy Buffett—people remember Trudeau and company coming by for dinner. It must have been a splendid vacation, but Trudeau was unwise to go there. The trip demonstrated both arrogance and incompetence. After working fiendishly hard and vanquishing his foes on the hustings, Trudeau deserved to give his family a winter getaway, but the trip was out of step with Canadian cultural norms, and it made his team—who until that point looked like the smartest kids to ever lace up skates—look like amateurs. It entangled his government in an investigative process that consumed time, energy, and political capital. It is hard to understand it except as a case of princely capriciousness.

———

IN THE NEW YEAR, Trudeau shuffled his Cabinet for the first time. Karina Gould replaced Monsef as democratic reform minister, and, strikingly, her mandate letter didn't say anything about electoral reform. Veteran John McCallum, who had been immigration minister, became ambassador to Beijing to make way for Ahmed Hussen; and the irrepressible François-Philippe Champagne, who represented Chrétien's old riding, became minister of international trade.

The big news was that Chrystia Freeland was the new foreign affairs minister. It was a no-brainer, says Butts. "She was definitely someone who was probably, because of her background, most comfortable in the United States. And we knew that we were going to need someone who was obviously unquestionably a loyal Canadian and a charter member of the team, but who could be very comfortable there."

Freeland is a "front-row kid," in the words of American photographer Chris Arnade—a driven, self-motivated, well-educated member of the global elite. After heroic democracy-building work in Ukraine, she worked as a journalist for the *Financial Times, Globe and Mail,* and Reuters, always hustling, always upwardly mobile. At the *Globe,* she was known as the "billionaire whisperer." She was the ideal candidate for the foreign ministry at a time when Canada's most important trade relationship was at risk of being destroyed.

Trudeau praised Freeland slavishly. "Quite frankly there probably isn't a day that goes by where I don't thank my lucky stars for having been able to convince her to leave her great job in New York to run in an uncertain by-election where I couldn't even guarantee she was going to win the nomination, and then come to sit with the third party in the House," Trudeau told Aaron Wherry for his 2019 book *Promise and Peril.* "She was the kind of person I knew Canada needed serving within Parliament and hopefully serving within government, if we were able to form that. She is exactly the right person to do what she's doing."

The only problem was that Canada already had a foreign affairs minister—Stéphane Dion. There is no evidence that Trudeau let any warm personal feelings for his former leader prevent him from firing him. When Chrétien was prime minister, he and Dion sometimes went trout fishing together at Harrington Lake, talking about the world. There was none of that with Trudeau, whom Dion never got to know on a personal level. On the day Trudeau met with Dion in Ottawa to give him the bad news, Dion dismissed his ministerial driver and hopped a bus for Montreal. Trudeau did offer him another job: ambassador to both Germany and the European Union. As it turns out, the Europeans didn't think that was a good idea, so Dion was made ambassador to Germany and a special envoy to the European Union, until 2023, when he was appointed ambassador to France, the most desirable diplomatic post available to former Quebec politicians.

———

THE TRUDEAU TEAM WAS focused on one foreign capital—Washington—which was sensible given the challenge of coping with Trump's chaotic White House and the crucial trade relationship. If they had been caught flat-footed, as Mulroney says, by the election of Trump, they were now making up for lost time, frantically researching the players in the new government, strategizing, trying to make sure they would not preside over the destruction of the Canadian economy for lack of homework.

In February, Trudeau flew to Washington for meetings with the new government. The first step was to avoid fights. At the end of January, Trump had signed an executive order banning immigration from Muslim countries, including refugees fleeing war in Syria—to keep "radical Islamic terrorists" from coming to America. Trudeau, who had campaigned on settling Syrian refugees and been celebrated for doing so, resisted the temptation to speak against the policy but sent several tweets highlighting Canada's position: "To those fleeing persecution, terror & war, Canadians will welcome you, regardless of your faith. Diversity is our strength."

Trudeau walked a fine line: he resisted criticizing Trump policies but highlighted progressive Canadian values. He had already made a personal connection with Trump on the phone, his team had linked up with Kushner and Ivanka, and he had a star quality that initially appealed to Trump. "If you look at the people that Trump has surrounded himself with over the years, they are celebrities," former diplomat Colin Robertson told the *Guardian*. "And they are all highly attractive people. Trudeau has that aura. And my view is that Canada should take advantage of whatever we've got."

Trudeau appealed to Trump's vanity, bringing a photograph of Trump and Pierre Trudeau that had been taken at a 1981 event in New York. On the flight down, Butts and Trudeau strategized how to manage the handshake to come. The week before, when Trump welcomed Japanese prime minister Shinzō Abe, he took him in a death grip, jerking and holding his hand for eighteen seconds while Abe struggled to maintain his poise. Trudeau made sure the same thing wouldn't happen to him. When he arrived at the White House, he stepped close to Trump, which made it impossible for the US president to jerk his arm. Trudeau even grabbed the president's bicep. He looked in control, vigorous and grinning, unintimidated by Trump, which was the message the Liberals wanted to send to voters back home.

The rest of the trip went as well as could be hoped. Ivanka was photographed smiling adoringly at Trudeau during a meeting of the Canada-United States Council for Advancement of Women Entrepreneurs and Business Leaders, a project dreamed up by Telford and Ivanka. Freeland, Sajjan, Goodale, Garneau, and Morneau accompanied Trudeau, trying to establish a rapport with Trump and his people. It went fairly well. "In the joint press conference, I was ready to throw up," recalls Butts. "I was so anxious about what was going to happen in that press conference, because you just never know. I'm in the Blue Room in the White House looking out over the lawn, kind of looking at it on TV, and Trump says, 'We talked about NAFTA. I said, maybe a few tweaks, a few tweaks.' And I was like, victory. That is everything we came to accomplish."

———

IN OCTOBER 2015, TYLER Meredith, the research director for the Institute for Research on Public Policy, attended the forty-ninth annual conference of the Canadian Economics Association at Ryerson University (as it then was) in Toronto. In one session, Dr. Michael Wolfson discussed his research into income inequality, which he had learned was worse than statisticians realized because the tax system was allowing well-off Canadians to shield income from the Canada Revenue Agency by transferring part of it to family members through private corporations. Another economist told Wolfson he was naive to think any government would change the policy: "No government in their right mind would be so stupid as to actually go after this thing, because who uses it?" he asked. "Small businesspeople and farmers and doctors and lawyers. And who's going to be noisy if they go after it? Small businesspeople, farmers, doctors, and lawyers. No one would ever want to fight with them, would they?" Two years later, when Meredith and Bill Morneau went after those groups, he remembered that discussion. Morneau released a discussion paper that July proposing to change the tax system to close loopholes for about three hundred thousand corporations, thereby raising about $250 million a year. "What we're trying to do is ensure that people who are getting their income through a typical salary . . . are not in a situation that is worse off than someone who might be able to use a private corporation to sprinkle income among family members or to turn regular income into capital gains," he said.

The system gave an advantage to those who could funnel their income through a corporation, allowing them to pay less tax than neighbours with similar incomes. The proposal made sense, but it would cost a lot of people. Eventually, doctors, lawyers, "high-net-worth individuals," and the Canadian Federation of Independent Business all pushed back, complaining angrily that they were being portrayed as tax cheats. They put pressure on their MPs, who found it uncomfortable. "All these people, they're not used to that, having been in opposition for a long time," one MP told me. "All these people in my riding are shitting on me about something. It was just sort of a novel experience."

Many of the people who were most upset were medical professionals who had voted Liberal. In 2000, the Ontario government had encouraged doctors to incorporate—to give them a tax break. Now the feds were going to disrupt their arrangement, which had become much more common in the intervening years. All those doctors were making the MPs sweat, and they in turn criticized Morneau in caucus at the same time that he was getting hammered in the House.

To make matters worse, Morneau's personal finances kept making headlines. In October, the CBC's Elizabeth Thompson discovered he had neglected to declare to the ethics commissioner a holding company he owned in France that managed his villa in Provence, even though he had declared the villa. It was an oversight, a minor error in the massive filing required to disclose all his wealth—the most complex filing ever handled by the commissioner's office. He was fined $200, a sum he wouldn't have noticed, but it was embarrassing, and it allowed the opposition to portray him as so rich that he forgot he owned a villa in France even as he was sticking it to small businesspeople.

After decades of dealing with deferential business journalists, Morneau was surprised by the toughness of the reporters in the Press Gallery and the viciousness of the attacks from opposition MPs. When they raised legitimate questions about an apparent conflict of interest between his pension policy and his stake in his family company, which managed pensions, Morneau bristled. Under pressure, he eventually sold his shares in the company and donated the profit they had accumulated to charity.

Morneau is wealthy and a generous philanthropist, and he regarded questions about conflicts of interest as personal insults. His foray into politics—which he saw as an act of public service—undoubtedly cost him millions of dollars. Yet the opposition kept attacking him, and the media kept reporting on these issues. He resented the attacks, particularly those from the ruthless Pierre Poilievre. His resentment had a brittle quality, as though he couldn't believe that people would criticize him after all he was doing for his country. He hadn't even had a chance to enjoy his villa in Provence! Instead of parrying opposition attacks, he took umbrage. In February 2017, a reporter at iPolitics discovered that his four teenage children had donated $12,098 to the Liberal Party. It seemed noteworthy, and we got a story ready. When I contacted his office for comment, a staffer let me know that the minister was personally upset that we would invade his family's privacy in this way, by writing about public financing of a political party. At a time when we should be encouraging young people to participate in politics, why would we be attacking them?

Morneau was an effective manager, but he never mastered political communications—and that limited his political capacity. Finance officials wanted to put a stop to income sprinkling because the gap between the small business tax rate and personal income tax rate had grown to the point that individuals could save money by incorporating. But Morneau failed to soften the ground for his policy, used rhetoric that insulted small business owners, and failed to effectively parry opposition attacks. He ended up having to retreat in December, leaving the loophole open for some taxpayers and promising to cut the small business tax rate to 9 percent from 11 percent—all of which cost the treasury about $3 billion. Money that the government wanted to redistribute, to reduce inequality, ended up staying sheltered, seemingly because Morneau could not sell his policy.

Meredith believes the government failed to sell a policy that he believed was necessary, first by putting out a vague policy proposal. "It let some people imagine the most horrific example of how we were going to affect their business, and it enabled tax accountants to whip up their clientele being super worried about how much money they were going to pay." The government didn't even explain why it wanted to raise the money. "So that secretary who makes a pittance is going to get a little bit more of a benefit for their work," says Meredith. "That would've been a much tougher argument for all those wealthy people to push back against this. We had no villain and no Robin Hood."

———

IN MARCH 2016, AFTER the triumphant state dinner with Obama, Trudeau gave a crowd-pleasing speech to students at American University, striding on the stage with his shirt sleeves rolled up and talking about the importance of feminism and diversity with cheerful enthusiasm. One student, originally from the Punjab, congratulated him for having so many Punjabis in his Cabinet. Trudeau grinned. "I've got more Sikhs in my cabinet than Modi does," he said, laughing.

The line went over well in the room, but not so well in India, where it was covered by media outlets that keep a close eye on the role of Sikhs in Canadian politics. Trudeau had four Sikhs in his Cabinet—Harjit Singh Sajjan, Navdeep Bains, Amarjeet Sohi, and Bardish Chagger. Narendra Modi had just two.

There are more than twice as many Chinese Canadians as Sikh Canadians, but Sikhs play a much more prominent role in our political parties, especially the Liberals. They are culturally inclined to participate in politics, perhaps as a natural outgrowth of their spiritual and cultural life in the gurdwaras or because as a minority that is vulnerable to persecution (in India and in diaspora communities around the world), political involvement provides a reassuring sign of prominence in public life. Some are motivated by a desire to advance the cause of Sikh separatism. The dream of an independent Khalistan in the Punjab, an idea long dead in India, lives on in the minds of many Canadian Sikhs.

Whatever the reason, Sikhs are ever present in nomination and leadership battles wherever a busload of voters might make the difference in a close race—and the federal Liberals are acutely aware of their importance. Trudeau's friend Bains was likely the most successful organizer in the federal party in the leadup to the 2015 vote, and not just with Sikhs.

Trudeau's offhand, lighthearted comment at American University likely did not please Modi. Hindu nationalists like Modi see Canada as soft on Sikh nationalism and fume at the sight of Canadian politicians looking for votes in gurdwaras where Sikh terrorists are venerated, including those involved in the 1985 terrorist bombing of Air India Flight 182, which killed 329 people. The RCMP and Canadian Security Intelligence Service failed to prevent it and then bungled the investigation—a record Indians saw as a disturbing failure.

In 2014, Modi led his Bharatiya Janata Party to victory, bringing an aggressive Hindu nationalism to the heart of power in India. He had been accused of condoning mass ethnic violence in 2002 when he was leader of the state government of Gujarat, leading the United States to ban him from entry to that country for almost a decade. But in 2018 he seemed to casual outside observers like a mild and pleasant new figure on the world stage. It later became clear that his brand of Hindu supremacism would result in violence, with religious minorities, especially Muslims, being humiliated and attacked by mobs associated with his party, but that it is not how it looked then. In 2016, during a successful meeting with Ontario premier Kathleen Wynne in New Delhi, Modi had urged Trudeau to visit India to promote trade. In January 2018, after India imposed import duties on chickpeas, peas, and lentils, hurting Canadian exporters, a visit seemed an excellent idea—not to mention the photo opportunities!

It was not a good idea—and it got off to a bad start. Modi, who is famous for hugging world leaders, didn't even show up at the airport to greet Trudeau and his family, instead sending a secretary of state for agriculture in his place. The Trudeaus then began a tour of the most photogenic sights in India, showing up at each with different Indian outfits, smiling and making the *namaste* gesture. They were photographed at the Golden Temple, the Taj Mahal, and the Swaminarayan Akshardham temple, ticking off boxes for Sikh, Muslim, and Hindu voters in Canada. It was too much. Although the greetings on the streets were positive, Indians started making fun of the Trudeaus and their elaborate costumes. Omar Abdullah, leader of the National Conference party, found the whole spectacle excessive. "Is it just me or is this choreographed cuteness all just a bit much now?" he tweeted. "I thought it was a little too Indian for Indians," said Indian fashion designer Anand Bhushan on Indian TV. "A little tacky in terms of sartorial choices. He looked like a complete backup dancer for a cheap Bollywood movie."

Back in Canada, Louis-Alexandre Lanthier, Trudeau's former executive assistant, was watching it go badly and thinks he knows why it went awry. "When Justin goes to Park Extension in his riding, and he's surrounded by the Indian and the Pakistani community in the parade, and he is wearing the garb, they love it. They go totally nuts for it. But then when you show up in India and you do the same thing, it's like, 'Is he mocking us?'"

The trip was not a disciplined business mission with a photo op or two thrown in. It was set up like a royal tour, as though Justin and Sophie were Will and Kate. The Trudeau people should have seen the reaction coming. The week before, British journalist Piers Morgan had described Trudeau in his column in the *Daily Mail* as "the worst kind of hectoring, bully pulpit smart-ass; dripping with virtuous self-aggrandizing sanctimony"—and it had gone viral globally. The progressive poster boy was starting to irritate people like Morgan, and they were ready to attack. Trudeau had lived by the photo op. Now he would die by it.

There are moments in the evolution of a brand when the people running it have to change their game. Trudeau had reached that point but did not realize it, and he was suddenly a figure of fun, with comedians around the world making jokes about his outfits. Overnight, he set a new global threshold for cringe.

Vandana Kattar was part of the contingent of young Liberals from the Greater Toronto Area who moved to Ottawa to work for Trudeau, a multicultural, urban group who were excited and energized by his openness to progressive young new Canadians. She had returned early from maternity leave for the India trip and was excited to help the family with their outfits, many of which had been contributed by members of multicultural communities in the GTA. When they arrived in Mumbai, she unwisely ate a paneer, which didn't agree with her. She started to feel ill before the cultural event that she was to attend with the Trudeaus and hundreds of guests that night. Instead of enjoying herself with the glittering crowd inside, she was outside, clutching her belly and regretting the paneer. "This is my favourite thing. I'm just going to eat it anyways. That was stupid." She decided to head to her hotel and get some rest.

Kattar was trying to sleep when John Zerucelli, director of operations for the PMO, knocked on her door. "We have a problem," he said. He told her what had happened at the reception she missed. "I knew it was bad," she recalls. "It was a comms battle. We'd have to figure it out and drive the narrative."

Back in Ottawa, where it was 6 p.m., CBC reporter Terry Milewski had just reported that a British Columbia man named Jaspal Atwal had attended the event that evening in Mumbai. Milewski was filling in as host of *Power & Politics*, the CBC's late afternoon news show. He had recently retired after a thirty-eight-year career. A stubborn and fearless scrutinizer of the powerful, he had been treated as an enemy combatant by both Jean Chrétien and Stephen Harper. That morning, someone had sent Milewski pictures of Atwal at the Trudeau reception, and he knew right away what it meant. Atwal had been one of five men who ambushed Malkiat Singh Sidhu, an Indian Cabinet minister, in an attempted assassination on Vancouver Island in 1986. They forced his car off the road and put several bullets into him. (Other assassins succeeded in killing him in India in 1991.) Atwal, then a member of the International Sikh

Youth Federation, which was later listed as a terrorist organization, was convicted of attempted murder.

Milewski had covered the Air India terror attack, spent time with the families of the victims, and pursued the story relentlessly ever since. He had interviewed Atwal and knew that, in addition to the attempted assassination conviction, he had been charged, and eventually acquitted, in the 1985 beating of Ujjal Dosanjh, a secular Canadian Sikh politician who ended up with a broken hand and eighty stitches in his head.

Despite his history as a terrorist, Atwal had remained active in Liberal politics at both the federal and the provincial level, posting pictures of himself with politicians on his Facebook page. It is hard to imagine that a terrorist associated with a movement attacking Israel, the United States, Britain, or France could have the kind of access he enjoyed. By not taking Indian security complaints seriously, Canada had shown disrespect to a rising global power.

The day of the Mumbai event, Atwal posted pictures of himself with Amarjeet Sohi and Sophie Grégoire Trudeau—who had no idea who he was—and also an image of his invitation to a dinner the next night in New Delhi. His presence at the event was a disaster for the Trudeau team. "I immediately thought it was an absolute blunder," Milewski told me later. "Because anyone who knew anything about these issues, and Canada's sorry history with this file, would know that this was a disaster and would know that Atwal was convicted. You know, this was a picture of a convicted terrorist posing with the prime minister's wife in India."

The *Times of India* wrote that the incident "threatened to further strain India-Canada ties" ahead of Trudeau's meeting with Modi. The Liberals sought to quash the whole thing by rescinding Atwal's invitation to the Delhi event and throwing Surrey Centre MP Randeep Sarai under the bus. He put out a statement saying he "alone facilitated his request to attend this important event." Trudeau said he would have a talk with Sarai when they got back to Canada.

The incident highlighted Canada's repeated failures to quarantine and isolate Sikh radicals from Canadian politics. The Liberals appeared to have failed to vet the list of invitees, an amateurish mistake, but, publicly, the Indian government was saying reassuring things. Atwal had denounced his terrorist past and made a deal with New Delhi that allowed him to travel to India. Modi's people understood his presence was an embarrassing mistake and were ready to move on.

But Daniel Jean, the national security advisor, decided to call John Ivison at the *National Post* to tell him what really happened—the Trudeau government had been set up by spies working for Modi, or something. Just when the story was ready to die, Ivison had a front-page scoop giving it fresh energy. The column was headlined "The Indian Government Removed Jaspal Atwal from Its Blacklist. Why? It Doesn't Make Any Sense—Until You Start to Consider Who Stands to Benefit from Atwal's Attendance This Week."

Jean, identified as "a senior security source within the Canadian government, who spoke on condition of anonymity," said that the incident "was not an accident," that the Indian government had given Atwal a visa, and that it stood to benefit from embarrassing Canada. The puppet masters behind the whole thing were likely the Indian intelligence service.

Later, Jean testified that he approached Ivison out of concern that security agencies were going to be blamed for failing to properly vet invitees. Instead, he ended up seeding an explosive story blaming India for Canada's failure. Jean then gave a similar story to the reporters travelling with Trudeau, ratcheting up the tension before Trudeau's visit with Modi.

Back in Ottawa, Milewski couldn't believe what he was watching. "There seemed to be two different streams of uncoordinated information coming into the travelling PMO. The political track was saying, 'Okay. Quick. We've got to fix this. Milewski's ranting about it on CBC . . . What are we going to do? I know. We rescind the invitation. That's easy. We admit that it was a mistake, we undo the mistake, and we find somebody to blame, and it might as well be Randeep Sarai. It's probably true that he put him on the list. So you have that slight advantage of it being true. Hey!

That's a bonus!' Then there's the other track," Milewski continues. "The professionals, you know, for whom the political types are beneath them. The professionals said, 'We've got to blame the Indian side.' I don't know what the hell the idea of that was. I mean, it's just very unprofessional, very ill-advised."

Nobody thinks the Indians engineered the invitation to the event. And if they had, in some hard-to-imagine scenario involving slippery double agents, Canada only made itself look bad by saying so. The Indians "find this whole thing an absolute farce," says Milewski. "I mean, that Canada is still treating these people with respect, giving them the time of day, just beggars belief."

It looked different to the Trudeau team. They saw two problems with the trip. The first was the outfits, which were at least partly the responsibility of Sophie, who was repeatedly photographed with her hands clasped, looking like a glamorous visiting yoga saint. "There was the cringe factor, which she is definitely responsible for much of that," says one insider. But nobody voted for Sophie. It was up to Trudeau to deal with that. And he was responsible for the political miscalculation around Modi.

"I think there was a view that Modi was going to try and fuck us," says a member of Trudeau's team. "But I would also say I don't think anyone anticipated how aggressively he was going to try and fuck us." The delegation was loaded with Canadian Sikhs who the Indians believed to be Khalistani extremists. That "upped the temperature on Modi going like, fuck these guys."

The Trudeau people felt jammed. "To be fair, I think it's a really hard line for us to walk, because you can't look like you're backing down to Modi, and you can't look like you are disavowing the Sikh community in Canada, and specifically Nav, who obviously is like incredibly important to us," says one Trudeau team member. "And so you have to kind of do this fine balance. But it was over-rotated I think, in terms of making sure that the Sikh community felt comfortable with the trip and then, in doing so, completely pissed off Modi to the point where 'We're just going to actively fuck you' as opposed to like a mild fucking, which is I think what people were kind of hoping for."

The Modi people were out to get Trudeau. "I did many foreign trips with the prime minister," says a senior staffer who could not believe how the Indians behaved behind closed doors. "I have never been on a trip where it was more obvious that the host country wanted the prime minister to be embarrassed and/or thwarted whatever his efforts or objectives were on the trip." And they didn't see it coming. "I think there was an underestimation of how much he was hated by the government there."

The trip did nothing in the end to improve market conditions for Canadian pulse producers. India increased its tariffs in March, which the Conservatives blamed on the Mumbai mistake. And, crucially, Trudeau damaged his reputation as a progressive media darling.

British comedian John Oliver said later that Trudeau had "overshot the runway of his own popularity. It felt like, for the first time, he singed his fingertips on people going, 'You're not quite that charismatic to pull off a trip like that.'"

Canadians noticed. Trudeau had done the country proud when he visited Washington and dealt manfully with Trump. Now he had gone to India and looked foolish. The trip diminished his political capital at home, permanently reduced the value of his global brand, and set back relations with one of the fastest-growing economies in the world. Modi may have laid traps for Trudeau, but it was the prime minster's job not to walk into them. It might have been the worst trip by a Canadian leader in history. Until that point, the slick operators on Team Trudeau had gone from triumph to triumph. Suddenly, they looked like they didn't know what they were doing.

6

THE LAST PIPELINE

On April 8, 2018, two months after his disastrous passage to India, Justin Trudeau got bad news from Houston. Kinder Morgan, the American petroleum giant, announced it was suspending work on the $7.4 billion Trans Mountain Expansion Project, 980 kilometres of new pipe to connect the upgraders of Edmonton to the Pacific Coast at Burnaby, along the route of an existing pipeline. Kinder Morgan Canada Limited, a subsidiary of the American giant, pulled the plug because of "extraordinary political risks that are completely outside of our control and that could prevent completion of the project."

The mother company's CEO, Richard Kinder, was making a smart play, the most recent of many he'd made in the process of becoming a billionaire. Kinder had been president of Enron until 1996, getting out before the shenanigans that led the company to what was then a record-setting bankruptcy, with $11 billion in shareholder losses and executives behind bars for conspiracy, fraud, and insider trading. According to *The Smartest Guys in the Room*, the bestselling 2003 book about the spectacular collapse of the company, Kinder "was an utterly practical businessman who saw his job as solving problems and making sure Enron delivered on the earnings targets it promised to Wall Street."

Before he got away from the fools who would destroy Enron and burn mountains of money with their fraudulent accounting practices, Kinder bought a $40 million Enron pipeline subsidiary, which he built into Kinder Morgan, a behemoth that was worth $140 billion by 2014. He didn't get to be a billionaire by blowing money on doomed projects, and the political risks of the pipeline expansion were real enough. Indigenous British Columbians and environmentalists had sworn to do whatever they could to stop the pipeline project from bringing 890,000 barrels of diluted bitumen—"dilbit"—a day to load on tankers at a terminal in Burrard Inlet, a deep, beautiful, wooded cove, home to chinook and coho salmon and orcas. People who live there are terrified of a spill and were determined to stop the pipeline. A 2010 Enbridge spill put a million gallons of Canadian dilbit into Michigan's Kalamazoo River, and the company had to spend $1.2 billion on the cleanup, including dredging, because the tarry bitumen in the dilbit sinks after it separates from the diluent, leaving a toxic, gooey mess.

In March 2018, five thousand people showed up for a protest at the Burrard Inlet site, which Kinder Morgan had to protect with ten-foot chain-link fences topped with razor wire. To make matters trickier for Trudeau, the premier of BC, John Horgan, was on the side of the protesters.

On election night in British Columbia the previous year, business-oriented Liberal premier Christy Clark, who was seeking a third mandate, came up short. She won forty-three seats, two more than Horgan's NDP, but Andrew Weaver's Green Party had three seats—the first time Greens elected more than one representative in a Canadian election. Weaver, a well-regarded climate scientist from the University of Victoria, made a deal with Horgan, trading the support of his party for several promises, including a commitment to "immediately employ every tool available to the new government to stop the expansion" of the Kinder Morgan pipeline. That gave Horgan the votes he needed to become premier, a job he could keep only so long as he tried to block the pipeline. In January 2018, his government proposed regulations that would restrict shipment of dilbit until there was a better plan for dealing with a spill, an attempt to do with regulations what the government couldn't do openly—block Trans Mountain.

Horgan was playing the role he was obliged to play, but his heart didn't seem to be in it. He comes from the moderate side of the party and, according to his advisors, was sympathetic to the political challenge facing his colleague Rachel Notley, the NDP premier of Alberta.

Albertans were furious. The lack of pipeline capacity meant that Alberta crude was selling at a $20-a-barrel discount. The province desperately needed pipelines. When Trudeau took office, he banned oil tanker traffic on the north coast of British Columbia, effectively killing the proposed Northern Gateway pipeline to Kitimat, near Prince Rupert. He did nothing to boost the proposed Energy East pipeline, which would have moved dilbit through Quebec to the Irving refinery in Saint John, New Brunswick, a project so unpopular in Quebec that it likely never could have happened. Obama had killed the Keystone XL pipeline that would have connected Alberta oil to the refineries on the Gulf Coast of Texas, and although Trump had revived it, Keystone was no sure thing. The one new outlet for Alberta oil was now being blocked by their neighbours in BC. Albertans, dispensers of largesse to the rest of the federation through oil and gas royalties, were being thwarted and treated with disrespect at every turn. Notley had no choice but to go after Horgan. Otherwise, Jason Kenney, who had unified the right in the province, would be happy to step in and take over.

A restaurant owner in Fort McMurray, heart of the oil sands, made headlines when she dropped BC wine from the menu. A few days later, Notley announced the whole province would follow suit. That was not far enough for many Albertans. Former Alberta energy minister Rick Orman, for instance, called for Trudeau to send in the Canadian Armed

Forces to deal with protesters. In April, Notley tabled a bill that would allow her to cut off the flow of gasoline and aviation fuel to BC if she judged that Horgan was treating her province unfairly.

These squabbles were bad for Trudeau. Many of the voters who elected both Horgan and Notley voted Liberal federally. His electoral coalition included BC voters who wanted climate action, and Alberta oil workers who couldn't believe that the rest of the country was making it so hard for their province to get the world price for its oil. In the leadup to the election, Trudeau had insisted that he could reconcile the differences and end the struggle over the oil sands. "In 2015, pretending that we have to choose between the economy and the environment is as harmful as it is wrong," he said in a speech to the Canada 2020 think tank. He argued that Harper had failed to build a social consensus around the industry. Where Harper had sought to polarize the issue, Trudeau promised sunny ways that would lead to greater certainty. He also promised to introduce carbon pricing—a price on emissions that would encourage reductions—a plan he would work out with the provinces.

The political bargain rested on the construction of Trans Mountain, a single compromise pipeline that he would defend to angry protesters in British Columbia while also denying Albertans the other pipelines they felt were their due. Without Trans Mountain, there would be no bargain. Richard Kinder had Trudeau cornered. The prime minister had no choice but to buy the pipeline.

———

THE BARGAIN TRUDEAU HAD built was never solid because many people in the oil patch—Brad Wall, for instance—would never sign on to anything that blocks development. Wall had been leading a popular Saskatchewan Party government for a decade, building a new Alberta-style consensus around free enterprise and the growing oil and gas business that was making people in the province rich.

In 2015, Trudeau convened a First Ministers' meeting in Ottawa—the first in six years—to talk about developing a climate plan before the international climate summit in Paris. Wall, alone among the premiers, expressed grave reservations about the plan that Trudeau and Environment Minister Catherine McKenna had prepared. At the time, the provincial map was great for Trudeau, with Liberal premiers in Atlantic Canada, Quebec, Ontario, and British Columbia, and New Democrats in Manitoba and Alberta. After the meeting, the government sent a bus to the Château Laurier to take the premiers to dinner at Trudeau's residence, Rideau Cottage. Later, Wall became engrossed in looking at the art in the residence. When he was ready to leave, he realized that all the other premiers had gone before him in their cars. He was the only one on the environmentally friendly bus back to the Château. "Just carbon-tax Brad was on the bus," he recalls. "I'm the only guy on the CO2-free bus."

Trudeau and McKenna were determined to put a floor price on carbon emissions, allowing each province to decide how to get there but imposing a federal backstop if they didn't get in line. Alberta had already brought in a carbon-pricing system for large emitters, part of a plan to make carbon-intensive oil from the oil sands acceptable to international markets. Notley was open to a federal plan so long as Ottawa helped her get a pipeline. British Columbia already had a carbon tax, and Quebec and Ontario had cap-and-trading schemes. Saskatchewan was the odd province out, and there was no way Ottawa could go to Paris without a real plan to reduce emissions that included Alberta and Saskatchewan, which have vastly higher per-capita emissions than the other provinces thanks to their oil and gas industries.

In October, Trudeau laid down the gauntlet. With the provincial environment ministers gathered with McKenna in Montreal, he stood in the House for a parliamentary debate on the Paris Climate Accord. He announced his government's plan—a $10-a-ton price on carbon starting in 2018, rising $10 a year to $50 a ton by 2020. Any provinces that chose could implement their own systems, but if they did not do so, Ottawa would step in and return the revenue to the citizens of each province through rebates.

Wall had been pushing for Ottawa to continue consultations with the provinces. When Trudeau unilaterally announced his plan, he was not impressed. His environment minister, Scott Moe, called him from Montreal to tell him McKenna had brought in a monitor so all the premiers could watch Trudeau's speech. "That's when Scott said to me, 'I'm, frankly, interested in leaving this meeting.' And I said, 'Can you take anyone with you? Are there any other provinces that'll go?' He said, 'I don't know. Maybe Newfoundland.' I said, 'Well, whether there is or there isn't, you should go.'"

Moe walked out. Wall blasted the plan in the media—calling it a "betrayal"—and gave the same message directly to Trudeau in a phone call later. Saskatchewan would never be a voluntary participant in the bargain Trudeau had laid out. The province would eventually sue—joined by Alberta under Kenney, and Ontario under Doug Ford—and go all the way to the Supreme Court, fighting Trudeau's plan on constitutional grounds, losing at every turn. Sunny ways could not stop the lawyers.

———

THE NEWS FROM HOUSTON hit the Alberta government hard. Notley had agreed to sign on to Trudeau's climate plan against the wishes of the many Albertans who were skeptical about climate change. She was pushing British Columbia hard, without any support from federal NDP leader Jagmeet Singh, who was listening to left-leaning urbanites who opposed all pipelines. Now Kinder Morgan had pulled the rug out from under her.

Anne McGrath, Notley's principal secretary, grew up in Montreal and Ottawa and had lived in Alberta after university, working as a student organizer. (At twenty-six, she ran as a Communist Party of Canada candidate in Edmonton in the 1984 election, placing seventh of seven.) She had moved back to Alberta after Notley's victory. McGrath had gotten to know Telford well when they were involved in the convoluted and ultimately unsuccessful attempt to overthrow the Harper government by forming a parliamentary coalition with the Bloc. That hadn't worked, but the two women liked each other.

McGrath and Brian Topp—a long-time senior New Democrat who had run unsuccessfully against Mulcair for the party's leadership—pressed the PMO hard for action on the pipeline. "Brian and I had several meetings with them talking about how basically in Alberta social licence is turned upside down, and that in order to get social licence for climate leadership, the pipeline was part of that," McGrath recalls.

Inside the PMO, Ryan Adam, who was working the western desk, was on their side. Adam had grown up in Edmonton and moved to the United States after university. He worked on Barack Obama's successful 2008 campaign and then at CNN. After the inauguration, he came back to Alberta for a job with the provincial government. On evenings and weekends, he worked with the Trudeau team, bringing organizational lessons from American politics—and connections with the Obama people.

After Trudeau became prime minister, Adam had the unenviable task of trying to build the federal government's political operation in Alberta and promote the province's interests within the government. Because Trudeau is so despised in Alberta, Adam found family gatherings were sometimes difficult when relatives wanted to share their views with him. "I usually make a deal with my family," he says. "If you want to talk to me about politics, it's $500 an hour, and we can talk all day if you want."

Adam knew the Trans Mountain project well, having been among the Albertans who had helped calm the waters when Christy Clark was tussling with Alberta premier Alison Redford about it. He believed Alberta needed pipeline capacity and lamented the way Harper had polarized opinion around the issue. "I would go to Vancouver on the weekends, and it would be like, 'Well, I hate Harper. And Harper likes pipelines. So therefore, I hate pipelines.'" When Kinder Morgan suddenly pulled the plug, Albertans were not just angry—they were rattled.

Albertan New Democrats and Liberals wanted Trudeau to save the project, but environmentalists wanted him to just let it die. If we need to reduce emissions, they argued, it is crazy to invest in fossil fuel capital projects that will still be pumping oil when Xavier Trudeau has grey hair. Green Party leader Elizabeth May thought it was crazy. She tried to convince Butts to give up on the project. "I'd go talk to him and say, 'You can't approve the Kinder Morgan pipeline. The environmental assessment is flawed and this, this, this, and this, all the facts of the case. And Gerry would just say, 'Rachel needs a pipeline.' I said, 'Well, Rachel may think she needs a pipeline. Maybe Rachel needs a refinery. The pipeline is to ship out raw unprocessed bitumen, and you do not get a better price at tidewater, because it is the crappiest, worst quality fossil fuel oil you're going to find."

But the industry didn't want a refinery in Edmonton. There were lots of refineries in Texas. The industry wanted a pipeline from Edmonton to Burrard Inlet. And Notley, as Butts said, needed it. To maintain national unity, to convince Albertans that the federal government wasn't out to destroy them, Trudeau needed to buy the pipeline. As he tweeted: "Canada is a country of the rule of law, and the federal government will act in the national interest. Access to world markets for Canadian resources is a core national interest. The Trans Mountain expansion will be built."

In April, when Trudeau was in Peru for the Summit of Americas, with plans to go on to London and Paris for more meetings, he interrupted his trip and flew back to Ottawa to sit down with Horgan and Notley. Horgan, his hands tied by his political arrangement with the Greens in the BC legislature, could not say much. His message came down to "I got this job because of the Greens, and they're never going to go along with this."

Notley made her case: "Look," she said, as Adam recalls, "I'm the first non-Conservative premier of Alberta in the last forty-four years. I'm a practical climate change believer. I'm fighting for my industry. I'm fighting for my province. I'm willing to meet you on pipeline safety. I'm willing to meet you on tanker traffic. I'm willing to meet you on climate targets. I'm willing to meet you on Indigenous jobs. I'm willing to do what it takes to get us to a place where you can not necessarily sell it to your people but to begrudgingly sort of let it move forward."

After the meeting, Trudeau announced that Bill Morneau would talk to Texas. "I have instructed the minister of finance to initiate formal financial discussions with Kinder Morgan, the result of which will be to remove the uncertainty overhanging the Trans Mountain pipeline expansion project." Horgan was unhappy about that and hadn't promised to get out of the way, but he talked about one possible win for his province. "At the end of the day we agreed that there may well be an opportunity for us to have officials address some of the gaps that we perceive to be in the oceans protection plan."

———

TRUDEAU COULD NOT AFFORD to have the project die but wanted to find a way to avoid buying the damn thing. Morneau opened talks with Kinder Morgan and came up with a dodge. He held a news conference on May 16 in which he declared that Ottawa was ready to "indemnify the Trans Mountain expansion against unnecessary delays that are politically motivated."

The idea was that Kinder Morgan could keep building, and Ottawa would cut the company a cheque if political uncertainty bogged them down. "Kinder Morgan has been trying to hose the taxpayer, asking for money to support their pipeline or they will stop it altogether, and we just called their bluff," a senior government source told Evan Solomon, writing in *Maclean's*. "We were not going to be held for ransom."

Morneau said there were other options. "If Kinder Morgan is not interested in building the project, we think plenty of investors would be interested in taking on this project, especially knowing that the federal government believes it is in the best interest of Canadians."

That is not what happened. Morneau was the one bluffing, and Richard Kinder surely knew it. Nobody else wanted to buy the pipeline, certainly not TransCanada or Enbridge, whose pipeline dreams Trudeau had shattered when he killed Northern Gateway and let Energy East die.

Two weeks later, on May 29, Morneau held another news conference to announce that his government would pay Kinder Morgan $4.5 billion for the existing pipeline and the terminal in Burrard Inlet. He said, though, that there were other customers kicking the tires: "We've had expressions of interest from multiple investors over the course of this last month." And, he added, the government likely would not keep the pipeline forever. "We would not expect it to be a long-term hold. We would expect it to be a short- or medium-term hold for the government."

Kinder didn't get to be the richest man in Houston by folding good cards. Trudeau would have to pay. Canadians will keep paying for the foreseeable future. As of March 2023, the total estimated construction cost is estimated at $30.9 billion, four times higher than the estimate in 2018, the result of unanticipated construction challenges.

There is good reason to think Trans Mountain will be the last big pipeline built in Canada. Adam agrees, no matter who is prime minister, because the legal, political, and regulatory environment is just too difficult. "Who is going to want to wait ten years for permits? You won't find a single person in Calgary willing to take a bet on a new pipeline."

In his book, *Where To from Here*, Morneau laments having to buy it. "It was a decision I didn't want to take—owning a pipeline was not part of our plan—but that was necessary to complete the project and show international investors that Canada is a place where things get done." Brad Wall agrees: "I don't know if they had a choice. And I think they did the right thing. Notwithstanding the massive cost overruns, I think that was the only thing left to do."

Jagmeet Singh, who called it an "investment in the past," may turn out to be right in the end, although we won't know until Xavier is prime minister. The future of the transition to a low-carbon future is unknown. Carbon sequestration technology may make fossil fuels the energy of the future, or oil may be a thing of the past, with empty pipelines rusting while we zoom around in electric cars. If the past is any guide, though, Trans Mountain will eventually pay off. In 1990, John Crosbie convinced Mulroney to put billions into Hibernia, the first big project off Newfoundland. Oil prices were low, Mulroney was unpopular, and central Canadian editorialists were outraged. But it has provided $15 billion for Newfoundland and Labrador, and $4 billion for the federal treasury.

Opposition politicians regularly point out that Trudeau's government has missed its emission-reduction targets, which is true, but it is also clear that the government has pushed hard to achieve the reductions that it has achieved, paying a political price for taxing carbon and stopping projects, galling would-be friends in the business community, for instance, by failing to get behind more liquified natural gas exports. But if you believe that Canada should be taking action on climate change, it is difficult to fault the Trudeau people for being too tough on the industry. There is no way to cut our emissions without affecting oil and gas.

The government can be faulted, though, for failing to get behind the transition, investing in geothermal, offshore wind, or tidal projects that would cut emissions and create employment for people who might otherwise resent the government for undercutting traditional industries. People who work in carbon-intensive industries will not believe promises from distant governments, but they can see things differently if good jobs are being created in a new industry. That is not easy, and it might mean spending money in areas where the Liberals don't have much hope of winning seats, which governments rarely do.

"They need a much more focused approach on creating the type of industry and economy that would actually create employment and long-term prosperity, export products, energy exports, all those things that the rest of the world is involved in, instead of being so obsessed with meeting the needs of the oil industry," says Tim Gray, executive director at Environmental Defence Canada. "They haven't done enough."

Still, Trudeau has remained true to the grand bargain he proposed—supporting the oil and gas industry while trying to cut emissions. In the process, he's disappointed almost everyone.

7

WRONG SIDE OF THE LINE

A t 10 a.m. on April 13, 2012, RCMP Inspector Lise Faucher showed up at the towering headquarters of engineering firm SNC-Lavalin on boulevard René-Lévesque in downtown Montreal with a search warrant authorizing her to seize documents related to the company's business in Libya.* Outside, uniformed Mounties attached yellow police tape to the polished granite pillars at street level. Faucher took the elevator to the twenty-first floor, to the office of CEO Pierre Duhaime, where the receptionist told her that he and everyone from senior management were out.

The bosses knew they were in trouble. Three days earlier, Riadh Ben Aissa, executive vice-president in charge of construction, had been arrested on corruption charges in Switzerland. They were all in a conference room at the nearby Queen Elizabeth hotel attending an anti-corruption presentation from Hentie Dirker, the regional compliance officer for Siemens, a massive German engineering company that, in 2008, had paid

---

* Faucher's story is told in full in the excellent 2021 book *La Saga SNC-Lavalin*, by longtime *La Presse* investigative reporter Vincent Larouche.

$1.6 billion in fines to the United States and Germany to settle a bribery case. Dirker was there to tell them how SNC could bounce back "even if things happened and there were issues and bad people doing bad things."*

Alerted to the raid, the executives rushed back to headquarters, where they found the Mounties already at their workstations beginning the huge task of downloading and transferring six to eight terabits of corporate records. They were looking for the paper trail showing money from Libya to Swiss bank accounts controlled by the company, and then back to the Gaddafi family.

So began a seven-year nightmare for the slippery businessmen who headed SNC-Lavalin. By the end, several were in prison, and both the company and the Trudeau government had been brought to the brink of collapse.

The story dates back to 1995 in Libya, the oil-rich North African republic ruled by Muammar Gaddafi. Immediately after he captured power in 1969, he nationalized the oil industry and improved literacy rates and living conditions, but he became increasingly cruel, erratic, and megalomaniacal. In the late 1980s, he was suspected of ordering the bombings of airliners over both Lockerbie, Scotland, and the Congo, killing 440 people in all.

When Libya refused to co-operate with international investigations, the United States imposed sanctions. That created an opportunity for SNC-Lavalin, and in 1995 the company won a $230 million contract drilling wells and laying concrete pipe to build Gaddafi's Great Man-Made River, which pumped water from Saharan aquifers to cities on the Mediterranean coast. SNC-Lavalin, which had built the massive James Bay Project in northern Quebec, knew about pipes and pumps—and also how to win contracts. It paid bribes to Al-Saadi Muammar Gaddafi, the second of the dictator's eight sons, a playboy with the power to approve

---

* Dirker, who eventually went to work as SNC-Lavalin's chief integrity officer, recounted the strange moment at the Trace International Bribery and Economic Crime Summit in Vancouver in June 2019, as described by Bob Mackin of the Breaker.com.

massive projects. From 2001 on, the company paid 6 to 6.5 percent commissions on the monstrous contracts it won in Libya, moving the money through Swiss bank accounts to Saadi Gaddafi, a total of $160 million over the years—dirty money diverted from projects that ought to have benefited the people of Libya.*

SNC-Lavalin was doing similar things in other countries, brazenly paying off local bosses to win contracts in Algeria, Bangladesh, Cambodia, and Tunisia. "Everybody hated SNC," recalls a former diplomat. "In Asia in the nineties, we had to bail SNC out of a bribery problem in almost every country in East Asia. They were just the cowboys of the industry. They didn't give a fuck about anybody. They'd break every rule and brag about it."

Libya was a special case, producing huge amounts of revenue—more than $2 billion in the first decade of the century. The conduit for the dirty money was the high-living Ben Aissa, who moved it through his personal Swiss bank accounts. Saadi used money from SNC to buy a 150-foot yacht and a $1.6 million condo on the waterfront in Toronto, among other extravagances. Until the Libyan government fell in 2011, SNC was a key part of Team Gaddafi.

The company was also paying bribes to win lucrative contracts in Canada—$2.3 million to the corporation that maintains the Jacques Cartier and Champlain bridges, for example, and $22.5 million to Montreal's new mega hospital. SNC-Lavalin seemed invincible until, in February 2015, after months of unsuccessful settlement negotiations between prosecutors and the company, the RCMP charged the company with one count of fraud, a Criminal Code offence, and, more worryingly for the company, one count of corruption under the Corruption of Foreign Public Officials Act.

The company reacted with horror, warning that a conviction could

---

* The company's board knew "absolutely nothing" about kickbacks paid to Saadi, then-chair Gwyn Morgan told the CBC in 2019.

lead to it being broken up or destroyed—a disaster for Montreal. In 2014, the Harper government had introduced a ten-year automatic ban from federal contracting for companies convicted of bribing foreign officials, part of a package designed to comply with the Organisation for Economic Co-operation and Development (OECD) anti-corruption regime. SNC could not afford to lose its contracting business.

The business community rallied. Economist Jack Mintz and former Liberal Cabinet minister John Manley wrote op-eds proposing that the federal government do what other countries had done—pass legislation allowing for deferred prosecution agreements, which would allow the company to settle without being convicted. Manley, CEO of the Canadian Council of Chief Executives, wrote in the *Globe and Mail* that DPAs offered a way of combatting "corporate crime and punishing the guilty without hurting others who have done nothing wrong."

SNC needed this workaround, so it launched what Michael Wernick, the clerk of the Privy Council and the most powerful public servant in the country, called the "most extensive government relations effort in modern times," an aggressive campaign in the backrooms of Ottawa, twisting arms. Trudeau would have to bail them out.

———

WHEN PIERRE TRUDEAU PATRIATED the Canadian constitution in 1982—the triumph of his political career—it did not initially recognize Aboriginal title, a concept that had been part of the legal framework since the Royal Proclamation of British North America in 1763. Bill Wilson, a Kwakwaka'wakw hereditary chief from Comox, British Columbia, wanted to change that, successfully pushing for an amendment—section 35—which became the key tool in the crucial legal battles that Indigenous peoples have won in court in the decades since. The second Indigenous person to graduate from the University of British Columbia law school, Wilson was a formidable speaker and a confident, poised politician, qualities he inherited from his mother, Ethel Pearson, an Elder who had played an important role in preserving the culture of the Kwakwaka'wakw people and resisting the cruel and exploitive colonial policies imposed by Indian agents and continued by various governments well into the twentieth century.

In 1983, that struggle brought Wilson to Ottawa, where he wrangled with Trudeau *père* at a constitutional conference in which the prime minister and the premiers sat with Indigenous leaders at a big table in the government conference centre. "I have two children in Vancouver Island, both of whom for some misguided reason say they want to be a lawyer, both of whom say they want to be prime minister, both of whom are women," he said. The conference broke out in laughter, the government dignitaries incredulous at the prospect of Indigenous girls leading the country.

Trudeau took off his reading glasses. "Tell them I'll stick around till they're ready," he said, cracking up the room.

Wilson, poised and smiling, responded with another joke: "Mr. Chairman, I'm informed by the government of British Columbia that one of them could be out here on a plane this evening."

The younger of those daughters, Jody Wilson-Raybould, was sworn in as justice minister on November 4, 2015.

———

BILL WILSON'S DAUGHTER WAS mostly raised by her mother, Sandra Wilson—a teacher of European background—but she credits her grandmother, Ethel Pearson, with shaping her. When Jody was eight, her grandmother held a potlach where she named her Puglaas, "woman born of noble people."

Like her father, Wilson-Raybould graduated from the University of British Columbia Faculty of Law and, like him, she became influential in Indigenous politics. In 2009, she was elected as the regional chief for

British Columbia in the Assembly of First Nations, the only woman at that level. Paul Martin talent-spotted her, and in 2013 Justin Trudeau arranged to meet her in Whitehorse during the AFN annual general meeting. He asked her to run for the party, and she eventually agreed. She gave a speech at the 2014 Liberal convention, outlining a "rights recognition framework" to remake the relationship between the Crown and Indigenous communities.

Butts and Telford pulled strings to get her the nomination in Vancouver Granville, convincing local Liberals to get on board. A few days after she won by acclimation, Trudeau came to town for a celebratory picnic in the riding, and they travelled together in northern BC to meet with Indigenous leaders.

When the election came, she was delighted to be made justice minister, and at her Cabinet swearing-in, the official photographer captured her and Trudeau embracing warmly. She threw herself into the unfamiliar world with gusto, with briefings and meetings filling the day. She was hopeful she could remake the relationship between First Nations and the Crown, as her father had worked for thirty years earlier.

Behind the scenes, though, from the beginning, there was tension between Wilson-Raybould and the staffers in the PMO. Normally, ministers in senior portfolios like Justice, Finance, Defence and Foreign Affairs get their jobs after spending years in the trenches, learning how to work on a team. These jobs are incredibly demanding, requiring long hours, difficult judgment calls, and disciplined communications. Wilson-Raybould did not have the experience of most of her predecessors in partisan politics and ended up having little patience for it, pushing back hard when staffers tried to discuss politics. Trudeau had been elected promising "real change" and needed to put newcomers in the front bench, but the change didn't mean that everyone was supposed to forget about the need to win elections.

The Trudeau-Butts-Telford triumvirate, after producing a miraculous victory and electing 148 new Liberal MPs, including Wilson-Raybould, pressured ministers to hire chiefs of staff recommended by the PMO. Morneau wanted John Zerucelli to be his chief of staff, for instance, but Butts and Telford had told key organizer Richard Maksymetz he could have his pick, and he wanted Finance. For Wilson-Raybould, they wanted a veteran staffer from Queen's Park, someone familiar with the players at big Toronto law firms. Wilson-Raybould reluctantly agreed to their choice, but the relationship was strained and it didn't last. She hired Lea Nicholas-MacKenzie, a long-time colleague, friend, and confidante, who was not a lawyer.

Any focus on electoral considerations, which is at the heart of modern Canadian politics, was off-putting to Wilson-Raybould. She found an ally in Jane Philpott, another rookie MP who had been elevated to preside over Health Canada. She too had been talent-spotted by Paul Martin. She joined the party in 2011, the day after Harper won a majority government, motivated by concern for the direction in which he was taking the country. Having spent the 1980s in Niger working as a doctor and training health workers, she opposed cuts to refugee health benefits imposed in 2012 by immigration minister Jason Kenney. She got involved in her local riding association, won the nomination, and was elected on the Trudeau wave.

Philpott and Wilson-Raybould were responsible for some of the biggest files in the first year of the new government—legalizing marijuana and medical assistance in dying—and in the process of working together they became close, often unwinding together with a glass of wine after work. Wilson-Raybould, who called herself MOJAG, for Minister of Justice/Attorney General, took to calling Philpott MOC, Mother of the Country. They shared a similar sense of mission, a similar impatience with partisan concerns.

Not everyone in Team Trudeau was on board with them. Their relationship with Carolyn Bennett, the minister of Indigenous and northern affairs, was tense. And several MPs and senators objected to the way they handled the contentious medical assistance in dying bill (C-14). In 2015, in *Carter v. Canada*, the Supreme Court had ruled that the Criminal Code prohibition on medical assistance in dying for those with "a grievous and irremediable medical condition" violated the Charter of Rights and Freedoms. Toronto MP Rob Oliphant, who as a United Church minister had provided spiritual counsel to many people facing the end of their lives, co-chaired a committee considering the matter, which recommended a more liberal regime than the bill Wilson-Raybould and Philpott tabled. Oliphant openly opposed it, arguing that it was not constitutional—a view borne out in 2019 by the Superior Court of Quebec. When a frustrated Oliphant complained about Wilson-Raybould, Butts told him she could not be moved. "She's too big to fail," he said.

Butts, who had pushed for Wilson-Raybould to be made justice minister, met with her more often than with other ministers and saw himself as her protector, but their relationship became strained over time. She resented the idea that she needed a protector, which she saw as a sign that the Laurentian Elite—the clubby network of powerful businesspeople, politicians, and public servants who run the country—could not accept her on her own terms.

In her book, *"Indian" in the Cabinet: Speaking Truth to Power*, Wilson-Raybould describes reacting with anger to PMO efforts to get her and Philpott to change course on assisted dying. She considered the intervention "ill-informed, superficial, political, and mostly just a series of ideas disengaged from the very serious and real issues at hand."

There were similar tensions behind the scenes with marijuana legalization. Wilson-Raybould and Philpott worked with veteran MP Ralph Goodale, the public safety minister, and with former Toronto police chief Bill Blair, who was Wilson-Raybould's parliamentary secretary. None of them had ever used marijuana. Some Liberals felt the approach they were taking was too restrictive and would make it hard for Canadian firms to capitalize on the business opportunities they expected would emerge (wrongly, as it turned out) from being one of the first countries to legalize cannabis. When someone in the PMO pressed for changes, Wilson-Raybould bridled, writing that the intervention "caused confusion and slowed things down."

In 2015, when Trudeau announced his Cabinet, he promised that a new era was at hand, that the days of micromanagement from the PMO were gone: "Government by cabinet is back," he said. Over time, however, the unelected people in Trudeau's orbit started to exert more control, and Wilson-Raybould kept pushing back. But the ones she resented were the same people who wrote the platform, arranged for her nomination, and engineered a majority election victory.

Every backroom veteran will tell you that "politics is a team sport." It regularly requires the subordination of individual desires to a broader group, reaching decisions through a frustrating process in which partisan considerations must be balanced. That's how it always works, but Wilson-Raybould found it harder to take than career politicians, who had learned to accept it over time.

Like Morneau, Wilson-Raybould was frustrated with Trudeau's remoteness. She resented having to go through Butts, who sought to insulate Trudeau from Cabinet ministers, and complained that she didn't have Trudeau's phone number. She found it "puzzling that a person in such a high leadership position would not make himself directly accessible," she wrote in *"Indian" in the Cabine*, her bestselling 2021 book.

Wilson-Raybould was also upset at the lack of progress on reconciliation and on repealing mandatory minimum sentences for criminal offences, which disproportionately affect Black and Indigenous people. Frustration was building on the other side too. In October 2016, Trudeau met with Wilson-Raybould and asked whether she was being properly supported by her office and the department, apparently in relation to delays in judicial appointments, which were causing backlogs in the courts. She had been refusing to give lists to partisan staffers who checked to see if candidates for the bench had donated to the party. Adam Dodek, dean of the University of Ottawa Faculty of Law, who was working with the government on proposed changes to the Supreme Court appointment process, blamed her: "They'd been in office for a year, they haven't appointed anyone because Jody Wilson-Raybould is reforming that process, meaning she's not doing anything," he said in an interview later. She didn't see it that way. She took the meeting with Trudeau as a "gut punch," and her relationship with the PMO went from bad to worse.

In 2017, Wilson-Raybould pushed to replace retiring Supreme Court Chief Justice Beverley McLachlin with Manitoba Justice Glenn D. Joyal, a Harper appointee who had criticized the court for overstepping its bounds in Charter cases. She sent Trudeau a sixty-page memo promoting Joyal's candidacy, which disturbed Trudeau, whose father had created the Charter. Eventually, Joyal withdrew his candidacy for personal reasons.

The prime minister and the justice minister were on a collision course. Compared with previous prime ministers, who would regularly have dinners and one-on-one meetings with their ministers, Trudeau had outsourced Cabinet management tasks to Butts and Telford. Trudeau, who gets energy from glad-handing in a crowd, is by nature introverted and gets drained by one-on-one meetings. "He's very introverted," says one person who has worked closely with him. "He finds personal engagement tiring, difficult, hard. If you're introverted, you're energized by crowds. You can keep your distance. You're not yourself." Trudeau tries to reduce the amount of time he spends with ministers and caucus members, some of whom wonder if he would recognize them on the street. While staffers who work closely with him find him warm and caring, to those outside the charmed circle he seems distant, like a celebrity protected by his entourage.

As the government aged, the relationships that had built it were under increasing strain. The triumvirate at the heart of the Trudeau operation was about to break down.

———

IN 2015, WHEN TRUDEAU became prime minister, he appointed Scott Brison as president of the Treasury Board, a powerful but low-profile role where he supervised and coordinated the government's ambitious left-wing agenda. Brison had first been elected to the House of Commons as a Progressive Conservative in 1997, in the Nova Scotia riding of Kings–Hants, but crossed the floor to join the Liberals after Stephen Harper and Peter MacKay created the Conservative Party. As a gay man, he was uncomfortable with the social conservatives in the new party but comfortable with Paul Martin's business-oriented Liberalism. He remained a progressive conservative at heart, and he appears to have found the interventionist approach of Trudeau and Butts excessive. When he spoke up in Cabinet meetings, counselling a more restrained approach to public spending, he felt that the prime minister treated him like a member of the opposition.

With Brison president of the Treasury Board, his office dealt with the paperwork for the big-ticket items being shuffled between the PMO and the bureaucracy. He observed that Trudeau's office would always choose the most expensive of the options presented by public servants, and he joked that the PMO would sometimes ask for even costlier choices than whatever was on offer: "Can we get that with Corinthian leather seats?"

He was out of step with Trudeau, and he wanted to have more time for his family. He and his husband, Maxime St-Pierre, were raising two young daughters. Also, he was dealing with a legal headache that might be handled more easily if he were out—the messy prosecution of Mark Norman, commander of the Royal Canadian Navy, who was charged with leaking Cabinet confidences in a fight over supply ships.*

Brison wasn't accused of doing anything wrong in that matter, but it looked like a looming headache for him. Norman's defence strategy seemed to hinge on portraying Brison as a stooge of the Irvings—an unpleasant scenario, not least because he was not close to the company.

On December 19, at the last caucus meeting of the year, the day of

---

* On May 8, 2019, the Crown dropped its case against Norman and the government reached a settlement with him, the terms of which have never been made public.

the Liberal Christmas party, Brison took Butts aside and told him he had decided to leave politics and would be announcing it to his constituents within days. Butts was alarmed to hear this news; it would require a Cabinet shuffle at a time when the government had its hands full. What's more, they would be in an election the following fall. He asked Brison to meet with Trudeau. Brison agreed, met the prime minister, but refused to reconsider. In February, the Bank of Montreal announced he would become vice-chair of investment and corporate banking, a job that demanded less of his time and likely paid a lot more.

Brison's departure—with an election around the corner—might have been good news for his family and his bank account, but it was bad news for the Liberals.

———

TRUDEAU MADE HIS SHUFFLE on January 14, 2019. Philpott, who was universally admired for excellent work at both Health and Indigenous Services, moved into the Treasury Board vacancy opened by Brison. Seamus O'Regan moved to Indigenous Services from Veterans Affairs. Wilson-Raybould took his spot, and David Lametti, a well-regarded law professor from Montreal, was made justice minister. Bernadette Jordan, the low-profile MP for South Shore–St. Margarets, was made minister of rural economic development, which kept a Nova Scotian in Cabinet without disrupting the gender balance.

At Rideau Hall, before the swearing-in ceremony, Wilson-Raybould went up to Lametti and said, "Be careful. All is not what it seems." Michael Wernick was within earshot. Wearing a striking red and black wrap decorated with Kwakwaka'wakw wolf motifs, Wilson-Raybould looked pained as she read the oath of office held up for her. Outside, when a reporter asked her if she saw the move as a demotion, she stuck to the script. "No, and I would say I can think of no world in which I would consider working for our veterans in Canada as a demotion," she said.

In an interview on the CBC, Lametti kept to the same script. "I am honoured to follow Jody Wilson-Raybould in this. I thought her appointment was a historic one and I agree with her that she's accomplished a great, great deal. And I think she's moving to a portfolio which requires an equal amount of success as she moves forward."

The script was nonsense. Wilson-Raybould had been demoted—and was widely seen as having failed. In the *Toronto Star*, Chantal Hébert wrote that "it had become an open secret on Parliament Hill that at least in the eye of her political masters but also in many quarters of the legal community her performance had not lived up to the advance billing." Wilson-Raybould put a statement on her website that read "as if it were written in anger in the middle of the night," as John Ivison wrote in the *National Post*.

Wilson-Raybould wrote that there was "very little, if anything, in my mandate letter" that she hadn't completed and attached "an overview" of other accomplishments. She continued at length about the role of the attorney general, pointedly reminding readers of "the unique and independent aspects of the Attorney General of Canada" and, ominously, that she "expect[ed] this to continue."

Wilson-Raybould had gone off script, raising questions about the independence of the attorney general. At the *Globe*'s Ottawa bureau, Bob Fife wondered why. Eventually, someone whispered to him that she had been shuffled because she wouldn't do what the government wanted—to overrule the prosecutor and order a deferred prosecution agreement for SNC-Lavalin. "Once I got the tip, then a light went off in my head," he says.

Fife worked the phones and found three knowledgeable sources who confirmed that officials in the PMO had pressured Wilson-Raybould to give SNC-Lavalin a get-out-of-jail-free card. Working with indefatigable colleague Steven Chase from the Ottawa bureau, and Sean Fine, the *Globe*'s justice specialist in Toronto, Fife started to put a story together. They knew they had an explosive scoop, but they were afraid of what would happen if they published. "My big problem was that I didn't know whether she was going to deny it and then I'd be screwed," he says.

A few days later, Fife approached Wilson-Raybould at Cabinet Outs, when reporters gather to pose questions to ministers. "I was waiting outside the Cabinet, and she came out and she gave me a big smile. I go down the steps. I catch her on the way out. I asked her the questions. She neither confirmed nor denied. She didn't say no and she didn't say yes." Before she left, though, she touched Fife on the arm and said, "Oh, you're a good reporter."

Wilson-Raybould messaged Butts to let him know that Fife had scrummed her: "Bob Fife seems to be doing a story on SNC. I did not say anything—have convo recorded. He seemed to know a great deal. Not sure how this could be . . ."

The exchange gave Fife what he needed. "I went back and I said, 'Okay, we can go with the story.' She didn't confirm it, but I felt confident. And then that's when we went to the PMO . . . and we wrote the story."

Fife and the *Globe* were taking a gamble. If Wilson-Raybould contradicted the story, it would not stand, and he would look like a fool. "It was terrible," Fife recalls. "I didn't sleep for two weeks."

———

THE STORY WAS AT the top of the front page of the *Globe* the next day: "PMO Pressed Wilson-Raybould to Abandon Prosecution of SNC-Lavalin." It said that Wilson-Raybould "came under heavy pressure" to have the Public Prosecution Service of Canada change its mind about prosecuting SNC-Lavalin, negotiating instead a "remediation agreement." The story included a brief statement from the PMO, which stated that the office "did not direct the attorney general to draw any conclusions on this matter."

The PMO's response was lawyerly. It was true that Trudeau had not directed Wilson-Raybould to overrule the director of public prosecutions,

Kathleen Roussel, but that isn't what the story reported. At a transit announcement in Vaughan, Trudeau went further. "The allegations in the
Globe story this morning are false. Neither the current nor the previous
attorney general was ever directed by me or by anyone in my office to take
a decision in this matter."

The reporter pressed Trudeau—the allegation was that the government pressured her, not directed her. Somewhat robotically, Trudeau
repeated his lines, but his non-denial denial could not kill the story.
NDP MPs Nathan Cullen and Charlie Angus wrote to Mario Dion,
the new conflict of interest commissioner, and he launched an investigation.

The NDP and Conservatives announced they would seek to have
Justice Committee hearings to look into the matter, bringing Wilson-
Raybould, Butts, and other officials in to testify. Wilson-Raybould was
saying nothing, though she found the pressure intense. "The world had
exploded around me," she later wrote.

Trudeau, it seems, was also concerned. He went to British Columbia three days after the story broke and met Wilson-Raybould in a private terminal at the Vancouver Airport. She described the exchange in
her book. He told her he wanted her to stay in his government, but she
wanted him to "acknowledge that the attempts to apply pressure were not
proper and take concrete steps to address the wrong actions"—and that
was not going to happen.

Trudeau began by telling her he didn't believe she leaked the story to
the *Globe*. Wilson-Raybould bridled at the very suggestion. She told him
she didn't trust the people around him. He said he wouldn't fire them. She
offered him an ultimatum: He could keep changing his story, in which
case she would resign. Or he could "come clean."

The meeting was inconclusive. They agreed to meet again early the
next morning in his suite on the top floor of the Fairmont Pacific Rim,
overlooking Burrard Inlet. Again, the meeting did not go well. She insisted his office had interfered, pressured her on the matter, and he denied

it, adding that he didn't shuffle her because of SNC-Lavalin. She didn't believe that line and asked him to "clean house," fire some people.

"If we did, we would not be the government in October," he said. He became increasingly agitated at her intransigence and told her she "experienced things differently."

"In that moment, I knew he wanted me to lie—to attest that what had occurred had not occurred," she wrote in her book, "to lie to protect a Crown government acting badly; a political party; a leader who was not taking responsibility. He must be delusional." She told him she was uncomfortable and wanted to go. Her only option was to consider whether to stay on as veterans affairs minister or to resign. She was done with Trudeau.

———

AFTER THIS MEETING, TRUDEAU headed to North Vancouver, where he made an announcement and took questions from reporters. He said he welcomed the news that the ethics commissioner would investigate him and said he had asked Lametti to look at the issues of solicitor-client privilege that were preventing Wilson-Raybould from commenting. He pointed to her continued role in his government as evidence that everything was fine. "In our system of government," he said, "her presence in cabinet should actually speak for itself."

Back at home, Wilson-Raybould was watching the news conference with her partner, Tim. When she heard the line about her presence in Cabinet, she turned to him and said she had to resign. She set up a meeting with the prime minister that evening where she told him she was done. They argued about the actions of his officials, but he could not convince her. "We have all tried to help you," he said. "We have all tried so much to help you be successful."

Wilson-Raybould left the meeting and flew back to Ottawa, where she issued her resignation letter. In it, she thanked her constituents, her staff, and Canadian veterans, but not Trudeau. She held out the possibility that she would eventually be able to speak publicly about SNC-Lavalin. "I am aware that many Canadians wish for me to speak on matters that have been in the media over the past week. I am in the process of obtaining advice on the topics I am legally permitted to discuss in this matter." She had hired former Supreme Court justice Thomas Cromwell to advise her so she could tell her story at Justice Committee.

There was misery in the PMO but great relief in the Ottawa bureau of the *Globe*, where Fife had been fretting ever since breaking the story. "I'm grateful to Jody for being an honest and ethical person. You know, honestly, if she'd denied it, [editor-in-chief David] Walmsley and I would've been fired."

Trudeau saw it differently. He told reporters he was "puzzled" by her resignation, which was "not consistent" with their recent conversations. "If anyone, particularly the Attorney General, felt that we were not doing our job fully, responsibly, and according to all the rules as a government, it was her responsibility to come forward to me this past fall and highlight that directly to me. She did not. Nobody did."

These comments did not convince many in Indian Country. Bill Wilson went on the CBC to denounce Trudeau for demoting his daughter. "For all Indians across the country that was a real slight . . . I would have resigned immediately and I wouldn't have taken as important a portfolio as . . . Veterans Affairs as some way to keep quiet, which seems to be what the prime minister tried to do to a woman who has integrity and won't listen to that kind of stuff."

Liberals, horrified at the widening crisis, whispered that Wilson-Raybould was responsible for the mess. The Canadian Press ran (and then withdrew) a story quoting anonymous insiders who said she had been moved from Justice "because she had become a thorn in the side of the cabinet, someone insiders say was difficult to get along with, known to berate fellow cabinet ministers openly at the table, and who others felt they had trouble trusting."

The government did not know what to do. If Wilson-Raybould has accurately described their conversations before her resignation, Trudeau was not listening to her, or he thought she would suffer in silence to keep the trappings of power. Once she quit, there was little he could say. If he sought to make her the villain of the story, few Indigenous people would believe him, and his progressive electoral coalition would not enjoy watching the most powerful white man in the country malign an accomplished Indigenous woman who had challenged him on an ethical issue.

Wilson-Raybould was clearly more interested in getting the matter into the open than Trudeau was. He was under pressure to explain, but nothing he said seemed to help. On one occasion he said she had not been shuffled because of SNC-Lavalin: "If Scott Brison had not stepped down from cabinet, Jody Wilson-Raybould would still be minister of justice and attorney general." Brison's witty husband, Maxime St-Pierre, responded dryly on Twitter: "It's OK. I usually blame my husband for everything too."

People were laughing at Trudeau. Inside the PMO, Trudeau's team was scrambling to figure out how to respond. Trudeau, Butts, and Telford, who had been so close they could finish each other's sentences, could no longer be sure if their interests were aligned.

I wrote in *Maclean's* on February 13 that Trudeau needed a fall guy. I was surprised, though, five days later, when Butts accepted that role. He put out a statement—retweeted by the boss—saying the allegation that Wilson-Raybould had been pressured was "simply not true." "The fact is that this accusation exists. It cannot and should not take one moment away from the vital work the prime minister and his office are doing for all Canadians . . . It is in the best interests of the office and its important work for me to step away."

Butts had tried to resign several times, but Trudeau kept turning him down. The prime minister was "very confident that he had not done anything wrong," he told Aaron Wherry. But Butts felt his long friendship with Trudeau made it impossible for others to have confidence in the judgment calls they would make as the scandal played out. He didn't want anyone thinking Trudeau was constrained in his decisions by worry about how they might affect his old buddy from their days as shaggy-haired undergrads at McGill. "If someone was going to get fucked in this, it was going to be me," says Butts. "So I'd rather go on my own terms and explain myself. Because I could see that the issues-management strategy was fucking losing."

In a way, Butts was responsible, having worked closely with Wilson-Raybould. "Some Cabinet ministers kind of have a relationship with him, and some Cabinet ministers kind of have a relationship with Katie," says one staffer. "And Jody was very clearly in Gerry's column. And so when that blows up that makes that challenging."

In the short term, the departure of Butts was part of the SNC-Lavalin story, but it had broader implications for the future management of the government. "Gerald Butts wasn't just Trudeau's right-hand man, he was his right hemisphere," Mulcair said on CTV. "He decided everything."

Critics liked to mock the relationship, calling him Prime Minister Butts and suggesting he was the puppet master pulling the strings of the empty-headed marionette in the big job. Butts was closer to Trudeau, more central to the operation, than any staffer had been in other PMOs, but nobody who worked with them thought Trudeau was Butts's puppet. But it was a useful line of attack. "The way the opposition killed Gerry was to lean in on that narrative," says Pitfield. "It's a classic manoeuvre."

The unusually close working relationships with Butts and Telford created a formidable team. When they started, Trudeau was the third-party critic for amateur sport (youth). With the help of Butts and Telford, he took over the party, won government, and built a worldwide brand. Trudeau would have to proceed now without Butts. In the future, he would have to trust his own instincts, for better or for worse.

As with Brison's departure, Butts's decision posed problems for those left behind. Telford had immediately to reorganize the operation. Close observers believe the government never fully recovered, because nobody with the same strategic skills—particularly for narrative-building—ever replaced him in a central role. For the rest of the Trudeau era, the government was reactive, dealing successfully with crises but never again managing to seize the agenda. And the government would lose its central focus on inequality—the middle class and those working hard to join it—and focus more on the feminism and diversity issues that Telford embraced, which ultimately led to a narrower electoral coalition.

The same day that Butts resigned, Wilson-Raybould wrote to Trudeau, asking for the opportunity to address Cabinet. He agreed, and she got to talk to them the next day. Such meetings are secret, but we can guess that she explained why she felt she had been forced to resign and had called for Trudeau to apologize and clean house. Her colleagues were not persuaded, however. This dispute would not settle behind closed doors. Rather, the entire saga was hashed out publicly in televised testimony at the Justice Committee, in a study titled "Remediation Agreements, the Shawcross Doctrine, and the Discussions between the Office of the Attorney General and Government Colleagues Relating to SNC-Lavalin."

———

THE SHAWCROSS DOCTRINE, NAMED after Hartley Shawcross, attorney general in British prime minister Clement Attlee's government after the Second World War, held, in essence, that an attorney general must consider the public, not the partisan, interest of the government and make decisions without interference. Advice from Cabinet colleagues "is confined to informing him of particular considerations which might affect his own decision, and does not consist, and must not consist, in telling him what that decision ought to be. Alone in cabinet, the attorney general must make decisions with a 'judicial mind.'" This doctrine eventually worked its way into the legal systems of all countries following a Westminster system. It is a crucial line that prevents politicians from sticking their fingers into the criminal justice system.

The MPs who gathered in a windowless room in the West Block for the Justice Committee on February 21, 2019, were there to find out if Team Trudeau had violated the Shawcross doctrine by pressuring Wilson-Raybould to intervene in the SNC-Lavalin prosecution. The Liberals would play defence; the Conservatives and NDP, offence.

Michael Wernick was the first important witness. A public servant since 1981, he had attended Cabinet meetings under Chrétien, Martin, and Harper. In 2006, he was appointed deputy minister for the Department of Indian and Northern Affairs, a role that put him on a collision course with Indigenous leaders when he implemented Harper policies that they saw as dismissive and confrontational.

Wernick was accustomed to testifying in front of MPs, but the stakes were higher at this meeting: Wilson-Raybould had brought the government he served to the precipice, and he was implicated. He began with an emotional lament for the state of Canadian democracy. "I'm deeply concerned about my country right now, its politics and where it's headed," he said. "I worry about the rising tide of incitements to violence when people use terms like 'treason' and 'traitor' in open discourse." This was a radical departure from the normal formulaic statement delivered by public servants at committee, which typically begin with an expression of restrained pleasure at the opportunity to account for themselves. Wernick was implying that casting doubt on the rule of law in Canada—as Wilson-Raybould was doing—could lead to chaos, assassinations even. And he wasn't done. "I worry about the reputations of honourable people who have served their country being besmirched and dragged through the market square," he said. "Most of all, I worry about people losing faith in the institutions of governance of this country."

Wernick was ill at ease, responding aggressively, and he was acting as a spokesman for the government, forcefully dismissing suggestions that anyone had pressured Wilson-Raybould. If she had felt pressure, she could have contacted the ethics commissioner, he said, or the PMO switchboard, which is staffed 24-7.

MPs quizzed him about one particular phone call he had with Wilson-Raybould, on December 19, in which he said he stayed on the right side of the Shawcross line. "I can tell you with complete assurance that my view of those conversations is that they were within the boundaries of what's lawful and appropriate." NDP MP Murray Rankin pointed out that he hadn't attended all the meetings she had with other officials. "Therefore, to say that she had no inappropriate pressure at any time is really a conclusion you're not able to draw."

Wernick said the ethics commissioner could sort it all out. "I think the matter may come down to the ethics commissioner's view on a conversation between two people and between what was sent and what was received. I think the ethics commissioner is the appropriate person to decide what was undue and what was inappropriate."

As things turned out, Canadians would not have to wait for the ethics commissioner to decide whether he crossed the line. A week later, in the same room, Wilson-Raybould told the same Justice Committee her story in great detail, and it was not as Wernick described.

Resolute and confident, she spoke for almost forty-five minutes. "For a period of approximately four months, between September and December 2018, I experienced a consistent and sustained effort by many people within the government to seek to politically interfere in the exercise of prosecutorial discretion in my role as the attorney general of Canada in an inappropriate effort to secure a deferred prosecution agreement with SNC-Lavalin," she said. She had brought receipts describing in detail how eleven people from the PMO, Finance, and the Privy Council Office had raised the SNC-Lavalin matter with her in ten meetings and ten phone calls beginning in September—when the director of public prosecutions told the company they could not have a remediation agreement—until December, when she had the final conversation with Wernick. They did everything but actually twist her arm, even after she told them she had made up her mind and would not intervene on behalf of the company.

On one side of the table sat the prime minister, his clerk, his chief of staff, his principal secretary, the finance minister and his staff, and the prime minister's lawyers. On the other side were Wilson-Raybould and her chief of staff, Jessica Prince, a graduate of McGill and Oxford who had come to Ottawa from a boutique firm on Bay Street.

Trudeau's people, Wilson-Raybould said, kept insisting she should think carefully about the consequences of not intervening. She kept saying no, reminding them that it was a decision for her alone. They pointed out that an election was imminent in Quebec, warned that SNC-Lavalin might move from Montreal (which the company could not actually do) and mentioned that former Supreme Court justice Frank Iacobucci was representing the company. They proposed seeking an opinion from Beverley McLachlin, who, they intimated, would see things their way.

A cold appraisal of the facts as Wilson-Raybould presented them left little room for doubt. She had been pressured, relentlessly, for political reasons, by Wernick and Trudeau among others, thereby violating the spirit, if not the letter, of the Shawcross doctrine and bringing electoral decisions into conversations where they did not belong. At one meeting in September, Wernick said: "There is a board meeting on Thursday, September 20, with stockholders. They will likely be moving to London if this happens." He mentioned the upcoming Quebec election. Trudeau jumped in to point out that he was "an MP in Quebec—the member for Papineau."

In October, long after everyone knew that Wilson-Raybould had made up her mind, Mathieu Bouchard, a Montreal lawyer advising the prime minister, told Prince, "We can have the best policy in the world, but we need to get re-elected." Later, Telford and Butts summoned Prince to a meeting in the PMO to discuss getting an outside opinion. She pushed back, raising the spectre of improper interference. "Jess, there is no solution here that does not involve some interference," Butts said. Telford added, "We don't want to debate legalities anymore." Prince texted Wilson-Raybould: "They keep being like 'We aren't lawyers, but there has to be some solution here.'"

The final intervention was the phone call from Wernick on December 19—the conversation he hoped the ethics commissioner would judge. Wilson-Raybould said he warned her in stark terms that she ought to change her mind and repeatedly pointed to the will of the prime minister. "I think he is going to find a way to get it done, one way or another," he said. "So he is in that kind of mood, and I wanted you to be aware of it."

Wilson-Raybould warned him that he was crossing a line, pressuring her on a matter of criminal law. "I said that I was having thoughts of the Saturday Night Massacre," she said, referring to the night in 1973 when Richard Nixon started firing Justice Department officials who were involved in prosecuting the Watergate matter. Even in the face of this pushback, Wernick spoke again about the strength of the prime minister's feelings on the matter. Then—just after the holiday period—she was shuffled out of Justice.

She testified that after the shuffle, the deputy minister of justice told Prince that Wernick told her replacement, Lametti, to get up to speed on the SNC-Lavalin file, that they would want to deal with it quickly. She said she had been watching the *Canada Gazette* for a notice of a remediation agreement and planned to resign if it appeared.

She concluded her opening statement by invoking her heritage. "I come from a long line of matriarchs and I am a truth-teller in accordance with the laws and traditions of our Big House. This is who I am, and this is who I always will be."

———

AFTER HER BRAVURA PERFORMANCE, Wilson-Raybould retreated to her office to watch the reaction. Philpott arrived with a bottle of wine.

Philpott was still in Cabinet, but she was finding her situation increasingly difficult. She liked and admired Wilson-Raybould and felt she had been badly treated by the prime minister. "She's an extremely smart person who knows how to do reconciliation," Philpott says. "And she was treated differently because she is a smart Indigenous woman. We're not used to dealing with smart Indigenous women."

Philpott had been worried about the SNC-Lavalin file since before the shuffle. When Trudeau asked her to take on Indigenous Services, he mentioned his plan for Wilson-Raybould. Philpott warned him that her friend might think she was moved because of the "DPA issue." Trudeau was surprised by the suggestion, he said later, which was the furthest thing from his mind. "There were a lot of different reasons. If I were to list a number of reasons why we felt this was the right thing to do and the right move to make, [the DPA] would not have been in the top five or ten reasons for that."

Philpott tried to keep Wilson-Raybould onside with the government, but it got harder as the story snowballed. She interceded with Trudeau again. "I said to him, when you go to medical school and you practise as a doctor, you get taught how to manage mistakes, medical mistakes," she told me later. "Sometimes those mistakes are so bad that people die, but what you get taught is that you have to admit that something terrible happened." She told him he should approach the problem in the same spirit.

Trudeau did not agree, saying this whole incident happened because of Brison's departure. That made Philpott see red because a much simpler shuffle could have filled that hole. "I was in the state where if you or another reporter had come up to me and said, 'Do you have confidence in the prime minister? Do you think they did the right thing?' I am not able to lie. And I knew that if I did speak the truth that it would put me at odds with my obligation to Cabinet solidarity . . . So I just have to say, I'm going let my Cabinet position go."

She did so on March 4. The departure of Philpott, his best minister, was a devastating blow to Trudeau's credibility, but most Liberal MPs rallied around the prime minister. Freeland said she couldn't imagine Trudeau applying pressure. Morneau put it down to friendship. "Jane

Philpott is a close personal friend of Jody Wilson-Raybould," he said. "She took a decision. I respect her decision."

Four years later, that comment still bothers Philpott. "It's like, oh, the girls need to go to the bathroom together . . . Actually, they were trying to tear down the fundamental tenets of democracy and they don't admit it. And I don't want to be part of a government that does that and won't admit it . . . A secondary reason was of course that they, in the process, just tried to destroy the reputation of a brilliant Indigenous woman. I think that was wrong too. But my primary reason for resigning was because they were undermining the foundations of democracy."

———

TWO DAYS LATER, ON March 6, Butts testified before the Justice Committee. Courteous and relaxed, he did a good job of casting doubt on Wilson-Raybould's story without attacking her. It was a subtle performance by a backroom operative forced into the spotlight. He had not been intimately involved in the file, he said, and was shocked at the outcome: "When you boil it all down, all we ever asked the Attorney General to do was to consider a second opinion."

Butts disarmed Lisa Raitt, the most dangerous Conservative MP on the committee, who, like him, had grown up in Cape Breton. "I respect you a lot, Ms. Raitt, and we've known each other a long time . . . You know, we grew up around the same time in the same place. We know what it's like to see a company or a community collapse. Can you imagine, when we were kids and the coal mines closed or the steel mill closed, if the best explanation someone could give us was that someone thought about it for 12 days in Ottawa? That's what concerned us."

He said it was not clear that Wilson-Raybould had made up her mind about the matter or even could do so. "My understanding, which was informed by the public service and lawyers in the PMO, is that the Attorney

General's power to direct the [director of public prosecutions] extends until the time a verdict is rendered. My further understanding is that the Attorney General is free to take advice on the decision up until that point and is obligated to bring fresh eyes to new evidence."

Butts also provided new context on the Cabinet shuffle, explaining why Brison's exit led to Wilson-Raybould's demotion. He explained that a small shuffle wouldn't have sufficed because it would have left a hole at Cabinet for Nova Scotia. The initial plan, he revealed, was to move Wilson-Raybould to Indigenous Services, but she refused. "She said she could not do it for the reason that she had spent her life opposed to the Indian Act and couldn't be in charge of programs administered under its authority."

Wilson-Raybould agreed that the offer came as a shock to her. "I had made it abundantly clear I could never serve as minister of [Indigenous Services]," she wrote later. "I could not and would not be the Indian agent. They knew this, and had been told on multiple occasions—including the first time I met the prime minister and was vetted for cabinet."

Perry Bellegarde, who was then national chief of the Assembly of First Nations, does not agree with Wilson-Raybould's view. "You have to get more and more First Nations peoples around decision-making tables, you have to get more and more First Nations people around the Cabinet table, more and more First Nations people around the deputy ministers table, more and more First Nations people on boards of directors tables in the private sector and public sector," he told me later. "So any time you do not get a First Nations person's voice at a senior table, you miss an opportunity . . . If you say no to that whole position of being Minister of Indigenous Services, what a missed opportunity, because you could help drive positive change within a department that's so colonial, going back to 1876. How do you bring about change but get in there and start stirring the pot?"

When Wilson-Raybould turned down the job, Butts advised Trudeau to move her to Veterans Affairs. "My advice was this: If you allow a minister to veto a Cabinet shuffle by refusing to move, you soon won't be able to manage Cabinet."

Butts succeeded in raising questions about Wilson-Raybould's story—not contradicting it but suggesting it was more complicated than she had explained. "I think he probably managed to sow some seeds of reasonable doubt as to whether there was just one way to look at this, and not two ways," said Chantal Hébert on a CBC panel that night. "I don't think the story is played out, but I think this is as much good as he could do to the government's story."

———

THE STORY HAD NOT quite played out. The scandal had already cost Trudeau his veterans affairs minister, his Treasury Board minister, and his principal secretary. Ten days after Butts left, Wernick announced that he, too, would go. By linking himself so closely to the partisan interests of the government, he had made it impossible to stay above the fray. "It is now apparent that there is no path for me to have a relationship of mutual trust and respect with the leaders of the Opposition parties," he wrote in a letter to Trudeau. "Therefore, I wish to relinquish these roles before the election."

Ten days after that, when Wilson-Raybould sent the last of her ammunition to the Justice Committee, it seemed merciful that he was already gone. She had recorded the infamous seventeen-minute call with Wernick when he repeatedly appears to pressure her. "So [Trudeau's] quite determined, quite firm. He wants to know why the DPA route, which Parliament provided for, isn't being used. And I think he's going to find a way to get it done one way or another."

Wilson-Raybould told him to back off. "Again, I'm confident in where I'm at, and my views on SNC and the DPA haven't changed. This is a constitutional principle of prosecutorial independence that, Michael, I have to say, including this conversation, previous conversations that I've had with the prime minister and many other people around it, it's entirely inappropriate and it is political interference."

Wernick, recall, had testified that "There was no inappropriate pressure put on the minister at any time." When asked if she had raised that with him, he spoke at length about all the avenues open to her to complain, not mentioning that she had explicitly warned him personally.

The recording vindicated Wilson-Raybould, proving that her story was much closer to the truth than the government's version. Other players in the PMO say they were surprised to hear how hard Wernick had pushed. It is unclear whether he was directed to do so.

There are disturbing racial and gender politics at play. One of the most powerful old boys' clubs in Canada—the men at the pinnacle of the Laurentian Elite—bullied an Indigenous woman and then sought to deny it. It undercut Trudeau's image as a feminist and an ally to Indigenous people.

Trudeau's credentials as an ally to Indigenous voters had also taken a hit earlier in the week when protesters from Grassy Narrows First Nation interrupted a Liberal fundraiser in Toronto to draw attention to mercury poisoning in that community, the result of dumping from a pulp mill in the 1960s. "Thank you for your donation," Trudeau joked when they spoke up. Liberals in the room laughed at the joke, but it was an offensive way to talk to people from a community struggling with a horrible multigenerational health crisis. He apologized for his remarks the next day.

After Wilson-Raybould released the tape, Wernick's lawyer objected, calling it "inappropriate." Many lawyers found it unsavoury, and staffers, who must be able to speak freely behind closed doors, were generally indignant. Wilson-Raybould wrote that when she recorded it she "had reason to believe that it was likely to be an inappropriate conversation," which, as it turns out, it was. It is significant that Wernick was not forthcoming about its nature in his testimony.

The existence of the recording turned Liberal MPs against Wilson-Raybould. They called it a betrayal of trust, and they lobbied for her and Philpott to be ejected from caucus. By April 2 that seemed like a good idea, setting aside questions of right and wrong, if the Liberals wanted to carry on running the country.

It had been two months since the *Globe and Mail* story broke, and the government let the saga drag on, dominating headlines and raising questions about what Trudeau's people had done and what they were doing. Trudeau seemed unable to decide what to do. The determined leadership he had shown running the third party, when he expelled sex abusers and senators and laid down the law with his caucus, seemed to be gone. The government was drifting, buffeted by revelations, exposed as prevaricating nincompoops. The only active step he had taken was appointing Anne McLellan, a well-regarded former deputy prime minister, to give him a report on the role of the attorney general, which eventually ended up gathering dust.

Trudeau defended his position: "I believe in doing politics differently," he said in an interview with Aaron Wherry in March 2019. "And I think that part of that is showing a willingness to work things through, and being a strong leader doesn't mean imposing or being rigid but actually trying to leave lots of room for different perspectives."

But many Liberal MPs are critical of Trudeau's caucus management style. While earlier prime ministers would survey the room before putting down a marker on an issue, Trudeau begins by stating his position, which makes it difficult for others to disagree. If they do, they are "immediately slapped down." MPs have been shocked at how aggressively he handles criticism behind closed doors. But during this period he seemed to be clinging to a vain hope that somehow he could reverse the catastrophe. Intermediaries were sent to try to bring Wilson-Raybould around. Inside the PMO, Telford and Trudeau were insisting on keeping the lines of communications open while others were arguing for an expulsion. Trudeau called her to brief her when he appointed McLellan, for instance. They seem not to have understood her. She wanted him to apologize, and he would not.

There was no going back. Trudeau went to the Liberal caucus, behind closed doors, and told them he had decided to dismiss the two women. It was a lively meeting. One MP called Wilson-Raybould a cow. Another urged the pair be banished to the worst seats in the backbench: "It's time to send those two women up to the back row on the far side with the sex offenders." They had few defenders in caucus by this point. Trudeau gave a fiery speech in which he denounced them, which at least one MP thought was arrogant. When it was over, Trudeau marched out to the lobby, where the cameras were waiting, and took a defiant tone: "The will of caucus was very clear, but I made the decision," he said.

After two months of drifting, Trudeau had finally moved to cauterize the wound.

———

ON AUGUST 14, ETHICS commissioner Mario Dion released his report, which showed that basically everything Wilson-Raybould said was true. He ruled that Trudeau had used his office "to circumvent, undermine and ultimately attempt to discredit" her. He found Trudeau guilty of violating section 9 of the Conflict of Interest Act, which prohibits "improperly furthering another person's private interests." This section of the act is meant to capture sharp dealing to benefit friends or relatives, but Dion found that Trudeau's actions were improper because "they were contrary to the Shawcross doctrine and the principles of prosecutorial independence and the rule of law."

The report contained new information about behind-the-scenes contacts between Trudeau's team and two important businessmen—Bank of Montreal board chair Robert Prichard, who was also chair of law firm Torys, which was representing SNC-Lavalin; and Kevin Lynch, the former clerk of the Privy Council, who was chair of the board of SNC-Lavalin and vice-chair of the Bank of Montreal board. They met with Brison, who later worked for the Bank of Montreal, and also with Morneau and other members of the Trudeau team "so often last fall they should have been allowed to choose the furniture," as business columnist Andrew Willis put it in the *Globe*.

Faced with a prosecutorial decision they did not like, the team proposed workarounds, employing two former Supreme Court justices—Frank Iacobucci and John Major—and wanted to involve a third, former chief justice Beverley McLachlin. Throughout, instead of telling SNC to focus its efforts on the legal process, Trudeau's people kept trying to help them avoid the prosecution. The Privy Council Office and Finance officials "actively assisted SNC-Lavalin in developing" a legal argument that the prosecutor had failed to properly consider the "public interest." By giving the SNC-Lavalin executives the idea that there was a back door to avoid prosecution, the government encouraged them to spend time and money lobbying and paying lawyers to pursue a dead end instead of focusing on dealing with the person they should have been trying to convince: the prosecutor.

Wilson-Raybould would have had to publicly overturn the judgment of Kathleen Roussel, an independent, highly regarded prosecutor, something no government has ever done. "You can imagine there's certain factors that you consider as the director of public prosecutions in terms of whether or not something would be used, and it didn't meet the criteria, basically," says a source who knows the file.

The enduring mystery at the heart of the matter is why Trudeau and his people didn't accept that decision. In some cases, they still don't, even now. Morneau, for instance, wrote in his book that a DPA would have been "an entirely appropriate remedy for her to agree to." The Laurentian Elite is hard to convince.

———

IN SEPTEMBER 2023, SNC-LAVALIN, the company the Mounties busted back in 2012 to begin this sorry saga, changed its name to Atkins-Réalis in an effort to leave its legal and image problems behind. It still offers engineering services, including mining projects in the developing world.

Half the world's mining capital is raised on the Toronto and Vancouver stock exchanges. Mining projects in the Global South are particularly prone to bribery, leading to environmental degradation, rape, and political murders. A 2016 study by Osgoode Hall's Shin Imai found that from 2000 to 2015, forty-four people died as a result of violence linked to Canadian-owned mines in Latin America.

The OECD Working Group on Bribery in International Business Transactions, established in 1997 to try to stop multinationals from paying off corrupt leaders around the world, determined in 2010 that Canada was a laggard compared to comparable countries. Canadian laws had loopholes that made conviction next to impossible. Since Canada passed the Corruption of Foreign Public Officials Act in 1999, there had been only one conviction. None of our provincial securities commissions had issued any fines, and the Mounties were not up to the job.

When the working group delivered its report, Canada was furious. Mark Pieth, the Swiss anti-corruption lawyer who was chair of the OECD, put it this way: "Basically we said, look, guys, we gave you a critical evaluation . . . and nothing has happened, and you are a very critical place in the world for mining so there's a high risk of corruption." Alan Kessel, a lawyer for Canada's Department of Foreign Affairs, told Pieth he would pay for his intransigence. "I'll see to it that you are going to be kicked out," he said.

Pieth refused to water down the report, but he says Kessel was successful in forcing him out of his job, although he was able to arrange an orderly departure in 2013. Because of the report, though, Canada was forced to act, closing loopholes and putting more effort into enforcement. One of the key measures was a ten-year ban on federal contracting, brought in by Harper—and that is what drove SNC-Lavalin to its extraordinary lobbying efforts. If we don't want companies doing what SNC did, they must be prevented from getting a get-out-of-jail-free card from politicians. All the reasons cited by Trudeau's people—the desire to prevent economic misery in Montreal, to save jobs—are explicitly forbidden from consideration by prosecutors because of Article 5 of the OECD convention.

Pieth watched the SNC-Lavalin case unfold from Switzerland. Dismayed by what the Trudeau government did, he is happy that the tough report that cost him his job has led to reforms in Canada. "The bad marks had to do with laws that had not been ameliorated, that the advice had not been followed at all and . . . there were hardly any cases. Now, a few years on, the situation looks much better."

David Lametti, who replaced Jody Wilson-Raybould, did not overrule the director of public prosecutions to order that SNC be given a deferred prosecution agreement. It would have looked terrible if he had, but because attorneys general are not supposed to factor political considerations into their judgments, and because he was seen as an upstanding and careful lawyer who took his obligations seriously, we have to conclude that when he read the prosecutor's reasons, he, like Wilson-Raybould, must have decided they were sound.

SNC-Lavalin ended up making a deal, but not with any politicians. On December 18, 2019, a subsidiary pleaded guilty to a single charge of fraud and agreed to pay a $280 million fine. The Crown dropped the corruption-of-foreign-officials charge. The company did not go bankrupt or leave Montreal. The CEO who had pushed so hard for a backroom deal had quietly resigned.

The Trudeau government was badly damaged by the SNC affair. In a way, it would never recover. Trudeau, paragon of progressive virtue, had gaslit an impressive Indigenous woman in greasy backroom machinations and had managed the fallout in a way that cast doubt on his competence. It was a waste of political capital.

But there is a second point of view, widely shared by the staffers and fixers who populate Liberal Ottawa, that Wilson-Raybould was intent on revenge when Trudeau demoted her. She was already working on her book, gaming out an exit that would make her look good and him bad.

This view of her is not really persuasive, but even if you buy it, what does it say about Trudeau? The people who hold this uncharitable view often blame Trudeau for being clueless enough to let it happen. "They were contemplating shuffling her out of Justice, every single Cabinet shuffle from the time she was appointed until the time that it actually happened," says one ministerial staffer. "There was a dysfunctional relationship from the beginning."

Morneau, who had a front-row seat to the whole affair, eloquently summed up the government's mishandling of the episode in his book. Trudeau, he writes, has an "inability to develop significant relationships with his colleagues." Wilson-Raybould could not raise her concerns directly with him. And by leaving her in the job, despite the fact they did not have a good relationship, he created "an impossible position" for himself. He did not have faith in her, but she would not accept a demotion. "The ingredients for the SNC affair were set, and in my estimation the resulting fireworks had little to do with the file itself."

8

TALKING TO AMERICANS

In April 2017, an official from the Privy Council Office, the permanent bureaucracy under the prime minister, called Canada's ambassador to the United States, David MacNaughton, to tell him he would have some company at the next briefing of Trudeau's Canada-US Cabinet committee. "Prime Minister Mulroney's going to be there," the official said. "He's going to speak for the first forty-five minutes, and then you're going to speak for the next forty-five minutes. Can we have the material you're going to use?"

"I said no," recalls MacNaughton. "And they said, 'What do you mean?' I said, 'I'm never going to get to talk. So there's no point in preparing any material . . . We let the prime minister talk for as long as he wants to talk . . . I get my chance every meeting."

In those days, Mulroney spoke frequently to Trudeau—more often, likely, than he ever spoke to Stephen Harper. Trudeau did not have any scores to settle with the man from Baie-Comeau. He wanted help. Mulroney knew a lot of Republicans, and he enjoyed sharing war stories about his glory days negotiating trade deals. He arranged for a Cabinet committee briefing from Trump advisor Stephen Schwarzman, slapped backs, made connections, whispered in ears.

Mulroney told the Canadians that the Americans would be foolish to tear up NAFTA. "I tell Chrystia and the others that when they say NAFTA is the worst deal ever, remind them of what it has done," he told the *New York Times* at the time. "There are 500 million people who are 7 percent of the world's population producing 29 percent of the world's wealth. Trade has allowed America to reach high levels of prosperity and a historically low unemployment rate of 3.9 percent." He advised the Trudeau Cabinet "to take it easy, keep your head down and don't say anything—don't take the bait." The Americans "know a good deal when they see one. There would be a pitchfork revolution in the Midwest when the farmers realized what would happen to their markets."

But Mulroney was also explicit in warning that the Americans were not playing games, says Brian Clow, whom Trudeau made director of Canada-US relations after Trump's election. "One thing he would definitely emphasize is take these guys very seriously. If Trump says, 'I'm willing to tear up NAFTA,' he means it. And we've got to prepare for that."

Mulroney thought the Canadian team would be wise to cultivate friendships. "We've got allies in the United States, particularly in the Republican Party and in the business community," says Clow. "So whether it's the US Chamber of Commerce, or Steve Schwarzman, who we already knew and helped us get to know better, Congress for sure."

Clow is a smooth professional—tall and slim, with a diffident air, well dressed and well regarded. He had worked as chief of staff to Freeland at International Trade and brought over two young colleagues from that office to the PMO: Diamond Isinger from British Columbia and Simon Beauchemin from Quebec. "We were very much a package deal and we were never more than ten feet from each other," says Isinger. "Clow is a real maniac, and I mean that in the most loving possible way. He is an extremely smart person."

Clow's group eventually hired former journalist Michael Den Tandt to help with communications. Together, they set up a little war room in the PMO and started an unprecedented campaign to send earnest Canadians around to bore Americans about the importance of the trade relationship. No state fair, no Rotary Club meeting could take place anywhere in the United States without some Canadian emissary popping by to remind the Americans how much both economies depend on keeping goods moving across the border. Isinger set about her work with zeal, dispatching Canadians far and wide. To keep track of all her glad-handing Canucks, she got a school map of the United States and stuck pins in it, labelled with their names—"I would be like, 'Okay, Champagne is here, and so and so is here.'"

The traditional diplomatic approach wouldn't work with Trump. "His influence didn't come from the same traditional network," says Clow. "You know, every past president went to the Brookings Institution, different think tanks that would provide opinions, this cabal of Washington insiders. Trump took his best advice from the owners of sport franchises and hoteliers and all these random people."

While Clow and Isinger sought levers to pull, Trudeau was putting his case directly to Trump. After a call in April, Trudeau reported that Trump said "he was very much thinking about cancelling." Trudeau told him that was a bad idea. "I highlighted quite frankly . . . that a disruption like cancelling NAFTA, even if it theoretically eventually might lead to better outcomes, would cause a lot of short- and medium-term pain."

Trump had promised that new pipelines in the United States would be built with American pipe made from American steel, posing a problem for Evraz's Regina steel mill, which was manufacturing the pipe for the Keystone pipeline. Although the fine print in NAFTA prohibited that kind of unilateral action, Trump's bombast introduced an element of uncertainty, and Keystone told Evraz it would lose the work. Wilbur Ross, Trump's secretary of commerce, was talking tough. "The Mexicans know, the Canadians know, everybody knows times are different. We are going to have new trade relations with people. And they all know they're going to have to make concessions," he'd said in March, when he was appointed.

Ross is a hard-nosed businessman. He had been doing business with

Trump since the 1980s, when he brokered a deal between Trump and his investors in the bankrupt Atlantic City casinos. Chrystia Freeland, now foreign affairs minister, decided the best tactic was to mix with the Trump people, so she went to see Ross in Washington. When she met with Mac-Naughton beforehand, he warned her that Ross might refuse to bend on the steel order. He had already encountered an irrational stubborn refusal on the softwood lumber problem. After working on it for two months, Robert Lighthizer, the US trade representative, simply said, "David, look, I know what you're trying to do, but it's not going to work. And the reason is that the president wants one of his legacy items to be [the Trans-Pacific Partnership], and in order to get TPP, we need some key senators onside, including Ron Wyden from Oregon, and he's never going to agree."

The situation was similar now. Trump had promised the Rust Belt that he would clear the way for American steel. But it was one thing for the Americans to impose tariffs, and another for them to violate the terms of NAFTA and throw people out of work in Saskatchewan. Mac-Naughton advised Freeland that if Ross wouldn't bend, she should be resolute: "That is totally unacceptable," she should say. "I'm calling the prime minister. He's going to call the president. We are going to do all sorts of countermeasures." She should tell Ross she was going for drinks at the Four Seasons with MacNaughton and Trump advisor Dina Powell, who had worked with her on the women's entrepreneurship project. And so it happened: as they sat in the bar at the hotel, Ross called Freeland to say that Regina could keep producing the steel.

MacNaughton advised her to keep the whole incident quiet. "We can't go and do a victory lap and say, we just saved five hundred jobs." Trump wouldn't like that. So Freeland quietly called the plant with the news along with Saskatchewan premier Brad Wall. During the next First Ministers' call, Wall praised the government for the way it handled the file. As he explains: "I tried, whether it was Harper or Trudeau, if the federal government did something good, that we thought was positive for Saskatchewan, well, we should say so."

Wall, who led a popular Saskatchewan Party government for a decade, built a new consensus in his traditionally NDP province around free enterprise and the growing oil and gas business. He didn't often have common political ground with Trudeau, but when it became necessary to rally around Ottawa to work out a new trade deal, he was happy to do what he could. He had a great relationship with MacNaughton, whose views were more business-oriented and centrist than the government's. "I thought he acquitted himself very well as our ambassador," says Wall, "and that my dealings with him were always positive."

Trudeau requested that all the premiers help carry the pro-trade mission to their American contacts. MacNaughton in turn asked Wall to go to Des Moines, Iowa, to talk to the state politicians and agricultural trade groups and meet with Governor Terry Branstad, a Republican. A plain-spoken son of the northern prairie, Wall was likely better able to get his pro-trade message across than members of Trudeau's party would manage in the Hawkeye State. He reminded everyone in Iowa that Saskatchewan farmers bought a lot of tractors from John Deere, which had been manufacturing in the state since 1918. He urged them all not to take the trade relationship for granted. "I think even at that time people thought, well, this is more sort of bluster from Trump. Is he really serious about what he said? And my message then is let's be intentional. Let's not leave this to chance. Let's use our networks and our associations to advocate for a continued trade between our two countries."

Freeland created a NAFTA advisory council to send more emissaries and build more support for the negotiation process. It included Conservative politicians Rona Ambrose and James Moore, New Democrat Brian Topp, AFN National Chief Perry Bellegarde, and Canadian Labour Congress president Hassan Yussuff. "We wouldn't have been able to get as good a deal as we got had it not been for the phenomenal help—federal, provincial, business, labour, like everybody," says MacNaughton. "The Team Canada thing was real."

The PMO targeted people in Trump's orbit. "Who are Trump's key people and how do we befriend them?" Isinger asked. "So the PM would spend all kinds of time with unlikely characters while he was in the US." Trudeau met, for example, with Robert Kraft, owner of the New England Patriots, a long-time friend of Trump. "The idea was to get Bob Kraft to be an ally and a champion of Canada, to be in the ear of the president."

Canada's chief negotiator, Steve Verheul, supported this frantic emissaries' campaign. "It was important as a means of trying to get some intelligence gathering, trying to figure out what their thinking was, what their plan was," he says. "So it was more of a basis to direct our own thinking about how we should respond."

It was next to impossible in the early days of the Trump administration to know what Trump would do, given his poor understanding of his job. The West Wing was full of weirdos and chancers, people who didn't know how to run the government and didn't care to learn, like contestants on a third-rate White House reality show. Trump "second-guessed people's motives, saw conspiracies behind rocks, and remained stunningly uninformed on how to run the White House, let alone the huge federal government," John Bolton, his national security advisor, wrote in his book *The Room Where It Happened*. "It is undeniable that Trump's transition and opening year-plus were botched irretrievably."

While the Canadians were strategizing, Trump was hiring and firing flunkies, getting into Twitter feuds and making policy based on what he saw on *Fox & Friends*. But not all his people were knaves or idiots. Members of Team Trudeau speak respectfully of Robert Lighthizer. Like Bolton, Steve Bannon, and Peter Navarro, he wanted to change America's trade relationships, especially with China, but unlike them he had the experience, patience, and insight to mount a credible plan to negotiate better terms. In his book *No Trade Is Free*, he wrote that he saw the job as "a chance to fight a battle that I had been preparing for my whole life: the battle to build trade policy that supports a society in which American workers, including those without college educations, can build better lives for themselves and their families through the stable, well-paying jobs that no healthy country can do without."

Lighthizer passionately believes that NAFTA cost hundreds of thousands of good American jobs, and he has a point. While an elite cross-party consensus around trade agreements hardened in Ottawa and Washington, the American Rust Belt was hollowing out, with good jobs moving to Mexico, China, and other low-wage jurisdictions, leading to misery in the places where Americans used to build things. Lighthizer grew up in Ashtabula, Ohio, a small manufacturing town that had fallen on hard times during the NAFTA years. He had worked for decades at the highest level in trade law, and he knew what he wanted to do to make NAFTA a better deal for American workers. He was particularly focused on rules of origin for auto parts, so that manufacturers in other countries could not get around trade barriers with the United States by assembling foreign-made parts in Canada and, especially, Mexico.

In August 2017, when Freeland and her Mexican counterpart Ildefonso Guajardo Villarreal went to Washington to open the talks, they both made blandly upbeat remarks, but Lighthizer began defiantly. Trump "is not interested in a mere tweaking of a few provisions and a couple of update chapters," he said. "We feel that NAFTA has fundamentally failed many, many Americans and needs major improvement."

Canadian officials knew they were facing a challenge, Verheul agrees. "We knew what he'd been saying—the worst agreement ever. It was going to be an uphill battle." He was not rattled, though. After two decades of negotiating trade deals for Canada, he had developed an unflappable persona. He has a reserved presence, mild and pleasant but watchful, and his refusal to move from a position sometimes unnerves his opposite numbers. In one negotiation with the Europeans, Italian negotiator Mauro Petriccione became so upset by Verheul's stubbornness that he stormed out. But they were negotiating in Petriccione's office, so Verheul simply waited until he returned, somewhat sheepishly, to continue the talks.

Verheul needed to call on that same stubbornness in the early sessions because the Americans were putting forward positions that would have left Canada and Mexico at a huge disadvantage. The proposals on rules of origin for auto parts would devastate Canada's industry; the changes to government procurement would leave Canada with worse access to US government contracts than Bahrain; and, crucially, the erasure of the dispute-settlement mechanisms would deprive Canada of the system it relies on to settle disagreements.

For decades, under pressure from domestic lumber producers, the Americans have repeatedly imposed duties on Canadian mills—a multi-billion-dollar drag on an industry that sustains towns across the country. American producers, who buy their wood from privately held timber lots, find it difficult to compete with Canadian producers who cut on Crown land and complain that the low stumpage fees amount to a government subsidy. Canada always wins, eventually, through dispute-settlement mechanisms. Without that process, the Canadians would have no recourse when the Americans lash out.

Verheul's US counterparts were professionals and did what they were told, but it was obvious they did not want to make these foolish proposals. "At one point one of the negotiators came up to me and said, 'I apologize. This is what we've been told to do.' Because he knew it was ludicrous." Verheul suspected these boorish ideas were coming straight from Trump. He had repeatedly mused about tearing up NAFTA and asked that officials draw up an executive order ready for his signature. "That's his negotiating style, right? You come up with something extreme and put it out there."

Early on, Verheul felt he had to signal that Canada would not be bullied. In one session, when the Americans refused to talk about the dispute-settlement mechanism, he responded: "If you're not prepared to talk about those issues to us, then we're not prepared to talk about some of your issues. So, we might as well stop." He left the room, called Ottawa, and told his political bosses what he had done. They had his back. He was confident the Americans would yield on what was, essentially, a small matter. True enough: next morning they called to say, "Fine. We'll talk about your issue."

Lighthizer realized what was going on. "I can't recall a single meaningful concession that Canada or Mexico made during the first nine months of the negotiations," he wrote. "They clearly were coordinating all their moves. I guess they simply hoped to wear us down or hoped that Congress would roll us in the end."

———

EVEN PEOPLE CLOSE TO the former US president don't know if he understands international trade and purposely sows confusion as a negotiating tactic or if he has such a short attention span that he never managed to learn how it works. Early on, when Trudeau and Trump were meeting with senior aides in Washington, Trudeau mentioned the decades-long softwood lumber dispute. Trump asked Wilbur Ross to explain it to him. Ross said the Canadians subsidize their industry and the Americans were working on negotiating a quota arrangement as a way to break the impasse. "I like tariffs," said Trump. "Tariffs are good, but quotas are bad because they raise prices."

A senior staffer kicked MacNaughton under the table, as if to ask him to explain that tariffs raise prices. MacNaughton did not take the hint. "What do you think I'm going to do? The first time I meet the guy, I'm going to say, 'Mr. President, you're stupid?' You kind of sit there and go, 'Really? Seriously?'"

In his book, *Breaking History*, Jared Kushner describes several occasions when his father-in-law seemed prepared behind the scenes to wreck the whole negotiation. At one point an alarmed Agriculture Secretary Sonny Perdue, who had previously run a Georgia agribusiness, went to Trump's office with an oversized map of the United States to show him all the agricultural counties that would have their economies ruined if Trump tore up NAFTA. By convincing even those closest to him that he might do something erratic, Trump set in motion panicky calls and meetings, with Kushner and the Mexicans and Canadians trying to figure out how to mollify him and keep everything on track.

Throughout the negotiations, Freeland was Canada's lead political negotiator. Trudeau trusted her and was content to let her do her job. Over time, Freeland and Lighthizer developed a warm relationship—at the end of the process she had him to her home in Toronto for dinner—but there were tense moments and sharp words during the months that the negotiations dragged on. They met repeatedly, flying to all three countries, with officials sitting around a conference table while Freeland and Lighthizer held forth. "You could see Bob Lighthizer getting quite frustrated that he wasn't getting out of Chrystia Freeland what he wanted, and that's what ultimately built to some pretty heavy frustration from the Americans and from Lighthizer himself," says Clow. "He came to the view that the Canadian strategy was to just not give an inch on anything, ever. And, I mean, that ultimately ended up not being true, but I think it was a good strategy on our part."

The Americans disliked Freeland's frequent but largely content-free scrums on her way in and out of the sessions. "She wouldn't say much at all," Clow recalls. "But it would be wall-to-wall coverage up here, the networks would cut away and Chrystia Freeland is talking again, and she would just give the most minor update. But Lighthizer, and I think the Trump administration generally, was very anti-media and media-adverse. And they did not look at that kindly. So talking to the media, talking to Congress, they didn't love it, but they understood it."

In the spring of 2018, Trump and Lighthizer made a move designed to break the logjam. Trump announced he would impose a 25 percent tariff on steel and aluminum imports, which violated NAFTA rules, justifying it with a paper-thin national-security exemption. Lighthizer wrote that it "sent an unmistakable signal that business as usual was over."

Trudeau and Freeland held a news conference in the National Press Theatre. "Let me be clear. These tariffs are totally unacceptable," said Trudeau, in both official languages. He discussed the long military alliance between the two countries, portraying the tariffs as a betrayal. "Canadians and Americans fought shoulder to shoulder with one another in two World Wars and in Korea. From the beaches of Normandy to the mountains of Afghanistan, we have fought together and mourned our fallen together."

Then Freeland announced the response: dollar-for-dollar tariffs on certain American products. It was a strange list, including yogurt, cheese, pork, maple syrup, bourbon, and Wisconsin gherkins. Clow's team in the PMO had worked hard on the list, targeting individual American businesses and politicians with influence in Washington. Senate majority leader Mitch McConnell would be sure to hear from distillers in Kentucky. Wisconsin pickle producers and dairy farmers would talk to House speaker Paul Ryan. "The whole plan was that we were trying to exert pressure in unlikely ways because those Kentucky bourbon distillers would be the first people to be on the phone to [McConnell] saying, 'What the F? Sort this out because my personal business is being impacted right now,'" Isinger says.

On June 9, at a G7 meeting in beautiful Charlevoix, on the north shore of the Saint Lawrence River, Trump had a temper tantrum that brought relations between the two countries to the lowest point since the War of 1812. He arrived for the summit late and left early. Throughout, he felt put upon by the other leaders, who did not share his agenda and harangued him about tariffs, the unilateral American decision to withdraw from the Paris Climate Accord, and the Iranian nuclear deal. They flatly rejected his proposal that Russia be invited back into the fold. A picture from the event captures the vibe. German chancellor Angela Merkel is leaning on a table, looking exasperated while Trump, arms folded, looks back, defiant. She is flanked by Emmanuel Macron and Shinzō Abe. Bolton stands next to Trump. The top of Butts's head is visible behind the leaders.

In his book, Bolton describes the tone of his meetings with Trudeau and Macron: "Trump didn't really like either Trudeau or Macron, but he tolerated them, mockingly crossing swords with them in meetings . . . I assume they understood what he was doing, and they responded in kind, playing along because it suited their larger interests not to be in a permanent tiff with the U.S. president."

In the bilateral with Trudeau, Trump kept talking about how the markets had responded positively when he and Trudeau shared a friendly handshake. The leaders and their sherpas spent many hours wrangling over a communiqué that was of more concern to diplomats than voters in the countries back home. Butts was working closely with Larry Kudlow, director of the National Economic Council of the United States, and Canadian deputy minister Peter Boehm, trying to find language that Trump and the other leaders could agree on, which they ultimately did. Trump left early, bound for Singapore and then North Korea, where he would hold a summit with dictator Kim Jong Un. He was ready to blow up generations of patient American diplomacy on nuclear non-proliferation in exchange for the opportunity to portray himself as a statesman.

On Air Force One, Trump apparently watched Trudeau's remarks at the closing news conference and became enraged. "Canadians, we are polite, we are reasonable, but we also will not be pushed around," Trudeau had said. "I reiterated to President Trump that these tariffs threaten to harm industry and workers on both sides of our border." It was the same kind of thing Trudeau always said about the trade talks, but there was a difference this time: Trump happened to see the interview. "Suddenly he saw that for the first time," Trudeau told me in an interview later.

In two tweets, Trump attacked Trudeau and withdrew US support for the communiqué everyone had been wrangling about for two days. "PM Justin Trudeau of Canada acted so meek and mild during our @G7 meetings only to give a news conference after I left saying that 'US Tariffs were kind of insulting' and he 'will not be pushed around.' Very dishonest & weak." And then the bombshell: "Based on Justin's false statements at his news conference, and the fact that Canada is charging massive Tariffs to our U.S. farmers, workers and companies, I have instructed our U.S. Reps not to endorse the Communique as we look at Tariffs on automobiles flooding the U.S. Market!"

Butts was enjoying a celebratory drink in Quebec, toasting a successful summit, when press secretary Cameron Ahmad came in, looking distressed. Ahmad had been relieved that the summit had gone well until he saw Trump's tweet. "His eyes are bulging," says Butts. "And he hands me his BlackBerry and I look at him, 'Is this a joke?' And then I see the little blue check mark by Donald Trump and it's like, 'Nope. It's not a joke.' So I call Larry Kudlow immediately."

Trump asked Kudlow and Navarro to attack Trudeau on the Sunday panel shows, Bolton wrote in his book: "Just go after Trudeau. Don't knock the others. Trudeau's a 'behind your back' guy." Navarro may have exceeded his brief on Fox News the next Sunday. "There's a special place in hell for any foreign leader that engages in bad-faith diplomacy with President Donald J. Trump and then tries to stab him in the back on the way out the door," he said. "And that's what bad-faith Justin Trudeau did with that stunt press conference."

It was ridiculous, coming from the man-child leading the most powerful country in the world, but Canada could not respond by telling him to get lost. We are destined to be hewers of wood and drawers of water, exporters of raw materials. And our biggest customer was led by an impulsive, television-addled fool.

Trudeau had to stay away from the bait. Freeland responded calmly but firmly. "Canada does not believe that ad hominem attacks are a particularly appropriate or useful way to conduct our relations with other countries," she said. Canadians, including critics of Trudeau, were angered by Trump's outburst, and Conservatives, including Candice Bergen, Doug Ford, and Stephen Harper, objected.

Trudeau had to hold his tongue. It was difficult throughout, says Ahmad. The Liberals were hearing, "Your neighbour is saying all these horrible things and doing all these terrible things, why won't you condemn it?" Trudeau had to reflect his values but also, "say my job is to work with anyone who's in the office." He was threading a needle.

Freeland had a freer hand. She delivered a riposte a few days later while in Washington to receive an award for Diplomat of the Year from *Foreign Policy* magazine. She denounced the tariffs as "illegal," called them a "naked example of the United States putting its thumb on the scale, in violation of the very rules it helped to write," and warned about the rise of "angry populism." She spoke with confidence and passion about the values her government stood for—the rule of law—sending the message that Canada was not intimidated by Trump's antics. She didn't name him, but the message was clear. It was pitch perfect, brave, and articulate, even poetic. She quoted W.B. Yeats's "The Second Coming": "The best lack all conviction, while the worst / are full of passionate intensity." "It's time to turn the tables," Freeland said. "It is time for liberal democrats to rediscover that passionate intensity."

Trump didn't like it. In a call with Trudeau two weeks later, he called Freeland a "nasty woman" and said she had delivered a "nasty speech" about him—a call described in Aaron Wherry's *Promise and Peril*. When MacNaughton heard about the spat, he was delighted. "I phoned Chrystia and said, 'I don't know exactly what you've been doing, but whatever the hell it is, keep doing it.'"

In an interview in 2024, Trudeau told me that while he was briefed on every aspect of the deal, Trump focused on only a few points. "There were things where we knew we could find common ground and where Mr. Trump was in a slightly different place. There were a lot of people in the system, a lot of things, a really complex deal to work through. As a leader, I was very much aware of all the different lines going on—when to push Chrystia on this, when to pull someone else back on that. And Mr. Trump had a very clear focus on a few elements that he felt he knew and wanted to run with, and we just worked around that for the whole deal."

Trump was bellicose in public, but behind the scenes he was not so difficult. "In direct conversations, he would fully expect me to be pushing hard for Canada's interests because he knows that's my job," Trudeau says. "And his job is to push hard for American interests."

The Canadians had done their homework, kept their cool, ragged the puck, but the game was going into sudden-death overtime. Frustrated with Canadian foot-dragging, the Americans had succeeded in opening one-on-one negotiations with Mexico. The populist left-winger Andrés Manuel López Obrador, known as AMLO, a sort of a Bizarro World Trump, had been elected as president of Mexico on July 1 but would not take office until December 1. His people told Lighthizer that AMLO would support a new deal, but only if it was complete before he was sworn in. Since a new deal would have to be presented to Congress ninety days before it could be signed, that gave the Americans a deadline of August 29. Lighthizer set up secret talks with the Mexicans, cutting the Canadians out. "The Mexicans were much more panicked than we were because of the scale of the threat against them compared to what it was against us," says Verheul.

Trump made the most of the opportunity to jab at Ottawa. "We're not negotiating with Canada right now," he said in August. "Their tariffs are too high; their barriers are too strong. So we're not even talking to them right now."

With Canada on the sidelines, and the Mexicans facing a deadline weeks away, Lighthizer and the Mexican secretary of the economy managed to reach agreements on the things the Americans wanted—higher labour standards for Mexico, stronger auto parts rules of origin, and some assurances about the politically sensitive Mexican energy industry.

The Trudeau people saw this deal as a betrayal and called the Mexicans for a meeting in Washington. Freeland "spoke to them in a tone that would make your blood run cold," says Butts. "She didn't use these words, but she basically said, 'You told us you would never do this and you did it. You stabbed us in the back.' But she was so cold in the way she was saying it to them. It was chilling, frankly."

In the media, it looked as though the Canadians had been shut out, but Verheul was getting updates from both sides because the other players still hoped the Canadians would eventually join the evolving US-Mexico deal. "In fact," he said, "we were still talking to the Americans through this process. I had a pretty good picture of what was going on, but the US saw their biggest issue being with Mexico, not with Canada. For Canada, it was supply management and a handful of other issues."

Lighthizer "needed to get this done before the midterms," says Butts. "And we knew that. So we thought he was bluffing when he said he'd go with Mexico alone, and he was."

On August 27, Trump announced a new deal with Mexico from the Oval Office, with outgoing Mexican president Enrique Peña Nieto on speakerphone. Nieto said he hoped that Canada would be incorporated. Trump threatened to impose tariffs on Canadian-made autos if Canada didn't "negotiate fairly." He demanded concessions on dairy.

Every day of 2017, $1.6 billion in goods crossed the 8,891-kilometre border between Canada and the United States, so local politicians and chambers of commerce all along the long and peaceful frontier know how many livelihoods depend on keeping the trucks rolling. Canada had pestered them effectively for the previous year, but there was one group that would be impossible to convince—Wisconsin dairy farmers. Canada has had a supply-managed dairy market since the 1970s, with a system of quotas and tariffs that keeps prices artificially high, Canadian farmers happy, and foreign competitors out. Economists dislike the arrangement because it is bad for consumers, but Canadian dairy farmers are a well-organized, widely dispersed, and highly motivated bloc of voters—much like American softwood lumber producers—who exercise an exaggerated influence over vote-seeking politicians. For that reason, the original NAFTA had a dairy exemption, with Canada keeping out imports of protected products with tariffs of over 200 percent. American dairy producers would like Canada to scrap that system so they can flood the northern market, but what was really galling them in 2017 was a new regulatory regime in Canada that had closed the door to American milk powder. The angry Wisconsin dairy farmers gave Trump a constituency he could noisily champion on Twitter.

Freeland was frustrating the Americans, refusing to give ground at the table, and then going out to scrum, telling the folks back home that she was holding firm. She showed up for one session wearing a T-shirt her kids had made, with "Keep Calm and Negotiate NAFTA" on the back and "Mama ≠ Chopped Liver" on the front.

Verheul also got on Americans' nerves. "You decide that you want to rag the puck, but then somebody's got to go in there and rag the puck," says Butts. "And Steve was the guy who had to skate around his own end with the puck. He annoyed Bob [Lighthizer] so much, but it was worth it."

Trudeau credits Verheul for keeping the deal together. "Steve was doing amazing work, working brutally hard. The stakes couldn't have been higher, but the level of difficulty and chaos was also extremely high, and he was absolutely masterful in pulling it all together."

The Americans put pressure on Trudeau to get onside. According to Kushner, Nieto called to urge him to become more involved personally, give Trump a win, and join the US-Mexican deal. In his book, *What It Takes*, Stephen Schwarzman describes setting up a meeting with Trudeau and American CEOs and talking with him privately, giving him the hard sell. "If he refused to meet the U.S. demands of a deal, Canada would almost certainly go into a recession, and no politician wins re-election in a recession. If he did a deal, at least he'd have a chance of political survival."

Schwarzman advised Trudeau to "empty your pockets on dairy," find other concessions, refuse to move on dispute-resolution mechanism and culture, write it up in a proposal, and send it to Trump. "The prime minister looked at me from the couch. He said it would be tough, but he would do it." Later that day, Schwarzman met Trump, who agreed on the broad outline of what they had discussed. Schwarzman called the Canadians and let them know they might have a deal.

Katie Telford sent the Americans an offer that included the dairy concessions the Trudeau team were willing to make. They had been waiting for the right time to present them. Lighthizer was not impressed. As Kushner relates in his book, Lighthizer complained it was "all rubbish. They don't want to make a deal." Kushner convinced Lighthizer to brief him on the details, and he then phoned Telford. They spent two hours going over the changes the Americans wanted.

Lighthizer had been frustrated by Canada's delaying tactics. "While the politicians in Canada clearly had decided it was time to make a deal, the professional bureaucrats were continuing to fight for every inch of turf—or, in this case, every litre of milk. Every time we thought we were close to finalizing the text, the Canadian negotiators would come back with some cleverly worded caveat designed to undermine the spirit of what had been agreed to at the political level." But the Canadians were not going to be rushed. "Every number matters," says Clow. "Every rule matters. Every line matters and it takes time to work through." "One of the things that is clear is that we have red lines that Canadians simply will not accept," Trudeau said in a radio interview as the tension cranked up. "We need to keep the Chapter 19 dispute resolution because that ensures that the rules are actually followed, and we know we have a president who doesn't always follow the rules as they're laid out."

With forty hours until the deadline, Lighthizer put his foot down, demanding that the Canadians stop the "sneaky shit."

In Ottawa, the pressure was on. Telford, Butts, Clow, Verheul, Isinger, Michael Wernick, and a huge rotating crew of extras set up camp in Telford's office. Rob Silver, Telford's husband, brought in a smoked brisket. They worked through the weekend, going back and forth with the Americans. Unifor president Jerry Dias came in to help the government find its bottom line on auto export quotas. They were facing a hard deadline to get the deal done so that the ninety-day congressional clock could start ticking before AMLO's inauguration. Trudeau was working in his office and would come and go as needed.

"We had to continually ask him if he was okay with different things, because there were things moving right up to the end," says Butts. "He was on top of it."

There was a lot of pressure on them all. One key official felt terrible that he wasn't able to spend time with his daughter, who was running for high-school class president. When Trudeau found out about that, he called her at home and offered to have PMO speech writers help her out while her dad kept going over niggling details.

They wrangled over dairy, dispute settlement, and auto rules—and with powerful people in Washington and Ottawa focused on compromise, resolved them one by one until they had a deal. At one minute to midnight on September 30, 2018, the deal was posted on the US government website.

Trump had delivered his dismissive talk on Wednesday. On Thursday, Telford sent a proposal. By Sunday night the deal was made.

Trump announced it the next day in the Rose Garden, bragging about a campaign promise kept and a good deal for American workers. "It was just an unfair deal, whether it was Mexico or Canada, and now it's a fair deal for everybody. It's a much different deal. It's a brand-new deal. It's not NAFTA redone." He even praised Trudeau. "There was a lot of tension, I will say, between he and I, but he's a good man. He's done a good job. And he loves the people of Canada."

Trudeau was more circumspect. "The relationship between the U.S. and Canadians is much deeper than just the relationship between two individuals who happen to be prime minister and president."

Trump had won a deal, but at the cost of a respectful relationship. He had offended Canadian sensibilities, insulted our leadership, introduced existential uncertainty where it was not necessary. Pew Research Center polling showed only 39 percent of Canadians had a favourable view of the United States, down from 68 percent before Trump.

But Canada would live to fight another day. Disaster had been averted. The deal looked pretty good to most Canadians. We had given some ground to the Americans but had minimized the damage. Dias was content, as were the premiers, business groups, and manufacturers. The Dairy Farmers of Canada complained that the government was "willing to sacrifice our domestic dairy production," but dairy farmers were eventually compensated for the market share they had to surrender. Nobody should ever feel too bad for Canadian dairy farmers, who enjoy protections from market forces at the expense of dairy consumers.

Andrew Scheer did his job as Opposition leader and said the Liberals had failed. "I would have focused on economic issues. I would have focused on making sure that we saw an end to softwood lumber tariffs, an end to steel and aluminum tariffs," he said. The attack did not resonate. The Trudeau team deserved credit for bringing stakeholders into the process, pressing hard for advantage, withstanding pressure, taking Trump's guff and staying focused on saving the furniture. They have to share that credit with all kinds of people, including officials, business and labour leaders, premiers, and Conservatives.

"I said at the beginning that there is no Conservative or Liberal way to negotiate a free trade agreement—there is only a Canadian way," Mulroney said when the deal was done. "This has been the government's approach as well, and I commend all—from the prime minister down—who contributed to writing this vital new chapter in the ongoing drive for greater Canadian strength and prosperity."

There was real peril all through these negotiations. It would have been disastrous for the Americans to blow up their most valuable trade relationship, but Trump made many foolish moves. "I think he did a number of things while in office that he probably understood at some level would be hurtful to himself and his country, but did it anyway for whatever reasons beyond me," says Wall. Though no fan of the Trudeau Liberals, he thinks they deserve credit for saving NAFTA.

One person who doesn't deserve any credit was Stephen Harper, who was attacking the government from the sidelines and had at least one secret meeting with the Americans during the negotiations. The government found out about it when a junior official from John Bolton's office called the Canadian embassy to arrange for the "prime minister's" visit. The Canadians were confused—Trudeau was in Ottawa—until the American official realized they were setting up a visit for the previous prime minister.

Harper wrote a memo in October 2017 that was leaked to newshound Alex Panetta, the Canadian Press man in Washington, in which he attacked the Liberal approach to the negotiations, arguing that the Canadians ought to have given more ground sooner and never hitched their wagon to Mexico. "I also believe that President Trump's threat to terminate NAFTA is not a bluff . . . I believe this threat is real. Therefore, Canada's government needs to get its head around this reality: it does not matter whether current American proposals are worse than what we have now. What matters in evaluating them is whether it is worth having a trade agreement with the Americans or not."

Freeland responded with a tweet: "We will continue to defend Canadian interests. Capitulation is not a negotiating strategy."

Happily, the negotiators did not let Harper's critique rattle them. It seems likely that his long-standing visceral hatred of the Liberals, as chronicled in Lawrence Martin's 2011 book, *Harperland*, explains his intemperate remarks.

Verheul, who worked closely with both Harper and Trudeau, thought Trudeau's approach was successful, although he was less detail-oriented than Harper. Trudeau "doesn't feel like he needs to get into the fine details of every issue, which is appropriate," he says. "I think he sees a big part of his job being he's the public face. He's for the delivery of the messages, he's for overall guidance, not someone that gets into the fine, fine details of issues. He leaves that to others, as he should. I think he's very realistic about the role that he plays."

We can't know whether Harper would have managed the crisis better than the Liberals did. He did not drive a hard bargain with the Chinese when he negotiated a trade deal with them. Perhaps it would have been better to let Mexico worry about Mexican interests, to have let the Americans divide and conquer. What we do know is that the Liberals worked hard, found creative solutions, and ended up with an acceptable arrangement. The only real critique is that they neglected other files because they were forced to focus on these negotiations. The SNC-Lavalin affair, for instance, although it dominated headlines after Jody Wilson-Raybould walked out, was not a first-tier issue until she was shuffled from Justice to Veterans Affairs.

The Trudeau team saved the auto industry, stuck to their red lines on dispute settlement and culture, and gave up some ground on dairy. It was a better deal for the Americans than for us, in a way. You can tell because Senate Democrat Chuck Schumer, a sworn enemy of Trump, had to give him credit: "As someone who voted against NAFTA and opposed it for many years, I knew it needed fixing. The president deserves praise for taking large steps to improve it."

The deal remains positive for both sides. In 2016, Canada-US trade was worth $627.8 billion. By 2022, it had increased to $1.2 trillion, exactly as it would have, probably, if there had been no renegotiation. Trump had made a lot of noise, but business carried on. "He initially started saying that NAFTA was the worst agreement ever," says Verheul. "And then by the end of the whole process, the new agreement was the best agreement ever negotiated. And there was very little difference between the two of them."

"My motto through the whole thing was, Never have so many people worked so hard to make nothing happen," says Butts. "That was our motto. And we did."

9

SHAME-FACED

Truro, Nova Scotia, where I grew up, is the kind of place where you hear country music playing out the window of passing pickup trucks. The home of former Progressive Conservative leader Robert Stanfield, it is the biggest town in the riding of Cumberland–Colchester, a naturally Conservative riding—largely rural, white, and English-speaking, with little immigration—but Harper's brand of conservatism was not popular there, and the Liberals won in 2015 with a popular former Tory MP, Bill Casey. He was ready to retire, so he recruited Lenore Zann, a well-known actor and former provincial NDP member, to stand for the upcoming election in 2019. The race would be razor-close: Conservative Scott Armstrong, a well-liked school principal, had been the MP until 2015. The Liberals decided to send in Trudeau to give Zann a boost at a rally in downtown Truro on September 18.

A good crowd turned out. Zann was there outside her headquarters, waiting for the big bus with a picture of Justin on the side. "It was looking like we had a very good possibility," she says. "The momentum had been building and building and building. There was a lot of excitement around the campaign, around me. So we were very positive."

When the bus rolled up, Trudeau got out and started glad-handing, posing for selfies, working the crowd like few in Canadian politics can manage. The campaign song—"One Hand Up" by the Strumbellas—had everyone in the place tapping their feet. A local man had brought an ancient copy of *Chatelaine* with Margaret on the cover, and Trudeau stopped to chat with him and look at the pictures. Zann's supporters were pumped to see him. He ran up to the stage, gave Zann a hug, said how delighted he was that she was running for him, and gave his ten-minute stump speech, warning about Andrew Scheer's agenda and talking optimistically about Liberal plans for the future.

"He gave an incredibly empowering speech," says Zann. But something seemed off. "When I looked him in the eyes a few times, I got the feeling he was perhaps a little bit on . . . overdrive, as if there was a little bit of desperation behind his eyes. Like something was going on . . . I got an instinct, like a Spidey sense . . . Of course I didn't have any clue and I just thought, 'Oh, he's probably on a schedule.'"

Trudeau was likely preoccupied with a story that was about to break—a scandal that had the potential to end his political career. It is impressive, in a way, that he had the gumption to carry on.

———

UP TO THAT POINT, the campaign had been going well for Trudeau. He had the good fortune to be facing Andrew Scheer, who had won an upset victory in 2017 to become Conservative leader after a tumultuous campaign that featured thirteen candidates. As they criss-crossed the country, they produced a cacophonous, politically incorrect din for months, inveighing against Trudeau and subjecting the world to horrible French.

The race was noteworthy for the dismal showing of Kellie Leitch, who positioned herself as the Trumpian, race-baiting candidate; the braggadocio of reality TV mouthpiece Kevin O'Leary, who quit before it ended; the articulate, poised, and measured campaign of Michael Chong, who was booed by party members at every debate; the practical but dull candidacy of Erin O'Toole; the folksy charm of Deepak Obhrai; and the risk-taking libertarian messaging of Maxime "Mad Max" Bernier, who had the courage to oppose supply management, equalization, and other sacred cows.

In the end, Scheer, the establishment candidate, the man closest to Stephen Harper and with the most support in caucus, squeaked out a win that surprised everyone at the Convention Centre in Toronto. Bernier, whose populism had ignited the grassroots, had been polling well ahead. He was shocked to lose, and his campaign manager, Kory Teneycke, smelled a rat. CTV learned that the number of votes exceeded the number of eligible voters. The party, staffed by people whom Bernier would have fired if he had won, rejected accusations of wrongdoing. Bernier grumbled for a few days, but there was not much to do. The ballots had been destroyed.

What he could do, and did, the following year was denounce the Tories as "fake Conservatives" and launch the People's Party of Canada, a populist vehicle that immediately vacuumed up the red-meat-loving ideologues across the country who think the government should stay out of their business. The new party was going to steal Scheer's votes during the campaign. Rachel Curran, former policy director to Harper, tweeted: "I hope Justin Trudeau and his cabinet colleagues are breaking out the champagne in Nanaimo this morning. Congratulations to @gmbutts & co. who have secured an easy win in 2019 despite a mostly terrible summer."

That's the way it looked until Trudeau got to Truro. Earlier that day, the campaign had learned that *Time* was about to go live with a story—and, crucially, a photo—that would change the face of the campaign.

———

AFTER TESTIFYING IN THE SNC-Lavalin affair, Butts had been licking his wounds and reconnecting with his family after the brutally long hours he had worked in the PMO. His wife, Jodi, joked she should send Jody Wilson-Raybould a present to thank her for engineering her husband's exit from politics. But on a trip to Tuscany to celebrate their twentieth anniversary, he told her he thought he should go back for the 2019 campaign. She reluctantly agreed. "You know what? If you don't go back and they lose, you're going to blame yourself for the rest of your life. So just go do it. But you've got to promise me on election night it's all over."

Butts returned as a senior advisor for the campaign, to strategize, as he had done in Trudeau's successful election of 2015 and in earlier elections for Dalton McGuinty in Ontario. On his first day back, Brian Clow, the issues manager on the campaign, told him that BC Liberals had heard that a reporter was making inquiries about a yearbook photo involving Trudeau. Anna Kodé, a plucky twenty-two-year-old cub reporter with *Time* magazine, had heard about a brownface picture of Trudeau. She set out to track it down and eventually found it through the father of a university classmate, Vancouver businessman Michael Adamson. He had a family connection to West Point Grey Academy, where Trudeau had taught. Adamson had a copy of the yearbook. He was not involved in politics and didn't want to be in the public eye, but he thought Canadians should see the picture before the election.

The photo had been taken at an "Arabian Nights" party Trudeau attended when he taught drama at the school in 2001. It shows him standing with four women, all smiling and enjoying the party. He is wearing a robe and a turban decorated with feathers and a large jewel.

The picture came from *The View*, the private school's yearbook, which Trudeau helped produce. It includes several other pictures of him too, wearing a kilt, a bowler in the style of Charlie Chaplin, and a tux, James Bond–style. They are pictures of a popular, exuberant, attention-seeking young man.

The photos are all black and white, but the troublesome picture showed him wearing dark makeup on his face and hands. In fact, it was blue. He was dressed as Aladdin, from the 1992 Disney animated movie.

Though not prime-ministerial, it was not particularly shocking. If it was the only picture, he could have pointed to the context and shrugged it off. But it was not the only picture. In February 2019, when reporters found yearbook pictures of Virginia governor Ralph Northam in blackface and a Ku Klux Klan robe, Trudeau had confided to Butts and Telford that he had also done blackface. "I knew the story was out there, but I had no idea there were so many," says Butts.

Butts was pushing for the campaign to release the picture and get ahead of the story. "Guys, we've got to get this up there or it's going to come out. And people are like, 'No, maybe it won't come out.' Like, no. It's coming out."

The team wouldn't budge, and Butts, frustrated, went back to his office. Before long, Zita Astravas, media relations lead for the campaign, who was not in the loop, came in, her face white with shock. "*Time* magazine just called me," she said. "They have a picture of the prime minister in blackface."

Butts burst out laughing. "Oh my God," he said. "This could be the biggest disaster in the history of Canadian politics."

Astravas, a savvy operator who had previously worked for Kathleen Wynne, broke the news to Kate Purchase, her boss on the campaign. "We often called her Kramer because she would burst into rooms," says Purchase. "She burst into my office and said, 'I have to talk to you right now.' I was on a very important phone call and I said, 'I can't talk to you.' And she said, 'Hang up.' So she told me and said, 'They're sending me the photo.'"

Purchase was flabbergasted. "All our reputations are now on the line."

The senior people were worried how the young multicultural staffers in the war room would react to the news. Before the story broke, campaign manager Jeremy Broadhurst gathered them together and broke the news, followed by Butts. Some of them cried; others took time off to think things through. "Jeremy especially was really excellent and in a terrible position there, running his first campaign, having to go and do that," says Purchase.

Senior managers also called in Vandana Kattar, who was working on multicultural outreach. "Here is this whole office full of very senior people," she says. "I thought I was getting fired." Butts was looking at her in a fatherly way. "I was like, 'Did my husband get shot? What happened? Did my parents die? What happened?'"

Kattar liked the way they handled it. "I appreciated the warmth of my colleagues, who were all white and didn't really know how to best support me but realized they had to support me somehow." They needed her help, and they got it. She knew Trudeau well enough to be sure the photos didn't reflect some kind of secret racism. "I didn't think he was a racist. I thought, he was young once and didn't know better. I have known him since 2009. I have worked for him since 2012 or 2013. We went on tour driving in my 2005 Chevrolet Cobalt together. And that really brings you together."

After the Truro rally, the senior people got on the phone to Trudeau and strategized how best to handle the bombshell. They knew it would be a global story, a bad one, and he had to respond quickly. They threw questions at him—the kind of practice news conference that staffers do to prep leaders. Someone asked how many times he'd worn blackface. Trudeau didn't know. That seemed like a tough thing to have to explain to Canadians.

After the meeting, Purchase was gloomy. This looked like the end. "Well, it's been swell," she said to Butts and Broadhurst.

The Conservatives had found a video of Trudeau in his early twenties clowning around in actual blackface, almost minstrel-style, from when he worked as a whitewater rafting guide on the Rouge River in Quebec. The Conservatives gave it to Global News, but they hadn't broken the story yet.

When Trudeau had been a student at Brébeuf, he had performed "Banana Boat (Day-O)," the Harry Belafonte classic, on stage in blackface. I am told that he also wore blackface at McGill on Halloween in 1993, going out as Ted Danson, who had offended Americans that year by wearing minstrel-style makeup to a comedy roast (at the instigation of his then girlfriend, Whoopi Goldberg, who is Black). Any one of the pictures could perhaps have been waved off, dealt with, rationalized. Together, they posed a problem that could not be explained away.

It is surprising that none of the photos had surfaced earlier. If they had come up during the 2015 election campaign, for example, they would have reinforced the Conservative message about Trudeau and raised doubts within his multicultural progressive coalition. He likely would not have won the election. "The opposition—Conservatives and NDP—they should have found this," says Clow. "They didn't."

———

TERESA WRIGHT, A JOURNALIST from Prince Edward Island, was on the media bus covering the 2019 campaign in Nova Scotia for the Canadian Press. In Truro, she had noticed that Trudeau seemed "even more Energizer Bunny than usual, like feeding off the crowd in a way that normally he doesn't. He was just extra happy. He took extra time shaking people's hands to get up to the stage."

After the event, the reporters filed their stories, did their standups, and got on the bus for Halifax, where they were to board the plane for Winnipeg. No events were scheduled that night. Usually, that would mean it was time to break out the beer. But it was not party time: "All the staffers were super somber."

Glen McGregor was on the bus for CTV when the story broke. "All of a sudden, everybody's phone starts going off. And it's like a rock concert, when people hold their phones up." The assignment desks were looking for the reporters on the bus to match *Time*'s explosive scoop. McGregor was trying to figure out how he had been beaten on the story. "Surely somebody would have gone and pulled his high-school yearbook photo, because that's what you do. But then I realized nobody thought to pull the high-school yearbook at the high school *where he taught*."

Nobody had by then told the reporters that Trudeau would respond before the plane took off for Winnipeg. McGregor talked to his colleagues from other outlets and decided to push the matter. "I walked three or four rows back to where [press secretary] Cameron [Ahmad] and the cameras were, and I said, 'Before we leave Halifax, we need your guy or we're not getting on the plane.' And Cameron's like, 'Yeah. We know.'"

On the plane, Trudeau scrummed from the front of the cabin, wearing a suit, frowning, apologizing. "I deeply regret that I did that," he said. "I should have known better, but I didn't."

The journalists, having been scooped by their American counterparts, were not going to go easy now. The normal rules—where they take turns and wait for follow-ups—were out the window. "It's just a mob scramble of people shrieking questions," says McGregor.

Trudeau didn't say much, repeating his apology. David Akin asked if he would resign. Trudeau was experienced enough not to say, "No. I won't resign," which would have been the media clip rather than the obvious one of him apologizing.

Even if Trudeau handled it well, it was a nightmare. The story went viral around the world. Global sent Kate Purchase an image from the video they had, of Trudeau in actual blackface from a rafting camp. The staffers couldn't tell if it was actually him, so she sent it to the plane for Trudeau's confirmation. Global put the story out, meaning there were now at least three incidents of Trudeau in blackface. He was a global punchline. The election was up in the air.

For young racialized people on his staff, the story was especially painful. Not only had their leader been shown to have done something, repeatedly, that they found hard to understand, but the reporters shrieking at him were all white. "Obviously, as soon as blackface broke, people tweeted pictures of us," says Wright. "There was [a picture] of us on the plane. And they're like, 'Wow, look at the press. Those are all white people.' And I thought, 'Oh, crap.'"

The Press Gallery is what you might call a lagging indicator in Canadian society. It is less diverse than the institutions it covers, largely because the media organizations who do the hiring have been financially struggling for decades, shedding rather than adding jobs while other institutions were welcoming newcomers who better reflected Canada's growing diversity. On expensive leaders' tours, all the outlets tended to send only their most experienced people—and they in turn represented the industry as it was in the past.

It was a long, grim flight to Winnipeg for the Trudeau people, McGregor says. "They don't know really until the next day if their campaign is fucked, if the Trudeau experiment is over."

When explosive news breaks, it is not always clear how voters will react. The most famous Canadian example is the "Shawinigan handshake," when Prime Minister Jean Chrétien throttled protester Bill Clennett at a 1996 Gatineau protest. His staff was terrified he would be seen as a thug, but the polls showed that people liked it, and it is now part of Chrétien's schtick. The big question for staffers on the Liberal plane was whether Trudeau would be cancelled. He worked the phones all the way to Winnipeg, apologizing, asking for advice.

Jagmeet Singh, who had been struggling to connect with Canadians since taking over the NDP after Thomas Mulcair's exit, released a note-perfect video on social media, pointing out that the story would be painful for people who had experienced racism and been marginalized by white bullies. "When I was growing up, I fought racists. I dealt with them myself and I fought back. But I got a message from a friend and it reminded me that there were a lot of people who couldn't do that . . . And I think it's going to hurt to see this. It's going to hurt them a lot."

Singh's video was the ideal illustration of why representation matters, why Canada's political class must reflect the country. Singh is a Brampton lawyer who drives a BMW sports car and wears Rolexes and tailored suits. His advocacy on economic justice issues often seems hollow, as though he is delivering lines by rote. He doesn't have the effortless command of legal and constitutional issues that Mulcair had, and he sometimes gets himself in trouble, particularly in Quebec, where voters are not ready to warm to a leader in religious headgear. The party had sixteen seats in Quebec at the time, and Singh was going to lose all but one. But when the blackface video dropped, he helped Canadians understand why the pictures were problematic. It gave his struggling campaign a boost and made the election more competitive. The Conservatives typically do well in Canadian elections only when the NDP is doing well, because of the vote splits on the left in tight ridings.

For the Liberals, especially Black Liberals, the incident was a gut punch. They networked frantically while they tried to figure out how to react. Greg Fergus, the Liberal MP for Hull–Aylmer, had founded the Black Liberal Caucus, a group where Black staffers and MPs from across the country met on an equal footing to discuss Black issues. They had worked with Trudeau to get the picture of Viola Desmond—the Black woman jailed in Nova Scotia in 1946 after refusing to leave her seat in a movie theatre—put on the ten-dollar bill. As the story was breaking, Butts set up a call with Fergus and Trudeau. Fergus told the prime minister he had his back.

There was a distinct generational divide. "Anybody over the age of forty had the exact same reaction I had. 'This is shit, but, you know, move on. We know where he is at,'" one prominent Black Liberal told me. "And under thirty, the reaction was 'Who the hell does that?'" Some of the conversations were tense. "Look. This is your come-to-Jesus moment," one Black Liberal recalls saying. "Are you in or are you out? Because if we shit on him, we lose this." Barack Obama must have reached a similar conclusion, because he tweeted an endorsement of Trudeau as the campaign entered the home stretch.

In Quebec, where American cultural dynamics have less force, the story did not resonate in the same way as in English Canada. Haitian Canadian novelist and professor Dany Laferrière laughed at it in TV interviews, accusing Trudeau's opponents of attacking him hypocritically. Trudeau had been silly, he said, not racist.

The next day, in Winnipeg, Trudeau did a long scrum in a downtown park, accompanied by Robert-Falcon Ouellette, an Indigenous MP. He talked for forty minutes, until journalists ran out of questions. He made an abject apology: he didn't excuse himself, didn't say he was sorry if people were offended. He said that what he had done was wrong and that he should have known better. It was wrong because of the harm it does to people who have dealt with discrimination. "I didn't see that from the layers of privilege I have," he said.

By the end of the news conference, there was not much that anyone could say that Trudeau had not said himself. Reporters eventually cornered him into admitting that he didn't know how often he had worn blackface, but otherwise the event was free of news. At one point, when he asked for forgiveness, people in the park spontaneously applauded.

Cameron Ahmad was relieved to hear the people clapping. He was twenty-seven, the child of Pakistani immigrants. For his generation, the idea that someone would don blackface was hard to swallow. He knew Trudeau, whom he considers the "most inclusive, diversity-loving prime minister we've ever had," but was finding it hard to absorb the whole thing. Ahmad believed Trudeau's earnest apology was genuine, and it helped clear the air. Party canvassers and pollsters soon learned that many Liberal voters felt the same way. The campaign pivoted quickly to guns, flying into Toronto to announce a ban on "all military-style assault rifles, including the AR-15."

Trudeau was able to skate away from this scandal, but it would follow him around for the rest of his career. One of the things that his critics—especially white men of a certain age—find most galling about him is his tendency to virtue signal, letting on that his opponents should move closer to enlightenment by emulating him in mouthing pious bromides. Yet he seemed to have bullied an Indigenous woman in the SNC-Lavalin affair and now it had been revealed that he'd repeatedly worn blackface, like a 1960s Alabama frat boy. His team would have automatically rejected prospective candidates with blackface pictures in their background. He, in contrast, was protected, as he said, by layers of privilege. He is a prince, and the rules don't apply to princes.

Before the story broke, Telford had mentioned casually to reporters on the campaign that Trudeau liked to dress up, perhaps planting a seed so they would have some context in mind when the story came out—a subtle bit of spin, which works, like all good spin, because it is true. Trudeau has all his life sought the limelight. That desire is what makes him such an extraordinary campaigner and gives him the discipline to undergo the humiliations and travails that leaders must endure. Now he was paying for it. "He wanted to have the best costume at the Arabian Nights thing at West Point Grey, in India, at Halloween," says one Liberal who has known him well for a long time. "He's always got to have the best costume. Well, now he's ruined that for himself."

———

PROGRESSIVES WERE MADE TO feel queasy by Trudeau's blackface schtick, but they stuck with him because they preferred him to the alternative. Scheer did not do as well as I expected him to do. I had gotten to know him a little bit over the years because he was Harper's Speaker of the House, and I found him pleasant—a tall and friendly family man with boyish dimples and an easy way with people. He did not distinguish himself as Speaker as his predecessor, Peter Milliken, had, but he was pleasant and inoffensive. If he toed the Conservative line more often than a Speaker should, he did not attract attention to it.

Scheer, forty years old when the campaign began, was a former Reform Party guy, part of the contingent of fresh-faced young people who learned at the knee of Preston Manning and Stockwell Day before Harper brought them to power. Originally from Ottawa, Scheer grew up in an intensely religious Catholic family. His father is a deacon and an adherent of the Latin mass who travelled to Europe to network with other activists opposed to the liturgical reforms brought in by the Second Vatican

Council in the 1960s. Quebec journalists speculated that Scheer might be a member of Opus Dei, the hyper-devout and secretive organization of Catholics, some of whom practise self-flagellation. He seems not to have been a member of that group, but he was devoted to his religious beliefs and unwilling to talk about them with candour.

In the first debate where all the leaders squared off, on Quebec's private TVA network, the initial question dealt with abortion. Mulcair was in the studio for a pre-debate show with journalist Emmanuelle Latraverse, and, once done, they headed to the green room to have dinner and watch the debate. "By the time we walk from the studio, take our things off, it's like six minutes and the debate's already over," he recalls. "We come in and Scheer is sputtering because Trudeau's gone after him on abortion. Scheer had nothing. He was unprepared for the first obvious line of attack."

Scheer had the same stated position as Harper, saying he would not reopen the issue, but he was not at ease discussing it. He was actually less categorical than Harper had been about restraining MPs from debating it. Pro-life Tories have long sought to bring the issue up in the House, looking for subtle ways to get the issue on the agenda—by highlighting sex-selection abortion, for instance. The Liberals are always waiting for that, ready to exploit it and warn Canadians that the party wants to restrict abortion rights. Conservative leaders must balance this issue with great care, keeping social conservatives in the tent but silent. Harper, who had won the Canadian Alliance leadership in a race against the more openly pro-life Stockwell Day, found the right balance. Scheer had moved a shade toward social conservatives, and that left him, in Mulcair's words, looking like a "deer in the headlights." His performance did not put the matter to rest with Quebecers, who are in general suspicious of religiosity. Trudeau, Singh, and Bloc Québécois leader Yves-François Blanchet all accused him of hiding his views, creating the impression he would not come clean.

The Liberals were delighted. "It sank him in Quebec," says Clow. "From that first abortion answer it was over for him."

The next day in New Brunswick, Scheer sought to clarify his position by saying he opposed abortion, but his government would not. "I am personally pro-life, but I've also made the commitment that as leader of this party it is my responsibility to ensure that we do not re-open this debate, that we focus on issues that unite our party and unite Canadians."

Pro-choice voters were not obliged to take him at his word, and they appear not to have done so. He got another bloody nose in New Brunswick, when the *Globe and Mail*'s Bob Fife and Janice Dickson reported that he had dual citizenship—Canadian and American—and had not bothered to mention that to voters.

Scheer looked bad. Not only had he kept his dual citizenship secret from Canadians but he had previously attacked former Governor General Michaëlle Jean, a Black woman, for having French and Canadian citizenship, a hypocritical cheap shot at someone who broke through a glass ceiling. And he had failed to deal proactively with his own issue: If he had declared his US citizenship and announced plans to renounce it, he would have been fine. Instead, he had hoped it wouldn't come out, just as the Liberals had hoped Canadians would never learn about Trudeau's many blackface incidents.

Scheer seemed to be reluctant to give forthright answers about anything. Earlier in the campaign, the *Globe* questioned whether he really had been, as he claimed, an insurance broker in Saskatchewan in his youth. "I did receive my accreditation," he said. "I left the insurance office before the licensing process was finalized." It was a significant issue because it suggested Scheer had fibbed about his not-very-illustrious pre-political career. Still, it was the blandest possible scandal, sending political reporters down impossibly dull Saskatchewan-insurance-regulation rabbit holes.

Between Trudeau's blackface incidents and Scheer's stumbles, the race remained tight. It would be a photo finish. Scheer's campaign had a shot at victory—if they had a strong finish. They did not.

The Conservative campaign seems to have misjudged their position, trusting internal polls that showed them ahead. Only that would explain the counterproductive messaging in the last week of the campaign when Scheer decided to say that "only a Conservative majority government can prevent a government with Justin Trudeau as the spokesman but the NDP calling the shots."

There followed several days of talk about whether Scheer would have the right to form a government if he won more seats than Trudeau—all calculated, apparently, to soften the ground for a post-election struggle for legitimacy that was not going to happen. If Scheer had spent the last week of the campaign talking about anything else—tax credits for community volunteers!—it would have been better for him, because his message was foolishly giving credence to the traditional Liberal end-of-campaign pitch at NDP and Green voters who can be stampeded to the Liberals out of fear of a Conservative government.

The party's voter-ID and get-out-the-vote efforts, once miles ahead of the competition, were as bad as its polling. In the last week of the election, as veteran Conservative campaigners spread out across the country to help their friends in tight races, many were surprised at the paucity of data. The party had decided to spend less money on political phone banking than it had in previous elections, reasoning that, as fewer people have landlines or answer calls from political parties, the old approach was producing diminishing returns.

As a result, riding-level campaigns had fewer identified votes to pull on election day than in previous elections. To make matters worse, the campaign sent extra volunteers to ridings where they were not in contention—such as Kings–Hants, Scott Brison's old riding in Nova Scotia—instead of ridings they ended up losing by a few hundred votes—Cumberland–Colchester, for instance, where Zann managed to squeak out a win over Armstrong. The Liberals did not make similar mistakes. Under Trudeau's old friend Tom Pitfield, the Liberal data operation was functioning at a high level, precisely targeting the ridings they needed to win, finding their supporters, and getting them to the polls where it mattered. He and Sean Wiltshire, who has a PhD in genetics, had learned how Obama's people built computer models to find their voters and then adapted those techniques for a more complicated multi-party parliamentary system. That made the difference between winning and losing.

It was a desperate affair, as close elections always are, but it was uglier than it ought to have been. The Conservatives, running against Prime Minister Blackface, the man who brought Canadians the SNC-Lavalin affair, should have been on the moral high ground. But on the last day of the campaign, during Scheer's final media opportunity, Glen McGregor asked him about a *Globe and Mail* report that the party had hired former Liberal strategist Warren Kinsella to run a social media campaign against Maxime Bernier. Kinsella was well suited to the task: his bestselling 1996 book, *Web of Hate*, sounded the alarm about the threat posed by organized hate groups. The pugilistic Kinsella, who had worked in Chrétien's war room, was not on good terms with the Trudeau people, who had prevented him from running for the party in Toronto. His firm, Daisy Group, took on a contract from the Tories to "seek and destroy" Bernier's populist, far-right People's Party, highlighting racist posts associated with the party on social media. A Daisy Group employee who left the company after a conflict with Kinsella leaked recordings of company meetings in which Kinsella told staffers, "I want the hatred you have for Maxime Bernier to wash over you as a purifying force." He said that Scheer campaign manager Hamish Marshall and party president John Walsh wanted to see results. The contract raised questions about what Scheer was doing, secretly hiring an outside company to attack his former colleague Bernier.

McGregor had left reporting on the Liberal campaign and was on the Conservative campaign as the election wound down. He wanted Scheer to explain the contract. Scheer smiled and declined to answer: "We don't offer comments on contracts that may or may not exist on vendors we may or may not have a relationship with," he said. "Why not?" McGregor asked. Scheer repeated his answer. McGregor asked again. Scheer declined to comment twenty-three times, which looked ridiculous and spoiled his chance at getting out a final message to voters.

The Conservatives looked desperate. They had issued a news release asking about Trudeau's departure from West Point Grey. A fake-news operation in the United States posted several false stories alleging terrible wrongdoing by the prime minister which were widely shared on social media by Trudeau-despising Conservatives, who no doubt believed them to be true. A journalist from Rebel News Network, where Scheer's campaign manager, Hamish Marshall, used to work, pressed Trudeau on the matter. A *Globe* reporter even asked Trudeau why he left the school. It was ugly. Politicians should not face unfounded accusations as a condition of their work.

The Conservatives seemed, not for the first time, to have their judgment impaired by their hatred for Trudeau, wagering that voters would reject the blackface-wearing rascal, the virtue-signalling phony whom people liked only because of his good looks and famous name. They were too intense. Scheer was warning of Trudeau's secret plan to form a coalition with the NDP to raise the Goods and Services Tax and legalize hard drugs. But he failed to deal with ethical issues in his own operation and failed to deliver a message on abortion that would make swing voters comfortable. His climate change policy amounted to little more than an expensive pamphlet and a promise to get rid of the carbon tax. It was an undisciplined campaign, characterized by wishful thinking and a failure to communicate policies designed to appeal to people who had voted for Trudeau in 2015 but now had buyer's remorse.

Even so, he almost won and actually got more votes than Trudeau: 6,239,227 across Canada—220,000 more than Trudeau's party, and 625,000 more than Harper's campaign won in 2015. But they were in the wrong places. Scheer ran up huge numbers in Alberta (69 percent of the vote) and Saskatchewan (64 percent), where many voters see the carbon tax as a dirty eastern plot dreamed up by the same family that brought them the National Energy Program, which Trudeau *père* foisted on the west. Scheer needed votes in the close ridings, especially in the GTA. He didn't get them.

There is a constant tension in the Conservative Party between west and east, country and city. The party builds in toward the Liberal cities from its rural strongholds. Its members, and donors, are much more conservative than the median voter. The membership wants its red meat—policies on guns, abortion, resource extraction—but the voters in the towns and suburbs, whom the Tories must convince before they can form a government, have different values, different worries. Harper had, through patience and a natural fearsomeness, managed to walk the fine line, keeping the base happy while gradually broadening his appeal. Scheer had given the base too much, but in a way it was the membership of the party, the libertarians and social conservatives, who lost the election by backing Scheer. They wanted their red meat, and they got it, but they then had to watch when Trudeau gave his victory speech and Scheer conceded.

Peter MacKay, who had decided not to run in the leadership race that Scheer won, summed up the situation well at an event a week later in Washington, blaming Scheer for not having dealt with abortion. "That was thrust on the agenda and [it] hung around Andrew Scheer's neck like a stinking albatross, quite frankly. And he wasn't able to deftly deal with those issues when the opportunities arose. To use a good Canadian analogy, it was like having a breakaway on an open net and missing the net."

Still, it was not a terrible night for the Conservatives. They picked up twenty-six seats. The Liberals lost twenty and the NDP fifteen, including all but one of their Quebec seats, while they failed to break through in Toronto, where members might have hoped a son of the GTA would have coattails. The biggest winner, in a way, was the Bloc Québécois, which had a solid leader in Blanchet. He won thirty-two seats, after inheriting only ten. Mad Max missed out, but he likely took some satisfaction in getting 294,092 votes that otherwise may have gone to his former colleagues in the Conservative Party.

Trudeau was going back to Ottawa with a minority government. It was disappointing, but despite the blackface scandal, he'd somehow managed to win re-election, demonstrating a capacity for shame-eating and a resilience that is, in a way, impressive.

10

THE TWO MICHAELS

On December 1, 2018, Meng Wanzhou, the deputy chair and chief financial officer of Huawei, the Chinese technology giant, got on a plane in Hong Kong bound for Mexico City, where she was to meet with President Andrés Manuel López Obrador to try to convince him to let Huawei into the Mexican market. It was a routine business trip for Wanzhou, then forty-six, but a brief stopover in Vancouver ended up lasting for almost three years because, earlier that day, RCMP Constable Winston Yep got an arrest warrant for her in response to an extradition request from a New York judge.

Meng is the daughter of Huawei's founder, Ren Zhengfei, and was known in China as the "Princess of Huawei." Ren, a former engineer in the People's Liberation Army, founded the company with $5,000 in 1987 to manufacture cellphone parts. He lived modestly and worked such long hours that he slept in the factory, setting an example he expected his workers to emulate. His diligence paid off, and as cellphone networks expanded rapidly in the early part of the century, Huawei grew at an extraordinary pace, undercutting foreign competitors by reverse-engineering their products and manufacturing them at a fraction of the price. In 1994, President Jiang Zemin visited the company, and Ren told him a country unable to manufacture telecoms switches was like a country without a military. Jiang seems to have listened. Huawei won a key contract to build a network for the People's Liberation Army, and later obtained an estimated US$75 billion in loans and grants from the Chinese government.

To acquire the technology it needed to build high-tech capabilities, China offered foreign companies joint ventures, trading know-how for market access. This arrangement offered advantages to Ottawa-based Nortel—in the 1980s a big player in telephone switching systems. Nortel reacted quickly, closing its factories in North America and outsourcing its manufacturing and engineering to China. In the late 1990s, CSIS warned the company that China was stealing its secrets. "We went to Nortel in Ottawa, and we told the executives, 'They're sucking your intellectual property out,'" said Michel Juneau-Katsuya, director of CSIS's Asia-Pacific unit at the time. "They didn't do anything." In 2004, sophisticated hackers vacuumed up hundreds of technical documents from the company and forwarded them to a front company in Shanghai. Its Ottawa campus was eventually found to be full of listening devices. In 2009, Nortel, which could trace its origins to Alexander Graham Bell's Brantford, Ontario, farm, filed for bankruptcy protection.

As Nortel struggled, Huawei thrived. It was increasingly demonstrating more sophisticated technological capacities, beating out Nortel and other Western companies in competition for big contracts. The company benefited from China's official "Go Out" policy, which encouraged direct Chinese investment abroad, and expanded aggressively in the Global South, where cellphone networks were offering communications in places that had never had landlines. By 2018, the company was selling two hundred million mobile phones a year and had become the dominant global player in 5G technology, with US$107.13 billion in annual sales around the world. It was a crucial generator of soft power for growing Chinese business expansion—and an enormous source of national pride.

The Americans do not see it that way. They view Huawei as a threat to their own business interests, a wholly owned subsidiary of the Communist Party of China, and an arm of the Chinese security state in thrall to China's vast intelligence apparatus. US intelligence officials were warning allies that the Chinese could create back-door vulnerabilities through Huawei systems in Western mobile networks, allowing them to gather intelligence or even shut down networks in the event of conflict. By 2018, Australia, the United Kingdom, the United States, and New Zealand had shut the company out of their 5G networks, and the Americans were pushing Canada to do the same.

In 2016, the US Department of Commerce released documents from Chinese telecom firm ZTE that seemed to show it believed its competitor, Huawei, was using arm's-length companies to break US sanctions by selling equipment to North Korea, Cuba, and Iran. In 2013, Reuters reported that one such subsidiary, Hong Kong–based Skycom Tech Co. Ltd., had sold Huawei equipment to Iran. To reassure representatives of HSBC Bank, who were worried about violating sanctions, Meng, who was on the board of Skycom, had briefed bank officials that the two enterprises were not linked.

That assurance amounted to fraud in the eyes of US intelligence officials—and also to Constable Winston Yep, who was waiting for Meng when she landed in Vancouver. Meng owned two homes in the city, one assessed at $5.6 million and the other, in the swanky First Shaughnessy neighbourhood, for $16.3 million, but she wasn't planning to stay over.

Meng, casually dressed for travel in a hooded sweatsuit and running shoes, was brought into the terminal and directed to a secondary inspection area. There Canada Border Services Agency officers went through her luggage and interrogated her while Constable Yep waited and watched. They took her electronics—a Huawei phone, an iPhone, an iPad, a MacBook and a USB stick. They placed them in Mylar bags provided by the Americans, beyond the reach of cell signals. Meng, likely hoping they would let her go, voluntarily gave the passwords to the border security officers just before the Mounties came in and arrested her. They charged her with fraud and took her to the lockup at the Richmond RCMP detachment, a far cry from the luxurious world to which she was accustomed.

———

THE CHINESE WERE NOT amused by the arrest of Meng. Given the importance of Huawei and the close relationship between the company and the government, the arrest was seen as a terrible insult. "Obviously, Washington is resorting to a despicable rogue's approach as it cannot stop Huawei's 5G advance in the market," the nationalist *Global Times* wrote. In the opinion of *China Daily*: "The U.S. is trying to do whatever it can to contain Huawei's expansion in the world, simply because the company is the point man for China's competitive technology companies."

Canada was in a pickle. The arrest in Vancouver had been carried out in response to an American extradition request, which Canadian courts must honour if the offence is against the law in both countries and carries a potential jail sentence of more than a year. The government had no choice unless it overruled the judge who granted the arrest warrant. Foreign Affairs Minister Chrystia Freeland quickly signalled that they would not do that. She told reporters she had sent a message of reassurance to Beijing through her former Cabinet colleague, John McCallum, Canada's ambassador to China. "He has assured China that due process is absolutely being [followed] in Canada and consular access for China to Ms. Meng will be provided, and that we are a rule-of-law country and we will be following our laws as we have thus far in this matter, and as we will continue to do."

That response did not satisfy Beijing. A week after the arrest, Meng was given $10 million bail and provided with an ankle bracelet to track her whereabouts. The next day, Le Yucheng, the deputy foreign minister, summoned McCallum and demanded her release. "China strongly urges the Canadian side to immediately release the detained person, and earnestly protect their lawful, legitimate rights, otherwise Canada must accept full responsibility for the serious consequences caused," he said.

The consequences were immediately apparent. The Chinese arrested two Canadians resident in China: Michael Kovrig, a former diplomat with the Global Security Reporting Program who worked for the International Crisis Group, a non-governmental organization that tries to minimize the harm caused by armed conflict; and Michael Spavor, who worked for an NGO that facilitates exchanges with North Korea. They were charged with espionage under the National Security Law, brought in by President Xi Jinping in 2015, which allowed for the men's detention on suspicion of "engaging in activities endangering national security." The same law was being used on pro-democracy protesters in Hong Kong, on Uyghurs in re-education camps in western China, and on dissidents throughout China.

Chinese officials treated Kovrig and Spavor harshly, interrogating them at length and keeping them isolated in cells where the toilet was a hole in the floor and electric lights burned twenty-four hours a day. They were denied regular consular visits and access to legal representation. In Vancouver, in contrast, Meng was living in one of her fine homes, able to host family and friends in the lap of luxury and travel around the city until 11 p.m. every day, when her curfew kicked in.

Nobody outside the Chinese government considered the charges against the men legitimate. They were hostages, and Canada was powerless to get them out. One person who might have been able to exert influence and find a way to persuade China to release the Canadians was US president Donald Trump, but he was indifferent to their plight. Rather, he seemed pleased that Meng had been detained because it gave him an edge in his wrangling with President Xi. Trump had campaigned on a promise to get tough on trade with China, which was a huge challenge to the economy. In 2017, China had a $375.2 billion trade surplus with the United States. Critics such as Robert Lighthizer argued that it had been a mistake to let China into the World Trade Organization in 2001, giving open access to Western markets to a country that cheated, stole intellectual property, and used its new economic power to threaten its neighbours and oppress its own people, especially minorities. Trump had a mandate to seek better terms in the trade relationship and relished being the man in the spotlight, talking tough, standing up for America, imposing five successive rounds of tariff increases on China after taking office.

When Meng was arrested, Trump and Xi had just enjoyed a working dinner together at the G20 in Argentina. Trump, having signed the United States-Mexico-Canada Agreement, now moved on to wheeling and dealing with Xi, agreeing on high-level talks to tackle irritants in exchange for a promise to stop raising tariffs while the talks continued. The agreement was reached before the news of Meng's arrest reached the Chinese. "Had it been known, Ms. Meng's arrest could have completely scuttled the agreement reached by the two presidents," Lighthizer wrote later.

Back in Washington, after the successful Argentina trip, Trump told Reuters that he might intervene with the Justice Department in the Meng case if it was good for his country: "If I think it's good for what will be certainly the largest trade deal ever made—which is a very important thing—what's good for national security—I would certainly intervene if I thought it was necessary."

It was a stupid thing to say. To look important and decisive, Trump proposed interfering in a criminal matter to advance his political interests. His comment gave Meng's lawyers an argument: by linking politics with the process, they could say in court that she was being used as a political pawn. His interference also made it harder for Canada to argue to the Chinese that the case had nothing to do with politics—the central message the Canadian government had to make unless it wanted to give in to hostage diplomacy and spring Meng.

Canada could expect that kind of thing from Trump, who appears to have a poor understanding of the separation of powers, but it was alarming when Ambassador McCallum made a similar argument in January. An accomplished and articulate economist and university professor, he had long-standing connections to China—his wife is of Chinese descent—and a sophisticated understanding of politics. But the stress of the situation seemed to overwhelm his judgment. During a news conference with Chinese-language journalists in his riding of Markham, he said that Meng had good arguments to make in court and might beat the case: "One, political involvement by comments from Donald Trump in her case. Two, there's an extraterritorial aspect to her case, and three, there's the issue of Iran sanctions which are involved in her case, and Canada does not sign on to these Iran sanctions. So I think she has some strong arguments that she can make before a judge." He went on to say that Canada would not interfere in a "purely judicial process," but that "there may come a time when the justice minister is required to give a view."

At the time, Chrétienites—many of whom had business ties with China—were arguing that Canada should make a deal. Former deputy prime minister John Manley, for example, urged a prisoner exchange, as in the Cold War days in Berlin, "as crass as that may seem."

McCallum may have agreed, but that was not the official line. When Trudeau was asked about his ambassador's comments, he stated clearly: "Canada is a country of the rule of law, and we will make sure the rule of law is properly and fully followed. That includes the opportunity for [Meng] to mount a strong defence. That is part of our justice system."

McCallum apologized, saying that his comments didn't reflect Canadian policy, but two days later, at a luncheon in Vancouver, he told a reporter that it would be "great for Canada" if the United States dropped its extradition request, again embarrassing the government. Trudeau called him to ask for his resignation. It was a sad end to an impressive career, but the stakes were too high for loose talk.

Meanwhile, on January 14, 2019, Robert Lloyd Schellenberg of Abbotsford, BC, was sentenced to death in Liaoning for trying to smuggle

222 kilograms of methamphetamine to Australia from China. Schellenberg, who claimed innocence, had previously been convicted and sentenced to fifteen years in prison. Legal experts believe the death sentence was linked to the arrest of Meng, and he remains imprisoned in China under sentence of death, a victim of politics.

The Chinese insisted that the detention of Kovrig and Spavor had nothing to do with the Meng case, but few believed that argument. The *Globe and Mail* reported in 2023 that Spavor is seeking a settlement from the federal government because Kovrig was engaged in intelligence gathering and implicated him without his knowledge. Soon after, Kovrig responded in an interview in the *Toronto Star*, rejecting the allegation that he had anything to do with intelligence gathering. We will likely never know the truth.

Beijing had clearly ordered its diplomats to behave belligerently. In an op-ed in the *Hill Times*, China's ambassador to Canada, Lu Shaye, laid it on thick: "The reason why some people are used to arrogantly adopting double standards is due to Western egotism and white supremacy. What they have been doing is not showing respect for the rule of law but mocking and trampling the rule of law."

Canada kept working the phones and won public support from the United Kingdom, France, Germany, the European Union, the United States, and Australia, drawing attention to the crime China was committing against the two Canadians. In late January 2019, 27 diplomats from seven countries and 116 scholars and academics from 19 countries signed an open letter calling for China to free the men, pointing out that both were engaged in work aimed at creating bridges. "We who share Mr. Kovrig's and Mr. Spavor's enthusiasm for building genuine, productive and lasting relationships must now be more cautious about travelling and working in China and engaging our Chinese counterparts."

———

TRUDEAU WORKED HARD TO bring about the release of the two Michaels. When Zita Astravas went through the consular files in the PMO, she was struck by "how much time and effort he spent on that, on personal engagement with foreign leaders, etc., in the pursuit of those wrongfully held." Trudeau appointed Dominic Barton as Canada's ambassador to China after McCallum's departure, and he in turn did what he could to get the men freed. The former managing director of McKinsey & Company, Barton had lived in China from 2004 to 2009. As an unusually effective businessman, he had the connections and experience to try to move the file.

The Chinese were not going to give up Canada's innocent hostages until their princess was free to leave Vancouver, so Barton worked on the Americans, whose case against Meng had started the whole horrible mess. He visited the Canadians in their prisons, exchanging messages with them using code because their Chinese jailers did not allow them to meet privately. He spent weeks in Washington, twisting arms in the new Biden administration and trying to get the Democrats to sort this out, which they were reluctant to do. Any record of interfering in the Justice Department could hurt them, they feared, when the department eventually got around to charging Trump. Trudeau pressed Joe Biden on the issue, and Barton pressed the Justice Department and Huawei executives. When Meng's legal team realized she would not beat the extradition case, they agreed to consider a deferred prosecution agreement in which, by agreeing to the charges against her, she was allowed to board a plane for China.

On September 9, Biden and Xi had a ninety-minute telephone call aimed at getting the bilateral relationship back on track. That discussion seems to have broken the logjam, and the greasy quid pro quo was sorted out that allowed the hostage exchange—an unsavoury end to the whole business.

On September 24, 2021, after 1,020 days in detention in China, Michael Spavor and Michael Kovrig were finally released. Trudeau announced the happy news in Ottawa, with Foreign Affairs Minister Marc Garneau by his side. He flew out to Calgary to greet them—and Dominic Barton—on the tarmac when the Royal Canadian Air Force plane Canada sent for them touched down. It was a moment of joy, seeing the men in the arms of their loved ones again after losing almost three years of their lives to the Chinese Communists.

Trudeau had done what he could to get the Michaels out without giving in to the Chrétienites who had called for Canada to unilaterally release Meng, giving in to hostage diplomacy. In an interview in 2024, Trudeau told me that he never considered doing that because Canada, as a medium-sized country, depends on the international rule of law. "The rules-based order matters," he said, and Canada can't afford to break the rules. "It's not that we're not going to break our extradition treaty with the United States because they would be mad at us. We're not going to break our extradition treaty because Canada signed an extradition treaty, and we commit to it. So if we 'accidentally' let Meng out a back door to get on a plane and go home, that would be us breaking the rules that we are saying matter. And the fact that we got through that horrible situation for those two Michaels by being completely anchored, and then having integrity around those rules, was really important."

But the entire drawn-out incident revealed the limits of Canadian power. In a multipolar world, when China's wolf warriors challenged us, we had no recourse but to plead for help from Uncle Sam. If Trump had won re-election in 2020, our pleading would have been in vain. Canada looked weak because, in foreign affairs, it is weak.

PART THREE

IN A FLOODED ZONE

2019–2023

A prince can never make himself safe against a hostile people.
There are too many of them.

Niccolò Machiavelli, *The Prince*

11

A PLAGUE AND ITS CASUALTIES

I was in Florida when I first learned about COVID-19. I had bought an old boat to sail to the Caribbean and was fixing it up in a marina in Punta Gorda. On March 11, 2020—the day the NBA suspended play for the season—I listened to a webinar by Dr. David Fisman, an epidemiologist at the University of Toronto. After a while I put down my sander and gave the doctor my full attention. Fisman said he had been startled by the news from Europe, where the Italian papers were adding extra sections to accommodate all the obituaries, and he didn't believe Canada was ready. "Everyone should be very scared," he warned. COVID was coming, and it would take a terrible toll.

I called Fisman and wrote a column for *Maclean's* titled "Cancel Your March Break." The same day, Ontario premier Doug Ford told families they should board their flights for sun destinations during March break: "I just want the families, and their children, to have a good time. Go away, have a good time, enjoy yourself—and we're going to be monitoring the situation."

For Justin Trudeau, it was already too late to keep the virus out. That same day, the Prime Minister's Office announced that Sophie Grégoire

Trudeau had come back from London with COVID. She and Margaret Trudeau had flown over for a WE Day event at Wembley Stadium, a celebration of youth volunteering organized by the Canadian charity. The program was headlined by actor Idris Elba. On Instagram, Sophie posted a picture of herself with Elba and some other British celebrities with a vague but cheerful message: "My heart is full after spending time working with my own family and the WE family. Our message in London: Show yourself love and offer that same love to the world." She likely caught the coronavirus in London and then apparently gave it to Elba. After he saw the news about Grégoire Trudeau, he got tested and learned he was also positive.

Rattled by the apparent indifference of Floridians to the coming plague—the dad bands were still packing them into the bars on the boardwalk in Punta Gorda—I moved my boat to storage, rented a car, and started driving north, twenty-four hundred kilometres, from palm trees to snow, past many golden arches and Exxons. I was part of an enormous movement of Canadians coming home—the flight of the snowbirds.

On March 16, Trudeau announced that Canada was finally taking dramatic action, closing its borders to most foreigners. "If you're abroad, it's time for you to come home," he said. About a million Canadians returned that week—in planes from airports around the world, and a huge wave from trailer parks and retirement villages in Florida and other US states. It was an unprecedented influx.

Trudeau had called Canadians home, but there was no plan to safely handle all the returnees. The airports were a mess. Travellers were jammed together in waiting areas. Masks were still not recommended, and few were wearing them—a shocking contrast for Canadians returning from Asia, where everyone was masked. On March 13, Public Safety Minister Bill Blair had tweeted: "We have enhanced screening measures in place at all international airports, as well as land/rail/marine ports of entry. We are taking the necessary steps to ensure that Canadians are safe in the face of COVID-19." But travellers were quick to respond on social media with stories and pictures showing that those measures were not being implemented. Glen Canning, a Nova Scotian resident in Toronto, shared pictures of a jammed terminal at Toronto's Pearson International Airport: "I've been in the Canada customs line at Pearson for over an hour along with hundreds of people. Six agents on duty, zero screening, no masks, no sanitizer in site. This is as unsafe as it can get."

Dr. Theresa Tam, the chief public health officer of Canada, was trying to get the message out. "We are asking that all travellers that come back self-isolate," she said to reporters on March 15. "This is a voluntary self-isolation. It is impossible to keep tabs on every single traveller who comes in. This is a social phenomenon. This is a societal response, and everybody must take that responsibility. Public Health is going to do what it can."

But travellers weren't consistently being advised to self-isolate everywhere. It remains a mystery why the measures announced by Trudeau and Bill Blair were not being implemented.

———

CANADA WAS NOT AMONG the countries that responded successfully to COVID's early spread. South Korea, Singapore, Taiwan, Australia, and New Zealand all saw what was coming and took early action to contain the disease, closing borders and imposing mask mandates and other public health measures, buying precious time. Canada moved more slowly.

On March 5, Trudeau told reporters that Canada wouldn't be rushed into a "knee-jerk reaction" to COVID by restricting international travel, as other countries had done. "We recognize there are countries that make different decisions. The decisions we make are based on the best recommendations of the World Health Organization (WHO) and the tremendous health experts who work within Canada and around the world."

That delay was a mistake. Donald Trump had imposed travel restrictions on China in February, taking a helpful measure for probably the wrong reasons. On the same day that Trudeau warned against knee-jerk reactions, Australian prime minister Scott Morrison extended that country's travel bans to foreigners coming from many countries, including China, Iran, and South Korea. Trudeau, presumably, was listening to Dr. Tam, who'd told reporters a day earlier that closing borders was not a good idea. Time has shown that was bad advice. The experts aren't always right, and their recommendations are not always apolitical.

Dr. Tam should have been giving the best advice available anywhere. Born in Hong Kong and raised in the United Kingdom, she was chief of respiratory disease at Canada's Centre for Infectious Disease Control and Prevention in 2003 when a Toronto woman contracted SARS on a trip to Hong Kong and brought it back to Canada, where it quickly spread through an ill-equipped Ontario health system. Tam literally wrote the book on how Canada should manage a pandemic. In 2006, she co-authored *The Canadian Pandemic Influenza Plan for the Health Sector*, a complex, detailed 550-page map for Canada facing a viral invasion. With a role as an expert at the World Health Organization, she was well placed to understand the threat from the mysterious viral pneumonia spreading in Wuhan, China. Yet she was slow to sound the alarm.

On January 23, Dr. Tam was among the dozen advisors who helped WHO director general Dr. Tedros Adhanom Ghebreyesus decide it was not yet time to declare the coronavirus "a global health emergency." Health officials have to balance the need to impose travel restrictions with the interests of the countries that would be affected by them. In order to maintain the co-operation of any country acting as a disease vector, they can't counsel draconian measures that will destroy their economies. Making those judgment calls isn't easy. With COVID, they were wrong, and we would have been better off if Trudeau had ignored her advice and acted more quickly to shut down the massive movement of people in and out of Canada.

Quebec was hit hardest early on. It has travel corridors with Europe

and the northeastern United States, and its March break was a week earlier than other provinces. When Quebecers returned from trips south,
they went to visit their relatives in care homes, infecting vulnerable seniors. On April 11, a report from Dorval, on the West Island of Montreal,
made it clear how bad things would get. The *Montreal Gazette*'s Aaron
Derfel learned that residents' family members had observed a stream of
funeral vans coming and going from Résidence Herron, a private home
in such dire conditions that its frightened staff abandoned it. When in-
spectors arrived, they found few people working and patients in filthy
diapers, so dehydrated they couldn't speak. Families, spending as much
as $10,000 a month to keep their loved ones there, were horrified. Que-
bec's coroner found that thirty-eight residents died at the home between
March 26 and April 16.

On April 15, with 14,860 COVID cases and 487 deaths in his province,
Quebec premier François Legault asked Trudeau to send military help for
long-term care homes. A week later, Ford asked for troops in Ontario as
well. As the death toll mounted among vulnerable seniors in care homes
across Canada, many of them were dying in conditions that would not
have been allowed in the poorest of countries, where family members
were not prevented from coming in to care for their loved ones as they
were in Canada.

Canadian Armed Forces personnel recorded their observations of
what they saw at five LTC homes in Ontario in a report that was made
public in May 2020. It paints a picture of neglect and maltreatment that
is difficult to absorb. The homes had been understaffed for weeks. Skel-
eton crews, supported by temporary agency staff, could not maintain
whatever standards of care had existed before the pandemic. Supplies
were kept locked up by cost-conscious management. CAF personnel
observed residents who were dehydrated, malnourished, dirty, and suffering from untreated injuries. They saw cockroaches and flies, and
stacks of stinking days-old meal trays next to patients' beds. Infected
and uninfected patients were in rooms together. Disabled residents

had not been turned or put in their wheelchairs. Staff were not using personal protective equipment appropriately or disinfecting medical devices to prevent infection.

What happened in care homes in Ontario and Quebec was disgusting, with scores dying miserable deaths. Those who could have saved them, or eased their suffering, will never face accountability or justice.

———

TRUDEAU'S GOVERNMENT FAILED TO take dramatic early steps to stop the disease from entering Canada—as Taiwan and Australia did. He might have slowed the disease and saved lives if he had, but once we all knew what we were dealing with, the Liberals made sure that Canadians would not go broke.

On February 27, Bill Morneau was meeting with senior finance officials to plan for that year's budget—due on March 30—ahead of a meeting with Trudeau planned for the next day to discuss options. In the middle of the meeting, the Toronto Stock Exchange halted trading. Markets around the world had been falling for weeks as investors pondered their portfolios in a world stricken by a pandemic. That day, global markets lost $1.83 trillion in value. Amid those losses, the TSX shut down at 2 p.m. because of a technical "problem with order entry."

Tyler Meredith, who had left the PMO to work as Morneau's director of policy, remembers the scene. "Someone rushes in and says, 'The TSX has just halted trading. The market is down. Trading has been suspended. Things are going wild.'"

Morneau left to get the head of the TSX on the phone. It was an ominous sign. After the phone call, he called Meredith, Elder Marques, and some other political staff into his office. "I remember vividly that the snow is coming down outside," says Meredith. "It's pretty dark that afternoon. And Bill says to us, 'I believe that we are going to have a recession. I believe that COVID is going to cause a major economic recession. And the only thing we can hope for is that we have enough time between now and then that we can present a budget and then prepare ourselves for that.'"

In fact, there would be no budget that year, no budget until April 2021, and Morneau wouldn't deliver it. He and the PMO would soon be focused on the biggest bailout in Canadian history—a massive cash infusion aimed at keeping Canadians from going broke or losing their houses. The first and most important program was announced on March 25: the Canada Emergency Response Benefit—CERB—a $2,000-a-month payment for those thrown out of work by COVID. Suddenly, many Canadians were able to stay home and order Uber Eats rather than go to the office. This cash inflow kept the economy going and also kept everyone, except Uber Eats drivers and all the other essential workers, from mixing and spreading the disease.

Morneau and Trudeau rolled out dozens of programs in the months that followed, identifying sectors in crisis and throwing money at them. They worked with the Office of the Superintendent of Financial Institutions and the Bank of Canada to keep Canadian institutions liquid. It was the most aggressive response among the G7 countries. Trudeau, bearded and isolating at Rideau Cottage, appeared on TV and announced a new program almost every day. The debt piled up. In March 2020, the federal debt was $721 billion. A year later, it was $1.2 trillion. Morneau was uncomfortable with it, as with a lot of decisions the government took while he was finance minister, but he reasoned it was best for Ottawa to borrow. The federal government could borrow at the lowest rates, and it had fiscal capacity to spare.

There was grumbling about all that money going out the door, which became louder as the pandemic wore on. Businesses found it difficult to get anyone to work when people could get $2,000 a month to stay at home, where they wouldn't risk getting infected. It rankled, but that was the point—if everyone stayed home, it was hard for COVID to spread. The health care system was at the breaking point, with exhausted doctors and nurses intubating deathly ill patients around the clock. The income supports helped to reduce the pressure.

Some of the spending is hard to justify. Economist Miles Corak, whose work on inequality was a major influence on Trudeau policy makers, published a paper in 2021 in which he pointed out that the 75 percent wage subsidy to employers cost $286 billion, four times more than the $73 billion CERB. It funnelled huge sums to institutions that appear not to have needed it. The Royal Ottawa Golf Club, where senior civil servants mingle with the most powerful lobbyists in the country, and both kinds of Ottawa senators—the kind who lose in the playoffs and those who doze in the Red Chamber—received more than $1 million from the program. The program cost a lot for every job it saved—as much as $25,000 per person month of employment, according to one estimate.

Morneau had not approved such a big spend. His officials worked frantically to figure out how to shape the wage subsidy and sent the report to Trudeau by 10 p.m. the night before it was announced. "At a press gathering the next morning, about 12 hours after he had agreed with all aspects of the program I had presented," he wrote in *Where To from Here*, "I watched and listened as he introduced the program to Canada." He was alarmed to learn, with everyone else watching, that Trudeau was announcing a figure "significantly higher" than what they had agreed upon.

This largesse was typical of Trudeau in that period. In his book, Morneau complains that after he and his officials would come up with a plan and submit it to the PMO, they would then "discover that the decision announced . . . to the public was framed according to the impact the PMO believed it would make on the daily news cycle."

The real power was being exercised in the PMO, where senior advisor Ben Chin was influential on communications, and Mike McNair, who had left at the end of 2019, returned to help the government figure out how to put money into people's pockets. McNair points out that people can quibble with individual programs, but the fact they were able to get the money out at all was extraordinary. "Part of the problem too was our systems in place in government—you didn't have a lot of mechanisms by which you get significant amount of cash out the door. And so this was a way to do it that worked and was successful."

The wage subsidy was crucial because it allowed the government to do two things. "One, convince employers don't lay any more people off," says McNair. "Because if you've taken the hits to your revenues, that means you qualify for the wage subsidy. We'll subsidize that and keep you going. But two, it was a way to inject very quickly a lot of money into the economy."

Finance officials could not figure out how to get so much money to businesses so quickly. "The prime minister was calling time on the play," says Meredith. "He was like, 'Guys, I need an answer. I need a program. Every other country is going ahead with the program. What is our program going to be?' And they were unable to come up with an answer. So it fell to people like Mike and me to sit there and write it out."

Funnelling the money through employers—keeping people linked to their jobs—helped when people eventually returned to work. "We put more weight on the wage subsidy than on the direct handouts," says Meredith. "And that seemed to work better because what it did was it preserved the relationship between the employer and the employee . . . When the economy could reopen, people could go around and spend all this extra cash that we'd given them and they hadn't been spending on other stuff cause they were sitting at home."

Still, huge amounts of money were wasted. A 2022 auditor general's report found $27.4 billion in suspicious COVID-19 benefit payments: "The Canada Revenue Agency and Employment and Social Development Canada did not manage the selected COVID-19 programs efficiently." Critics, including Pierre Poilievre, insist the government was too slow to taper off supports, leading to inflationary pressure.

Kevin Page, a former senior Finance official who served as the first parliamentary budget officer and founded the Institute of Fiscal Studies and Democracy, thinks the Liberals deserve credit, even if some people got money they didn't need or deserve. "The moral hazard was, you can't have too many checks and balances and still flow money really quickly. If you look at just the data, the drop-off when you turn off the lights in the economy, all the social distancing, it just was so dramatic, right? We've never seen a quarter-to-quarter decline like that since the Great Depression. Even then, I don't even know if we had one that steep. It was enormous. And so those early, big programs to get money into households and businesses, they flew the money out the door, right? And you want people to get that money so that they're not going bankrupt in that sort of environment. They could pay the rent, pay the mortgage, put food on the table—and they did that."

———

ON APRIL 17, 2020, five days after British prime minister Boris Johnson was released from the hospital where he had been treated for COVID-19, the UK government announced that it had established a vaccine task force. In Canada, Dr. Alan Bernstein decided to write a letter to the Trudeau government proposing it do something similar.

Bernstein is the president and CEO of CIFAR, a Canadian research-granting organization. Before that, he headed an HIV vaccine organization in New York and the Canadian Institutes of Health Research, a federal agency. He knows a lot about vaccines, and a lot about how government works. When Bernstein's email arrived, Canadian health officials paid attention. "The government acted very quickly," he says. "There was a mandate put together. I think there's roughly twelve of us and co-chairs were put together and it went through Cabinet . . . It took them about three or four weeks to do all that, which for the government is pretty fast. And we started, and it ruined my summer, basically."

Bernstein and the other task force members, including pharma executives and scientists, met online twice a week, going through submissions from would-be vaccine manufacturers, hundreds of pages of documents, looking for winners. They made recommendations to the government, which negotiated the deals. That led to contracts with eight companies, including five that by February 2021 would either be distributing vaccines or awaiting Health Canada approval: Moderna, Pfizer-BioNTech, Astra-Zeneca, Johnson & Johnson, and Novavax.

Canada ensured access to huge numbers of vaccines—eventually. In February, Canada was trailing not just Israel, the United States, and Britain, but France, Germany, Morocco, Turkey, Serbia, and Chile. Canadians could see, every day, evidence of rapid progress in the United States. For most of the pandemic, Trump bungled pandemic management, giving mixed signals and bad advice to Americans, but his vaccine moonshot, Operation Warp Speed, was a huge success. As of February 19, Canada had distributed 1.8 million vaccine doses. The United States government had distributed 78 million.

The opposition attacks wrote themselves. For everything Trump did wrong—and at times he appeared to be an agent for the virus—he got one big thing right. Canada was slower, but Bernstein says voters should understand that Canada doesn't have that much leverage with the pharma giants. "The US has ten times the population," he said. "So they have ten times the buying power we do. So where we're buying a total from any one company of 40 million vaccines . . . Let's say then the US is buying 400 million. If you're the company, who are you going to pay more attention to? I think the answer's obvious."

The Trudeau government was slower off the mark than the United States or Britain, but eventually caught up. By May 2021, half the Canadian population had received at least one shot—about a month behind the United States. By July, Canada had surpassed the United States, reflecting a better public health system and a less divisive political culture. Hucksters and paranoiacs were spreading toxic anti-vaccine messages through social media in both countries, but in the United States they were often amplified by conservative politicians and media outlets, which saw Big Brother behind the push to share life-saving vaccines. That cost lives. A Yale study of mortality rates revealed that death rates among registered Republicans were 43 percent higher than the rate among Democrats, which appeared to be a result of conservative suspicion and misinformation.

Overall, Canada did much better than the United States during the pandemic. We lost more than fifty thousand people to the disease, compared with 1.1 million in the United States. In the G7, only Japan had a lower death rate, likely a consequence of a strong public health system, a cultural willingness to act collectively, and a lower incidence of obesity—a major risk factor in COVID. Whatever else people think about the Liberal record in government, a lot of Canadians are alive who would not be if the Trudeau team had messed up the response.

———

THROUGHOUT THE PANDEMIC, TRUDEAU held news conferences from Rideau Cottage, announcing new programs, offering mildly upbeat messages, standing socially distanced on his front porch, wearing a salt-and-pepper beard and shaggy hair. Like a lot of Canadians, he was working from home, trying to run the country from his office there while the family life continued in the rest of the house. "He'd have to step out in front of his house where his family lives and do a press conference every single day for which he prepared before, and after which he would have meetings, endless meetings with his team, even with his Cabinet about tomorrow's announcement of tomorrow's policy," says Cameron Ahmad.

In those news conferences, he often sounded like a teacher trying to keep the spirits of his students up after a field trip took an unexpected turn for the worse. He refrained from naming and shaming premiers who were implementing policies that would cost lives, emphasizing the advice that the feds were offering but declining to point to Jason Kenney, for example, and warn that he was going to kill a bunch of Albertans by opening up too soon. It may be that he was wisely respecting provincial jurisdiction, keeping the vital working relationship going with other levels of government, or it may be that he instinctively shrinks from public confrontation. "He's funny because you've got the boxer narrative thing, right?" says a staffer who worked closely with him for years. "And he is a fighter and all of that, but he doesn't like to be seen as that. He likes to be seen as the uniter guy, and that means not throwing a punch, it means not picking a villain in the story."

—

ON APRIL 5, 2020, in the early days of the pandemic, Bill Morneau told Justin Trudeau in a phone call that he had been thinking about the way COVID was disrupting the lives of students and that the government should "do something to make sure their dreams weren't derailed and they could continue to pursue their education." Trudeau agreed, and the next day Morneau asked his deputy at Finance to talk to other departments about how they could tackle this problem.

Two days later, Morneau's friend Craig Kielburger, co-founder of the WE Charity, spoke to Mary Ng, minister of small business, telling her about WE's Social Entrepreneurship Program proposal, which he forwarded to her office on April 11. A lot of bureaucratic paper shuffling followed, and on June 25, Trudeau announced the Canada Student Service Grant—a $912 million program that would provide $1,000-to-$5,000 grants for post-secondary students doing volunteer work—to be administered by the WE Charity. When asked why that particular charity had been chosen to hand out the money, Trudeau said they were the "only possible option," that the public service had "determined that the WE organization was the only one that could deliver that program as ambitious as it was this summer." This explanation came as a surprise to the YMCA, the United Way, and other national volunteer organizations with more experience and capabilities, but they were not given the chance to make proposals.

Rachel Wernick, sister to Michael, an assistant deputy minister with Employment and Social Development Canada, later told the Finance Committee that she was the one behind the recommendation of WE Charity. Emails released to the committee showed that an assistant deputy minister at Finance had let her know that the Kielburgers and Morneau were "besties," which was true. His daughter worked for the organization, another daughter had done so, and he had taken two trips to see WE Charity projects overseas. The charity was linked to Trudeau as well. His mother and brother had received $300,000 in speaking fees from the group, and Sophie had also spoken but not taken a fee. Both the NDP and the Conservatives wrote to Mario Dion, the ethics commissioner, and asked him to investigate.

Dion eventually found that Trudeau was in the clear, but that Morneau had violated the Conflict of Interest Act because Marc and Craig Kielburger were his friends. As Morneau prepared to testify, he discovered he had failed to reimburse the charity for $41,000 in travel expenses related to a junket to Kenya.

Poilievre roasted him at committee. "It was a $41,000 expense," he said. "You didn't know about a $41,000 expense? How is that even possible?"

Morneau and his wife had donated more money to the charity than he received as a benefit. He was not looking to line his pockets, but he came across as self-satisfied and chummy, an elitist sharing tax dollars with his friends—smug, well-meaning wealthy people who resented having to explain themselves to taxpayers. Morneau was sloppy and, when this carelessness was exposed, his strongest defence was that he was so rich his honesty should not be questioned. This defence in no way endeared him to the vast majority of Canadians.

The Kielburgers, who were also put under the magnifying glass of the national media, seemed habitually pleased with themselves, do-gooders who resented having to answer questions about their involvement with a grant of almost $1 billion. Some of the journalism that was published during that period is now the subject of legal proceedings, and the charity's supporters say the organization was badly treated by opposition politicians and media that smeared it unfairly to drag down the government. The Kielburgers ran a charity that accomplished good work in desperately poor countries. They also created a for-profit company that arranged voluntourism, held huge youth rallies, and created corporate partnerships that critics found ethically questionable. During the scandal, a number of board members resigned.

It was kind of an empty scandal, in a way. No tax money was misspent. So far as we are aware, nobody sought personal advantage, but the whole episode raised questions about the judgment of both Morneau and Trudeau. Even if they didn't seek money for themselves, they helped people who offered inducements to members of their families. Are Justin's mother and brother such great speakers they were worth tens of thousands of dollars in speaking fees, or were the people behind the charity trying to get close to the government? Likely, they were worth the money. Margaret has performed a successful one-woman show. Sacha can pack a room. But we have conflict-of-interest rules so that we don't have to ask ourselves such questions. Both Morneau and Trudeau were too close to the charity to be giving it $912 million of our money. They ought to have known that.

The whole idea was dropped early in July, which meant there would be no program for students that summer. Trudeau apologized: "I made a mistake in not recusing myself immediately from the discussions given our family's history, and I'm sincerely sorry about not having done that," he said. "I didn't know the details of how much [my mother] was getting paid by various organizations, but I should have and I deeply regret that."

Morneau also said he was sorry: "I did not recuse myself from the discussions on this topic and, given the fact that my daughter works for the organization in an unrelated branch, I now realize I should have in order to avoid any perception of conflict. I apologize for not doing so, and moving forward, I will recuse myself from any future discussions related to WE."

But in his book, Morneau expresses resentment at his critics and the media, who are ultimately to blame. He writes that the Dion report "confirmed I had no opportunity to further my own interests, but that a potential conflict of interest meant I should have recused myself from the decision on WE. You may have missed the story. Most people did."

Morneau's skin was too thin for politics.

———

MORNEAU HAD HAD ENOUGH of Trudeau, enough of the whole thing. He resigned in August, saying he had never intended "to run for more than two federal election cycles." "Since I'm not running again, and since I expect we will have a long and challenging recovery, I think it's important that the prime minister has by his side a finance minister who has that longer-term vision," he said. He was interested in making a bid to be secretary general of the Organisation for Economic Co-operation and Development. The government supported him in that endeavour, but he didn't win enough support from other countries and ended his candidacy early in 2021. He went to Yale to lecture and now serves on the board of the Canadian Imperial Bank of Commerce.

In his book, Morneau describes his last meeting with Trudeau, on August 17, 2020. He went to see him at Rideau Cottage, where they met alone, which was rare. His criticism of the remote prime minister echoes that of Jody Wilson-Raybould. "That kind of thing simply didn't happen in Justin Trudeau's world. Virtually any topic you wanted to discuss with the prime minister—official or informal, strategy or gossip—had to be shared in the presence of members of his staff. This was an acknowledged fact among everyone who had reason to converse with him. While he appeared as a charming individual who could mingle among crowds of strangers, sharing hugs, smiles and selfies, he seemed to avoid solitary encounters."

Morneau complained to Trudeau about leaks that cast him in a bad light. Most damaging was a *Globe and Mail* story in which Bob Fife reported that Trudeau was "uncertain whether Mr. Morneau is the right fit to navigate the country into a post-pandemic economic recovery" and was considering shuffling him. Trudeau, the story said, had been disappointed to learn about Morneau's trips with the WE Charity. The story was a hint: get out or be pushed. Morneau saw no choice but to quit.

Trudeau told him he had no idea about the source of any leaks. Morneau didn't buy it, and how could he? Trudeau's senior people can't brief against the finance minister without the boss's approval. At an impasse, the two men agreed that Morneau had reached the end of the road, and Trudeau agreed to support him in his quest for the OECD job.

Mark Carney, the superstar central banker, was then being romanced by the Trudeau people, sought after as a potential replacement for Morneau. Seeing Morneau being treated so shabbily seems to have given Carney pause, and he did not allow himself to be seduced. They spooked him by putting the shiv in Morneau.

It is a sad story, an unfortunate end to a political career that started with promise, a partnership that was productive and useful until it wasn't. Morneau was a talented manager and deserves credit for implementing, often reluctantly, a once-in-a-generation re-engineering of the Canadian welfare state. And he is right to blame Trudeau for the breakdown in the relationship. During the pandemic, the prime minister asked other people to start to do his job for him, pushing out programs and policies that Morneau had not agreed to. Morneau was correct to complain that Trudeau's people were making some decisions based on "sound bites, not sound policy," and it is clear that they, and not he, were making the policies.

"Justin Trudeau has many talents as a politician, all of them apparent to anyone who observes him in a public forum," Morneau writes. "But he also possesses a number of weaknesses. These had become evident during discussions of programs dealing with the pandemic, and one of the most striking was his lack of focus on policy details. Leaving the development of policy responses to his PMO staff meant that debates were conducted and conclusions reached without his presence. The real clashes happened over things that we had never discussed."

It does not seem like the best way to run an office or a country. But Trudeau didn't want to have discussions with Morneau. "He doesn't want to have the direct confrontation," says one senior staffer who participated in the tense wrangling over policy that led to Morneau's departure. "That isn't who he is. He doesn't like to be confrontational. It actually is worse, because what it then means is that it's up to staff to have these kind of debates."

Trudeau would not say, "We need to do X. Let's debate it, or I'm going to tell you to do X." He let his staff wrangle over the files, treated Morneau like one of them, avoided the confrontation, and eventually his people leaked to Fife that Morneau should maybe be making other career plans.

On August 18, 2020, Chrystia Freeland was sworn in as finance minister, the first woman to hold the job.

12

A $600 MILLION CABINET SHUFFLE

A week after Bill Morneau resigned as finance minister, Erin O'Toole won the leadership of the Conservative Party. He beat Peter MacKay, who began as the front-runner but lost steam as the race went along.

When the campaign started, MacKay, a charismatic and competitive progressive Conservative from Pictou County, Nova Scotia, looked like the perfect anti-Trudeau—a mirror image in a way. The son of Elmer MacKay, who served in Mulroney's Cabinet, MacKay had the pedigree and a star quality similar to Trudeau's, the ability to turn heads when he entered a room. He was, like Trudeau, somewhat gaffe-prone, inclined to say things that later required clarification, but that is not a fatal quality in a politician. He had good name recognition and a network of connections going back decades, from his leadership of the Progressive Conservatives and his time as foreign affairs and defence minister. He is not a Red Tory, in the mould of Robert Stanfield or Joe Clark, but his mother, Macha, was a peace activist, and her influence seemed to make him more open to progressive concerns than most Tories in Harper's party. He also had many frenemies, particularly former Reformers in the west who didn't want to see someone from the Mulroney wing take over their party. He could be competitive to the point of arrogance and had sharp elbows, which left some in his own wing of the party hoping he wouldn't end up in charge. He began with a commanding lead, but in March, when COVID struck, the party had no choice but to suspend the race and postpone the convention. That delay gave O'Toole a chance.

MacKay's accurate but impolitic description of social conservative issues as a "stinking albatross" hurt the feelings of social conservatives, who are increasingly powerful in the party. In May, Jason Kenney, a trusted figure to the devout, endorsed O'Toole, saying he respected everyone in the big tent. He took a shot at MacKay. "No one will have their deeply held beliefs dismissed as 'stinking albatrosses' under Erin O'Toole's leadership." MacKay still might have managed to win, but fellow Nova Scotian Fred DeLorey—one of the best organizers in the country, who had run in MacKay's old riding in 2015—had been on O'Toole's team in the previous leadership race, and he stayed there. MacKay's team, in contrast, relied more on expensive strategists than ground-level organizers, and he outspent O'Toole by more than $1 million.

O'Toole positioned himself as a "true Blue Conservative," the candidate of the right. I found that odd: I had watched MacKay and O'Toole over the years and would have described them as ideologically identical, despite the positions they might take for tactical reasons in a leadership race. Both men are blue eastern Tories—a shade to the left of Stephen Harper, about where Jim Flaherty hung his hat—pro-business, pro-petroleum, pro-military, and pro-law and order, advocating lower taxes and smaller government, but not that much lower or smaller. They were both in the sweet spot for Canadian Conservatives—conservative enough to be a real alternative to the Liberals, but not to a degree that would scare the suburban voters who decide Canadian elections.

The difference between MacKay and O'Toole came down to personal qualities, the effectiveness of their campaigns, and their positioning. DeLorey and O'Toole knew that the only way to beat MacKay was from the right, so that's where they went. They hired Jeff Ballingall, who had founded the social media brands Ontario Proud and Canada Proud, to run campaign social media. Ballingall knew how to crank up engagement with clickable memes, and he sent his flying monkeys out into cyberspace to connect with all the angry old grumps who log into Facebook, sharing MS Paint graphics that portrayed climate change as a hoax. He needed to convince that base that O'Toole, not MacKay, was a real Conservative. Some of it was silly. "I'm not the media's candidate," said one O'Toole meme. "I'm not going to go Liberal-light to earn the fake approval of the Press Gallery. Add your name if you're with me." It was ridiculous. O'Toole was a Press Gallery *darling*. He didn't have to get our fake approval—he had the real thing.

O'Toole promised to respect the conscience rights of medical providers and kept his door open to the social conservatives, including Leslyn Lewis, a corporate lawyer who had emerged as the standard-bearer of the devout. As in the previous leadership race that Scheer won, the so-cons again played kingmaker and gave O'Toole the votes he needed to top MacKay.

In his victory speech, O'Toole identified the party's top priority: "Today, you have given me a clear mission: To unite our party." But the party, as usual, would remain divided, with deep antipathy below the surface. On the night of the convention, for instance, MacKay received no sympathy from Scheer's camp. After the results came in, Hamish Marshall, who had been Scheer's campaign manager, sent reporter Alex Boutilier a text: "Peter MacKay losing this leadership is like missing a shot on an empty net."

The race took place because Scheer had been ousted kicking and screaming after his old friend Kory Teneycke decided that the party must have a new leader if it wanted to be competitive in the next election. He found "whistle-blowers" who revealed that Scheer had used party money to pay for his children's private school fees—not what donors have in mind.

Scheer did not seem pleased to have to give up his job. At the convention, he gave a fire-and-brimstone farewell speech denouncing communism—"Nobody ever got shot trying to jump the wall into East Berlin or paddled a raft to get to Cuba"—and media people, whom he seemed to see as Communist fellow travellers. "Don't take the left-wing media narrative as fact. Please check out smart, independent, objective organizations like the Post Millennial, or True North," he said, naming right-wing digital start-ups with shadowy funding sources.

The mask was gone. Scheer, who had often had drinks with reporters during the campaign, affable and friendly, was revealed as an unhappy warrior, a conservative who blamed the media for his loss to Trudeau in 2019. O'Toole, in contrast, presented himself as a cheerful unifier, a middle-of-the-road dad who could scarcely contain his excitement as he shared all his great plans for this amazing country.

A former navigator on the navy's ancient Sea King helicopters, O'Toole had worked as a corporate lawyer before he ran for Parliament. He seemed to me a good representative of the officer class of the Royal Canadian Air Force, with a sense of duty and well suited to the job at hand. Somewhat cherubic, with a ready smile and receding hair, he didn't light up a room as Trudeau or MacKay did but was thoughtful and earnest, a bit of a policy wonk, with boring but carefully considered policy positions at the ready. He was hard-working and ambitious, driven to succeed, perhaps to a fault.

The day after the leadership convention, he held a news conference in which he veered suddenly toward the middle, smiling, answering questions, saying he was personally pro-choice and would march in a Pride parade under the right circumstances. "I am an MP with a clear track record for standing up for human rights, whether it's women, whether it's the LGBTQ community. I won the leadership of the Conservative Party as a pro-choice Conservative MP, and that's how I'm going to lead as leader of the opposition and that's how I will be as prime minister." The True Blue Conservative was suddenly sounding progressive, which was disquieting to the more strident Tories who had voted the day before for the conservative choice.

DeLorey, looking back, thinks they made a mistake. "We made him True Blue, and we abandoned that way too fast. And that fucked us. It was too much. It was stupid."

The pivot raised doubts among these Conservatives, but if they had buyer's remorse, they had to keep it to themselves for the time being. The Liberals were up in the polls after their successful pandemic management, and they were being urged to call an election and win a majority government. Chrystia Freeland was settling into her new role as finance minister, where, merely by accepting the position, she had broken a glass ceiling. That was no comfort to Bay Street, accustomed to having a finance minister with business experience, or to fiscal conservatives, who were worried about the deficit—projected to come in at $343 billion. Tories who had doubts about O'Toole could not afford to express them because the alternative was more Trudeau, but they would remember their new leader's opportunistic flexibility.

———

AS THE PANDEMIC GROUND on, with lockdowns lifted and reimposed, and stressed-out nurses and doctors working past their breaking point, Trudeau kept appearing on television screens, trying to reassure people and remind them of all the hard work the government was doing to look after everyone. O'Toole received a post-convention bump in the polls and then sagged—and kept on sagging for the better part of a year as the Liberals kept the focus on their pandemic recovery plans, and voters, stuck at home, looked on fearfully and approvingly.

O'Toole tried to maintain his viability, to keep his coalition together without agitating mainstream voters. In January, he convinced his caucus to vote to expel social conservative MP Derek Sloan, who had (apparently unknowingly) accepted a campaign donation from a neo-Nazi. When

Saskatchewan Tory MP Cathay Wagantall's bill outlawing sex-selective abortion came to a vote, O'Toole voted against it, but most of his caucus supported it. It was easily defeated by MPs in other parties.

In the spring, Freeland delivered her first budget, promising $101.4 billion in new spending, including $30 billion for child care, a significant spend toward a national $10-a-day system, modelled on that in Quebec. O'Toole called the budget a "massive letdown" and complained there was no plan to end the pandemic, but he was not pushing for an election for the good reason that the Liberals were well ahead in the polls.

The Liberals, who could already taste the celebratory champagne they would drink when they won their majority, were keen for an election, but no other party wanted one. In May, the Bloc Québécois brought in a motion urging the government not to hold an election until after the pandemic. It passed almost unanimously. Only Sloan voted against. The Liberals might have wanted a majority, but the idea of a socially distant campaign in the midst of a pandemic was not appealing to Canadians, who were hoping for nothing more than a summer with no lockdowns.

The Conservatives were especially leery. O'Toole had hired Hanbury Strategy, a British political data consultancy, to research their election prospects and offer a plan to replace Trudeau with O'Toole. Hanbury conducted in-depth polling in October and November 2020. When they crunched the numbers, they had bad news for the Tories: The Liberals were benefiting from a "crisis halo." "They basically said if Trudeau calls the election during the pandemic, virtually impossible for you to win," O'Toole said later. "Most people have it already baked in, they're doing a pretty good job managing the pandemic and a lot of the swing voters you want don't want to change horses midstream."

The Brits told O'Toole they were struck by how difficult it is for Conservatives to win elections in Canada, compared with the United Kingdom, Australia, and New Zealand. Their message as he related it was grim: "You guys are the hardest for the Conservatives to ever win a majority because of the disparity between what it means to be conservative from

Above: Justin Trudeau does the peacock yoga pose in a Liberal caucus meeting room on Parliament Hill in 2011. MPs Anthony Rota (*left*) and Mark Eyking look amused. Some of his colleagues resented Trudeau in those days as he effortlessly attracted attention and did not seem to apply himself to the grind of legislative work.
Greg Kolz

Right: Jody Wilson-Raybould and Justin Trudeau beam at one another after she is sworn in as justice minister and attorney general at Rideau Hall on November 4, 2015. By the time the SNC-Lavalin affair concluded, Trudeau had lost two ministers, his principal secretary, and the clerk of the Privy Council.
Adam Scotti

Left: Craig Kielburger, Sophie Grégoire Trudeau, Justin Trudeau, and Marc Kielburger wave from the stage at the Canadian Tire Centre in Ottawa during a WE Day event on November 10, 2015. Trudeau eventually apologized for failing to recuse himself from a decision to give WE a $912 million contract.
Adam Scotti

Left: Tsuut'ina Chief Roy Whitney-One-spot puts a headdress on Justin Trudeau during a ceremony in the Alberta First Nation on March 4, 2016. Trudeau has invested more time, money, and political capital in Indigenous reconciliation than any prime minister before him, but also opted to go to the beach rather than attend the first National Day for Truth and Reconciliation.

Adam Scotti

Above: Bill Morneau and Justin Trudeau walk in the Toronto Pride parade on July 3, 2016. Morneau resigned in 2021 when sources close to Trudeau told the *Globe and Mail* the government was thinking of dropping him.

Adam Scotti

Left: Katie Telford and Gerald Butts look on as Trudeau speaks during a first ministers meeting in Ottawa on December 9, 2016. The triumvirate took Trudeau from a backbench critic to a worldwide celebrity, but their close relationship broke down during the SNC-Lavalin affair.

Sean Kilpatrick/The Canadian Press

Right: Sophie Grégoire-Trudeau, Michelle Obama, Justin Trudeau, and President Barack Obama pose together before a state dinner at the White House on March 10, 2016.

Adam Scotti

Above: Justin Trudeau and President Donald Trump walk along the colonnade at the White House on February 13, 2017. Trudeau's visit to Washington was successful, but Trump would eventually send his people out to attack Trudeau as a backstabber.

Adam Scotti

Left: Justin Trudeau serves pancakes at the Calgary Stampede on July 15, 2017.

Adam Scotti

Left: Canadian Ambassador to the United States David MacNaughton, Foreign Affairs Minister Chrystia Freeland, Justin Trudeau, and Donald Trump in the Oval Office, October 11, 2017. Trudeau and his team managed to save Canada's economy by deftly handling the Americans in the NAFTA negotiations.
Adam Scotti

Right: Justin Trudeau announces Brenda Lucki as the first female commissioner of the RCMP in Regina on March 9, 2018. Trudeau, like his predecessors, has failed to do what is necessary to reform the RCMP.
Adam Scotti

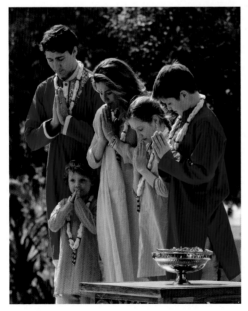

Left: Justin, Hadrien, Sophie, Ella-Grace, and Xavier visit the Sabarmati Ashram in Ahmedabad, India, on February 19, 2018. Indians found the daily costume changes on the trip to be a bit much.
Adam Scotti

Above: Justin Trudeau and President Emmanuel Macron have a drink on the grounds of the prime ministerial residence at Harrington Lake, Quebec, June 6, 2018.
Adam Scotti

Right: Prime Minister Narendra Modi and Justin Trudeau talk during a G7 meeting in Biarritz, France, August 26, 2019. In 2023, Trudeau accused Modi's government of being behind the assassination of a Sikh activist in British Columbia.
Adam Scotti

Left: Justin Trudeau and Conservative leader Andrew Scheer exchange words during the French-language election debate in Gatineau, Quebec, on October 10, 2019.
Adrian Wyld/Getty Images

Above: Justin Trudeau sports a Canada mask in Ottawa on June 11, 2020.
Adam Scotti

Right: Prime Minister Trudeau holds a media availability outside Rideau Cottage in Ottawa on June 16, 2020. During his pandemic news conferences, Trudeau sounded like a teacher trying to raise the spirits of his students after a field trip took an unexpected turn for the worse.
Adam Scotti

Left: Justin and Sophie get their first dose of the AstraZeneca vaccine at a Rexall Pharmacy in Ottawa, April 23, 2021.
Adam Scotti

Above: Justin Trudeau at his desk on February 14, 2022, the day he invoked the Emergencies Act to respond to the occupation of Ottawa and protests in other parts of Canada.
Adam Scotti

Left: Justin Trudeau shows Hadrien the official portrait of his grandfather, Pierre, on Parliament Hill, December 9, 2022.
Adam Scotti

Right: President Volodymyr Zelenskyy embraces Justin Trudeau at a G7 meeting in Hiroshima, Japan, on May 21, 2023. Trudeau responded quickly and firmly to Russia's invasion of Ukraine in 2022.
Adam Scotti

Above: President Volodymyr Zelenskyy accepts applause after a speech in the House of Commons on September 22, 2023. The Ukrainian leader's visit turned into a PR disaster when MPs applauded a Ukrainian Canadian who fought for the 14th Waffen Grenadier Division of the SS during the Second World War.
Adam Scotti

Below: Finance Minister Chrystia Freeland delivers the 2023 fall economic statement on November 21, 2023. "The Canadian economy faces global headwinds from a position of fundamental strength," she said—the kind of thing politicians say when the bottom is falling out of the boat.
Adam Scotti

east to west. But the Quebec piece . . . we're constantly kind of hammered in Quebec, and the best we could maybe achieve is fifteen seats, outside of a once-in-a-generation Mulroney scenario. But even that, Mulroney was pre-Bloc. So they basically said, 'Wow, it is frigging hard. And [in relation to Australia, New Zealand, and the United Kingdom] you guys are much more progressive than the other CANZUK countries.'"

"One thing they quickly identified was how toxic our party brand is," says DeLorey. "They had no idea coming in. They worked for conservative parties in Australia, UK, mainland Europe. And we had such a toxic brand in our country. And they also identified, surprisingly to me, how progressive Canada is versus most European countries."

The news wasn't all bad. O'Toole had managed to present himself to some voters in a positive way, giving him "a nascent reputation as a decent and moderate voice for Canada," according to a memo from Hanbury. But he had a "serious problem with cut-through," meaning most people did not know much about him. Trudeau was on TV every day for much of the pandemic while Parliament was shut, denying O'Toole the chance to get his message out. A lot of people hated Trudeau, and a lot of people loved him. In contrast, Hanbury wrote, "most people are ambivalent about Erin O'Toole."

In a memo on election strategy, Hanbury suggested there would be a short window where the Conservatives could win an election after the worst health risk had faded but before the post-COVID economic recovery kicked in. During that window, the Conservatives could argue that "the Liberals bungled vaccine deployment and the early stages of the Covid recovery, and therefore can't be trusted to manage Canada's broader economic recovery."

But the Liberals didn't bungle the vaccine rollout. By the time Trudeau dropped the writ calling the election, the Canadian vaccination rate was higher than the American rate. The real issue for the Liberals was that most people did not want an election until COVID was out of the way, at which point the Conservatives ought to have a shot at winning, because everyone would be thinking about the economic recovery. By then the Conservatives would have a brand advantage in economic arguments, just as the Liberals do in debates about health care.

The provincial election that spring in Newfoundland and Labrador made it plain why calling an election too soon might be a mistake—sort of. There was a COVID outbreak right before polls were due to open, on March 25, 2021, so the chief electoral officer delayed the vote and ordered that it be conducted by mail, making the whole exercise a depressing shambles. The provincial Liberals won a majority, though, so the possibility of an election might not have looked *that bad* to Trudeau's people.

On August 15, Trudeau went to Rideau Hall to announce Canadians would vote on September 20. His news conference did not go well, with reporters pressing him on why we needed to have an election. He seemed taken aback. "In this pivotal, consequential moment, who wouldn't want a say? Who wouldn't want their chance to help decide where our country goes from here? Canadians need to choose how we finish the fight against COVID-19 and build back better." This justification seemed weak to Canadians. The last election had been less than two years before. Everyone knew that Trudeau wanted a majority, but even Liberal voters didn't share that goal right then. They wanted to get on with their summer.

Former staffers watched with dismay as Trudeau failed to explain the reason for the election. "That opening scrum," says one. "It was the stupidest thing ever. It was awful. I remember watching it in my backyard being like, What is happening? Right. Is this happening?"

That same day, Kabul fell to the Taliban, a disaster for Afghanistan, a historic defeat for the West, and a bitter blow to the tens of thousands of Canadians who had served in that country in a vain attempt to keep the forces of barbarism at bay. I had travelled to Afghanistan to report on the war in 2013 and was impressed by the calm bravery of our troops. I was horrified by the prospect of the Taliban returning to power and depressed by our role in the losing battle we were fighting as part of the doomed American-led strategy. The Afghans I met were terrified of the return of the Taliban, and although the invasion seemed to have been a mistake, I came to believe that the West should make sure that Kabul, at least, would never fall to the fanatics. But the Americans eventually grew tired of the steady drain of money and blood and left, like the British and Russians before them, leaving the educated urban Afghans to face their horrible new masters.

As Trudeau was telling Canadians that they should be excited to have an election that nobody wanted, Afghan interpreters who had worked with our soldiers were waking up to the horrifying realization that the Taliban would soon be in a position to exact revenge on them for helping us. The airport was a humanitarian disaster, with thousands of vulnerable Afghans camping there in the desperate hope of getting on a flight before the Taliban killers could get their hands on them.

Unlike the French, whose superior on-the-ground intelligence had convinced the country that the city might fall, the Canadians and other allies were caught flat-footed by the departure of President Ashraf Ghani on August 15 and the sudden collapse of the city's defences. Canadian special forces arrived to get our people out in transport planes as the Taliban watched outside the airport. It was a hellish scene, and it did not reflect well on Canada or on the West in general.

This calamity was the backdrop to the first days of the campaign. While Trudeau insisted that the election would not prevent the government from attending to the desperate business of getting our people and our allies out of Afghanistan, Foreign Affairs Minister Marc Garneau resumed his duties, working the phones with his counterparts around the world. "I think it played a part in how Canadians felt about whether or not we needed to have an election at this time," he told me in an interview later. "I, for example, received lots of comments on social media about . . . why are you diverting all your attention to running in your election, when there's all these important things that you should be doing in foreign affairs? . . . It was a very tough time."

The whole campaign looked like a terrible idea. I wondered then if

Trudeau, having lost Butts, his key strategist, had given in to vanity. Did he think that Canadians would be so pleased to get another chance to vote for him that the campaign would be easy? Canadians had been through the most difficult two years in modern history, accepting government intrusions into their lives on a scale nobody could have imagined before the pandemic. Then, at the first sign of normality, the Liberals were seeking to take advantage and win the majority they dreamed of.

In fact, Trudeau was stating a reason—he needed a mandate for a post-COVID society. "Listen to the tapes," says Azam Ishmael, the national campaign director. "The prime minister said it time and time again, as to why we thought we were having a campaign. But nobody was listening to that reason. What people wanted to believe was that we were having a campaign because they thought we thought it was time for a majority."

Nothing was connecting. Trudeau was warning against the evil right-wing plans of the Conservatives, but O'Toole kept smiling, saying he was pro-choice, pro-LGBTQ, and against climate change but worried about Liberal mismanagement of the economy. Trudeau seemed to have overestimated his own appeal and the firmness of the support he picked up during the pandemic. He dramatically underestimated the political skills of O'Toole, a disciplined and blandly cheerful guy with lots of plans.

Since the beginning of the pandemic, in Canada and around the world, incumbents had generally been re-elected. But on August 17, just two days after Trudeau went to Rideau Hall, Nova Scotians sent the Liberals in that province packing, electing Progressive Conservative Tim Houston rather than opting for Liberal Iain Rankin, who had taken over from Stephen McNeil.

By Labour Day, when Canadians reluctantly turn from their sweet summer pastimes and start to pay attention to politics again, O'Toole was leading in the polls. On September 3, pollster Nik Nanos called O'Toole "a political freight train" and reported a Tory lead: CPC 36, LPC 31, NDP 20.

Trudeau was behind but not out. He found a weak spot during the

French-language TVA debate, the same venue where he had cornered Scheer on abortion in the previous election. On home ice, he pressed O'Toole effectively on whether the Conservatives would reverse a ban on assault weapons, which O'Toole denied. "It's written on page ninety of your platform," Trudeau said. "You should read page ninety of your platform." O'Toole, demonstrating both poise and a professional level of disingenuousness, declined to be pinned down, insisting he would not reverse the ban. The question hinges on how you define an assault rifle. After the mass shooting in Nova Scotia in April 2020, the Liberals added a number of semi-automatic rifles to the prohibited list, and that ban is what Trudeau was referencing. O'Toole was referring to a ban on automatic weapons that had been brought in by Trudeau *père* in 1977.

The next day, O'Toole refused to clarify what ban he was referring to—typical clever-politician-slithering-off-the-hook behaviour. He already had the kind of "message discipline" that Trudeau took years to learn. You had to admire his professionalism, but he couldn't skate backwards forever. The *Globe and Mail* kept pressing, and, going into the long weekend, the headline on its site read: "Conservatives Would Repeal Ban on Guns Used in École Polytechnique, Nova Scotia Mass Shootings." That explanation would not appeal to the suburban women whose votes O'Toole wanted, so the next day he reversed himself, saying he would leave the Liberal gun ban in place until it could be reviewed in some way. "We should have a public discussion of difficult issues related to public safety, and it should not be politicized."

O'Toole was in a jam. He was not planning to legalize assault weapons. What the Liberals were banning were guns that look like assault rifles—non-automatic AR-15s, for example. But journalists—most of whom couldn't tell a Howitzer from a BB gun—wouldn't point that out. "This is one of my problems with the Press Gallery," O'Toole says. "There's never really been an analysis of the Liberal position on an 'assault-style weapon.' That means nothing. That's not a real term. That means a black semi-automatic gun that can scare a soccer mom from Oakville."

O'Toole thought the confusion was going to get worse. "The Liberals were doing [literature] drops with pictures of assault weapons onto homes in Burlington, all the swing seats. Immediately they deployed that. And we heard they were going to fly around the country, PolySeSouvient people* to go to my events with pictures of their dead family members and scary looking black guns. And that's when I made a quick command call to say we could not have that."

The reversal backfired, suggesting he would say anything to win the election. The high-priced British consultants had warned he should be extra careful. He had only a brief window in which to introduce himself to Canadians, and he needed to present himself as trustworthy. "A particular risk is that EOT's likeable and friendly persona, if combined with any unforced errors, could make him an easy source of ridicule for Liberal-aligned media or cultural shows," Hanbury cautioned, advising he "cannot afford any unforced errors or gaffes that diminish his credibility as a steady pair of hands for the country."

The reversal allowed the Liberals to portray O'Toole as unreliable. "What actually happened is the prime minister opened the door in the debate and then the campaign drove a truck through it," says Ishmael. "On guns, and the whole idea that they're saying one thing here, and they're going to do another thing when they get into government, as exemplified by guns. When was the last time somebody had changed their platform mid-campaign? I can't even think of a campaign that's ever done that."

Still it was far from over. O'Toole kept smiling, and Trudeau flailed and trailed in the polls. At the English leaders' debate, O'Toole did what he needed to do, which was seem not scary. He managed to be as reassuring as a glass of milk, serene and cheerful, excited to tell you about his plans, like an unusually ambitious economic development officer for a suburban Toronto municipality. He lowered the temperature, smiled,

---

* Activists from l'École Polytechnique, the Montreal school where a woman-hating shooter killed fourteen women on December 6, 1989.

talked vaguely and optimistically, and was able to avoid tough questions or parry them with a smile.

I was anticipating that Trudeau would score some points in his head-to-head debate with O'Toole on climate, especially as the centrepiece of O'Toole's climate plan was an impractical-sounding carbon consumer reward system. Instead of rebating money to consumers through the tax system, as the Liberal system does, O'Toole was going to set up "personal low carbon savings accounts," which sounded like Esso Extra points. Collect enough and you get a set of steak knives! It sounded absurdly complicated, and likely never would have been implemented, but it allowed O'Toole to say that he had a climate plan. Trudeau couldn't make any clear points on the woolly scheme, and O'Toole shut him down when he pointed out that Trudeau had failed to meet his own targets.

O'Toole was looking good, but COVID was coming to rescue the Liberals. Cases were spiking, as they normally do after schools open. That made voters ask not which leader might have the best economic plan but who might keep them from getting sick.

In January, Trudeau had said he didn't like the idea of vaccine mandates, because they would be divisive. "We are certainly encouraging and motivating people to get vaccinated as quickly as possible, but we always know there are people who won't get vaccinated and not necessarily through a personal or political choice."

Looking at the election ahead, Trudeau changed his mind. The polling was strong. The Greater Toronto Area had been through some of the longest lockdowns in the world, grinding out the months in the cold while COVID ravaged the city. Peel Region, to the west, had been hardest hit as street-level "essential" workers there, many of them immigrants in multigenerational homes, found it harder to shut COVID out than country people or members of the laptop class. Support for vaccine mandates was high. Those were the voters Trudeau wanted, and he needed to get them onside, needed to use COVID as a wedge. He rolled out a new policy two days before the election that would require all federal employees, and anyone who wanted to board a plane or a train, to prove they were vaccinated. He attacked O'Toole for being soft on COVID. "We're unequivocal that civil servants must be vaccinated. If anyone doesn't have a legitimate medical reason for not getting fully vaccinated—or chooses to not get vaccinated—there will be consequences."

On the eve of the election, O'Toole spoke to Janice Charette, the clerk of the Privy Council, who briefed him on the caretaker convention and other election rules. O'Toole, who knew Charette from his time as minister of veterans affairs in Harper's government, asked if she had produced a Charter opinion on the just-announced mandate policy. "Two days ago, the prime minister announced a vaccine mandate," O'Toole recalls saying to her. "Parliament had a vote to say no election during the pandemic. There's been no parliamentary debate, discussion, or even briefings on vaccine mandate. In fact, three or four months ago, the prime minister gave several interviews where we said, in Canada, we don't make vaccines mandatory. I want to know did your office give him a Charter opinion or any legal advice on this issue?"

The answer was no. "That's when," says O'Toole, "I knew they saw the polls and they were just taking the pin out of the grenade."

Another call that O'Toole remembers ruefully was from Mark Strahl, MP for Chilliwack–Hope in British Columbia. Strahl told O'Toole that he would lose eleven or twelve MPs if he made vaccines mandatory for MPs and candidates. O'Toole believed that a number of western MPs, including Shannon Stubbs and Chris Warkentin, might undercut the campaign if he brought in the kind of COVID policy that voters in Ontario wanted, which would have helped to neutralize the issue. It was not an empty threat. Mark's father is Chuck Strahl, who had first been elected as a Reformer and then led a breakaway group from the Canadian Alliance when Stockwell Day was leader. That hamstrung his leadership and paved the way for Harper's accension.

O'Toole jokes that the potential rebels were all veterans of the "Preston Manning Youth Bus," a cadre of Reformers who go way back together. They had been close to Scheer and were not enthusiastic about O'Toole winning the leadership. "They see themselves being betrayed and also now being replaced down the road by a progressive," says one of their colleagues. "But worse, not just a progressive, a progressive campaigning as a True Blue. And where the tipping point really fucking happened was the carbon tax shit." O'Toole had sprung a new climate policy designed to appeal to middle-of-the-road voters without consulting his caucus, and they would not accept that betrayal. They had it in for him, and during the campaign they made him pay.

O'Toole never considered firing them. "Some of [Doug] Ford's people were saying you got to do exactly what we do. When the writ comes, execute everyone that's not vaccinated and replace them all. All the seats were safe seats. We could have replaced them. But that's not my style. The narrative would have been, he just executed the Reform wing, right? So I didn't do it."

O'Toole was under pressure early in the campaign, struggling to answer questions about how many of his candidates were vaccinated, but he was toughing it out, smiling and changing the subject. That started to get a lot harder when the cases spiked in Alberta. On September 1, Ford gave in to public opinion and announced that Ontario would bring in vaccine mandates.

Jason Kenney, who had promised Albertans "the best summer ever," was now harvesting an autumn of COVID misery. By September 15, with the hospitals filling with intubated unvaccinated people, Kenney had no choice but to declare a public health emergency. Alberta, which has a population a third of Ontario's, had twice as many COVID patients in hospital. Trudeau started to campaign against Kenney and Saskatchewan's Scott Moe, pointing out they had prolonged the misery by pretending that COVID was over. "Because of leadership that will not commit to keeping them safe in the right way, or protecting the economy the right way, they are facing greater risks because of cancelled surgeries, they are facing emergency public health restrictions that may have to be brought in."

O'Toole thinks the Liberals could see it coming. "The brilliance of the

Liberal wedge was they knew they'd beat us up at the beginning. And they knew the modelling showed near the end of the campaign the Alberta hospitals would be filling up. And they knew they'd have a second round to beat me up on the vaccine mandate. In the last week, Trudeau was talking more about Jason Kenney than me, because my numbers were better than his by that point. But people . . . especially swing Ontario voters worried about COVID, thought Alberta was a fucking shit show."

O'Toole was also losing votes on his right, to the People's Party of Canada. After an unimpressive showing in the 2019 election, Maxime Bernier's party was looking like a doomed vanity project. But the mandates and lockdowns, and the spread of anti-vax misinformation online, injected energy and money into the party. Suddenly, Mad Max could draw a crowd again, and he started to participate in anti-lockdown rallies around the country. Rural western MPs, who were accustomed to running basically unopposed, suddenly were getting pushback from the right, from constituents who had always been faithful Conservatives but who now wanted to know why O'Toole was supporting measures that infringed on their freedom.

"You cannot tell the story of the mandates and Erin making the decision without understanding two things," says one Conservative MP. "The PPC influence on O'Toole was everything, because our rural caucus, that's all they cared about was the fucking PPC vote. So he was getting pressure from caucus. And the other thing was . . . Erin was more concerned about winning a leadership race or a leadership review than winning a general election, because I don't think Erin went into the general election thinking he could win the general election where the polls were at when we entered it. So he avoided a showdown with the caucus and then had to live with the consequences when COVID cases started to go up. He decided to be a noodle."

On September 7, Trudeau went to London, Ontario, where his bus was surrounded by an angry group of PPC supporters. As Trudeau boarded the bus, Shane Marshall, president of the Elgin–Middlesex–London riding association of the PPC, threw a handful of gravel at him (he pleaded guilty to assault in 2023, and was sentenced to ninety days of house arrest). In that riding, the PPCs actually thought they had a shot at winning. The candidate was Chelsea Hillier, daughter of Randy Hillier, who had been ejected from Doug Ford's caucus and had been organizing anti-mandate rallies around Ontario, appearing with Bernier and Derek Sloan, confronting police. But the video clip of the gravel assault backfired.

Randy Hillier, who knows Marshall, says the attack was "stupid and immature." "I think it was blown out of proportion, but that's what political campaigns do. You take any misstep or any error and you force it into a bigger error. O'Toole was getting heat from the PPC side, the anti-mandate side."

Politically, this Conservative split was bad for O'Toole and good for Trudeau. O'Toole wasn't encouraging violent protests. Bernier was. "When tyranny becomes law, revolution becomes our duty," he tweeted that week. But swing voters edged toward Trudeau. "Trudeau may be getting mobbed, but it is Erin O'Toole who stands to take a hit and not just because the Liberals have been trying to pin the turmoil on his party," wrote Chantal Hébert in the *Toronto Star*.

O'Toole thinks the Liberals went into PPC country hoping for conflict, hoping to further polarize the election around mandates. "Ford's mandate came in in the middle of the campaign and southwestern Ontario went fucking bonkers, and that's why the Liberals drove the truck in there," O'Toole said in an interview later. "They knew that there would be some crazies show up and they wanted to portray the crazies as my people. So the whole rock-throwing thing, we were told they went there on purpose for some sort of confrontation."

Brian Clow, who was deputy national director of the Liberal campaign, says they were not looking to get rocks thrown at them, but once it happened, it was right that it became part of the national discussion. "We do not want it. We do not welcome it and we don't look for it. That said, when it happens, at least my view is, it is what it is. People should see this. It is a reflection of a certain segment of the population that I think Canadians should know exists."

Clow points out that while O'Toole may have yearned to be moderate on mandates, his party was divided on the key issue facing Canadians. "The anti-lockdown, anti-mask, anti-vax sentiment in certain populations was growing. And that included some conservatives. Leslyn Lewis was running for them. [O'Toole] had a very fine line to walk. And I think it was impossible for him to walk it."

———

ON ELECTION NIGHT, EVERYONE ended up almost exactly where they had been when the campaign started. The Liberals won 160 seats, up three from in 2019. The Tories had the same number, 119, as did the Bloc, at 32. The NDP picked up one seat, at 25. It was, as Conservative Lisa Raitt put it on TV, a "$600 million Cabinet shuffle." Trudeau had gone out looking for a majority, and Canadians said no. It was a stalemate. Canadians could not agree on who should govern them. The Liberals had won power with just 32.62 percent of the vote, a dismal low record. The Conservatives had slightly more at 33.74 percent. It was the lowest total for the top two parties in Canadian history. As was happening elsewhere, the electorate was increasingly fragmented, a process driven by social media, with everyone getting information in their own silos.

O'Toole had tried to make his vote distribution more efficient by veering to the middle, and it might have worked, except that COVID saved the Liberals in Ontario.

"I'm not surprised the Liberals won a minority government when they got 39 percent in Ontario," says Conservative strategist Nick Kouvalis, who was polling for Doug Ford. "Why did they get 39 percent in Ontario? Because 40 percent of Ontarians are hard-core for making vaccines mandatory. And so they got that support."

It was close, but they got their votes out, largely thanks to the Liberal data machine, a slick operation for identifying and motivating voters in the ridings they needed to win. Tom Pitfield, the head of Data Sciences, and his team, deserve much of the credit. He and the actual scientists he employed had figured out how to use Facebook data, the voter list, and databases from other sources to divine exactly where Liberals voters were and, crucially, where they were not, so the party didn't waste its resources connecting with people who were not going to vote for them.

Pitfield grew up with Justin and was a groomsman at his wedding. His wife, Anna Gainey, was president of the Liberal Party until 2018. He could not have been closer to the Trudeau operation. Liberals grumbled about his chumminess with the boss and the way the party pressed local riding associations to hire his company when they would have preferred to use local competitors, but nobody could complain about the results. He saved the election.

Canadian election law imposes a low spending limit—$30 million per party for the whole campaign. That's peanuts compared to the United States. Georgia Democrat Raphael Warnock spent US$180 million to win a Senate race in 2022. Pitfield had figured out how to spend money where it mattered. "The whole game plan since 2015 is to be agile and to deploy limited resources as efficiently as possible to the places where they'll have the greatest impact," he said later. "It's a similar problem that every company or any individual with limited resources has to solve."

The Conservatives had been forced into big TV spending early in the campaign to introduce O'Toole and try to create a coalition that did not already exist. The Liberals, in contrast, were able to activate networks of volunteers and voters they had been building for a long time. They conducted eighteen million "knocks and calls on the way into this election," Braeden Caley, director of communications for the party, told me. They found their voters in the ridings they needed to win.

This dedication to finding and targeting voters in ridings that matter increasingly means that huge sections of the electorate are essentially uncontacted during a campaign. Of the thirty-three ridings with the largest margins of victory, twenty-nine are Conservative. In Foothills, a riding at the Alberta edge of the Rockies known for spectacular scenery, coal mining, and rodeos, Conservative John Barlow won by 37,240 votes, the largest margin in the country. The Liberal candidate came fourth with 4,441 votes, behind the NDP and the PPC. No party will waste any time trying to reach voters in Foothills, while swing voters in the Greater Toronto Area are constantly under siege from all the major parties. Over time, this entirely sensible strategizing, this slicing and dicing, leaves chunks of the country out of the conversation. O'Toole tried to bring the fight to the suburbs, trading votes there for excess votes in the west, but it didn't quite happen.

Trudeau says he sees O'Toole as different from Scheer and Poilievre, but he couldn't lead that way. "I think Erin O'Toole probably has more honest to goodness Progressive Conservatism in him than others did. I think he had to end up playing a role that meant he couldn't trust his own grounding and his own instincts, and he sort of got lost within it. He was someone who many people think was more thoughtful, but his caucus wasn't."

In a way, O'Toole's western MPs saw him as Trudeau did—as a frustrated Progressive Conservative—but they didn't welcome his moderation. They bitterly resented the uncomfortable policies he had forced on them, and they would not follow him for long.

13

A GREAT BIG CONVOY

The election had not gone as Trudeau had planned. After repeatedly criss-crossing the country giving speeches and shaking hands, spending $30 million and getting pelted with gravel, he was exactly where he had been before dropping the writ. The election had been a waste of time and energy, and it must have been sobering to realize that Canadians had not, after all, welcomed the opportunity to give him a majority government.

In an end-of-year interview, Trudeau told Terry DiMonte that the gravel throwing was unfortunate, but the whole thing turned out well. "I think we saw it in a very specific moment in the campaign that made a whole lot of people wonder, and we've seen since—a coming together of the country, a parliament that is working more collaboratively and things are on the right track. Canadians, overwhelmingly, regardless of the various parties they voted for, when you look at the common themes between most of the progressive parties, [they are] doing more on the environment, doing more on reconciliation, doing more on supporting vulnerable people and fighting intolerance."

It is noteworthy that in a relaxed setting, talking to an old friend,

Trudeau had stopped talking about inequality and the middle class as central to his mission. His government had shifted its emphasis to diversity and inclusion, and away from the economic issues that had won him a majority in 2015. In an interview in 2024, he acknowledged that the shift in emphasis had an impact with voters. "Canadians didn't see us as doing that [dealing with inequality] anymore, and they were able to be convinced, or they became convinced, that we weren't as focused on the thing that drove me into politics and continued to drive me every day. Maybe I said, 'Oh no, but people already know that of me.'" That was a mistake, Trudeau admits. "That is probably a very fair contention that over the ups and downs of the time in office, perceptions are that we didn't do as much there."

In early 2024, Trudeau wanted to turn that impression around. "Certainly, that is part of the reflection we're going through right now, to remind people that we believe in building an economy that works for all Canadians. That frame of the middle class—again being what I've devoted my time as a leader to do—we need to put that back more in the window."

———

TRUDEAU'S GOVERNMENT HAD WORKED hard on reconciliation with Indigenous people, although there were bumps along the road. A week after the election, people across the country were gathering to mark the country's first National Day for Truth and Reconciliation. It was a day to remember and commemorate the horrors of Indian residential schools, where for generations Indigenous children had been abused and neglected with state sanction, taken from their families, forbidden to speak their own language, and dressed in the garb of their colonizers. Known informally as Orange Shirt Day since 2013, the date—September 30—had been chosen because it marked the time of year when the children were taken from their parents. A grassroots movement to recognize the intergenerational trauma and encourage healing had spread across Canada under the slogan "Every Child Matters."

In 2019, Saskatchewan NDP MP Georgina Jolibois managed to get a private member's bill through the House declaring it a national holiday, but it was stuck in the Senate when Trudeau called the 2019 election, so it did not become law. In May 2021, the Shuswap community of Tk 'emlúps te Secwépemc announced that a ground-radar survey of the Kamloops Indian Residential School had discovered what could be the remains of 215 children. The discovery made headlines around the world, and the government rushed a new version of Jolibois's bill through the House, making September 30 a federal holiday. Trudeau seemed shaken by the discovery. He ordered flags be flown at half-staff and declared they would remain there until "we have worked enough with Indigenous communities and leadership to make a clear determination that it was time to raise them again and continue the hard work of reconciliation."

Trudeau—who has a tattoo on his left arm based on *Raven Bringing Light to the World*, a painting by Haida artist Robert Davidson—has made reconciliation a higher political priority than any previous government has done, but at times he has clumsily opened himself to charges of hypocrisy. On September 29, the day before the first National Day for Truth and Reconciliation, a federal court rejected the government's appeal of a Canadian Human Rights Tribunal ruling that required Ottawa to pay $40,000 to each child who had been removed from home by child-welfare authorities.

That same day, Trudeau attended a somber ceremony on Parliament Hill, where he heard survivors relate their stories. The nearby Centennial Flame was encircled with children's shoes, symbols of the lost lives of those not present. "Do not tell me, or try to explain, that the National Day of Truth and Reconciliation is a day for Indigenous Canadians," Trudeau said. "It is a day for all Canadians. Take a moment to listen to the stories of a survivor, to an Indigenous elder who shares their perspective and their experiences in this country. And know that that story, their story, is your story as well."

It was good advice, but Trudeau would not be around to celebrate this significant first anniversary—or to take the initial heat for the new COVID mandates policy he had announced. Instead, he, Sophie, and the three children flew to Tofino for some family time. They had rented an $18 million beachfront estate among old-growth spruce and cedar, billed on promotional material as a "surfer's paradise." It had a guest house, a separate building for servants, and a treehouse for the kids—the perfect place for a luxurious break after the bruising and pointless campaign that had kept him away from his family. He might even catch some waves on one of Canada's best surfing beaches.

The official itinerary released by his office said Trudeau was having private meetings in Ottawa. He was not. Flight-tracking information showed the path of the Challenger, and Global News filmed him and Sophie walking along the beach holding hands. The story led the news across Canada. Trudeau looked, once again, like a hypocrite, happy to lecture Canadians about what they should do while he enjoyed a luxurious retreat. It is the kind of thing that drives his opponents crazy and makes his allies roll their eyes in exasperation.

To make matters worse, during the campaign, Trudeau had said he would visit Tk'emlúps te Secwépemc to meet with the community about the graves when the time was right. Chief Rosanne Casimir sent two invitations suggesting he visit on the first reconciliation day, but he was not able to make it. "I was truly saddened that he was not able to join us today," she told Global. "I did hold out a hope that maybe he would be here." Jody Wilson-Raybould tweeted, "True reconciliation begins with showing up."

Realizing his error, a few days later Trudeau called Casimir to apologize and visited the community in October. "I am here today to say I wish I was here a few weeks ago, and I deeply regret it," he said.

Perry Bellegarde, who had stepped down as national chief of the Assembly of First Nations that July, was disappointed by what happened but still thinks Trudeau has been an important leader for reconciliation.

He points to a massive settlement Trudeau agreed to at the beginning of 2022 to end a child-welfare-discrimination lawsuit brought by tireless activist Cindy Blackstock. "Look at the mandate letters. Look at the throne speeches. Look at everything we've talked about in terms of the three or four key pieces of legislation. Look at the $40-plus billion that got done. There's $43 billion for child welfare—$23 billion in compensation, and then $20 billion to fix the system. So yeah. Okay. Was it a strategic error? I guess from a public relations perspective, yeah of course. It was a faux pas. There's no question."

The faux pas made it difficult for Trudeau to show leadership on Indigenous issues. Flags remained at half-staff until Remembrance Day, although polling showed most Canadians believed they should have been raised earlier. The country was in a state of extended mourning because Trudeau had failed to show up for an event he had brought into existence.

———

IN OCTOBER, TRUDEAU SHUFFLED his Cabinet. No one was surprised when Chrystia Freeland, his indispensable right hand, remained as deputy prime minister and finance minister. But the appointment of Steven Guilbeault as minister of the environment and climate change raised eyebrows in the oil patch and corporate boardrooms. The MP for Laurier–Sainte-Marie in downtown Montreal is a well-known environmentalist, and he could be expected to bend only so far to the will of the business community. Rather, he would act as a guardrail, keeping the government from veering from its commitment to the environment and infuriating those who wanted to develop natural resource projects.

Trudeau made Anita Anand defence minister, only the second woman to hold the role. The daughter of Indian doctors who had immigrated to Kentville, Nova Scotia, she was a professor at the University of Toronto Faculty of Law until she won a seat in Oakville in the 2019 election. As procurement minister, she had led the successful and high-stakes effort to secure vaccines.

At Defence, she faced another challenge: changing the culture of sexual harassment within the department. In February 2021, Global News reported that Canada's top soldier—Chief of the Defence Staff Jonathan Vance—was facing allegations of inappropriate behaviour with two female subordinates. It was eventually revealed that he had carried on a secret relationship with a subordinate for twenty years, fathering a child with her and encouraging her to lie when Global asked questions. Vance was just the first of a series of senior officers who would be forced out for sexual misconduct, exposing a toxic culture in the Canadian Forces that Harjit Sajjan, the previous defence minister, had failed to root out. Anand would do so.

Mélanie Joly became foreign affairs minister, an appointment that got bad reviews from the foreign-policy establishment. Joly, a telegenic and popular Quebecer, had spent time in the penalty box after an unsuccessful turn as heritage minister, but she did not seem experienced enough for Foreign Affairs. To make room for her, Trudeau pushed out Marc Garneau, who officials in other countries regarded as a serious, respected colleague. It looked shabby: Trudeau waited until after the election campaign to let Garneau know he was no longer in Cabinet and offered him the French embassy as recompense. Garneau declined, saying he would prefer to finish out his term as a backbencher. Many Liberals thought Trudeau wanted him out so that Anna Gainey could run for that seat, Notre-Dame-de-Grâce–Westmount, one of the safest Liberal seats in the country.* Garneau, a former astronaut and faithful servant to Canada, was shunted aside for one of Trudeau's friends.

Joly's appointment sent a message that foreign affairs was not a priority for Canada. It had not been for years, really. Since 2006, when Harper became prime minister, Canada had gone through eleven foreign ministers—a sign that neither party was ready to invest politically in Canada's relationships around the world.

---

* People close to Gainey said she did not ask Trudeau to ditch Garneau to make the seat free, but after he left, she ran and won the riding.

IMMEDIATELY AFTER THE FUTILE election, Trudeau chose to hold his first post-election news conference outside a vaccination clinic in suburban Ottawa. There he talked about his plans to bring in mandates, as he had promised during the campaign, to force public servants to get jabbed, and to keep the unvaccinated from boarding planes or trains. He was back to pep-talk mode, telling reporters the results meant "we get to move even stronger, even faster on the things Canadians really want."

He was wrong on that score. Canadians were tired of COVID and its restrictions, and groups across the country were increasingly hostile to mandates that would oblige them to be vaccinated. In November, Marilyn Gladu, the popular Conservative MP for Ontario's Sarnia–Lambton riding, announced she had formed a "civil liberties caucus" of fifteen to thirty MPs and senators—a working group that was researching the concerns of unvaccinated Canadians and reporting back to the party for discussion. Gladu, an engineer before entering politics, is an enthusiastic politician with a cheerful, can-do attitude about representing the views of her constituents. Her riding, on the border with Michigan, includes the Blue Water Bridge and the Port Huron–Sarnia border crossing, second only in traffic volume to the Ambassador Bridge at Detroit-Windsor. It is also just west of London, where Trudeau had recently been pelted with gravel, part of a larger area—sometimes called the Canadian Bible Belt—where feelings against COVID restrictions were more intense than elsewhere.

In an interview, Gladu veered into anti-vax territory, mentioning a 1954 incident in which eleven children were killed by a bad polio vaccine. Everything she said was true, but talking about a long-ago vaccine accident was not helpful when public health officials were trying to convince reluctant Canadians to get a jab that might save their lives and would help hospitals deal with their overcrowded waiting rooms. Gladu apologized, immediately and abjectly.

In his first speech to his caucus when MPs returned to Ottawa for their parliamentary struggles, Trudeau referenced her remark, saying it was an example of Conservatives "stepping up to stand against vaccination, to stand against science, to stand against being there for each other." O'Toole, who was struggling to persuade a few unvaccinated MPs to follow the rules when they returned to the House, was jammed. The Liberals had won the election primarily because of this division in Conservative ranks and wanted to keep up the pressure. The great majority of Canadians were with them and they had a mandate to push, so push they did.

On November 19, a day after Trudeau and Biden decided that both countries would impose a vaccine mandate on truckers, Canada announced that, as of January 15, no unvaccinated truckers could cross the border. It was a major challenge to an industry that had been under intense pressure since the beginning of the pandemic. Many truckers had a tough time during COVID when businesses closed their bathrooms to them, leaving them struggling as they did their vital work between two stricken countries. "We worked eight months with no sanitizer, no face masks. Nothing," Brigitte Belton, a trucker from Wallaceburg, "smack dab in between Windsor and Sarnia," later told the Public Order Emergency Commission. "We had no bathrooms. We had no showers. We were refused everywhere we went. You have no idea what it's like to pee in a park on your way home from work."

Because they were deemed to be essential workers, carrying essential supplies to keep the country moving, truckers had not been required to be vaccinated. Most of them were, but for thousands of them—mostly people who wrongly believed conspiracy theories about the vaccines—this mandate put them in the lurch. They could stop crossing the border, but that would mean a severe pay cut. Many had to get the jab or lose their trucks. Belton, a mother and grandmother, was facing bankruptcy. She testified that she contemplated taking her life because of the trauma around the border crossings.

On November 16, Belton had a hard time crossing at Windsor after a run to the United States. She can't wear a mask because, she says, she had been a victim of violence and covering her face makes her anxious. At the border, she was confronted by a Canada Border Services agent. "I tried to explain . . . that I could not wear a mask, that my visor that I usually used had been broken during the trip. But he would open the window and go, 'Put on a mask,' and he would slam it shut." He got fed up after a couple of exchanges, directed her to wait in a parking lot, and told her he was going to bring in the Windsor police. Frustrated, she recorded a TikTok video on her phone in a dark parking lot in which she vented all her anger and frustration: "In Canada we're no longer free," she said. "This may be the night where I go and ask for exile into the US, because this isn't my country, this isn't what my grandparents came for, being harassed at the border over a mask."

Chris Barber, a Saskatchewan trucker, was one of many who saw the video. He contacted Belton, and they started talking about organizing some kind of protest. Belton mentioned that she had once been stuck on the Blue Water Bridge during a Canada Border Services Agency union work stoppage. If CBSA agents could shut down the border, truckers could shut down a city. They had the beginning of an idea. Barber was networking with James Bauder, who had organized the 2019 United We Roll convoy to Ottawa—inspired by the Yellow Vest protests in France—which, like them, had been criticized for links to far-right and racist groups. Barber was also talking to Pat King, a far-right activist and conspiracy theorist in Red Deer with a big following on social media, and Tamara Lich, who had been active with Alberta separatist parties. A loose organization started to come together. By January 22, 2022, the trucks were rolling in two convoys, one from Red Deer and the other from Vancouver. A few days later, other convoys left Nova Scotia and southwestern Ontario. Supporters lined overpasses and held signs encouraging the protesters. Belton was touched by the support: "Canadians finally peaceful," she said. "Canadians supporting each other." The convoyers kept their spirits up through social media networks—and they were growing stronger by the day.

Trudeau denounced them. "The small fringe minority of people who are on their way to Ottawa, who are holding unacceptable views that they are expressing, do not represent the views of Canadians," he said in a news conference as they rolled toward Ottawa.

The convoyers wore his comments as a badge of honour. Belton could not believe that Trudeau was attacking people like her. "The wording that he used was division, the whole time," she testified later. "Pit one person against another, shame them, make them comply . . . I draw the line when my government wants to throw something into my body I cannot remove . . . Bodily autonomy, it is mine. It is not my government's."

Most Canadians supported the government's agenda on COVID, but there were millions who did not, and they had had enough. The convoy was forty kilometres long by the time it was rolling through eastern Ontario, with throngs cheering them on. On January 28, the trucks arrived in Ottawa in a cloud of diesel smoke. The city had no idea how to respond.

———

THE STORY OF HOW Ottawa failed to deal effectively with the protest is a particularly Canadian story. As with so many problems we can't fix, it involves jurisdictional overlap that allowed officials to do nothing because they would not be blamed for doing nothing.

Ottawa police are used to welcoming protesters, including farmers who annually park their bulky equipment in front of the Parliament buildings to remind MPs of their existence, so they helped the occupiers find places to park their vehicles and gave them an additional parking lot at Coventry Road, five kilometres away. It quickly became clear this group wasn't a normal protest. Unlike the farmers, the truckers were settling in for the long haul. By noon on Saturday, January 29, the protesters had gridlocked the frozen city. Big rigs lined the streets in the downtown core, their engines running constantly, their horns honking. The protesters thronged the downtown core in a spirit of joyful togetherness.

Randy Hillier, the former Ontario MPP who had been leading protests against health restrictions from the beginning of the pandemic, went in for the day to join the demonstration and was so struck by the festive spirit that he checked into a hotel. "You had never seen such overwhelming friendship and love," he told me later. "I think euphoria was the best word that I could come up with. It was festive." During the long lockdowns, people who doubted the science and rejected the authority of the state being extended into their lives had been isolated. Now they were all together, rising up, recognizing and hugging one another.

It was a joyful gathering for Belton. "Love, unity, people happy. This had been two years people had been suppressed, two years people were struggling, two years that our government had told us, 'Shame your family. Do not allow them to come to Christmas . . . if they are not vaccinated, if they don't wear a mask.' People were evil towards each other, and that is not what I saw in Ottawa. I saw love. I saw unity."

For the protesters, it was a great party, a joyful and peaceful expression of freedom and togetherness. Most of the protesters were not truckers, but many were tradespeople, and they knew how to do things. They built temporary shelters and set up hot tubs for adults and bouncy castles for kids. They were jubilant, ecstatic.

For people in Ottawa, few of whom agreed with the protesters, it was all bad, a sudden nightmare in their neighbourhood. The protest was peaceful, but a lot of the protesters were uncouth, drunk, and aggressive, taunting the masked and refusing to wear masks in stores and restaurants. The massive Rideau Centre mall had to shut; small businesses lost their customers. Protesters danced on the National War Memorial, put a protest poster and a ball cap on the statue of Terry Fox. Staff at the Shepherds of Good Hope soup kitchen reported being harassed and assaulted.

The residents of the many high-rise buildings near the Hill were constantly bombarded with the chaos in the streets, the stench of diesel fumes, and the sound of horns, making it difficult to sleep or relax. "The first thing you noticed when you stepped outside was all the snow, because services were unable to be rendered due to the occupation that was going on," Zexi Li, a young public servant who lived downtown, told the commission. "The snow was often coloured yellow or brown due to the public urination and defecation that took place gratuitously . . . And oftentimes there were illegal bonfires and just trash burning right next to cans of fuel or near the same areas where these individuals would later set off fireworks. And I just remember feeling like it was such a surreal sight." Running errands became a nightmare, she said. "I'm a small Asian woman. I wore a mask most of the time due to the situation that was going on. It made you a target because it signalled to the people on our streets that we were not supportive of their cause and that we were not one of them. And in turn, they would increase their honking, and target their honking, and shout at us, shout at me, about how they were doing things for us and that they were fighting for our freedoms when, at the same time, I was unable to walk the streets feeling safe."

The protesters laughed at the objections. They saw the residents of downtown Ottawa as Trudeau supporters, Liberal mandate-supporting voters who deserved what they got. "The honking will continue until freedom improves," ran one slogan.

Newfoundland writer Edward Riche described it well in a column for the CBC: "People were calling for 'freedom' but what they wanted was absolute licence; they were the entitled demanding to be indulged." It was obvious when you watched clips of foul-mouthed mobs of young dolts that gathered to heckle journalists doing their TV standups, acting like high-school bullies trying to pick fights in a rink parking lot after a hockey game. The convoy protesters had legitimate grievances, but many of them were living in a narcissistic parallel universe where they were freedom fighters liberating a grateful public.

The convoy movement was steeped in conspiracism, the toxin that spread through algorithmic social media networks during the pandemic, boosted by anti-vaxxers selling quack COVID cures, attention-seeking wellness hucksters, anti-Semites, and foreign propagandists who wanted to increase discord in our society. An increasingly agitated minority was convinced that United Nations troops were being flown in to establish the New World Order, that 5G towers caused the pandemic, that the World Economic Forum was going to force everyone to eat insects. Some of them were furious, believing politicians were in on a vile conspiracy, and their fury made them dangerous.

American historian Richard Hofstadter identified the psychological appeal of this kind of movement in his 1964 essay "The Paranoid Style in American Politics": "As a member of the avant-garde who is capable of perceiving the conspiracy before it is fully obvious to an as yet unaroused public, the paranoid is a militant leader. He does not see social conflict as something to be mediated and compromised, in the manner of the working politician. Since what is at stake is always a conflict between absolute good and absolute evil, what is necessary is not compromise but the will to fight things out to a finish."

Boring, staid Ottawa was in the grip of deluded militants who would not leave until the government handed power over to them. Bauder's group had posted a memorandum of understanding that laid out the protesters' demands, beginning with a quote from Thomas Jefferson—proof that they didn't care to know how their country is governed. The document demanded that the Senate and the governor general, by signing the MOU, "agree to immediately cease and desist all unconstitutional, discriminatory and segregating actions and human rights violations," deposing the freshly elected legitimate government.

The protesters wanted a meeting with Trudeau, and well-meaning people called for the government to extend some kind of olive branch and negotiate, but Trudeau, who had contracted COVID again, said no. "We are not intimidated by those who hurl abuse at small business workers and steal food from the homeless," he said in a news conference as the protestors settled in to their expanding protest camps. "We won't give in to those who fly racist flags. We won't cave to those who engage in vandalism."

Trudeau would not give in to convoyers. It was a police matter, but the police could not clear the streets.

———

PETER SLOLY HAD BEEN chief of the Ottawa Police Service for just over two years when the trucks rolled in, and things were going badly. His family had immigrated to Toronto from Jamaica when he was ten, and he played professional soccer before spending twenty-seven years with the police force in that city. He was an ambitious, well-educated, rising star, smooth and poised. He came to Ottawa as police forces everywhere were struggling to come to terms with a racist squad-room culture in the aftermath of the police murder of George Floyd in Minneapolis and the rise of the Black Lives Matter movement. Sloly said those events had "shaken me as a police professional and as a person," and he was pushing for change to improve the relationship between OPS officers and Black citizens. In 2020, he wrote an editorial about the traffic stop of a Black motorist, but the union considered it unfair to officers who were simply doing their jobs. Union president Matt Skof responded with a column saying Sloly had "lost the room."

At the beginning, Ottawa police seemed too friendly to the protesters, posing for pictures and generally trying to be helpful to a group of white people whose values and beliefs they found relatable. An OPS intelligence report later made public described the convoyers as "less a professional protest with the usual sad players, but rather a truly organic grass roots event that is gathering momentum." Under pressure from miserable residents, Sloly tried to get the police to act, but he was stymied by senior officers, some of whom resented his being promoted over them with a mandate to shake up the force, and by front-line officers who were increasingly reluctant to confront the protesters. Frustrated, he lashed out at subordinates, which only made things worse. Raids he ordered did not happen. He wanted more officers from the Ontario Provincial Police, but the operational plans he sent to that force were deemed inadequate, and his request went unanswered.

Ottawa was not being policed. Ticketing didn't start for days. Tow-truck companies hesitated to move illegally parked trucks for fear of losing business from truckers after the protests ended. Protesters were refilling their trucks with jerry cans of diesel. When the police were ordered to put a stop to that, protesters began to carry empty jerry cans en masse to overwhelm the police, but they needn't have bothered. Front-line officers were not following orders to stop them from gassing up. There were reports that sympathetic officers were sharing police intelligence with protesters. Anything the police did could backfire. Families with children were living in some of the trucks, and there were reports of firearms in others.

Throughout, Ottawa mayor Jim Watson and Police Chief Sloly were ineffectual. Premier Doug Ford, in distant Toronto, had direct constitutional responsibility for policing Ottawa, but he sensed that the public considered the standoff Trudeau's problem and stayed out of it. He never visited Ottawa and, instead, left town to go snowmobiling at his cottage.

In the PMO, Trudeau was focused and determined, says Zita Astravas, who was working for Bill Blair, minister of public safety and emergency preparedness, but they were struggling to get the risk-averse public service to come up with options to restore order. Public servants, like the Conservatives, thought it might be good to negotiate with the protesters. That looked naive to staff in the PMO. "Well, who is the leader?" says Astravas. "Is this a group that actually acts with one voice? Who do we talk to? What do we say? We're not going to get rid of vaccine mandates. They were also saying that we needed to get rid of the prime minister, and they're only going to deal with the governor general, because they're going to take over Canada and do all these things for ninety days, and then they can get it back. Right. The absurdity of that is one thing. But it was like a constant drum, the push for real advice from the public service, which required more flushing out."

For the Conservatives, the convoy brought a burst of energy to Parliament Hill. The city was suddenly full of people who felt about the prime minister the way many of their constituents did. An Angus Reid poll showed that the public mood was turning against mandates: 50 percent of Canadians wanted restrictions lifted, and that rose to 80 percent for Conservatives. O'Toole tried to straddle both sides: he couldn't embrace the convoyers, whom he viewed as lunatics, nor could he ignore them. He met with some truckers outside Ottawa, but not the convoy organizers. The Liberals still attacked him, and the freedom-loving members of his caucus criticized him. Scheer led a group of Saskatchewan MPs to meet with the convoyers to show their appreciation "for the hardworking, patriotic truckers who have kept our supply chains healthy & grocery shelves stocked for the past two years."

O'Toole tried to keep his MPs from siding with the protesters. "Let them blow their steam," he says. "I don't support people breaking the law, so we can't support this . . . Once we get through the COVID craziness the media focus will then be Trudeau running again. I said, get through this and we will crush the next election with the same approach we had." They refused. On January 31, a third of O'Toole's caucus signed a letter calling for him to step down. On February 4, MPs voted seventy-three to forty-five to end his leadership.

Pierre Poilievre was waiting in the wings.

———

PEOPLE IN OTTAWA HAD had it. Abandoned by the police, they were tired of the noise, the fumes, and the maskless louts peeing in snowbanks.

On the day the Tories stuck the knife into O'Toole, Paul Champ, an Ottawa human rights lawyer, was introduced to Zexi Li, who was fed up with her neighbourhood becoming an outdoor toilet. One of her neighbours had asked Champ to take legal action against the convoy, and Li agreed to be the lead plaintiff in a class action suit. The next day, Champ filed a statement of claim, seeking monetary compensation for those affected by the constant horn honking.

Days later, Champ won an injunction not only to stop the honking but also to freeze millions of dollars in bank accounts controlled by the organizers. Spurred by friendly coverage from Fox News and viral posts on social media, donations of about $20 million had poured in, helping to pay for hotel rooms, diesel fuel, and logistics in general. The normally quiescent citizens of Ottawa had finally reached their breaking point and were pushing back. On February 13, a neighbourhood dog-walking group from Ottawa South organized a counter-protest and blocked a small convoy of flag-bearing vehicles. Police pled with convoy opponents to avoid confrontations.

That same day, at the Canada-US border at Coutts, Alberta, Mounties arrested thirteen convoy protesters who had blockaded the crossing. They seized firearms, body armour, and ammunition. Four protesters were eventually charged with conspiring to murder Mounties. Two of them were linked to Jeremy MacKenzie, the Nova Scotia Afghan vet who had founded the far-right group Diagolon. Every day, MacKenzie was livestreaming with his friends from the convoy compound in Ottawa.

After the Coutts bust, police moved to clear the blockade at the Ambassador Bridge, the Detroit-Windsor border crossing, which had jammed supply chains for auto-parts manufacturers on both sides of the border. The convoy organizers had done many things right, paralyzing the capital with a deeply irritating but peaceful protest, but they made a mistake when they shut down the bridge. Ford might not have cared about a bunch of Liberal and NDP voters in downtown Ottawa, but he would not let the auto industry get shut down. In a phone conversation with Trudeau, he promised the Ontario Provincial Police would clear the border. "This is critical," he told Trudeau. "I hear you. I'll be up their ass with a wire brush."

After that border was cleared, the province began to shift police to

Ottawa, to augment the beleaguered local force. Trudeau invoked the Emergencies Act, which enabled him to take extraordinary measures to end the siege in Ottawa. He announced the crackdown in the National Press Theatre, flanked by Chrystia Freeland, Marco Mendicino, and David Lametti. "We cannot and will not allow illegal and dangerous activities to continue," he stated.

The act empowered the RCMP to play a greater role in policing Ottawa, froze bank accounts being used to fund the protests, and allowed the government to force reluctant towing companies to move trucks. It also stipulated that, within a year, a Public Order Emergency Commission would have to report on whether this use of extraordinary power was justified. Interim Conservative leader Candice Bergen, who had wanted Trudeau to negotiate with the protesters, said invoking the act was a mistake: "The prime minister had the opportunity to talk and listen to so many he disagreed with and he refused to do so, so this looks like a ham-fisted approach that will have the opposite effect."

Pierre Poilievre, preparing to launch his leadership campaign, confidently asserted what he thought Trudeau should have done: "Real simple. Listen to the science, do what other provinces and countries are doing, that is to end the mandates and restrictions so protesters can get back to their lives and their jobs. The only emergency is the one that Justin Trudeau has deliberately created to divide the country and gain politically." A new partisan divide was taking shape, with health measures as the dominant issue around which everyone would have to orient themselves. That had been Trudeau's choice. In danger of losing an ill-considered election campaign, he had polarized the electorate around vaccination mandates. His gambit worked—just barely—but it led to blowback, cranking up emotions that would have been better soothed. It even unnerved members of Trudeau's own party.

A few days earlier, Joël Lightbound, MP for the Quebec City riding of Louis-Hébert and chair of the Liberal Quebec caucus, held a lonely news conference in which he objected to Trudeau's rhetoric. "From a positive and unifying approach, a decision was made to wedge, to divide and to stigmatize. I fear that this politicization of the pandemic risks undermining the public's trust in our public health institutions. This is not a risk we ought to be taking lightly."

For public servants and office workers, the pandemic had been mostly about hunkering down at home, but for street-level workers, life was different. "I think it's time we stop dividing the population," Lightbound said. "Not everyone can earn a living on a MacBook at a cottage."

—

POLICE STARTED TO CLEAR the streets on February 19. They set up a hundred checkpoints, hemming in the area between the Queensway and the Hill, and slowly moved in, arresting some people. Protesters yelled "hold the line," but they couldn't, and slowly the police made them leave. "We are in control of the situation on the ground and continue to push forward to clear our streets," said interim police chief Steve Bell. "We will run this operation 24 hours a day until the residents and community have their entire city back."

Bell had taken over from Sloly, who had been driven to the point of collapse by the crisis and ultimately forced out. With reinforcements from across Canada, the Ottawa police finally had the resources and authority they needed to get the city back. Tamara Lich and Pat King were arrested and charged. Within forty-eight hours, the streets were cleared and the state of emergency lifted.

Trudeau later testified at length at the Public Order Emergency Commission as commission counsel took him through a record of his behind-the-scenes communication with officials and politicians throughout the crisis. Calm and friendly, he was able to explain his interactions and state of mind with a thoroughness and precision that surprised viewers used to his pep talks full of platitudes and virtue-signalling warnings about extremists who don't share Canadian values. He was accounting for himself thoroughly and convincingly. "I am absolutely, absolutely serene and confident that I made the right choice," he said. He had acted when he had to: "The situation was out of control, with the potential for violence, not just in Ottawa but across the country."

Trudeau's calm and competent testimony made the protesters' complaints look foolish. All their dire warnings of overreach on his part seemed overwrought when he was able to demonstrate how methodically the government had proceeded. The structure of the Emergencies Act, which was passed in 1988 by Mulroney's government to replace the overbroad War Measures Act that Trudeau *père* invoked during the October Crisis, has measures embedded in it—such as the need for an inquiry—that force politicians to justify their actions as they go. That likely explained why Trudeau was able to justify its use: he had had to do so internally as he proceeded.

Nomi Claire Lazar, a political science professor at University of Ottawa and author of *States of Emergency in Liberal Democracies*, believes things could have gone much worse. "I don't think anyone can contest the fact that the situation was resolved in a way which was far safer, better than anyone could have hoped." Lazar was a member of the research council for the commission, but also lived through the convoy. "I live just two or three blocks from the cordon area—and we were really expecting that things might go badly. Everyone thought that it might become violent. The situation got resolved without anybody being seriously injured, nobody being killed. It was resolved quickly, effectively, efficiently, safely. And from that perspective, you couldn't really ask for better. Whatever other problems I have with Trudeau, I challenge you to find another situation like that anywhere else in the world in recent history, or maybe, you know, at all, where there was a resolution that tidy. That just doesn't happen."

Commissioner Paul Rouleau, the Ontario Court of Appeal judge who presided over the inquiry, found that Trudeau had met the "very high" threshold necessary to invoke the Emergencies Act. "In my view, there was credible and compelling information supporting a reasonable belief that the definition of a threat to the security of Canada was met." He did, however, criticize Trudeau for calling the protesters part of a "fringe minority," which cranked up the tension and energized them. "More of an effort should have been made by government leaders at all levels during the protests to acknowledge that the majority of protesters were exercising their fundamental democratic rights."

However, this would not be the final word. In January 2024, Federal Court justice Richard Mosley issued a ruling agreeing with an application from the Canadian Civil Liberties Association and the Canadian Constitution Foundation. Mosley ruled that the government's invocation of the act did not "bear the hallmarks of reasonableness." A government "cannot invoke the Emergencies Act because it is convenient, or because it may work better than other tools at their disposal or available to the provinces," he wrote.

Mosley noted that the protests in Alberta and at the border had been cleared by police, that Ottawa could have been managed similarly, and therefore found that the Emergencies Act was not warranted. He also found that when the RCMP ordered banks to freeze the accounts of protesters without due process, the government violated Charter protection against "unreasonable search or seizure." And by ordering the streets cleared of all protesters, rather than merely acting against the lawbreakers honking horns and blocking roads, the government violated the political rights of law-abiding protesters.

Both Mosley and Rouleau took care to note that the questions are difficult. "Reasonable and informed people could reach a different conclusion," wrote Rouleau. "Had I been at [the government] tables at that time, I may have agreed that it was necessary to invoke the Act," wrote Mosley.

The government immediately announced it will appeal, so the Supreme Court will ultimately decide which of the two judges was correct. The question of whether the invocation of the act was justified is one for constitutional scholars, but Mosley's arguments are compelling as regards the suspension of the constitutional rights of political critics. Taken with Trudeau's lackadaisical response to Charter violations by the provinces, it undercuts his assertion that the Charter holds a special place in his heart because of the values he learned at his father's knee.

He has disappointed his friends by failing to defend the Charter more vigorously. "These things are so important that as a prime minister, he's done so little by contrast to defend them and reinforce them at a time when institutions like this have never been under more attack," says one.

The Mosley ruling was a blow to Trudeau, reinforcing Poilievre's long-standing critique of his handling of the convoy. "He caused the crisis by dividing people," Poilievre tweeted. "Then he violated Charter rights to illegally suppress citizens." Even if you were among those waiting impatiently for the police to clear out the horn honkers, it is hard, in light of Mosley's ruling, to discount Poilievre's critique out of hand.

And the invocation of the act opened Trudeau up to more intense attacks from outside Canada. Fox News treated the episode as proof that Liberal poster boy Justin Trudeau was a hypocrite, suppressing lawful dissent with the help of jackbooted thugs. Its exhaustive coverage of the protest had breathed life into the movement, helping the Canadians raise funds and get their message out. The restoration of order was portrayed as a harsh and violent crackdown—a mirror image of the channel's coverage of Black Lives Matter protests, which emphasized the lawlessness of the protesters. A Fox contributor visiting Ottawa from the United States tweeted falsely that a woman had been killed, a post that was shared millions of times before it was deleted. On February 21, Tucker Carlson, then the top-rated Fox talking head, warned that northern-style totalitarianism was coming to the United States. "Now, the Biden administration, you should know and not forget, has encouraged all of this. 'Vladimir Putin is the tyrant,' they tell us, 'not Justin Trudeau.' At this point it's pretty clear that if you want to know the future they are planning for us in the United States, look north to Canada."

—

THE ONLY INTERNATIONAL ORGANIZATION that gave the protest more airtime than Fox was Russia Today. The timing was perfect. The convoy clearing operation would give Russia's defenders a convenient target when Putin invaded Ukraine on February 24.

Canada responded quickly and firmly to the invasion, bringing in sweeping sanctions against the criminals in the Kremlin, pledging billions in military and humanitarian aid, and offering sanctuary to refugees, who began arriving that spring. Trudeau and Freeland—whose family roots are in Ukraine—were important diplomatic allies for Ukrainian president Volodymyr Zelenskyy, whose brave and deft leadership inspired people around the world.

Putin's allies in the West—on Fox News and in populist parties—used the convoy to defend what Putin was doing in Ukraine. Comedian turned far-right YouTuber Russell Brand called Trudeau a hypocrite. "You can criticize Russia for many, many reasons, you can condemn the actions of Russia, quite rightly, for many reasons. What you can't do is claim to be an exemplar of democracy if whenever you get the opportunity to be tyrannical, you take it."

Two days after the tanks went over the border, Trump denounced Trudeau in the keynote address at the annual Conservative Political Action Conference in Orlando. "The radical left is trying to replace American democracy with woke tyranny," he said. The crowd booed in agreement. "They want to do the same thing to America that Trudeau has been doing to Canada—and much, much worse."

Trump, who had once praised Trudeau and knew him fairly well, did not attack Putin. The real threat to freedom was in Canada: "The tyranny we have witnessed in Canada in recent weeks should shock and dismay people all over the world," he said. "A line has been crossed—you're either with the peaceful truckers or you are with the left-wing fascists."

Trudeau, who had once delighted the world with his nerdy socks, his good looks, and his progressive bromides, now had an enormous target on his back. He is likely to spend the rest of his political career as a whipping boy for populists around the world. He defends democracy and the rule of law, warning against extremism and disinformation, but he has not found a register for responding successfully to the likes of Carlson, Brand, and Trump. Perhaps it is impossible. The police operation that ended the convoy upheld the civil rights of the protesters according to the highest standards of law in the world. In contrast, Putin's soldiers have murdered, raped, and tortured Ukrainian civilians on a scale not seen in Europe since the Second World War. There is no way to argue rationally that the two operations are equivalent.

Trump's Svengali, Steve Bannon, figured out how to operate in the new online world when he was running Breitbart News and working with Cambridge Analytica during the Brexit referendum. "The Democrats don't matter," he explained in 2018. "The real opposition is the media. And the way to deal with them is to flood the zone with shit."

For the rest of his time in office, Trudeau would be operating in that zone.

———

IN OCTOBER 2021, I got a tip that Liberals and New Democrats were quietly discussing the possibility of a governing accord in which the NDP would agree to support the Liberals in the House in exchange for a commitment to work on NDP priorities. I couldn't confirm that there were formal discussions, but senior people on both sides were talking about it among themselves.

The idea had obvious advantages and risks for both parties—especially for the increasingly unpopular Trudeau. Liberal Nathaniel Erskine-Smith, an outspoken, left-leaning Toronto MP, was in favour of making a deal: "There are so many shared priorities, from climate action, to advancing reconciliation, to addressing affordable housing, to addressing the opioid crisis, to PharmaCare, to long-term care, to child care and on and on, that we should establish a working agreement for stability in parliament, and to ensure that we deliver on our shared priorities over the next— hopefully as many as three years." But business-leaning Liberals, who were already uncomfortable with the government's leftward tilt, were not enthusiastic, and neither were left-wing NDPers, who would find it hard to vote for the people who bought a pipeline.

In January, Gurkiran Kaur Sidhu, Jagmeet Singh's wife, gave birth to a daughter, Anhad. Trudeau called to congratulate the first-time father, and they had a warm conversation. He suggested they talk about a deal. The details were hammered out behind the scenes in secret meetings between Liberals Jeremy Broadhurst and Katie Telford and New Democrats Jennifer Howard and Anne McGrath.

Trudeau had nudged them to talk during a beginning-of-session meeting with Singh, where they discussed their priorities for the sitting. "Katie passed a note to me about making sure that we had each other's phone numbers, and that we should get together and blah, blah, blah," says McGrath. "And then when we were leaving, Trudeau said, 'You two should get together and talk.'"

Telford and McGrath trusted each other, having worked together before. McGrath had the impression that Trudeau was pushing the idea on the Liberal side, nudging his people to make it happen whenever they were losing momentum. The NDPers called BC colleagues, who had worked out a similar arrangement that allowed NDP premier John Horgan to govern that province with the support of the Greens.

In March, Singh and Trudeau announced the deal, an agreement requiring the NDP to vote with the Liberals on confidence and supply bills, which would mean the government would not fall before 2025. In exchange, the Liberals agreed to support a new dental care program for low-income Canadians and eventually a universal pharmacare plan. In addition, they would allow three days of voting in the next election and a corporate beneficial ownership registry, which would make it easier to crack down on tax cheats.

The deal was a huge win for Trudeau, who would no longer have to strategize around how to survive every vote in the House. He said it was "a responsible answer to the uncertainty we're in, to the challenges facing democracies with hyper-partisanship and toxic polarization." It gave some measure of job security to MPs and staffers in both parties, and the opportunity to plan beyond the next vote in the House.

The agreement opened the NDP up to attacks from the Conservatives, who portrayed it as an unethical coalition cooked up in the backrooms, without the consent of voters. Every time the Liberals relied on NDP votes to kill some politically dangerous committee hearing, the Conservatives could blame the NDP. In 2023, as the housing crisis deepened and inflation increased, Poilievre sharpened his attacks on the Liberals. And, as the Conservatives began to target NDP seats where blue-collar voters could be convinced to vote Tory, the deal looked less and less comfortable for Singh.

When the arrangement was announced, Singh had promised he would pull the plug if it didn't work: "If they fall short on what we've agreed to, then the deal doesn't continue. But I'm going into this with a strong conviction that we can get this done." The conventional wisdom holds that smaller parties usually suffer from these arrangements because voters tend to blame them for unpopular policies pursued by the larger party. A similar deal between British Conservative prime minister David Cameron and the centrist Liberal Democrats was disastrous for the smaller party, leading to near electoral wipeout. That, so far, has not happened to the NDP in this deal. The arrangement bound the two parties together, preventing the Liberals from tacking right—which may have been politically smart, given the electoral threat from the Tories—and producing results for NDP supporters. The polls show them maintaining their support as Liberal numbers drop and a growing number of Canadians warm to the message from Pierre Poilievre.

14

ENTER POILIEVRE

Pierre Poilievre first came to my attention in 2004, when we were both new to Ottawa, and I used to sit in the gallery of the House to watch Question Period. Poilievre, then a freshly elected twenty-five-year-old, stood out as unusually combative, smug, and partisan. He sought every opportunity to take cheap shots at his opponents, like a trash-talking hockey player, always slashing, trying to draw penalties. Every team needs a player like that, but they get on your nerves.

In those days, he was dating Jenni Byrne, an up-and-comer in the PMO, and he would often deliver over-the-top partisan rants in the House typed up by her brash young PMO staffers, who Tory MPs nicknamed "the boys in short pants." I found his harsh recitations chilling because he gave the impression he would deliver the attacks no matter what the words said, so fierce and remorseless was his partisanship.

But his skill and zeal made him a valuable player, and once Stephen Harper beat Paul Martin in the 2006 election, he made Poilievre parliamentary secretary to John Baird, the president of the Treasury Board.

Poilievre had a setback in 2008, on the day Stephen Harper formally apologized to Indigenous people abused in the residential schools

288 | STEPHEN MAHER

system—one of the most significant moments of Harper's time in government. Before the apology, I had an emotional interview with Katherine Sorbey, then a spritely and energetic sixty-five-year-old. Sorbey, a Mi'kmaq Cape Bretoner, had been taken away from her family as a child and abused at the Shubenacadie Indian Residential School, an experience she struggled to deal with over the years. "I've lived a good life," she told me. "I'm tough. But it took me a while to let the tears flow from these experiences. I'm getting on the road now. I'm almost dying out, but I'm on the right path. I'm going to go with a clear conscience, a clear heart, and my soul will be free of any pains and hurts, anger for anybody else."

Sorbey later brought up three children and fostered others, taught Mi'kmaq, fought for justice, worked as a journalist and a civil servant, and appeared in films. The apology was deeply meaningful for her, helping to close a painful chapter. She even wrapped herself in a Canadian flag to celebrate the occasion—something she would never have normally done.

Later that day, though, she was hurt and angered by comments that Poilievre made in a radio interview. Poilievre thought the settlement was too expensive. "Now, along with this apology, comes another $4 billion in compensation for those who partook in the residential schools over those years," he said. "Some of us are starting to ask: 'Are we really getting value for all of this money, and is more money really going to solve the problem?' My view is that we need to engender the values of hard work and independence and self-reliance."

Years later, Sorbey told me the comments hit her and the other survivors hard. "The older survivors told the younger ones, remember that he's just a man. He's human. He's not any worse or any better than any of us. That's what we were taught. Let him be and let it be. There's nobody going to cure the human race."

Poilievre's comments were disrespectful to people like Sorbey, who had spent their lives trying to recover from the suffering they endured, suffering that Poilievre must not have contemplated for a moment. His comments cast a shadow over the day, and Harper was furious. The *Globe and Mail* reported that Harper "dressed him down so sharply that people outside the room were embarrassed."

Poilievre apologized in the House the next day and eventually found his way back into Harper's good books. In 2013, Harper made him minister for democratic reform and put him in charge of overhauling the Fair Elections Act.* Opposition parties and civil society groups thought the new bill would weaken Elections Canada's enforcement arm and make it harder to vote, a milder version of Republican-style voter suppression measures. When Elections Canada head Marc Mayrand complained he hadn't been consulted and warned the amendments could hamstring the agency, Poilievre attacked him by implying he was a Liberal. The "referee should not be wearing a team jersey," he said, a statement calculated to weaken public faith in the independent agency that runs Canadian elections, one of the best in the world.

After the Liberals won in 2015, Poilievre blossomed as a critic, finding ways to hold the government's feet to the fire and tormenting Bill Morneau with particular relish. He pressed Morneau on the blind trust in which he had placed shares in the family pension management firm while he was making rules about the industry. When Morneau bent to pressure and divested, Poilievre went for the jugular. "The finance minister hid his offshore company in France until he got caught, and then he reported it. He hid from Canadians his millions of dollars in Morneau Shepell shares in a numbered company in Alberta, despite wrongly telling others it was in a blind trust, until he got caught, and now he is selling them."

Poilievre has a gift for quickly finding the most devastating line of attack and is thoroughly committed to the Conservative cause, quali-

---

* The impetus for a new act was a series of investigative stories I did with Glen McGregor on the so-called robocalls scandal, concerning Conservative dirty tricks in the 2011 campaign.

ties that earn him grudging respect from his opponents, including Trudeau. During the WE Charity controversy, when Trudeau testified by video hookup at committee, Poilievre roasted him over the speaking fees WE paid to his family members, demanding he say the amount. When Trudeau refused, saying he didn't have the number in front of him, Poilievre was scathing. "Nobody believes you," he said. Trudeau actually squirmed in his seat as Poilievre skewered him and tried to talk about his mother's advocacy work. Poilievre was not interested. "You don't know how much your family has received from this organization to which you tried to give a half billion dollars. Really?"

While O'Toole was leader, Poilievre worked hard on his social media game, regularly recording and uploading videos and finding an audience. It became clear that Poilievre had the leadership in mind: his comments had nothing to do with O'Toole's message track and never referenced him. To reach a larger audience, beginning in 2018, Poilievre, or—theoretically—someone working for him, used a hidden tag—#mgtow—which stands for "Men Going Their Own Way," an online anti-feminist movement adjacent to the incel movement.

Poilievre considered running for the Conservative leadership in 2020 but dropped out at the last minute for personal reasons, saying he didn't realize how hard it would be on his family. Anaida, his wife, born in Venezuela and raised in Montreal, had met Poilievre on the Hill, where she was working as a parliamentary staffer. They eloped to Portugal in 2017 and have two small children.

Like Sophie Grégoire Trudeau, Anaida has her own social media presence. In 2020 she founded the online magazine *Pretty & Smart* and wrote articles offering career advice and closet-organizing tips. One article, early in the pandemic, urged people to obey public health rules, listen to experts, and "#StayTheFuckHome."

When the convoy arrived in Ottawa, Poilievre delivered coffee to the protesters on the Hill. He cast their struggle in a libertarian framework, emphasizing the importance of personal freedom—something he embraced, at least according to his superhero origin story, when he discovered the writing of American economist Milton Friedman as a high-school student. Whether because of a passionate belief in liberty or a cold-eyed political calculation, he welcomed the Freedom movement and has taken care ever since to stay connected. "The Trudeau government has attacked small businesses, truckers and other hard-working Canadians," he said in the video he dropped to launch his campaign.

Out on the ground, hustling for support, he would make more explicit appeals to the conspiracy-minded convoy supporters. In April 2022, when he and Anaida were grilled by potential supporters outside the Elks Lodge in North Bay, Ontario, someone in the crowd uploaded the exchange to TikTok. An older woman told him she had driven four hours to meet him. "I want you to know that I have been following you and watching you, and you have given me so much hope," she said. But she had questions too: Had he confronted Trudeau about all the money he has made from vaccines? There were fake stories on Facebook and Twitter alleging that Trudeau's family had shares in a Vancouver-based biotech company. A man chimed in: "$70 million in two years." Poilievre said no, he hadn't spoken to Trudeau.

The woman went on. "I have heard you have shares in that company." Stepping away from her husband, Anaida took the woman's hand and gazed into her eyes. "I do not, darling," she said. "I really do not." The crowd applauded. "I hope to God that's true," the woman said. "I hope you guys are who we think you are."

The video provided a behind-the-scenes look at Poilievre's cultivation of what we might call disinformed Canadians. Standing in front of the lodge that day, Poilievre fielded questions about Bill Gates, the World Health Organization, and the World Economic Forum, all elements of the "Great Reset" conspiracy theory—the claim that elites are using the pandemic to collapse the world's economy and install a tyrannical global government. He parried and deflected, explaining away a 2015 photo with Gates by saying that the Microsoft co-founder was simply visiting

Parliament. His answers seemed to satisfy the group, but what he didn't do is contradict their mistaken beliefs or try to convince them that it is silly to worry about the World Economic Forum or Bill Gates injecting people with microchips. He was enthusiastically harnessing the energy of deluded people who get their ideas from social media fever swamps. He would ride that tiger to the leadership of his party.

Jean Charest challenged him for the leadership, but he never had a chance. Charest, one of the most talented politicians of his generation, seemed not to understand the race he was in. The days of genteel brokerage politics are long gone. Modern leadership races are about mass membership sales driven by social media messaging. Poilievre knew what he was doing. Charest looked like a relic of an earlier age. The polling showed that Canadians would have embraced Charest as a non-scary alternative to a tired Liberal government, but party members saw him as part of the Mulroney gang, a quasi-Liberal who could not be trusted.

It wasn't even clear that Charest would come second. Former Ontario PC leader Patrick Brown, who had figured out how to sell memberships in diaspora communities, had been driven out of Ontario politics by allegations of sexual wrongdoing (which he strenuously denied). He was a threat to Poilievre, until, in July, the party announced he was disqualified. He was summarily tried and found guilty by the party of having paid a campaign worker off the books. Canadians learned later that her legal bills had been paid by the Poilievre campaign.

In December 2023, Sam Cooper revealed that CSIS believed the Indian government had interfered in the leadership race, supporting one candidate and working against another. That is a disturbing allegation, but the leadership result could not have been clearer. After Brown was bounced, there was nothing in Poilievre's way. He won with 68 percent of the vote on the first ballot. More than five hundred thousand people had joined the party during the three-month leadership race, 311,958 of them to support Poilievre. He campaigned as an outsider who wanted to undo Trudeau's Canada. He promised to get rid of mandates, defund the CBC, and fire the governor of the Bank of Canada.

A friend who talked to Trudeau the day after the convention reports that he was "energized" by the prospect of facing Poilievre in an election. "He thinks that Poilievre is everything he dislikes," says another friend. "He's an asshole. He's mean. He's gonna hurt a lot of people who are already vulnerable. He can't stand him."

The mutual hostility is clear enough in every exchange between the two men. Poilievre took the fight to Trudeau in the next Question Period, two weeks later, showing his ability to find the weakest spot in an opponent's armour. "It is good to see the Prime Minister here, visiting Canada, to fill up the gas on his private jet," he said. Trudeau had just flown back from Queen Elizabeth's funeral in London, New York for the UN General Assembly, and was about to fly to Japan for the funeral of former Japanese prime minister Shinzō Abe. Poilievre pressed him on the impact of the carbon tax on home-heating oil in Newfoundland and Labrador, which was going to hit seniors on fixed incomes hard. "The leader of the Liberal Party has an opportunity to respect the fact that heating one's home in January and February in Canada is not a luxury, and it does not make those Canadians polluters. They are just trying to survive. This from a prime minister who burned more jet fuel in one month than 20 average Canadians burn in an entire year. Will the prime minister ground the jet, park the hypocrisy and axe the tax hikes?"

Trudeau responded by mocking Poilievre's support for unregulated cryptocurrency. "If Canadians had followed the advice of the leader of the opposition and invested in volatile cryptocurrencies in an attempt to 'opt out of inflation,' they would have lost half of their savings."

In retrospect, Trudeau might have been better off taking Poilievre's suggestion on the carbon tax. Under the threat of losing Atlantic seats, in October 2023, Trudeau agreed to let Freeland suspend the carbon tax on heating oil for three years, overruling objections behind the scenes from Guilbeault. Politicians in the rest of Canada, whose constituents would not get a break on natural gas, objected angrily. It looked like desperation, stoked regional resentments, and threatened to undermine Trudeau's central environmental policy. If he had acted sooner, he might have been able to change the policy without a humiliating backdown that undercut the rationale for the carbon tax.

Trudeau won in 2015 after campaigning to take action to help the "middle class and those working hard to join it," convincing Canadians that he, not Harper, would be more likely to look after their economic interests. At some point, the government stopped emphasizing that. Liberals can point to significant ongoing efforts to help people who are struggling, through child care and dental programs, for instance, but the government has stopped talking effectively about its commitment to the middle class. They did not see the cost-of-living crisis coming.

On the economy, Poilievre has been strong, overmatching Trudeau with a libertarian message delivered skillfully on social media. Once he dropped his crypto fixation, Poilievre had a good, simple message: the government should get out of the way, cut taxes, and go after "gatekeepers" stifling growth in other levels of government. "There are people in this country who are just hanging on by a thread," he said in his victory speech. "They don't need a government to run their lives; they need a government that can run a passport office. They need a prime minister who hears them and offers them hope that they can again afford to buy a home, a car, pay their bills, afford food, have a secure retirement, and God forbid even achieve their dreams if they work hard. They need a prime minister who will restore that hope, and I will be that prime minister."

The Liberals are out of touch. Three months after Poilievre became leader, Chrystia Freeland released a fall economic update warning that Canada might face a recession in 2023. "The Canadian economy faces global headwinds from a position of fundamental strength," she said—the kind of thing you say when the bottom is falling out of your boat.

Freeland, a brave and formidable person, sometimes fails to find the right tone. In an interview on Global's *West Block* a few days later, Mercedes Stephenson asked her if the government was considering program review—finding ways to save tax dollars. Freeland told her she had already found $3 billion in savings. "I personally, as a mother and wife, look carefully at my credit card bill once a month," she explained. "Last Sunday I said to the kids, 'You're older now. You don't watch Disney anymore. Let's cut that Disney+ subscription.' So we cut it. It's only $13.99 a month that we're saving, but every little bit helps. And I think every mother in Canada is doing that right now. And I want to say to all of those mothers, I believe that I need to take exactly the same approach with the federal government's finances because that's the money of Canadians."

It landed badly. The Canadian Press did an access-to-information request for emails to her office and discovered many angry messages accusing her of being "smug," "elitist," "clueless" and "entitled." She apologized. In the House, Poilievre attacked her for the comment and linked it to the carbon tax.

Poilievre exaggerates the economic impact of the carbon tax to the point of dishonesty. Most voters are better off for it because they receive bigger rebates than they pay in tax, but they notice only the increased bills, not the rebates. And in the symbolic sense in which voters absorb politics, Poilievre is right in a way. Trudeau has made decisions that have constrained resource extraction—mining, oil, and gas in particular, but also agriculture and transportation—and imposed restraints on sectors of the economy that would have grown faster if Harper, say, had continued as prime minister. Under Trudeau, it has become harder to build pipelines or mines. In response to climate, public health, and Indigenous concerns, Bill C-69, which critics call the no-more-pipelines act, opened new barriers for projects in these sectors. Conservatives were particularly angered that the bill required regulators to consider the possibility of violence against Indigenous women from the "man camps" that are established wherever resources are extracted, seeing it as an insult to the men who hew the wood and draw the water we all need.

296 | STEPHEN MAHER

Trudeau had promised to grow the economy and protect the environment. By 2022, the people who felt he put too much emphasis on the lat-
ter were growing increasingly frustrated, and Steven Guilbeault, who did
not shrink from exercising his authority, looked like a nightmare to the
oil patch, bringing back bad memories of Marc Lalonde's National Energy
Program under Trudeau *père*. Westerners accused Trudeau of preventing
them from putting bread on the table and Maseratis in their driveways.

For leaders trying to create economic opportunity for their people,
Trudeau's policies were unbelievably frustrating. "I just think he's been
the most divisive prime minister we've ever had," says former Saskatchewan premier Brad Wall. "More so than his father, even. I think his policies
are more of a danger to the West's economy, and willfully so." Wall questions the sustainability of the federation. "This Canada, it doesn't really
represent us in a meaningful way, or doesn't provide us remedies when
we feel like we're just being ignored or, worse, targeted. And I didn't think
that was the sense during [the] Chrétien and Martin [administrations].
I mean, they were pragmatic, they were fiscally responsible, they had to
support and promote a Canadian industry, including oil and gas."

If the Trudeau government wants to reduce Canada's greenhouse gas
emissions, however, it does not have many options. Per capita greenhouse
gas emissions are five times as high in Alberta and Saskatchewan as in
Ontario or Quebec, almost entirely because of the oil and gas industry—particularly the oil from the oil sands, which must be cooked out of
the sand. Any policy aimed at bringing down Canada's emissions would
hit that part of the country harder. On this issue, the government has
achieved some success: the Canadian Climate Institute reported in 2023
that Canadian emissions were 6.3 percent lower in 2022 than in 2005. But
opponents blame the government for changing market conditions that
are beyond its control. As pressure builds in global financial markets to
hold companies accountable for their pollution, the world's big oil companies have been moving out of the oil sands, selling their holdings to
local companies.

Even Blue Liberals think the Trudeau government has given Guilbeault too much leeway. They point to the failure to push liquid natural gas exports to Europe, which would reduce European reliance on Russian gas, and to Asia, where it could reduce the use of coal. And unlike Europe or the United States, Canada has not made it easier to get permits for critical mineral mines, which are necessary for the massive shift to a battery-powered world. Blue Liberals don't know why Trudeau doesn't bend and become more pragmatic on these questions, but at this point in his mandate, polling so badly and relying on the NDP for parliamentary support, it's not clear that he could change course. He couldn't afford to lose Guilbeault, a crucial communicator in Quebec, where Trudeau needs to maintain his support.

Despite western alienation, the environment and energy file is not the worst one for Trudeau or the best one for Poilievre. As always, bread-and-butter issues are the easiest way to get the attention of voters, and both bread and butter have become much more expensive while Trudeau has been prime minister, with annual food inflation pushing 10 percent—the result of the war in Ukraine and pandemic supply-chain issues. But Poilievre has been able to blame it on the carbon tax—a real but small factor in price increases—and on inflation caused by the government's free-spending ways.

Federal policy may or may not be responsible for inflation—which is worse in other countries than in Canada—but there is little doubt that the Trudeau government is responsible for the housing crisis. Federal governments have historically helped to build housing during moments when supply was tight, and Trudeau did not take the necessary action, even while increasing immigration to record levels—431,645 newcomers in 2022. There was nowhere for all those new people to live. And no place for the 551,405 international students Canada welcomed in 2022, plus an unknown number of undocumented foreigners—the migrants who somehow got into Canada without papers. Tent encampments started to appear in major cities, not only for the people afflicted by mental health issues or addiction but also those who could not find a place to rent. And forget about buying: home ownership is for baby boomers.

Although this crisis should have been foreseeable—that's why we have the Canada Mortgage and Housing Corporation and Statistics Canada— it seemed to come as a surprise to the Trudeau government. That created a huge political opening for Poilievre. "I think we're headed to a massive socioeconomic crisis in the next couple of years as an entire generation of young people are forced to give up on having kids, building home equity or even leaving their parents' basements," he told the *Sault Star* in July. "It was never like this before Trudeau, and it won't be like this after he's gone."

Poilievre was speaking for all the people stuck in their parents' basements, and they were listening. Trudeau, who had never had to worry about putting a roof over his head, had somehow failed to see this issue coming. His government had actually started putting money into housing—more than any prime minister since Brian Mulroney—but it was not enough to keep up with demand. Young people began to tell pollsters they planned to vote Conservative. This was an enormous shift from recent patterns and an existential threat to the Liberals, who had looked like the party of hope and change in 2015. Now it was Poilievre who was talking about hope—and young people who were listening. Underpinning the loss of support was a generalized gloom among the young, who got the dirty end of the pandemic stick and now can't find places to live.

"The most pessimistic group are young people," says pollster Nik Nanos. "In the past, young people tended to be the most optimistic, which means that, in 2015, for a leader that talked about sunny ways and appealed to young people, now he has taken that generation and turned them from the most optimistic and hopeful into the most pessimistic and negative when it comes to the country and when it comes to the future."

Trudeau, too late, came to see he had a problem, and he put the talented Sean Fraser—the towering, bagpipe-playing MP for Central Nova—on the housing file in July 2023. He started using carrots and sticks in an effort to get municipalities to approve more construction. It was a good start, but it would not produce results quickly enough to get those angry kids out of their parents' basements or give them much reason to vote for Trudeau.

And the gloom was not confined to young people. In November 2023, pollster Frank Graves did a survey and was shocked by the grim national mood. Seven out of ten Canadians felt the country was moving in the wrong direction, the worst score Graves has seen in thirty years of polling. Three-quarters thought the world was becoming more dangerous. And not even half said they had a strong connection to Canada. Canadians were increasingly distrustful of institutions, worried about political polarization, disinformation, and their own finances, and increasingly skeptical about immigration. "When you look at the collective expression of fundamental barometers of societal health and cohesion, this constitutes a legitimacy crisis," says Graves. "It's not sustainable."

Oddly, the government's approval numbers—though terrible—were worse than the score for the direction of the country. And the results in similar countries are even worse, Graves says. "The idea that this is authored by the missteps of the Trudeau government flies in the face of the fact that we're seeing similar kinds of pathology—nihilism, anomie, whatever you want to call it—these are like once-in-a century types of bad outlooks—they're going on basically in every other advanced Western democracy."

When it is time for a change, it is time for a change. At the end of 2023, the polls kept sending Trudeau the same grim message, and everything the Trudeau government did seemed to go sideways. "It's like watching somebody who's been on the ice too long," says one former senior staffer. "It doesn't matter how good of a hockey player they are, if they're gassed they're gassed, and they're just not able to do anything."

The next election is Poilievre's to lose, but he might find a way to do that. He signalled from the beginning that he would stay connected to the convoyers and appointed as director of communications Sarah

Fischer, who has passionate libertarian beliefs about government over-reach during the pandemic. He was insulting to reporters and friendly to anti-vaxxers. There is a sensible plan behind this stance. If he can perma-nently absorb supporters from Max Bernier's People's Party of Canada, the Conservative Party will not have to worry about its right flank in every election. But would middle-of-the-road Canadian voters find his openness to outlandish ideas off-putting? Would voters really want to entrust management of the national economy to someone who could be gulled by the hucksters selling crypto on YouTube?

Maybe not, but by the time Poilievre won the leadership, many Cana-dians were exhausted with the current prime minister. He had pulled off an election victory by polarizing voters around the pandemic, but frus-tration with him was growing. People who had never voted for Trudeau were increasingly unable to abide pious lectures about diversity from Prime Minister Blackface or about feminism from the man who threw Jody Wilson-Raybould under the bus. Worse, people who had voted for him repeatedly were tired of his schtick. "Every MP will tell you that their closest, most long-standing Liberal supporters all think it's time," a Liberal MP told me in late 2023. "Every MP."

Even his friends were telling him to go. "I think of him more as the leader for a time, and I think the times require a different kind of leader now," says one close friend. "That's how I look at it."

Governments naturally take special care to look after people in their electoral coalition—preferential treatment that, over time, becomes in-creasingly irritating to those outside that coalition. Trudeau looks hostile to rural people and those who make their living in resource extraction. He rarely makes appearances with police or members of the Canadian Armed Forces, and he doesn't speak often or effectively about issues that matter to working-class white men. His diverse, social-media-attuned staffers take pains to be politically correct, but a growing number of peo-ple outside his coalition think that the government ignores issues that are important to them. He has focused, perhaps by necessity, on the people in his coalition—and left the rest to Poilievre. But Trudeau does not want Poilievre to run the country. "He's been around this place a long time," he told me in 2024. "I have never seen the drive to service. What is the call to build a country? I've seen a tremendous, cutthroat competitor, someone who's willing to do whatever it takes to win, to score points, to make the goal. And there've been politicians in all parties who do that, but that's never been what drives me."

Trudeau is telling everyone he is keen to face Poilievre in an election. "I just see it as such a fundamental choice in what kind of country we are, who we are as Canadians. That, for me, is what I got into politics for: to have big fights like this about who we are as a country and where we're going. And that is what this next election is going to be—because the contrast between the vision that Mr. Poilievre is putting forward and what we continue to work for every single day couldn't be clearer, couldn't be crisper. As a competitor, as a leader, as someone committed to this country, being there for that conversation with Canadians touches me at the core of what I feel my purpose is in stepping forward into politics."

But it is not clear to Liberals, even some close to Trudeau, that he is the best candidate to face Poilievre. Some think he is uniquely qualified to lose to him, given the deep resentment and fatigue that many voters feel for Trudeau, and the dominance of cost-of-living concerns, which have destroyed many governments. Voters struggling to pay their bills do not believe that Trudeau understands their problems, and Liberals have been watching in dismay as the government has failed to connect on bread-and-butter issues. If there was a strong leader waiting in the wings, Trudeau would have to watch out for knives in his back.

There are no similar mixed feelings among Conservatives. They have rallied behind Poilievre, setting aside any squeamishness as he has shown greater poise and depth, and continued to expand his lead in the polls. He is doing so well and has been for so long that he is attracting prominent prospective candidates, as Trudeau did before the 2015 election.

And Jenni Byrne, the formidable strategist and organizer who helped Harper win his majority in 2011, is his chief advisor, bringing her focus, skill, and determination to his operation. She knows her candidate well, and neither of them will shrink from doing what is necessary to win. The smart money is on them, not Trudeau.

15

ANNUS HORRIBILIS

In April 2021, Kenny Chiu, the Conservative MP for the British Columbia riding of Steveston–Richmond East, introduced a private members' bill to establish a foreign influence registry. It would have required anyone trying to influence the Canadian government on behalf of a foreign entity to register publicly. Chiu, who immigrated from Hong Kong in 1982, modelled his bill after Australia's Foreign Influence Transparency Scheme, which Prime Minister Malcolm Turnbull passed in 2018 after becoming alarmed at Chinese "influence operations" aimed at controlling Australians of Chinese descent and manipulating Australian decision makers. Because China was also targeting Canada—a "direct threat to our national security and sovereignty," CSIS calls it—Chiu thought Canada should take similar steps.

The Liberal government did not agree, so the bill, like most private members' bills, went nowhere, but Chiu paid a price for suggesting it. In the 2021 election, his suburban Vancouver riding, where about 45 percent of the voters are of Chinese ancestry, was targeted with disinformation, articles in the Chinese-language press and a social media campaign on WhatsApp and WeChat portraying him as anti-Chinese. Some warned that the registry would result in internment camps for Chinese Canadians. The campaign, which appears to have been orchestrated by Beijing, hurt the Conservatives in ridings across Canada. Chinese Canadians lean Conservative, but the campaign succeeded in convincing many to vote for other parties or stay home. We can't know for sure, but it looks as though it cost Chiu his seat. He lost to Liberal Parm Bains by 3,477 votes.

Chiu believes many Chinese Canadians who voted for him in 2019 were convinced to stay home by Chinese disinformation. "If you are a Conservative supporter, when you see that your MP is proposing something that would hurt yourself and your family in the future, and that his leader has taken a very anti-Chinese position, you probably would feel disincentivized to go to ballot as well," he told me in an interview later. He had several meetings with CSIS officers, showing them printed examples of the disinformation and answering their queries. They refused to tell him what they would do with the information. "They're asking all these questions. And they would not tell me why or what they're going to be following up on."

Before the election, Trudeau's government established the Security and Intelligence Threats to Elections Task Force, a group of senior intelligence officials tasked with monitoring election interference during the campaign, with the power to raise an alarm if necessary. Walied Soliman, the co-chair of Erin O'Toole's campaign, attended task force meetings with other party representatives. The party was getting reports from across Canada of a foreign influence campaign, so he raised the issue with the task force. "Our concerns were never taken seriously," he tweeted later. "We were met with shrugged shoulders and complete ambivalence. It was truly unreal."

The Chinese Communists wanted O'Toole to lose the election because he had been speaking out forcefully about the threat that China poses to Canada and the world. In November 2020, Conservative foreign affairs critic Michael Chong tabled a motion in the House asking the government to ban Huawei from building Canada's 5G network and lay out a plan for fighting Chinese interference in Canadian politics. The Liberals voted against the motion, ignored the request for a plan, and delayed banning Huawei until May 2022.

O'Toole kept warning that Canada had to change its direction on China. "The democratic world must acknowledge that the approach to China over the last two decades has not worked. In fact, the situation has gotten worse," he said. "Canadians of Chinese origin have been threatened by foreign agents in our country. Anti–Hong Kong protests were organized in Canada to bully democracy activists. Uighur students in our universities have been de-platformed and menaced in coordinated actions led by Chinese consulates across our country. And the very values we hold dear, like openness, justice and tolerance, have been weaponized against us."

He was right. For decades, as China became the industrial powerhouse of the world and both sides enjoyed the ringing of cash registers, Beijing played nice with its customers in the West, and the West played nice with Beijing. But China has changed its tactics, likely because it has convinced so many countries to join the Belt and Road Initiative—a transportation infrastructure plan linking Chinese factories with materials and markets around the world. The network of ports and roads, built with Chinese capital and know-how, connects 155 countries with about three-quarters of the world's population, creating a sphere of influence that could make China a more potent threat to Western dominance than the Soviets ever were.

To throw their weight around, the Chinese were using what they call "wolf warrior diplomacy" to project power outside the web of belts and roads. That explains the insulting tone repeatedly taken by Cong Peiwu, the Chinese ambassador to Canada. In 2020, when Canada was considering asylum claims from Hong Kong democracy protesters, for instance, he warned that they would risk the safety of Canadians in that city. "If the Canadian side really cares about the stability and the prosperity in Hong Kong, and really cares about the good health and safety of those three hundred thousand Canadian passport-holders in Hong Kong, and the large number of Canadian companies operating in Hong Kong SAR, you should support those efforts to fight violent crimes."

The Chinese were creating problems for Canadian canola, pork, and lobster exporters, treating Canada like a petulant vassal state that needed to be put in its place. Trudeau stood back and did nothing to combat it. In fairness, he may have felt constrained at the time by the Chinese seizure of the two Michaels, but even after they were released, he did not press the reset button on the relationship, and nor did he bring in a foreign registry. Why, no one knows. Canada should be six to eighteen months behind Australia on this file—given that country's proximity to China—not three years.

Quebec's powerful Desmarais family, which has close business and family ties to Brian Mulroney, Jean Chrétien, and Paul Martin, and was connected to Trudeau senior, has been influencing Liberal thinking on China for generations. People who have watched Trudeau closely do not believe, however, that he failed to act as the result of pressure from the business community. "If you have three people sitting in the PMO who just show up unannounced, one is a union leader, one is an environmentalist, and one is a Canadian CEO responsible for fifty thousand jobs, I don't know who's going to get in first, but I can tell you who's going to get in last," says a former Cabinet minister. "It's the business guy. He doesn't trust business, doesn't take advice from business."

Trudeau first went to China with his father as a boy, and his brother has written of Chinese society with frank admiration. Perhaps Trudeaus just like China. Whatever the reason, it is hard to understand his inaction in the face of Chinese interference in our democracy, which is a threat to our sovereignty. The Australians understood it as such and reacted firmly while Canada did little.

O'Toole thinks the Canadian inaction can be traced back to politics, in particular to Queen's Park, where many of Trudeau's people began their careers and where some Liberal politicians have cozy relations with the Chinese consulate. It is not inherently disloyal for Chinese immigrants to support the government of China, and many recent arrivals naturally take pride in their homeland, seeing no conflict between supporting President Xi at home and Prime Minister Trudeau here. But that dual allegiance became increasingly problematic after Xi took our men hostage. The Chinese had to be stopped from working against Chiu and other candidates. Eventually, Trudeau's inaction became too much to bear and our spies began to leak, drawing the public's attention to what they saw as a failure on the part of the government.

There were a number of leakers, and they gave information to both Sam Cooper, who was at Global News until 2023, and the *Globe and Mail*, in what appeared to be a carefully managed series of information dumps designed to prevent the government from spinning its way out of the mess because there was no way to guess what might leak next.

The central allegation was that Trudeau had failed to respond adequately to intelligence reports that revealed Chinese interference in Canadian politics. This intrusion had two goals: to put friendly politicians in place and to defeat those less friendly—such as Chiu and Chong, who were speaking out against China in the House and urging Canada to take steps to defend its institutions from interference.

The Liberals complained that the leaks were inaccurate, but for security reasons they could not respond with detailed rebuttals. They pointed out that the kind of messages O'Toole and Chiu objected to—WeChat attacks—had previously been aimed at Liberal candidates, which is true. Retired intelligence officials were horrified by the implications for the secret sources and methods that were exposed by all the leaks, but eventually the revelations reached a point that the government could no longer ignore them.

———

ON MARCH 22, 2023, Han Dong, the Liberal MP for Don Valley North, stood in the House of Commons to announce that he was resigning from the Liberal caucus because of a Global News report that alleged, according to secret sources in Canada's intelligence agencies, he had urged a Chinese diplomat to keep the two Michaels in prison in China. Earlier, Global had reported that Dong, who was born in Shanghai, had won the nomination in the riding with the help of Beijing's Toronto consulate and that he was one of eleven candidates in Toronto secretly backed by China in the 2019 election.

Dong, with a little Maple Leaf pin on his lapel, read from a written state-ment. He said he had done no such thing, would never do such a thing, and broke down in tears as he sent a message to his family. "To my parents, who brought us here to Canada, to my wife, Sophie, and my kids, I love you. I thank you for all the support and love you give me." Dong started to weep piteously, bracing himself on his desk for strength. "The truth will protect us. Our honour and our family will get through this together."

We cannot know whether the allegations against Han Dong are true because they come from unnamed sources and rely on documents and recordings that can't be made public. The day after Global's report, the *Globe and Mail* reported that the Prime Minister's Office had reviewed a transcript of Dong's conversation about the two Michaels and determined that it contained "no actionable evidence." Dong has quietly told people he believes a translation error is likely responsible for the allegation. That makes sense because there would be no reason for him to urge the Chi-nese to keep the two Michaels locked up. Several days later, Dong filed a libel notice against Global News and three of its journalists, including Cooper, who has for years done praiseworthy investigative work on the question of Chinese interference in Canadian democracy.

This affair, which damaged Dong's reputation and put Cooper and Global in legal jeopardy, made it plain that Trudeau had failed to main-tain public confidence in Canada's elections. To try to reassure Canadi-ans, he appointed former governor general David Johnston* as a "special

---

* Johnston was appointed governor general by Stephen Harper, after he advised Harper to establish a public inquiry into the Airbus scandal without examining the Airbus deal.

rapporteur" to investigate the issue and make recommendations to the government. It was a bad idea.

—

JOHNSTON HAS BEEN AN admirable servant of the people of Canada, an honourable and talented man who fulfilled his vice-regal role with praiseworthy dedication, promoting voluntarism and exemplifying the spirit of public service. He had been a leader since his youth, when he was captain of the hockey team at Harvard and inspired a character in both the novel and the film *Love Story*. He is a great Canadian, but he was too close to Trudeau to play the needed role here. It soon became clear he could not expect Poilievre to play by the gentlemanly rules of the Laurentian Elite on the matter and defer to his sterling character.

Johnston was a former member of the Pierre Elliott Trudeau Foundation, a scholarly foundation endowed with $125 million by the Chrétien government. The foundation had received a $200,000 donation from Chinese billionaire Zhang Bin, who had also attended a Liberal fundraiser with Justin Trudeau. Zhang had wanted to erect a statue of Trudeau *père* shaking hands with Mao Zedong at the University of Montreal, but the university declined. The *Globe* reported, based on intelligence leaks, that a Chinese diplomat had instructed Zhang to donate to the Trudeau foundation and promised to reimburse him. Johnston had nothing to do with this donation, but it looked like a conflict of interest. Morris Rosenberg, the senior public servant who wrote a report on the 2021 election that cleared the government, was also a former president and CEO of the Trudeau Foundation.

Was Johnston the only person who could sort out this mess? It was asking too much to expect the Conservatives to accept him. In the days after the appointment, reporters revealed that Johnston had been friends with Pierre Trudeau and that his children and the Trudeau boys used to ski together at Mont-Tremblant. It looked as though Trudeau and

Johnston thought it would be vulgar to point out the long-standing relationship—that's not the way things are done in Rockcliffe—and Liberals reacted with cries of wounded dignity when called on it. Poilievre demanded that Johnston resign. "He is Justin Trudeau's ski buddy, his cottage neighbour, his family friend and a member of the Trudeau Foundation, which got $140,000 from Beijing. He has a fake job and he's unable to do it impartially. He needs to simply hand it over and allow an independent public inquiry into Beijing's interference."

Poilievre had a point—it was a fake job. An inquiry under the Public Inquiries Act empowers a judge, who is obliged to act independently. Johnston, however, was a "special rapporteur," a term borrowed from the United Nations that has no meaning in Canadian law. He did, as requested, produce rapport, a feeling of amity and comfort for the government.

Johnston, unwisely, disregarded private advice that he should quit and carried on, ignoring the fact that his work would be seen as illegitimate by Conservatives, who seem to be the injured parties in the 2021 election. While he was working on his investigation, the *Globe* revealed that CSIS had written a report showing that Zhao Wei, a Chinese diplomat in Toronto, had been collecting information about Chong's distant relatives in China so they could get leverage over him. In February, Chong had put forward a motion formally recognizing China's treatment of its ethnic Muslim Uyghur population as a genocide. The genocidal maniacs in Beijing wanted to discourage that kind of motion by putting pressure on Chong's relations in Hong Kong. The leakers got wind of it, likely from cellphone snooping, reported it up the chain of command toward the office of Public Safety Minister Bill Blair, and then . . . nothing happened. Chong learned about it from the *Globe*. The government was forced to admit that somebody messed up, although they wouldn't say exactly how, or why it was they had failed to get the report. They arranged for CSIS director David Vigneault to brief Chong on the matter. The government plainly did not know what it was doing.

Eugene Lang, a foreign policy and defence expert who dealt with risky and difficult security files as chief of staff to two Liberal ministers of defence under Chrétien and Martin, watched this saga unfold with horror. "If Vigneault is aware of this intelligence, and it's reliable, and it's about Michael Chong, a foreign affairs critic for the Official Opposition, a former minister and member of the Privy Council, and they're threatening his family, you go straight to the minister with that, your minister, not the PM, you go straight to the minister of public safety. And you advise that minister and you would do it in a verbal briefing. And then the minister would decide, okay, what am I going to do with this? And any competent minister would say, 'Well, the first thing I'm going to do is tell the PM, and tell the PM what I'm going to do. I'm going to Chong, unless you object.' That's the way it should happen. And this should be done within twenty-four hours, because people's lives are potentially at risk. People will say, 'Well, what could they have done?' Well, at least Chong's able to make his family aware that you may be at risk because of something I've done over here."

The mysterious missing report was filed in the summer, when nobody in Ottawa is at work and the role of national security advisor was being filled on an interim basis, so incompetence may be responsible for the mess. That is not much of a defence. The Conservatives are right to be suspicious. The worst-case scenario is that the Liberals turned a blind eye to nasty things because they wanted the support of Chinese Canadian voters and didn't want to know anything at all, if they could possibly avoid it, about dirty tricks the Chinese were playing on their Conservative opponents. It was insalubrious to question the loyalty of Chinese Canadians, the kind of thing that Conservatives would do, unlike virtuous Liberals, who embrace multiculturalism.

The Liberals had a legitimate desire to avoid creating an environment hostile to Chinese Canadians, but the Liberal record of donations and close high-level links to Canadians acting in concert with China's foreign influence organizations is disquieting. And who could blow the whistle if the Liberals were letting the Chinese play dirty tricks on the Tories? Everyone who had access to the intelligence reported to Trudeau, which is why he appointed Johnston to reassure us.

Johnston's report let Canadians know that everything within the government was fine, in spite of plentiful evidence to the contrary. "I have not found examples of ministers, the prime minister or their offices knowingly ignoring intelligence, advice or recommendations on foreign interference or being driven by partisan considerations in dealing with these issues," he wrote. But he did not go into detail about how it was that senior political staffers and ministers appeared not to be receiving briefings on specific incidents of foreign interference that targeted their opponents. And he said there should be no public inquiry. While calling one would be the "easy choice, it would not be the correct one," he said, because the secrets were too secret for a public airing. That argument was not persuasive; Commissioner Dennis O'Connor's 2006 inquiry into the wrongful rendition of Maher Arar successfully dealt with the darkest secrets in the Canadian security apparatus. Opposition MPs were asked to take Johnston's word on his findings, although they had the option of getting a secret clearance that would allow them to read the annex where he laid out his homework. Poilievre declined, but the Green Party's Elizabeth May accepted the offer. When she read the annex she found it did not answer her questions because most of the secret documents were still withheld. May, who likes Trudeau and would be inclined to give him the benefit of the doubt, could come to no conclusion on Johnston's report.

Johnston had assured us that the government had done nothing wrong, but it was hard to be sure he had examined the evidence with the right kind of skepticism. Then the *Globe* reported that his lead counsel had donated thousands of dollars to the Liberal Party and had attended a Trudeau fundraiser. Johnston hadn't asked her about that kind of thing and didn't see it as an issue. Her work was good. His excessive high-mindedness amounted to a kind of naïveté that cast doubt on all his secret judgment calls. Jagmeet Singh put forward a motion calling for him to step aside because of an "appearance of bias." Johnston, who had been privately advised he would be better off quitting earlier, finally accepted that he could not play the role he had tried to play and resigned.

Trudeau had wasted months and put Johnston in an untenable position. Nobody was reassured. The government finally accepted it would have to call an inquiry. Intergovernmental Affairs Minister Dominic LeBlanc, who is good at working with other parties, was tasked to negotiate with them and reach an agreement on the way forward. After watching Johnston get put through the wood chipper, the prospect of presiding over such an inquiry must have been formidable, but eventually they found someone to do it, and in September 2023 LeBlanc announced that Quebec Court of Appeal justice Marie-Josée Hogue would lead an inquiry examining foreign interference. Trudeau had ended up in the right place, but only after wasting time and energy, looking duplicitous and incompetent, and making a revered elder look like a fool.

"The main problem in this government is we are masochistic and love to extend our pain over a long period of time even though we know the person's going to die," a senior Liberal told me before Johnston resigned but after he should have. "So medical assistance in dying is my metaphor of this government."

———

ON AUGUST 2, 2023, Justin Trudeau and Sophie Grégoire Trudeau simultaneously announced, on Instagram, "after many meaningful and difficult conversations, we have made the decision to separate." Eighteen years after their fairy-tale wedding in Montreal, they could no longer live together. "As always, we remain a close family with deep love and respect for each other and for everything we have built and will continue to build."

The announcement was not a shock. Grégoire Trudeau, who had

handed out literature in a Papineau shopping mall when Justin was getting started, had stopped showing up to party events. Although they managed to keep details about their private life from leaking, the marriage had long been under strain. In the early years, she was an important part of his brand, their loving relationship celebrated as part of Trudeau's appeal as the dutiful and dashing feminist husband and dad. And Sophie was also a source of strength and balance at home, self-consciously working to keep both Justin and the family in a good place.

"We've been preparing for this for years," Sophie told the *Globe*'s Ian Brown before the 2015 election. "Once Justin decided to go on the political scene, all the spotlights were on him. I think we've done pretty well finding a balance and a centre. It can be very scrutinized. We see a lot of leaders and people in the public service and the political world reacting with fear, or intimidation, lack of respect for other human beings. I think not only Canada but the world as a whole is called upon to really choose leaders who can generate unity and compassion throughout the world. This is how you find peace, right? I think it starts from within. And Justin has that capacity to swim through crazy waters but keep his vision, keep calm."

At the time, she was devoted to their shared mission. "I feel all of this is made to happen. And it's making deep sense. This whole political journey. Yes, in our life. For Justin in his life, as a man, I understand how all of this life, and my life, in other ways, prepared us to serve, and to serve fully, and to be surrounded by brilliant minds and hearts. That's a pure honour."

The couple had seen a marriage counsellor. "We're super open, we don't have much to keep secret. It's boring, relationship stuff. We were adjusting to life and to marriage."

Sophie was with Justin on election night in 2021, smiling and holding hands on the stage, but by July 2023, when he was organizing a Cabinet shuffle, they were negotiating a formal separation. It was all done without the public becoming aware. She had not attended the Liberal convention in May 2022 but did manage to attend, with Trudeau, the funeral of

Queen Elizabeth in London in September, looking stylish in a black silk dress and jacket, a hat with a veil, holding her husband's hand. She went back to London with him for Charles's coronation, looking sharp in a pink Ted Baker dress.

Justin seemed to be devoted to her still, posting a birthday message for her in April: "Happy birthday, Sophie. From this, to this, and everything in between, there's no one I'd rather have by my side . . . I love you, mon amour." It was accompanied by a nice picture of them embracing on a hike in the beautiful Gatineau Hills.

But Sophie had already moved on. Given the political advantage to Justin of continuing to maintain the façade of a marriage, it seems likely the decision to split was hers. There are indications she had been making plans for a post-Justin life since 2022, when she began to pursue other interests. In November that year she incorporated a company, Under Your Light Communications. Also that month she appeared on a podcast hosted by Meghan Markle entitled "Good Wife/Bad Wife, Good Mom/ Bad Mom." Markle and Sophie had become friends in Toronto in 2016 when they met through Jessica Mulroney, around the time Markle began her romance with Prince Harry. On the podcast, Markle described Sophie as "a dear friend" who is "emblematic of strength that comes from embracing humanity, even in the face of all these family and home and public pressures." Markle noted that Sophie had a "full plate" as a wife and mother, knowing all about the "crushing guilt of expectations" women face. Sophie said all women "long to be free in who we are" because they carry "most of the load" at home.

After the split, ace journalist Glen McGregor tracked down some court documents showing that Sophie had a new relationship with an Ottawa surgeon. Divorce papers filed by his estranged wife in April alleged that the doctor had "re-partnered" with an unnamed "high-profile individual" whom McGregor identified as Sophie.

Grégoire Trudeau is not looking for a life outside the public view. In May 2023 she announced plans to publish a book, *Closer Together: Know-*

ing Ourselves, Loving Each Other, which the publisher described as "a self-discovery and wellness book for adults" that will take readers on "a deeply personal journey toward self-knowledge, acceptance, and empowerment."

Friends of Trudeau say the breakup was a long time coming and that Grégoire Trudeau was finding it increasingly hard to be a prime minister's wife. Trudeau might have saved his marriage if he had decided to step down in 2023 and let someone else take on Poilievre, but he did not want to do that. His friends say he put the country ahead of his marriage. "For those of us who had spent a long time around both of them, I don't think it came as a shock to anyone when it finally happened," says a friend.

Cameron Ahmad says people underestimate the difficulty of life under the spotlight, especially in the age of social media. "That's a real challenge. But I think [Justin and Sophie] made it work. To create the family and to handle the pressure and the criticisms, remarkably, for years, and make a personal decision, [it's] probably not too far away from a lot of other people, millions of adults who've been through something similar and will probably understand what it's like."

Ahmad is right about how awful social media has been for the family. In August, Trudeau tweeted pictures of him and Xavier dressed in pink for *Barbie,* and one with Ella-Grace at *Oppenheimer*—the two big movies of the summer. They were goofy, cheerful-divorced-dad selfies. The haters responded with vile attacks on him and the kids. Trudeau can no longer communicate with the public about anything without being immediately heckled by a vast brigade of vicious trolls.

The marriage and its dissolution are properly a private matter, a marriage that, sadly, has run its course, but the family's spending has been a matter of public debate. Conservatives have attacked Trudeau for having taxpayers pay for a nanny and for taking costly vacations, even after the Aga Khan debacle. The total bill for that trip came in at $271,000, including $56,000 worth of meals, accommodation, and jet ski rentals for RCMP officers who accompanied Trudeau and his party, all of which had to be remitted to the Aga Khan. The next year they went to India, which was a different kind of disaster, and then, in the Christmas holidays of 2019/20, they had a long vacation on the beach in Costa Rica, which produced no headlines except for the cost—about $200,000, mostly for shuttling planes around. The following Christmas, they stayed with wealthy friends in Jamaica in a resort that typically bills $9,000 a night. The travel and security cost taxpayers about $162,000. And in 2023 Trudeau took an Easter ski trip to Montana's Big Sky Resort, which cost taxpayers about $230,000. That made even less sense because, while you can't find sunny beaches in Canada in the winter, there are many ski resorts.

Trudeau's most extravagant personal spending came from renovations at Harrington Lake, the prime ministerial retreat across the border in Quebec, on which the government spent $8.6 million, including expenses related to a sauna. A lot of long-time Ottawa insiders roll their eyes at these stories, rightly pointing out that they encourage foolish penny-pinching and take up space that could better be used to explore the colossal sums spent on vast national programs. Because successive prime ministers have been reluctant to get blamed for spending money on 24 Sussex—the prime ministerial residence since 1951—it was uninhabitable by the time Trudeau was elected. It would cost $40 million to get it up to modern standards, and its location poses security problems. Trudeau never moved in and let it sit, getting more dilapidated, rather than endure public recrimination over spending money on it.

———

ON JUNE 19, 2023, a friend in British Columbia sent me a *Vancouver Sun* story about the murder of Hardeep Singh Nijjar, who had been murdered outside a gurdwara in Surrey. His lawyer, Gurpatwant Singh Pannun, told the *Sun* he had spoken to Nijjar the day before. Nijjar was concerned because a CSIS agent had told him there were threats to his life.

"This seems like a pretty serious issue," my friend said. "Unclear why this isn't setting off alarm bells."

"Sounds like it could be a local dispute," I replied. "Or it could be Modi."

Nijjar was a Sikh, born in India's Punjab region, who came to Canada on a false passport in 1997. He was not deported, though, became a plumber, and eventually got his citizenship. In 2014, India issued a warrant for his arrest through Interpol, alleging he leads a terrorist group and was involved in the 2007 bombing of a cinema in Punjab. He had been photographed with weapons and accused of running a training camp. But it is not illegal to support an independent Khalistan, and if there is proof that Nijjar broke the law, India has not presented it. In 2018 he was elected president of his gurdwara, which flies the flag of Khalistan outside its gates.

According to a video of the murder, Nijjar was leaving the parking lot in his truck when he was cut off by a car, which blocked him at the exit. Two bearded men on foot, wearing turbans and hooded sweatshirts, came out of cover and fired on the vehicle, more than fifty shots, thirty-four of which hit him, leaving the front of the vehicle a mess of shattered glass and blood. The shooters ran off to a waiting getaway car. The *Washington Post*, whose reporters have seen the video, described it as a large and organized operation.

———

ON SEPTEMBER 8, PIERRE Poilievre gave an overlong but successful speech to Conservatives gathered in Quebec City for a policy convention. Where once he seemed capable only of snarling and smug attacks, he was now able to reach for different notes, to inspire emotions other than glee at the prospect of the end of the Trudeau government.

"The most important job of any leader is to bring hope," he said, as sappy music played in the background. "Hope is what Canadians need now more than ever. Hope is something that you feel, but it's hard to picture it, so let me paint a picture for you." He spoke of safe, happy communities, full of prosperous families, with shopkeepers sweeping their storefronts, new houses going up, kids playing street hockey, Canadian flags flapping gently in the breeze. It was schlocky and nostalgic, but it worked.

The reviews were excellent. Mulcair, no fan of Poilievre, called it a "magic weekend in Quebec City, a tour de force." Mulroney, recovering from surgery, sent a message through his son, Mark. "I attended my first convention in 1956 for Mr. Diefenbaker. I was 17 years old then. I've seen a lot of convention speeches since then. Pierre's speech was probably the best convention speech I have ever witnessed." Fred DeLorey, whose former boss, O'Toole, had been pushed out to make way for the new leader, said Poilievre's election was all but assured. "If you think the question is whether Poilievre will win the next election, you're asking the wrong question. The real issue is the margin of his impending victory."

A week earlier, an Abacus poll found that only 27 percent of Canadians wanted Trudeau to stay on. Many people, including a lot who voted for him, thought it was time for him to go. His caucus, most of whom were elected on his coattails, were starting to complain anonymously. Every headline about inflation or the housing crisis undercut Canadians' sense that the country was being run as it should. As Poilievre basked in his post-convention adulation, Trudeau was getting on the Challenger to fly to New Delhi for two days of meetings with leaders from the G20.

———

IT WAS NOT PUBLIC at the time, but Trudeau was on a difficult mission. He intended to tell his host, Narendra Modi, that Canada had learned that India was behind the killing of Nijjar and ask for India's help in investigating his murder, which Modi might have personally ordered. National Security and Intelligence advisor Jody Thomas had flown to India in August to meet with Indian officials about the murder. Intercepted communications from both Canada and the Five Eyes allies had implicated Indian diplomats in the killing. The CBC reported that when Thomas went to see the bosses in India, they did not deny the killing or offer to help investigate it.

Trudeau had tense exchanges with Modi during the G20. Modi publicly chided Canada for allowing "continuing anti-India activities of extremist elements in [the country]. They are promoting secessionism and inciting violence against Indian diplomats, damaging diplomatic premises, and threatening the Indian community in Canada and their places of worship." Trudeau responded that he had talked to Modi about foreign interference, without mentioning the assassination of Nijjar. It was a frosty exchange, the lowlight of a difficult trip. Trudeau tried and failed to ensure that the closing communiqué included a mention of Ukraine. Then the Canadian plane broke down and the delegation had to wait until a replacement could be flown in from Canada. It was another terrible visit to India for Trudeau, and he didn't even get to dress up.

The *Hindustan Times* reported it this way: "Trudeau's India Agony: After Modi's Terse Khalistan Rebuke at G20, Plane Breaks Down." The reviews were no better at home. The *National Post* went with the headline "Trudeau's Positively Disastrous Trip to India." The *Toronto Sun* ran a picture of an awkward handshake and the headline "This Way Out; Trudeau Finds He Has Few Friends at G20 Summit in India." The Canadian Press wrote a story with Saskatchewan premier Scott Moe complaining that the Trudeau government had "once again put its own domestic political interests ahead of the national economic interest—particularly as it relates to exports and trade of western Canadian-produced commodities."

The PMO said little, which seemed odd. There was no pushback at critiques. It all suddenly made sense a week later when Trudeau stood in Parliament to announce that the government had reason to believe that India was behind Nijjar's murder. "Any involvement of a foreign government in the killing of a Canadian citizen on Canadian soil is an unacceptable violation of our sovereignty. It is contrary to the fundamental rules by which free, open and democratic societies conduct themselves."

Poilievre, who had been briefed before Trudeau's statement, backed him up. "Our citizens must be safe from extrajudicial killings. Canadians deserve to be protected on Canadian soil. We call on the Indian government to act with utmost transparency as authorities investigate this murder."

India reacted swiftly, declaring the allegations "absurd and motivated," and again complained that the Canadians were sheltering Khalistani extremists. It was a full-on row, with worrying implications for the relationship. There are about two million Canadians of Indian origin, and about three hundred thousand Indian students in Canadian schools.

Canada expelled an Indian diplomat. India responded by expelling one Canadian, then stopped issuing visas, and finally expelled forty-one Canadian diplomats. Nationalist Indians were furious with Trudeau and took to social media to denounce him. Tellingly, they did not deny that India had killed Nijjar. It should not have been necessary, in their view, if Canada had cracked down on Khalistani separatists. Sushant Sareen, a senior fellow at the Observer Research Foundation in New Delhi, put it this way on Twitter: "If we did it, it was right; if we didn't, you were wrong."

Canada said it had shared intelligence with India, but India ignored it. Poilievre shifted from supporting Trudeau to calling for him to show proof. Harper, who wields influence behind the scenes, has frequent and friendly contacts with Modi through the International Democracy Union, which Harper heads. Poilievre's newest MP, Shuvaloy Majumdar, used to work for Harper and has advocated in the think-tank world for closer ties between Canada and India. The Liberals want Sikh votes. The Conservatives are after the Hindus.

Eventually, the Americans came to the rescue, acknowledging that Canada had shared information with them. In December, an indictment was unsealed that showed an Indian, acting on instructions from a government official, had hired an assassin in the United States who turned out to be an undercover Drug Enforcement Administration officer. Modi's angry denials suddenly looked absurd, and Trudeau was vindicated.

But why had he got ahead of the story? He could have done what the

Americans did, which is leak the story and wait for the facts to show that he was right. After all the Chinese stories, Trudeau didn't want to be caught flat-footed, again, on a story about foreign interference. "For the first six months of this year, Trudeau and his team erred on the side of secrecy," wrote Susan Delacourt in the *Star*. "For the last few months of this year, it appears they've decided to risk erring on the side of transparency."

Modi should take away the licence to kill from his bumbling 007s, but India has a point when it complains that Canada has been soft on Khalistani separatists because of diaspora politics. Sikhs are vital to the Liberal electoral operation, and they seem to have exerted influence to prevent the government from taking a harder line on Khalistani separatists. The Charter of Rights and Freedoms prevents Canada from doing what India would like—rounding up all the separatists and deporting them to India—but the Trudeau government could have spoken out more often and more forcefully against Khalistani extremism, and would have done so if the movement threatened one of our traditional allies. This kind of diaspora politics is nothing new in Canada. The Harper Conservatives, for instance, pushed a strongly pro-Israel stance and did not shrink from seeking support in Canada's Jewish community, abandoning our traditionally more middle-of-the-road consensus position on the Middle East. Diaspora politics often take priority over security or sovereignty concerns because the rest of the world is far away, and we live under the security umbrella of the United States. Trudeau had to run to Uncle Sam for help once he made his statement on India, and the Biden administration dutifully exerted influence on our behalf, just as Uncle Sam did—eventually—during the two Michaels hostage taking.

But that umbrella is looking less reliable, and Canada needs to show more discipline in foreign policy, taking positions on Khalistan, for example, designed to be defensible internationally rather than help win in a Surrey nomination battle. The world is getting smaller and more dangerous, with more assertive and autocratic leaders. Trudeau has not articulated a strategy for dealing with this dangerous new world and has failed to take steps—a foreign-agent registry, for instance—that other countries have long ago accepted as necessary.

Progressives can look at Trudeau's record domestically and see real progress for children, women, families, and the most significant effort to fight poverty in a generation. He has demonstrated a greater openness to multiculturalism, done the difficult work necessary to bring in a carbon tax, and taken other steps to protect the environment and reduce emissions. On reconciliation with Indigenous people, despite his public failings, it is clear that his government has invested more money, energy, and political capital than any before it, taking steps to close the enormous gap in infrastructure and services that Canadians had accepted as a fact of life. This approach is expensive and not much of a vote winner, but it will pay economic dividends from productivity gains in the fast-growing Indigenous population and is necessary as a matter of national honour. After the Harper years, Trudeau rebuilt the multicultural, bilingual, liberal political coalition that his father had constructed; managed to deal with Trump, a pandemic, and the convoy; and became a global symbol of progressive politics. But, as 2023 wound to a close, there seemed to be significantly less demand for that symbol, in Canada and abroad.

Diaspora politics and foreign affairs collided again a few weeks later when Ukrainian president Volodymyr Zelenskyy came to Ottawa to address Parliament. He gave a powerful speech, praising Trudeau and Ukrainian Canadians who have rallied to the mother country. Trudeau, Zelenskyy, and every MP in the House applauded when Speaker Anthony Rota introduced Yaroslav Hunka, a ninety-eight-year-old Ukrainian Canadian by saying he "fought for Ukrainian independence from the Russians, and continues to support the troops today." It was a touching moment, but a few days later we learned that Hunka had fought for the 14th Waffen Grenadier Division of the SS—the Nazis—during the Second World War.

The news that Canada had praised a Nazi in the House was like Christmas, New Year's, and Victory Day rolled into one for Russian propagandists, who have tried to sell their genocidal war in Ukraine as a de-Nazification project. It was a disaster, humiliating for Zelenskyy, for Trudeau, who invited Hunka to a reception, and for Rota, who had invited Hunka, a constituent, to the House and praised him. Rota took personal responsibility and resigned, a day later than he should have. It was a terrible day. Canada—and Trudeau—looked foolish.

On the same day, the *Toronto Sun* ran a story headlined "Trudeau's Plane Had Cocaine During G20, Claims Former Indian Diplomat"—a story quickly matched by news sites around the world. It was trash. The prime minister had his son with him on the trip. Indian customs agents never boarded the plane. It was made-up mischief from India finding its way to eyeballs everywhere thanks to the *Sun*.

Trudeau, once the darling of the world's media, was now being portrayed as a Nazi-loving coke huffer. His global brand, once a huge asset to Canada, had become a drag. Pollster Nik Nanos hears it as he travels the world on business. "We're a laughingstock everywhere. We are not taken seriously, and it's going to take a generation to fix." That image is showing up in the polling. In 2022, almost half the Canadians polled told Nanos that the country's reputation has suffered in the previous year.

For Canadians on the right, Trudeau's continued presence in the PMO is infuriating, hard to believe. Worse for him, many people who previously supported him—who shared in the national pleasure when he was elected—are also irritated. He is like a cottage guest who came for a weekend and is still with us as Labour Day approaches. But he swears he intends to run again. He spent much of his time at the end of 2023 assuring anyone and everyone that he will not stop until he has bested Poilievre.

"Even if he knows he might lose, he wants to go down fighting against Pierre Poilievre, because I think he feels in his bones that there is a stark difference," says Trudeau's former executive assistant Louis-Alexandre Lanthier. "With another leader, like Erin O'Toole, I'm not sure that he would feel as compelled to want to fight."

In September 2023, when Zita Astravas decided to get out of government after eight years of long hours and high stress, Trudeau popped in to her going-away party at the Métropolitain Brasserie—a lively faux Paris bistro on Sussex Drive. She told him that she would come back from the private sector to help him in the next campaign.

"He is running," she told me later. "He's excited for the campaign."

She believes he remains the best candidate to take on Poilievre, "by a country mile." "I have never worked alongside a campaigner like the PM. The energy that he brings every day, but particularly during campaigns, is something you can't count him out for. And I think the Conservatives have seen that for three campaigns consecutively. There's nothing really to talk about other than I know that he's running, and I think that he's the best guy for the job."

Of course, leaders can't let on that they are considering other options, or everyone who works for them will suddenly send out their resumés, and opponents and rivals will bring out their knives. But in late 2023, with the world united in the opinion that Trudeau was a spent force, Telford drew in talented, experienced veterans from the private sector— Andrew Bevan, Kevin Coon, Supriya Dwivedi, Max Valiquette, and Peter Wilkinson—who took pay cuts to go to work for Trudeau. They had been convinced that Trudeau isn't going anywhere, that he will stay and fight.

"I'm not much interested in coming into a space that all of a sudden is thrown into even more chaos, because there's a leadership race of some kind," one of them told me. "Every indication I was given was he has no inclination to leave whatsoever."

Liberals don't know what to do. They know that Trudeau is unpopular, but they also realize he might do better than whoever they run in his place, especially in Quebec. Everyone knows who he is, and he is a formidable campaigner. His team may be weary, but they know what they are doing. And the alternatives all seem like a gamble electorally.

"He's my best bet because I think that in a fight, the way that this is lining up to be, we don't have anybody on the bench right now," says Lanthier.

Perhaps, with a separation behind him and a despised rival howling at his heels, with some smart new people in the operation, Trudeau can establish stability and try to do some useful things. But governments that have been in power too long start to tell themselves falsehoods. They get full of themselves, lose touch, and begin delivering messages that are crafted to make themselves feel better rather than addressing the priorities of voters. He's fighting gravity. But even after a year from hell, Trudeau does not want to go down without a fight.

16

NO MORE SUNSHINE

A few days after Nathan Cirillo was murdered under the war memorial in Ottawa in 2014, someone vandalized the mosque in Cold Lake, a city of fifteen thousand on the Alberta side of the Alberta-Saskatchewan border, a three-hour drive northeast of Edmonton. The hater broke the windows and spray-painted "Go Home" on the front of the modest building, which Canadians who worshipped there found profoundly upsetting. Shocked local residents, including Canadian Forces members from nearby CFB Cold Lake, came to help with the mess and put up posters reading "You Are Home" and "Love Thy Neighbour."

In 2015, six days after he became prime minister, Trudeau mentioned the incident to Guy Lawson, a *New York Times* reporter who had come to Ottawa to write a profile. "Countries with a strong national identity—linguistic, religious or cultural—are finding it a challenge to effectively integrate people from different backgrounds," Trudeau said. "Canada doesn't have that dynamic. There is no core identity, no mainstream in Canada. There are shared values—openness, respect, compassion, willingness to work hard, to be there for each other, to search for equality and justice. Those qualities are what make us the first post-national state."

Lawson called Justin "an avatar of his father's vision" of the country, which is accurate. Trudeau's comment echoes his father's words in a 1971 speech to the Ukrainian-Canadian Congress: "Uniformity is neither desirable nor possible in a country the size of Canada. We should not even be able to agree upon the kind of Canadian to choose as a model, let alone persuade most people to emulate it. There are few policies potentially more disastrous for Canada than to tell all Canadians that they must be alike. There is no such thing as a model or ideal Canadian . . . A society which emphasizes uniformity is one which creates intolerance and hate. A society which eulogizes the average citizen is one which breeds mediocrity. What the world should be seeking, and what in Canada we must continue to cherish, are not concepts of uniformity but human values: compassion, love, and understanding."

Canadian identity is inherently obscure. As William Lyon Mackenzie King put it: "If some countries have too much history, we have too much geography." Marshall McLuhan wrote that "Canada is the only country in the world that knows how to live without an identity." Novelist Yann Martel called Canada "the greatest hotel on earth." But if Canadians are just hotel guests, how can anyone rally citizens around a common project? The national myths at the heart of France or the United States may be artificial constructions, but they bind people together. In 2023, after eight years of Trudeau, it is hard to know who is speaking for the national project, with Trudeau playing the role of "head waiter to the provinces"— to use his father's dismissive words about Joe Clark.

Trudeau has used sunny ways, as promised, but they have not convinced Saskatchewan premier Scott Moe to collect the carbon tax, as required by law, or Alberta premier Danielle Smith, for instance, to abandon a plan to withdraw her province from the Canada Pension Plan. And he never seemed to know how to handle François Legault, whose nationalistic leadership of Quebec poses a challenge to the rights of linguistic and religious minorities around which the Liberal Party has traditionally built its brand.

In 2019, Legault brought in Bill 21, which prohibits public employees from wearing religious symbols at work—a law that prevents Jews, Sikhs, and Muslims from wearing religious headgear on the job. The bill had overwhelming support among the rural and suburban francophones who support Legault. In 2021, he invoked the notwithstanding clause pre-emptively to protect Bill 96—a new French language law—from Charter challenges from anglophone Quebecers whose rights to live and work in English were affected by the new regulations. In both cases, Trudeau said he opposed Legault's laws but declined to launch legal challenges. He wanted to avoid giving Legault a target to rally Quebecers against him in a nationalist battle that Trudeau could only lose. Legault made it clear he was ready to inveigh against federal interference and seemed to be itching for a fight on that turf. That was dangerous to Trudeau because he and Legault rely on many of the same francophone voters. But Trudeau's failure to act to defend the Charter rights of Quebec Muslims and anglos left them feeling abandoned by their federal government.

In late 2023, Legault went further still, imposing tuition hikes on English universities that threaten to bankrupt them, including Trudeau's own alma matter, McGill. Rather than fighting Bill 96 in court, Trudeau referenced it in Bill C-13, an update to the Official Languages Act, which led four of his Quebec MPs to vote against it.

Don MacPherson, a former *Montreal Gazette* columnist who has been covering Quebec politics since René Lévesque was a Liberal member of the National Assembly, thinks Trudeau has failed to respond to Quebec nationalism. "He doesn't quite know how to handle it, how to respond to it, unlike his father, who had very, very clear ideas on the subject. And I don't think Justin does . . . he thinks that it is possible to appease nationalists, and it's definitely not the case. Every time a federalist government has tried to do that, the reception on the part of nationalists has always been 'Well, it's a good first step, but it doesn't go far enough.' It really opens the door to new demands."

If Trudeau was intimidated by a showdown with Legault, he showed no similar deference to western premiers, who made a strong argument that Bill C-69—which they call the no-more-pipelines act—infringed on their turf. In 2023, the Supreme Court ruled that they were right and that sections of Trudeau's environmental assessment process overstepped federal jurisdiction by requiring certain projects, which ought to be assessed by the provinces, to be subject to a federal process. If Trudeau is the headwaiter, it seems clear that some guests—those in Ontario and Quebec—are more equal than others. In 2023, Ottawa put tens of billions into battery plants in Ontario and Quebec, matching subsidies that Joe Biden was offering across the border. Meanwhile, officials in Guilbeault's office were drawing up plans to force western oil producers to cut emissions by 38 percent by 2030.

Trudeau's failure to confront Legault over the use of the notwithstanding clause* in a law that breached anglophones' Charter rights appeared to send a signal to other premiers that they had a violate-rights-at-will card they could play whenever they wanted to pass a law that the courts might strike down. Ontario's Doug Ford used it three times, and Saskatchewan's Scott Moe invoked it for a law requiring schools to inform parents about the pronouns their children were using at school. Where earlier Liberal leaders had portrayed themselves as loyal defenders of the Charter, Trudeau could more properly be characterized as a supporter of the Charter—he won't fight for it if it is politically inconvenient. To be fair to Trudeau, no federal politician would want to pick a fight with Legault—neither Andrew Scheer nor Erin O'Toole showed any enthusiasm for standing up for minorities by taking on the then-popular premier.

Trudeau's passivity is mysterious. Politics is about storytelling, and every story needs a villain. He has repeatedly failed to pick fights, draw

---

* The notwithstanding clause allows premiers or prime ministers to pass laws that violate the Charter of Rights and Freedoms for up to five years, at which point the particular law must be renewed by a vote of the legislature. Premiers insisted on this clause in negotiations with Pierre Trudeau as the price for agreeing to enshrine the Charter in the Constitution in 1982. Its defenders argue that it preserves the supremacy of Parliament. Its critics argue that it allows governments to overrule fundamental rights.

lines, take on opponents. In some cases—with Ford and Legault, for example—it is because they are both relying on the same voters. In other cases—with Philpott and Wilson-Raybould—it was likely because he would not benefit from trash-talking women who had rejected his government. And his restraint in the face of Trump's provocations may have saved the trade relationship. But in fights with Prime Minister Modi and President Xi, Trudeau did not define the national interest and speak up for it as convincingly as Canadians would have liked. And, crucially, he has failed to take on Poilievre, declining to use attack ads to define the most dangerous challenger he has faced, as the Conservatives did effectively with Stéphane Dion and Michael Ignatieff. In 2022 and 2023, as Poilievre introduced himself to Canadians as a credible alternative prime minister, showing greater poise and maturity and connecting with new constituencies, Trudeau did not respond effectively, allowing him to define himself in the public mind.

This aversion to confrontation—private or public—has damaged the government, alienating key ministers whom Trudeau failed to engage. All his life, Trudeau has been surrounded by people trying to get close to him and has had to establish boundaries, but Morneau, Wilson-Raybould, and others weren't trying to spend time with Justin Trudeau because he's a celebrity. They needed to establish a rapport with their boss, the prime minister of Canada, and his remove made that impossible. He is kind and indulgent to members of the team around him, to people he trusts, but he maintains his distance from MPs and staffers he doesn't know. I was repeatedly surprised in researching this book to learn that he had never had meaningful exchanges with people in his orbit—MPs and staffers who have made important contributions to the country and his government. "He's not a nice guy," one of them said to me and shrugged. Others find that view astonishing, pointing to many acts of personal kindness.

Trudeau's passivity is most striking in his failure to speak up for Canada. The contrast with Jean Chrétien—who could don the Maple Leaf like a cape—was striking in May 2023 during the Liberal convention, when the former prime minister brought Liberals to their feet applauding a speech that linked love of country to disdain for Poilievre, who has convinced many supporters that "Canada is broken." Chrétien talked about the "millions and millions of people around the world that would give their shirt to come and share our so-called miseries. You know why? Canada is the land of freedom. Canada is the land of opportunity. Canada is the land of generosity. Canada is the land of tolerance. Canada is the land of the rule of law." The Liberals were on their feet, applauding steadily as he spoke. "No," he said, holding up his hand to quiet the crowd. "No. No, Mr. Poilievre, Canada is not broken. Canada is the land that made it the envy of the world. Canada is still the best. Vive le Canada!"

Trudeau won't, or can't, do that. He photographs better than the old guy, but he can't move a crowd as well. And he seems to have ambiguous feelings about Canada. He left flags across the country at half-staff for six months, which seemed unwise. Attacks on symbols of our shared heritage trigger an authoritarian, populist response in people who are predisposed to those emotions because they signal a feeling of shame rather than pride in our past. Trudeau's attacks on convoy participants had a similar triggering effect, riling up people who would have been better left unriled. And even those who don't share the complaints of the anti-vaxxers and convoyers have become fatigued with what they see as pious scolding from Trudeau. He has become "too woke, too precious, preachy in tone, exceedingly smug, lacking in leadership, fading in celebrity, slow to act, short-sighted in vision and generally getting more irritating with every breathlessly whispered public pronouncement," Don Martin wrote for CTV in 2022, reflecting widespread fatigue with Trudeau's pieties.

As Canadians gradually got tired of his schtick, foreigners were increasingly disdainful, portraying him as a smug hypocritical busybody. He is a target for right-wing politicians and commentators. Trudeau sees them attacking a symbol that threatens conservative American thinking. "I think the American right has increasingly noticed that Canada is a bit of a challenge to them," he said in an end-of-2023 interview with Terry DiMonte. Canada, with gun control and public health care, offers "a direct challenge to them, and also a direct opportunity."

More important, though, than how he fared in the inane Punch and Judy shows of Fox News is how well he has safeguarded the national interest in our relationships with other countries. After eight years of Trudeau, we are obviously in a weaker position.

When Trudeau came to office, Canada was seeking strategic room to balance our trade relationship with the United States by drawing closer to China. He seems to have approached it naively, wagering that China would be willing to accept human rights and labour concessions that clear-eyed observers knew were off the table. He wasted time and energy on a similarly vain attempt to win a seat on the UN Security Council, again overestimating the world demand for empty Canadian virtue-signalling.

In 2016, when Barack Obama spoke to Parliament, he riffed on the smug Chapters bookstore slogan "The world needs more Canada." "As your ally and as your friend, let me say that we'll be more secure when every NATO member, including Canada, contributes its full share to our common security. Because the Canadian armed forces are really good— and if I can borrow a phrase, the world needs more Canada. NATO needs more Canada. We need you. We need you."

But the world will have to settle for our pious words, our earnest lectures, because Canada does not spend much on defence. The budget for it has increased under Trudeau—from 1.15 percent of gross national product to 1.32 percent—but we are nowhere near the 2 percent target that the North Atlantic Treaty Organization has set as the voluntary cover charge. Trudeau agreed to big spending on the NORAD air defence system and F-35 fighter jets (after campaigning against them), but those are merely commitments to keep capacities that the Canadian Armed Forces had when his father was prime minister. Canada was left on the sidelines of a new defence agreement—AUKUS—between Australia, the United Kingdom, and the United States because, unlike the Australians, we are not buying nuclear submarines. The Forces can't buy anything at all with dispatch, and they can't hire. They are struggling with a severe personnel shortage—a 10 percent shortfall—which is severely limiting operational capabilities. The main Liberal focus during this period was not investing in people or kit but on ridding senior ranks of sex offenders—removing officers who had been accused but not convicted of sex crimes. When some were found not guilty, the Forces had no choice but to pay tens of millions of dollars in legal liabilities.

Canada's allies have noticed our reduced capacity to contribute to shared defence objectives. In April 2023, a document leaked from the US Joint Chiefs of Staff revealed that Trudeau had privately "told NATO officials that Canada will never reach 2% defense spending." The anonymous authors of the report observed that "widespread defense shortfalls hinder Canadian capabilities while straining partner relationships and alliance contributions."

Canada is little better on foreign aid, spending about 0.3 percent of GDP, far below the 0.7 percent level the United Nations agreed on under a commission led by Lester Pearson. Canada may think the world should listen to us when we talk about climate, about same-sex marriage in Italy, human rights in western China, and Ukraine's right to self-determination, but we should not expect them to listen very carefully. We speak loudly and carry a small stick.

In an interview in 2024, Trudeau was frank about Canada's ongoing difficulties with China and India. "We're in a vulnerable position because we are in such a great position," he said. "We are big enough to make an example of, for a country like China or India, but small enough that it doesn't hurt them too much. We are near the United States, so they can send messages, but we're not the United States, so they can do a little more. Countries around the world have figured that out about Canada—we have this glorious diaspora where people come from every corner of the world, but that also gives countries that feel threatened by our model, or our diversity, leverage to [try to] impact how Canada is doing. So we are very exposed in some sense, but we're also more resilient because of it."

The best protection Canada has, Trudeau says, "is the international rules-based order. When people are following the rules . . . they are there to protect us, to protect everyone. And it doesn't mean that on trade things—particularly when it comes to dairy—we're not willing to push and pull and defend ourselves, but the rules-based order matters."

It would be foolish to lay too much blame on Trudeau for Canada's weakness: he has modestly increased both defence spending and foreign aid, and Canada has long found security under Uncle Sam's apron. In a speech to the League of Nations in 1926, Senator Raoul Dandurand said that Canada was "a fireproof house, far from inflammable materials." That is less true than it was. The world has grown increasingly dangerous, and the United States less predictable. We need to manage our relationships with the rising Asian powers much more carefully. As 2023 drew to a close, who could say that Trudeau has done that well? China appears to feel it can bully Canada at will, and our relationship with India could not be worse. Both countries want to interfere in our democracy, and we have not taken the elementary steps necessary to discourage them.

Trudeau has put too much emphasis on two diaspora groups that are important to his coalition—Sikhs and Chinese Canadians—and too little emphasis on the national interest. Our strained relations with India and China appear to be the result of a lack of seriousness, a lack of discipline, the kind of thing Stephen Harper warned about when Trudeau was seeking the job back in 2015. It is noteworthy that many of the gaffes Trudeau had to apologize for at the time were related to national security, defence, and foreign relations. It is strange, because he grew up with every opportunity to learn about the world, travelling with his father. By the time he was thirteen, he had been to fifty-one countries. Perhaps he sees foreign trips as an opportunity for performance, without recognizing that the world stage is necessarily a place of struggle. Perhaps the world has just become a more treacherous place, and any prime minister would have faced similar struggles.

———

WHEN HAMAS INVADED ISRAEL in the fall of 2023, raping and butchering civilians and taking more than two hundred hostages, and Israel responded with air strikes that turned much of the Gaza Strip into rubble, Trudeau appeared paralyzed by the political ramifications of any response. His caucus was painfully divided, with some calling for a cease-fire and others urging him to speak up more forcefully for Israel's right to defend itself. This division is a consequence of geography—Liberals represent the cities where both Jewish and Muslim voters live. MPs on both sides of the terrible divide owe their loyalty first to their families and communities and could be expected to put the Liberal Party second. It was hard to know where Trudeau stood, but wherever it was, it was pleasing nobody.

Trudeau wanted to go to a Toronto mosque during Friday prayers to signal his support for Canadian Muslims, but several declined to host him. He found one in Etobicoke that welcomed him, and he attended without informing the media, posting photos on social media that showed him being welcomed. But cellphone videos posted online showed him being booed and heckled by worshippers angry that he had not called on Israel to stop raining bombs down on their co-religionists in Gaza. They were not interested in Trudeau's sunny ways. Neither, any longer, were Jews in other parts of Toronto, who were furious at his tepid support.

The war in Gaza did not pose any problem to Poilievre, who said simply and repeatedly that he supported Israel. Few Canadian Muslims vote Conservative, so events in the Middle East set up no tensions inside Poilievre's caucus or electoral coalition. Trudeau was in a political jam and seemed to be taking a position—about halfway between that of the United States and Europe—designed to do the least damage to his election prospects.

———

IN APRIL 2020, IN the heart of the pandemic, a deranged killer in an RCMP uniform and replica cruiser went on a killing spree in Portapique, Nova Scotia, a quiet community of 150 on the banks of the Bay of Fundy. By the time Mounties gunned him down thirteen hours later, he had killed twenty-two people, including a Mountie and an expectant mother. Three years later, a public inquiry confirmed what Nova Scotians came to realize in the weeks after the tragedy—the RCMP had let them down that day. For years, the Mounties had ignored reports about the threat posed by the perpetrator, a wealthy white man with a track record of violence—the result of "implicit bias" on the part of officers. After he started killing on the night of April 18, the Mounties were disorganized. Officers did not know the geography of the area. They did not listen to community members who told them that the perpetrator was driving a Mountie car. They decided he was dead when he was not. After shooting thirteen people, he escaped on an unmarked back road and continued his rampage the next morning. Mounties did not call in the Truro police for help, neglected to send an emergency alert that would have saved lives, shot up a fire hall where survivors were sheltering, and failed to find the perpetrator for several hours while he killed nine more innocent victims.

In the horrible aftermath of the rampage, before the families buried their dead, Trudeau announced that the government would ban "assault-style weapons" to prevent similar tragedies. I am in favour of gun control, but the announcement left me cold. I grew up in that area. The response in rural Nova Scotia, where the unreliable Mounties are far away and where many people have shotguns and deer rifles in their homes, is not the same as in cities, where people respond to shootings by seeking gun bans. A ban of "assault-style weapons" is of questionable value. "Assault-style" weapons look scary but have the same capacity as other unbanned rifles. Real assault rifles were banned by Trudeau's father. Besides, the killer brought three of his guns in illegally from the United States, so a ban would not have prevented the tragedy.

The Liberals tried to block the public inquiry that the families needed so they could learn how their police had let them down. Seen from the back roads outside Truro, the government looked as though it did not have the interests of the affected people at heart—that it was playing for votes in the cities and ignoring the wishes of the families. Nova Scotians supported the families and, when it became clear that stonewalling would put Liberal seats in jeopardy, Trudeau reversed himself and agreed to an inquiry with a broad mandate. The families wanted reform within the RCMP. "I pray that they fucking learn something," Darcy Dobson, who lost her mother, told me. "If nothing else, they learn something because they made some horrible, horrible mistakes. I'm trying to tread lightly . . . but they dropped the ball in Nova Scotia."

The inquiry report agreed: the RCMP has serious problems. The commission recommended that the Regina Depot boot camp—where every Mountie is trained, and where Louis Riel was hanged—should be shut down. Federal policing and "contract policing," the back-road work in places like Portapique, should be reformed after an independent review. The Liberals thanked the commissioners, helped pick up the tab, and placed the report on the shelf next to earlier reports, such as one by Michel Bastarache, that recommended the same things. Instead of ordering an independent review of contract policing, the government launched an internal review, which, given the history of the RCMP—a remarkably change-resistant organization—will not lead to the reform that is required. The RCMP, for its part, had by late 2023 implemented only two of the dozens of recommendations in the report.

Everybody who has studied the force knows that the RCMP needs to be torn apart and put back together again, and that the Mounties do not want to reform themselves. Only a determined government can do so. Trudeau does not have that determination. Pierre Trudeau did. In 1977, he ordered a public inquiry into dirty RCMP tricks and then implemented real reforms, taking away security intelligence and handing it to CSIS, a new agency. But fixing the RCMP again would be expensive and difficult, even perilous, because the Mounties can find ways of sandbagging politicians who threaten them. It would mostly be to the benefit of rural people and the officers driving down back roads, few of whom vote Liberal. Rural Canadians will likely have to wait for another prime minister to reform the RCMP.

———

EVEN PEOPLE WHO SUPPORT Trudeau acknowledge that his government is not effective in managing far down its to-do list. Insiders complain that everything gets jammed in Trudeau's office, so nothing gets done except for the top items that can be handled effectively by the small team of talented, hard-working staffers who are trusted by the boss. The best of the people around Trudeau are top-notch, but others seem to be there because he is comfortable with them, not because they are the best at what they do.

And Trudeau is a big-picture guy, not someone with the appetite or capacity to force progress on many different files. Anne McGrath, when she was negotiating a supply agreement on behalf of the NDP, was chiefly worried about whether the Liberals would manage to get done all the things they promised to do. "I would say implementation is their biggest weakness," she says. "And they know it."

These complaints are typical of all governments, but the record of inertia is undeniable. The linked issues of housing and immigration, for example, were allowed to get out of control until they reached crisis levels, at which point the government made a smart, sustained response. "They think the press release is the work product," one Ottawa insider told me. That is the conventional wisdom in Ottawa—the Trudeau operation is overly communications-focused and reactive. They do well on big files, but "even the top two or three, it's often in reaction to something as opposed to proactivity," says a friend of Trudeau. "I think, in response to COVID, in response to the threat to NAFTA, in response to x, y, and z . . ."

You could fill a whole book with examples of problems that have not been solved while Trudeau was prime minister. The RCMP, the CBC, and the Canadian Armed Forces—three vital national institutions—are all in worse shape than when he was elected. The federal public service, despite being 24 percent bigger, is not functioning better: the amount spent on outside consultants over the same period has almost doubled, up to $15.7 billion in 2023. To figure out how to bring that number down, the government hired KPMG, at a price tag of $669,650, to advise how to spend less on outfits like KPMG.

As the public service has grown, Canadians' faith in it has declined. It is easy to see why. There were long delays for passports when the COVID restrictions were lifted and Canadians were free to travel again. The surge ought to have been foreseeable, but many Canadians had to wait months, and some were forced to cancel or postpone trips.

Federal systems have become impossibly bureaucratic, so focused on human resources concerns and checking policy boxes that it has become very difficult to do anything. Senior Liberals talk frankly about it when they are sure they won't be quoted by name. "All the dotted lines, like the commissioner of environment and climate change, and getting a gender-based analysis, and the Official Languages commissioner and this list of accountabilities that a deputy minister has before you even get to talking to their minister," says one Liberal at the heart of the Trudeau government. "It's insane. We've layered on so much stuff that even good people, and there are lots of them, can't make their way through this. It takes two years to hire somebody."

When the Liberals govern, they are colonized by public servants, and colonize them in turn, until the country seems to be run by a remote and inward-looking apparatus for resisting accountability. The bad thing about this—for people who believe the government has a role to play in providing a social safety net and helping create opportunities for Canadians—is that it gets harder to have faith that government can accomplish anything. This doubt strengthens the arguments made by Poilievre, that it is time to get "gatekeepers" out of the way, to shrink government and focus on productivity—on "powerful paychecks."

It is tempting, when Canadians have grown so tired of Trudeau, to pass judgment, to point to his errors and say it is all his fault, that his government has failed, that Harper was right, that he wasn't actually ready. Robert Asselin, who helped convince Quebecers that Trudeau was ready, now has mixed feelings. He left the government in 2017 after serving as Bill Morneau's budget and policy director and is now senior vice-president of policy at the Business Council of Canada. He is critical of the government's approach to the economy. He gives Trudeau credit for work on diversity, pushing for meaningful climate policy, fighting poverty, and working on Indigenous reconciliation, but on other fronts he sees failure. "For me, the three tests for prime minister at the end of his tenure are: Are we better off on the world stage? No. The second is, Is the economy better? Has it been better for people, real wages, productivity, all this stuff? The answer, again, is no. The public finance stuff, too, is terrible. And the third is national unity. And I think on these three fronts—and I accept there were challenges that he could not control—but I think the country is worse off."

Brian Mulroney sees it differently. The former prime minister told me in 2023 that history will forget about the "trivia or the trash" that are often top of mind on Parliament Hill and look at Trudeau's accomplishments. "What has he done as a politician? Well, he took a third-place party, and he beat the shit out of a sitting prime minister. Then he turned around and defeated Andrew Scheer. Then he turned around and defeated O'Toole, and now he's gearing up to defeat Poilievre. So that's a pretty good political record. Then you have to look at, what did he do as prime minister? History will have lots of negative things to say about him, but I say that . . . he handled the pandemic, with the premiers, well, he did the negotiation with NAFTA well. Those are the big-ticket items."

At the beginning of 2024, it is difficult to have confidence that Justin Trudeau has the right answers, the right team, and the right ideas to tackle Canada's problems. Even if he did, it is hard to imagine him rallying enough support to bring Canadians together to do much of anything. Sunny ways have run their course, and Canadians seem ready for the wind.

Pierre Trudeau helps Justin climb a coconut tree at the Prospect Estate near Ocho Rios, Jamaica, in the 1970s. Trudeau has been going to the resort since he was in diapers.

National Library of Jamaica

BEING JUSTIN

On December 19, 2023, at the tail end of his year from hell, Trudeau sat down for an interview with the CBC's Rosemary Barton, who asked him to acknowledge that Poilievre had done a better job of understanding affordability concerns than he had. "Absolutely," Trudeau said, and then corrected himself. "It's not that he understood that. It's that he's done a really effective job of reflecting that back and amplifying that to people."

It's easier to blame everything on the government, Trudeau pointed out, than to do the complex and difficult things the government was doing to try to help people: "We're busy doing them and not just taking out YouTube space and amplifying those concerns."

Three days later, the Canadian Press had a story about Trudeau's holiday plans. On Boxing Day, the prime minister would be travelling to Jamaica with Sophie and the kids. CP reported that the office had cleared the details with interim ethics commissioner Konrad von Finckenstein and wrote that "the family will cover the cost of its stay."

That was not true. During the holidays, Glen McGregor saw a social media post of a family member that showed they were staying at Frankfort Villa in Ocho Rios, part of the Prospect Estate—a famously grand former slave plantation.

The villa, which rents for US$7,000 a night, is a stately two-storey manor built between verdant woods and a hundred-metre white-sand beach, with a swimming pool, an eight-person hot tub, six bedrooms with en suite baths, a chef, and concierge service. According to the website, it is "perhaps the most desirable north coast villa in Jamaica." Charlie Chaplin, Henry Kissinger, Noël Coward, and Ian Fleming all stayed there. Winston Churchill was fond of the turtle soup.

McGregor asked the PMO about the cost. Were the Trudeaus really spending US$7,000 a night to stay in such opulent surroundings? The PMO sent a clarification to the Canadian Press reporting that Trudeau was not paying for the trip but was staying "at no cost at a location owned by family friends." The headlines were not good. The Trudeaus had taken a free luxury trip from rich friends.

The Conservatives put out an attack ad contrasting Trudeau's lavish holiday with interviews with Canadians struggling to make ends meet. Conservative ethics critic Michael Barrett wrote to Konrad von Fincken-stein asking for an explanation. "A sitting prime minister accepting a gift of more than $80,000 in cash would certainly look suspicious and raise serious ethical questions," he said. "Accepting the non-cash equivalent should be no different."

The code allows MPs and prime ministers to accept hospitality from friends, and, unlike the Aga Khan, Trudeau had been close to the Greens for most of his life.

The Trudeau family has been going to Prospect Estate since Justin was in diapers. When he was an infant, Margaret convinced Pierre, who did not like vacations, to take her for a break at the nearby Jamaica Inn, in Ocho Rios. But that was not to be.

"Just a week before coming, my mom called down to find out if the Jamaica Inn had a diaper service or whether she needed to bring enough for the entire week," Trudeau told me in 2024. The inn wanted to know who the diapers were for. "For my baby, of course," said Margaret. "Oh, no, ma'am. There are no babies allowed. No children are allowed at the Jamaica Inn."

Margaret was rattled. She was afraid her longed-for vacation would be cancelled. She said, "'Oh no, I can't tell Pierre,'" Justin told me, "'because then he'll cancel the whole trip. And this vacation that we've been counting on, he'll just find it as an excuse not to go.'"

So she called the high commission in Kingston and asked them to find another place. The diplomats suggested they stay at the nearby Prospect Estate, a place owned by Sir Harold Mitchell, a British industrialist and politician who was vice-chair of the British Conservative Party under Churchill. The Trudeaus switched venues and became friends with Mitchell and his daughter, Mary-Jean. The families have been friends ever since, and the Trudeaus have often returned to the estate. In 1975, Mary-Jean married Canadian businessman Peter Green, and they had two sons, Alexander and Andrew.

"They had kids who were exactly two years younger than us," Trudeau told me. "So it was me, two years, Sach, two years, Miche, two years, Alexander, two years, Andrew. Right? So there are great pictures of the five of us. We used to spend every Easter together down on the beach."

An old photo shows Pierre helping Justin climb down from a coconut tree on an early visit. In 1989, a teenaged Justin planted a royal palm on the grounds, where it still stands with a little sign below. Pierre spoke at Mitchell Green's funeral, and Alexander, his godson, did a reading at Pierre's funeral. The two families often travelled together, and the Greens donated to the Trudeau Foundation.

The Greens were no doubt pleased to host the Trudeau family, just as many Canadians are glad to welcome old friends to a cottage. There was nothing unethical about it, but it was politically stupid.

The prime minister undercut his year-end message about how seriously his government was taking affordability, and, once again, he failed to communicate about his vacation plans proactively. In 2023, with so many Canadians counting their pennies in the grocery line, it seemed selfish to jet off to a luxury resort. The trip confirmed everything Poilievre and other critics were saying about him—that he is out of touch and disconnected from the struggles of ordinary Canadians. It is hard to argue otherwise.

Liberals in Ottawa gritted their teeth. Why couldn't the Trudeaus spare the government another messy holiday story? Trudeau had faced family pressure throughout his prime ministership to take Sophie and the kids to opulent holiday destinations, but now that he was separated he was still doing it. His senior staff, savvy veterans who knew very well how this story would land, surely made the same point before he arranged the stay, as they did before the Aga Khan trip. He has a blind spot about his vacations and won't be denied. After foreign trips have done so much damage to his brand, his insistence on carrying on this way seems perverse. He likely viewed the holiday as a chance for him to reconnect with his estranged wife in a place where they had enjoyed happy times, and for the kids to share his own history. "They have a walk they like to take, a waterfall they like to climb, and a view that they like to look at," says a friend. "And it's got sentimental value and memories to them that give them real joy."

He can almost be congratulated for putting family time ahead of politics, but it makes no sense. Trudeau may not be prime minister much longer, after all. He could have taken the children to a condo in Fort Lauderdale and slummed it among the middle class, just for a year, to avoid the terrible headlines, to ease things for his team. He could have paid for the trip. When you consider what is at stake—an election to lead the country he loves against an opponent he despises, with the hopes and dreams of so many people resting on his shoulders—it is hard to understand how he justified this holiday.

In an interview in 2024, I told him I didn't think it was a good idea because the cost-of-living crisis was top of mind for so many struggling Canadians.

"I understand that," he said. "Fair enough." He paused, thinking of how to explain himself. "We don't take a lot of vacations. Unlike some other political leaders in Canadian history, wherever I go, I get recognized," he said. "And most importantly, my kids sometimes ask, 'Dad, can you not come pick me up at my trampoline class, because it always makes such a big deal.' Giving my kids time where they can just be with me as I'm teaching them how to snorkel . . . there are limited places to go. Here's a place that I grew up in that I want to share with my kids. I mean, it's an impossible balance."

With his carefully guarded inner self, his stage-managed and scripted public appearances, and his unusual upbringing, Trudeau is hard to read. But he reveals himself through his actions. He believes he and his family belong at Prospect Estate—a beautiful place with special meaning for them—and he will not give up that legacy, even if it means angering typically parsimonious Canadians, handing ammunition to his critics, disappointing his team, and letting down the people who make personal sacrifices to get him elected. He sees this as his due, a conviction that comes from the same place as the confidence that allowed him to win Papineau, beat up Brazeau, take the third party to first, and trounce Harper, Scheer, and O'Toole.

That's just Justin.

ACKNOWLEDGEMENTS

A book like this takes a lot of conversations. I want to thank, first of all, all the people who agreed to talk to me but whose names appear nowhere in these pages. At Simon & Schuster Canada, I'd like to thank Kevin Hanson and Justin Stoller, who conceived of the idea for the book, and editors Rosemary Shipton, Jim Gifford, and Linda Pruessen, who corrected my many errors and patiently made the text better. I'd like to thank writers who gave me valuable advice: Mark Bourrie, Michael Harris, Lawrence Martin, Arthur Milnes, and Donald J. Savoie. I am indebted to many friends who helped me, in various important ways, while I was working on this book: Amir Attaran, Andrew Balfour, Kevin Bosch, Paul Champ, Lisa Cochrane, Carrie Croft, Dan and Danielle Davis, Moose Debone, Gary Dimmock, Donna Gabriel, Sophie Galarneau, Richard Greene, Frank Hall, Ana Ilha, Jenn Jefferys, Doug Jonah, Camille Labchuk, Jean-Frédérick Legendre, Quito Maggi, Susan MacQuarrie, Glen McGregor, Andrew Murphy, Greg Silver, Barb Stegemann, Robert Stevens, Melissa Stone, Gweneth Thirlwell, Mike Velemirovich, and Bruce Walsh. There are other names I have left out, erring on the side of discretion. You know who you are. Thanks to my mother, Elinor, who taught me to love books, Kelly and Bruce, Rena and Paul, Malcolm and Maggie, and cousin Dan.

SOURCES

The primary research for this book was conducted during more than two hundred confidential interviews carried out in 2022, 2023, and 2024 with current and former political staffers, public servants, politicians, lobbyists, and journalists. What follows is a partial list of documents, books, and publications consulted.

BECAUSE IT'S 2015

Peter Mansbridge, "Behind the Scenes with Justin Trudeau on His 1st Day as PM," CBC News, November 4, 2015.

Jennifer Ditchburn, "'Because It's 2015': Trudeau Forms Canada's 1st Gender-Balanced Cabinet," Canadian Press, November 4, 2015.

Jezebel (@Jezebel), "The sexiest thing about Canadian PM Justin Trudeau is his cabinet's gender parity," Twitter, November 4, 2015, 3:21 p.m., https://x.com/Jezebel/status/662001766989459456?.

Emma Watson (@EmmaWatson), "Why a gender balanced/50:50 government? 'Because it's 2015!' Coolest thing I've seen in a while. ❤U Canada. #Hefor she," Twitter, November 5, 2015, 9:20 a.m., https://x.com/EmmaWatson/status/662273218221314048?.

CHAPTER 1

Max Weber, "Politics as a Vocation" [published as "Politik als Beruf"], *Gesammelte Politische Schriften* (Munich, 1921).

Daniel Leblanc, "Trudeau's Vision for Liberals High on Ambition, Short on Firm Answers," *Globe and Mail*, October 2, 2012.

"Text of Justin Trudeau's Speech Announcing Leadership Bid," CBC News, October 2, 2012.

People, *Time*, March 21, 1977.

Justin Trudeau, *Common Ground* (Toronto: HarperCollins, 2014).

John English, *Just Watch Me: The Life of Pierre Elliott Trudeau, 1968–2000* (Toronto: Knopf Canada, 2009).

Jonathan Kay, "The Justin Trudeau I Can't Forget," *Walrus*, April 8, 2020.

Staff, "An Old Clip of Justin Trudeau Saying He Can't Do Simple Math Is Making Rounds," *Daily Hive*, April 21, 2022.

Kathy Larkin, "Margaret Trudeau Says She Likes Her New Freedom," *Toledo Blade*, November 30, 1977.

Jonathon Gatehouse, " 'When I Run': Justin Trudeau Considers Politics," *Maclean's*, December 23, 2002.

Lianne George, "When Justin Met Sophie," *Maclean's*, June 6, 2005.

John Powers, "Justin Trudeau Is the New Young Face of Canadian Politics," *Vogue*, December 9, 2015.

Daniel Leblanc, "Justin Trudeau Apologizes over French School Comment," *Globe and Mail*, May 7, 2007.

Meagan Fitzpatrick, "Justin Trudeau Apologizes for Swearing at Kent," CBC News, December 14, 2011.

Jessica Murphy, "Trudeau Backpedals on Separatism Comments," *Ottawa Sun*, February 14, 2012.

Aaron Wherry, "And Now a Word from Justin Trudeau," *Maclean's*, February 14, 2012.

Stephen Rodrick, "Justin Trudeau: The North Star," *Rolling Stone*, July 26, 2017.

Michael Den Tandt, "As Leadership Material, Justin Trudeau Is Nice but He's No Bob Rae," *National Post*, May 10, 2012.

Teresa-Elise Maiolino, "Identity Politicking: New Candidacies and Representations in Contemporary Canadian Politics" (PhD diss., University of Toronto, 2017).

Shannon Proudfoot, "Being Sacha Trudeau," *Maclean's,* September 8, 2016.

CHAPTER 2

Susana Mas, "Liberal MPs Murray and Garneau Challenge Frontrunner Trudeau," CBC News, March 3, 2013.

Glen McGregor, "Justin Trudeau Reveals Details of His $1.2-Million Inheritance," *Ottawa Citizen*, February 14, 2013.

Althia Raj, "NDP MP Breaks Silence on Allegations against Liberal MPs," *Huffington Post*, November 25, 2014.

Leslie MacKinnon, "Harper Slams Trudeau for Comments on Boston Bombings," CBC News, April 17, 2013.

Laura Payton, "Justin Trudeau Under Fire for Ukraine Joke," CBC News, February 24, 2014.

Aaron Wherry, "Further Clarifying Justin Trudeau's Position on Abortion Votes," *Maclean's*, June 18, 2014.

Andrea Janus, "PMO Decries Trudeau Joke That Canada Should Not 'Whip Out Our CF-18s,'" CTV News, October 2, 2014.

Kady O'Malley, "Eve Adams, Former Conservative MP, Joins Liberal Party," CBC News, February 9, 2015.

Simon Miles, "KGB Archives Show How Chrystia Freeland Drew the Ire (and Respect) of Soviet Intelligence Services," *Globe and Mail*, October 11, 2021.

Chrystia Freeland, *Plutocrats: The Rise of the New Global Super-Rich and the Fall of Everyone Else* (New York: Penguin, 2012).

CHAPTER 3

"Stephen Harper 'Gaming the System' with Early Election Call, Says Former Elections Canada Head," CBC Radio, August 1, 2015.

"Trudeau Will Exceed Expectations 'If He Comes on Stage with His Pants On': Harper Spokesperson on Debate," Canadian Press, August 5, 2015.

"Trudeau Suggests Policy on Quebec Secession, Bilingualism," Canadian Press, February 20, 2013.

Andrew Coyne, "The Moment Trudeau Had Mulcair's Number," *National Post*, October 14, 2015.

Bill Curry, "Mulcair Says NDP Would Balance Budget Despite Economic Woes," *Globe and Mail*, August 25, 2015.

"Justin Trudeau Accuses Tom Mulcair of 'Austerity' over Balanced Budget Pledge," CBC News, August 25, 2015.

"Justin Trudeau Says Liberals Plan 3 Years of Deficits to Push Infrastructure," CBC News, August 27, 2015.

Rachel Aiello, "Budget 2023 Prioritizes Pocketbook Help and Clean Economy, Deficit Projected at $40.1B," CTV News, March 28, 2023.

Denise Ryan, "Alan Kurdi: The Life and Death of the Boy on the Beach," *Vancouver Sun*, April 13, 2018.

Mark Kennedy, "Harper Defends Syria Stance after 'Heartbreaking' Death of Child Refugee," *Ottawa Citizen*, September 3, 2015.

Don Peat, "Trudeau Wants to Accept 25,000 Refugees," *Toronto Sun*, September 3, 2015.

"Appliance Repair Ripoffs Caught on Camera," *Marketplace* (CBC News), October 16, 2020.

"Jerry Bance, Conservative Caught Peeing in Mug, No Longer Candidate, Party Says," CBC News, September 6, 2015.

Stephen Maher, "Inside the Explosive Conservative Party Fight over Rick Dykstra," *Maclean's*, February 2, 2018.

Sean Fine and Gloria Galloway, "Ottawa Asks for Stay on Niqab Ruling Pending Supreme Court Appeal," *Globe and Mail*, September 18, 2015.

"Chris Alexander on 'Barbaric Cultural Practices': 'It's Why We Lost,'" CTV News, October 9, 2016.

"For the Record: Justin Trudeau's Rally Speech in Brampton," *Maclean's*, October 4, 2015.

"Pour un gouvernement Trudeau," *La Presse*, October 7, 2015.

Nancy Macdonald, "Trudeau Tours Western Canada with His Final Pitch," *Maclean's*, October 18, 2015.

David Frum (@davidfrum), "Like George W Bush campaigning hopelessly in California last weekend 2000, Justin Trudeau in Calgary to create false image of momentum," Twitter, October 18, 2015, 2:20 p.m., https://x.com/davidfrum/status/655810753509900288?.

"Liberal Campaign Co-chair Steps Down after Email to People behind Energy East with Lobbying Advice," Canadian Press, October 15, 2015.

Kevin Donovan and Jennifer Pagliaro, "Rob Ford: Crack Video Motive for Smith Murder, Police Told," *Toronto Star*, December 4, 2013.

Chris Selley, "Desperate Conservatives Embrace the Fords as Time Runs Out," *National Post*, October 18, 2015.

"Justin Trudeau, for the Record: 'We Beat Fear with Hope,'" *Maclean's*, October 20, 2015.

CHAPTER 4

Andrew Coyne, "Trudeau Cabinet Should be Based on Merit, Not Gender," *National Post*, November 2, 2015.

Julie Van Dusen, "Justin Trudeau Joyfully Mobbed by Federal Civil Servants," CBC News, November 6, 2015.

"Justin Jabs, Sophie Sings and Rona Rocks," *National Observer*, June 5, 2016.

Powers, "Justin Trudeau Is the New Young Face of Canadian Politics."

Catherine Porter, "How to Deal with an Angry Mob of Do-Gooders," *Toronto Star*, March 31, 2016.

"Welcome to Canada," *Toronto Star*, December 15, 2015.

Bill Morneau and John Lawrence Reynolds, *Where To from Here: A Path to Canadian Prosperity* (Toronto: ECW, 2023).

Andy Blatchford, "Justin Trudeau Says Vow to Balance Budget in 4 Years Is 'Very' Cast in Stone," Canadian Press, December 17, 2015.

Lucy Pavia, "Justin Trudeau: Full-Time Canadian Prime Minister, Part-Time Lover," *Marie Claire*, April 28, 2016.

Tonda MacCharles, "Justin Trudeau 'Manhandled' MP in Commons Uproar, Opposition Says," *Toronto Star*, May 18, 2016.

Marie Vastel, "Trudeau ne garantit plus une réforme électorale majeure," *Le Devoir*, October 19, 2016.

Chantal Hébert, "Electoral Reform Deck Appears Stacked by the Liberals to Fail," *Toronto Star*, May 12, 2016.

Robert Fife, "Hunter Tootoo's Messy Love Triangle Helped Spur Resignation from Cabinet," *Globe and Mail*, September 12, 2016.

John Paul Tasker, "Trudeau Offered Hug after Revelation of Addiction, Inappropriate Relationship, Tootoo Says," CBC News, September 7, 2016.

Laura Stone, "Top Trudeau Aides Butts, Telford Expensed over $200,000 for Moving Homes," *Globe and Mail*, September 21, 2016.

CHAPTER 5

John Ivison, "Trudeau Shows Trump Canada's Cards before He Sits Down," *National Post*, November 14, 2016.

Guy Lawson, "First Canada Tried to Charm Trump. Now It's Fighting Back," *New York Times Magazine,* June 9, 2018.

David Johnston (@GGCanada), "Where better to kick off #Canada150 than on Parliament Hill? That's where Sharon and I will be!" Twitter, December 31, 2016, 5:12 p.m., https://x.com/GGCanada/status/815319710514475012?.

David Akin, "As Canada Begins Celebrating 'Once-in-a-Lifetime' Anniversary, Trudeau Is in Some Other Country on Holiday," *National Post*, December 31, 2016.

Chris Selley, "It's 2017. Do You Know Where Your Prime Minister Is?" *National Post,* January 3, 2017.

David Akin, "Trudeau and Family Were New Year's Guests of the Aga Khan on His Private Bahamas Island," *National Post*, January 6, 2017.

David Akin, "Liberal MP, Party President Joined Trudeau for His Controversial Bahamas Vacation with the Aga Khan," *National Post,* January 11, 2017.

Adam Radwanski, "Meet Chrystia Freeland, the Woman Defining Canada's Foreign Role," *Globe and Mail*, August 12, 2017.

Aaron Wherry, *Promise and Peril: Justin Trudeau in Power* (Toronto: HarperCollins, 2019).

Justin Trudeau (@JustinTrudeau), "To those fleeing persecution, terror & war, Canadians will welcome you, regardless of your faith. Diversity is our strength #WelcomeToCanada," Twitter, January 28, 2017, 3:20 p.m., https://x.com/JustinTrudeau/status/825438460265762816?.

Ashifa Kassam, "Justin Trudeau Faces Tricky Balancing Act in Meeting with Donald Trump," *Guardian*, February 12, 2017.

Elizabeth Thompson, "Finance Minister Bill Morneau Waited 2 Years to Disclose Company That Owns His French Villa to Ethics Watchdog," CBC News, October 13, 2017.

Piers Morgan, "How Dare You Kill Off Mankind, Mr Trudeau, You Spineless Virtue-Signalling Excuse for a Feminist," *Daily Mail*, February 6, 2018.

Terry Milewski, "Convicted Attempted Murderer Invited to Reception with Trudeau in India," CBC News, February 21, 2018.

Sachin Parashar, "Dinner Invitation to Ex-terrorist Clouds Canadian PM Trudeau's Visit," *Times of India*, February 23, 2018.

John Ivison, "The Indian Government Removed Jaspal Atwal from Its Blacklist. Why?" *National Post*, February 22, 2018.

Bill Brioux, "John Oliver Says He Limits Trump Jokes, but Is Watching Canada-U.S. Trade War," Canadian Press, July 26, 2018.

CHAPTER 6

Bethany McLean and Peter Elkind, *The Smartest Guys in the Room: The Amazing Rise and Scandalous Fall of Enron* (New York: Penguin, 2003).

Richard Zussman and Karin Larsen, "NDP-Green Alliance to Focus on Electoral Reform, Stopping Kinder Morgan and Banning Big Money," CBC News, May 30, 2017.

Justin Trudeau, "Real Change in Canada-US Relations" (speech delivered to Canada 2020, June 23, 2015).

Evan Solomon, "Bill Morneau, Kinder Morgan and Texas Hold 'Em Bluffing," *Maclean's*, May 16, 2018.

John Geddes, "Why Trudeau Decided to Buy Trans Mountain—and Hopes to Sell It Again Soon," *Maclean's*, May 29, 2018.

Morneau and Reynolds, *Where To from Here*.

CHAPTER 7

Vincent Larouche, *La saga SNC-Lavalin, un thriller géopolitique* (Montreal, Éditions La Presse, 2021).

Dave Seglins, Rachel Houlihan, and Jonathan Monpetit, "What the SNC Board May Have Known about the Firm's Dealings in Libya—Like the Office Safe with $10M Cash," CBC News, April 15, 2019.

John Manley, "Canada Needs New Tools to Fight Corporate Wrongdoing," *Globe and Mail*, May 29, 2015.

Maurice Bulbulian, dir., "Dancing Around the Table" (National Film Board, 1987).

Jody Wilson-Raybould, *"Indian" in the Cabinet: Speaking Truth to Power* (Toronto: HarperCollins, 2021).

David Lametti interview, *Power & Politics* (CBC News), January 14, 2019.

Chantal Hébert, "Trudeau Plots a Steady Course with His Cabinet Shuffle," *Toronto Star*, January 14, 2019.

John Ivison, "Wilson-Raybould Couldn't Hide Her Disappointment at Move from Justice Minister," *National Post*, January 14, 2019.

Robert Fife, Steven Chase, and Sean Fine, "PMO Pressed Wilson-Raybould to Abandon Prosecution of SNC-Lavalin," *Globe and Mail*, February 7, 2019.

Trudeau news conference, *Power & Politics* (CBC News), February 7, 2019.

"PM Asserts Full Confidence in Wilson-Raybould amid Ethics Investigation," Canadian Press, February 11, 2019.

Robert Fife and Steven Chase, "Wilson-Raybould's Resignation Prompts Trudeau to Say She Failed in Duty to Voice SNC Concerns," *Globe and Mail*, February 12, 2019.

Mia Rabson, "Wilson-Raybould Entered Federal Politics Hoping to be a Bridge Builder," Canadian Press, February 9, 2019.

Stephen Maher, "The Incredible Miscalculation by Trudeau and Co.," *Maclean's*, February 13, 2019.

Wherry, *Promise and Peril*.

"Mulcair on Butts Resignation: 'They Know an Accusation Is Coming,'" CTV News, February 18, 2019.

The Federal Prosecution Service Deskbook (Ottawa: Her Majesty the Queen in Right of Canada, 2000, as represented by the Minister of Justice).

Morneau and Reynolds, *Where To from Here*.

At Issue Panel, *The National* (CBC News), March 6, 2019

Jesse Ferreras, "Trudeau Apologizes after Telling First Nations Mercury Poisoning Protester, 'Thank You for Your Donation,'" *Global News*, March 27, 2019.

"Jane Philpott Says Trudeau Broke the Law by Kicking Former Ministers out of Caucus," Canadian Press, April 9, 2019.

Andrew Willis, "Bank of Montreal Connection in the SNC Affair," *Globe and Mail*, August 14, 2019.

Nicolas Van Praet, "SNC-Lavalin Changes Name to AtkinsRéalis as Engineering Giant Looks to Forge New Identity," *Globe and Mail*, September 12, 2023.

CHAPTER 8

Lawson, "First Canada Tried to Charm Trump."

Daniel Dale, "Trump Tells Canada, Mexico He Won't Pull U.S. out of NAFTA," *Toronto Star*, April 26, 2017.

Alexander Panetta, "NAFTA Talks on Big Changes to Start This Year, U.S. Commerce Secretary Says," Canadian Press, March 8, 2017.

John Bolton, *The Room Where It Happened: A White House Memoir* (New York, Simon & Schuster, 2020).

Robert Lighthizer, *No Trade Is Free: Changing Course, Taking on China, and Helping America's Workers* (New York, Broadside Books, 2023).

Binyamin Appelbaum, "U.S. Begins NAFTA Negotiations with Harsh Words," *New York Times,* August 16, 2017.

Jared Kushner, *Breaking History: A White House Memoir* (New York: Broadside Books, 2022).

CNN Transcript, June 11, 2018.

Donald Trump (@realDonaldTrump), "PM Justin Trudeau of Canada acted so meek and mild during our @G7 meetings only to give a news conference after I left saying that, 'US Tariffs were kind of insulting' and he 'will not be pushed around.' Very dishonest & weak. Our Tariffs are in response to his of 270% on dairy!" Twitter, June 9, 2018, 7:04 p.m., https://twitter.com/realDonaldTrump/status/1005586562959093760.

Fox News, June 10, 2018.

Dan Bilefsky and Catherine Porter, "Trump's 'Bully' Attack on Trudeau Outrages Canadians," *New York Times*, June 18, 2018.

Mike Blanchfield, "In Washington to Talk about Trade and 'Absurd' Tariffs, Freeland Says 'Facts Matter,'" Canadian Press, June 13, 2018.

Aaron Wherry, *Promise and Peril.*

Ana Swanson, "Canada on the Sidelines as U.S. and Mexico Near an Agreement on NAFTA," *New York Times,* August 17, 2018.

Stephen A. Schwarzman, *What It Takes, Lessons in the Pursuit of Excellence* (London: Simon & Schuster, 2019).

Catharine Tunney, "Canada Needs Chapter 19 because Trump 'Doesn't Always Follow the Rules': Trudeau," CBC News, September 5, 2018.

Mark Landler and Alan Rappeport, "Trump Hails Revised NAFTA Trade Deal, and Sets Up a Showdown with China," *New York Times*, October 1, 2018.

Dairy Farmers of Canada, "Dairy Farmers' Livelihood Sacrificed Again," news release, October 1, 2018.

Kathleen Harris, "Trump, Trudeau Praise USMCA Trade Deal They Say Will 'Grow Middle Class,'" CBC News, October 1, 2018.

Stephen Maher, "Stephen Harper's No-Good Advice on NAFTA," *Maclean's*, October 30, 2017.

Chrystia Freeland (@cafreeland), "We don't agree w former PM Harper's advice. We will continue to defend Canadian interests. Capitulation is not a negotiating strategy #NAFTA," Twitter, October 27, 2017, 7:55 p.m., https://x.com/cafreeland/status/924061937264222210?.

Lawrence Martin, *Harperland: The Politics of Control* (Toronto: Penguin, 2011).

Ken Thomas and Rob Gillies, "Trump Hails NAFTA Revamp, Trudeau Calls It 'Win-Win-Win'," Associated Press, October 1, 2018.

CHAPTER 9

Anna Purna Kambhampaty, Madeleine Carlisle, and Melissa Chanup, "Justin Trudeau Wore Brownface at 2001 'Arabian Nights' Party While He Taught at a Private School," *Time*, September 19, 2019.

"Man Who Shared Trudeau Blackface Photo Says Canadians Had a Right to See It," CBC News, September 27, 2019.

Lawrence Martin, *Iron Man: The Defiant Reign of Jean Chrétien* (Toronto: Penguin, 2003).

Stephen Maher, "Jagmeet Singh's Moment. Andrew Scheer's Opportunity," *Maclean's*, September 19, 2019.

"Justin Trudeau Apologizes for Brownface and Blackface Photos," CBS News, September 19, 2019.

John Paul Tasker, "'I Am Personally Pro-Life,' Scheer Says, Vowing Not to Re-open Abortion Debate," CBC News, October 3, 2019.

Robert Fife and Janice Dickson, "Conservative Leader Andrew Scheer Holds Dual Canadian-U.S. Citizenship, Had Attacked Michaëlle Jean on Same Issue," *Globe and Mail*, October 3, 2019.

"Scheer Accused of Falsely Claiming He Was Once an Insurance Broker in Saskatchewan," Canadian Press, September 30, 2019.

Catharine Tunney, "Singh Distances Himself from Coalition Talk as Campaign Enters Final Week," CBC News, October 14, 2019.

Stephen Maher, "Andrew Scheer's Moment of Truth," *Maclean's*, November 5, 2019.

Warren Kinsella, *Web of Hate: Inside Canada's Far Right Network* (Toronto: HarperCollins, 1996).

Bill Curry and Tom Cardoso, "Kinsella Firm Hired to 'Seek and Destroy' Bernier's People's Party, Documents Show," *Globe and Mail*, October 18, 2019.

Andrea Bellemare and Kaleigh Rogers, "Recordings Reveal Details of Campaign to Attack Maxime Bernier, PPC as Racists before Election," CBC News, November 26, 2019.

Allison Jones, "Scheer Won't Say If Conservatives Hired Consultant to 'Destroy' People's Party," Canadian Press, October 19, 2019.

Kathleen Harris and Hannah Thibedeau, "Scheer's Conservatives Missed Scoring 'on an Open Net,' Peter MacKay Says as Leadership Talk Heats Up," CBC News, October 30, 2019.

CHAPTER 10

Fen Osler Hampson and Mike Blanchfield, *The Two Michaels: Innocent Canadian Captives and High Stakes Espionage in the US-China Cyber War* (Toronto: Sutherland House, 2021).

Helen Davidson, Vincent Ni, and Leyland Cecco, "Meng Wanzhou: 'Princess of

Huawei' Who Became the Face of a High-Stakes Dispute," *Guardian*, August 19, 2021.

Chuin-Wei Yap, "State Support Helped Fuel Huawei's Global Rise," *Wall Street Journal*, December 25, 2019.

Natalie Obiko Pearson, "Did a Chinese Hack Kill Canada's Greatest Tech Company?" *Bloomberg Businessweek*, July 1, 2020.

Steve Stecklow and Babak Dehghanpisheh, "Huawei Hid Business Operation in Iran after Reuters Reported Links to CFO," Reuters, July 14, 2020.

"Chinese State Media Says U.S. Trying to 'Stifle' Huawei with Arrest," Reuters, December 6, 2018.

David Cochrane, "Canada Had No Choice But to Arrest Huawei Executive at Washington's Request: Expert," CBC News, December 7, 2018.

Ben Blanchard and David Ljunggren, "China Urges Canada to Free Huawei CFO or Face Consequences," Reuters, December 9, 2018.

Nathan Vanderklippe, "China Charges Canadians Michael Kovrig and Michael Spavor with Espionage," *Globe and Mail*, June 19, 2020.

Jeff Mason and Steve Holland, "Trump Says He Could Intervene in U.S. Case Against Huawei CFO," Reuters, December 11, 2018.

John Paul Tasker, "Canada's Ambassador to China Says Meng Has Strong Defence to Fight Extradition," CBC News, January 23, 2019.

Catharine Tunney, "John McCallum Fired as Ambassador to China Amid Diplomatic Crisis," CBC News, January 26, 2019.

Austin Ramzy and Dan Bilefsky, "Chinese Court Rejects Canadian's Appeal of Death Sentence for Drug Trafficking," *New York Times*, August 9, 2021.

Robert Fife and Steven Chase, "Spavor Blames Fellow Prisoner Kovrig for Chinese Detention, Alleges He Was Used for Intelligence Gathering," *Globe and Mail*, November 18, 2023.

Stephane Levitz, "Freed China Detainee Michael Kovrig Breaks Silence, Says Allegations Linked to Michael Spavor Are 'Baffling' and 'Hurtful,'" *Toronto Star*, November 24, 2023.

Mike Blanchfield, "White Supremacy a Factor in Detainees Cases, Chinese Ambassador Charges," Canadian Press, January 9, 2019.

"Mr. Xi, Release These Two Canadian Citizens," *Globe and Mail*, January 21, 2019.

CHAPTER 11

Stephen Maher, "Cancel Your March Break," *Maclean's*, March 12, 2020.

Tom Cardoso and Chen Wang, " 'We Could Have Saved Lives': Did Ottawa's Spring Break COVID-19 Travel Advisory Come Too Late?" *Globe and Mail*, May 4, 2020.

Robyn Merrett, "Idris Elba and Sophie Trudeau Posed for a Photo Together Days before Testing Positive for Coronavirus," *People*, March 16, 2020.

Stephen Maher, "Escape from Florida: My 2,400-km Drive Back to the Sanity of Canada," *Maclean's*, March 24, 2020.

Mark Gollom, " 'Frustrating and Challenging': Canadians Abroad Struggle to Find a Flight Home," CBC News, March 17, 2020.

Bill Blair (@BillBlair), "We have enhanced screening measures in place at all international airports, as well as land/rail/marine ports of entry. We are taking the necessary steps to ensure that Canadians are safe in the face of COVID-19," Twitter, March 13, 2020, 9:50 p.m., https://x.com/BillBlair/status/1238643631218741248?.

Phil Tsekouras, "Travellers at Pearson Airport Report Lack of COVID-19 Screening," CTV News, March 15, 2020.

Stephen Maher, "Year One: The Untold Story of the Pandemic in Canada," *Maclean's*, March 24, 2021.

Kathleen Harris, "Trudeau Says 'Knee-Jerk Reactions' Won't Stop Spread of COVID-19," CBC News, March 5, 2020.

Teresa Tam and Karen Grimsrud, *The Canadian Pandemic Influenza Plan for the Health Sector* (Ottawa: Her Majesty the Queen in Right of Canada, December 2006).

Aaron Derfel, "Public Health, Police Find Bodies, Feces at Dorval Seniors' Residence: Sources," *Montreal Gazette*, April 10, 2020.

Peter Evans, "TSX Shut Down for 'Technical Halt' as Stock Markets Sell Off," CBC News, February 27, 2020.

Morneau and Reynolds, *Where To from Here*.

Darryl Greer, "More Than 1,000 Canadians Take CRA to Court over Pandemic Payments—and Some Win," CBC News, July 12, 2023.

Jordan Press, "No Evidence of Trudeau Contact with WE Charity before Deal Awarded: Top Public Servant," Canadian Press, July 21, 2020.

Paul Waldie, "Bill Morneau's Office, Kielburgers Described as 'Besties' in Newly Released Documents," *Globe and Mail*, August 19, 2020.

House of Commons, Standing Committee on Finance meeting, July 22, 2020.

Steve Scherer, "Canada's Trudeau Apologizes for 'Mistake' amid Charity Uproar," Reuters, July 13, 2020.

Marieke Walsh and Bill Curry, "Trudeau, Morneau Apologize for Not Recusing Themselves from WE Charity Contract Decision," *Globe and Mail*, July 13, 2020.

Ryan Maloney and Zi-Ann Lum, "Bill Morneau Resigns as Finance Minister amid WE Charity Controversy," *Huffington Post*, August 17, 2020.

Robert Fife, "Finance Minister Bill Morneau's Job Could Be in Jeopardy after Clashes with Prime Minister, Sources Say," *Globe and Mail*, August 10, 2020.

CHAPTER 12

Stephen Maher, "Jason Kenney's Endorsement of Erin O'Toole Is Unusual, but Could Also Deliver a Powerful Boost to a Campaign Already on the Upswing," *Maclean's*, March 5, 2020.

John Paul Tasker, "Conservative Caucus Revolt Triggers Vote on Erin O'Toole's Leadership," CBC News, January 31, 2022.

Stephen Maher, "What Wouldn't Erin O'Toole Do to Win?" *Maclean's*, February 14, 2020.

Brian Platt, "'You Have Given Me a Clear Mission': Erin O'Toole Wins Conservative Leadership Race on Third Ballot," *National Post*, August 24, 2020.

"Andrew Scheer Compares Left-Wing Rhetoric to Communism in Final Speech as Party Leader," Global News, August 23, 2020.

Tonda MacCharles, "Behind the Scenes, Conservatives Know That Erin O'Toole Must Make Party Unity His First Priority," *Toronto Star*, August 24, 2020.

Alex Boutilier, "After Riding Social Conservative Support to Leadership Victory, Erin O'Toole Reaffirms He's 'Pro-choice,'" *Toronto Star*, August 25, 2020.

Anja Karadeglija, "Budget Criticism but No Election Calls, Though O'Toole Seeks Change on Economic Growth," *National Post*, April 20, 2021.

Aaron Wherry, "Elections Matter—and This One May Matter More Than Most," CBC News, August 16, 2021.

Cameron French, "O'Toole a 'Political Freight Train' as Conservatives Take Clear Lead: Nanos," CTV News, September 3, 2021.

Stephen Maher, "If O'Toole Hopes to Keep His 'Freight Train' on the Tracks, He'll Need to Address a Lot of Tough Issues about the Economy, Climate, Race and Gun Control," *Maclean's*, September 5, 2021.

Marieke Walsh, Bill Curry, and Laura Stone, "Conservatives Would Repeal Ban on Guns Used in École Polytechnique, Nova Scotia Mass Shootings," *Globe and Mail*, September 3, 2021.

Darren Major, "O'Toole Reverses Course on Guns, Will Maintain Liberal Ban during Review of Classifications," CBC News, September 5, 2021.

David Lao, "No Plans for 'Divisive' Vaccine Passports for Canadians, Trudeau Says," Global News, January 14, 2021.

John Paul Tasker, "Trudeau Warns of 'Consequences' for Public Servants Who Duck COVID-19 Shots," CBC News, August 17, 2021.

Elizabeth Thompson, "Bernier's Talk of 'Tyranny' Echoes Far Right Militia Group's Slogan, Say Experts," CBC News, September 10, 2021.

Stephen Maher, "Canada Has Shifted to the Left," *Maclean's*, September 22, 2021.

Stephen Maher, "The Ruthless Math of Political Campaigns: Is Big Data Bad for Democracy?" *Walrus*, April 21, 2023.

CHAPTER 13

Toronto Star. "PM Justin Trudeau's Year-End Interview with Terry DiMonte," YouTube video, 32:09, December 30, 2021. https://www.youtube.com/watch?v= NWUXfwKlzLk.

Olivia Stefanovich, "Flags Will Remain at Half-Mast until Agreement Is Reached with Indigenous Leaders: Trudeau," CBC News, September 10, 2021.

"Residential School Survivors, Trudeau Speak on Eve of National Day for Truth and Reconciliation," CBC News, September 29, 2021.

The Current, CBC News, October 18, 2021.

Jody Wilson-Raybould (@Puglaas), "True reconciliation begins with showing up. #EveryChildMatters," Twitter, September 30, 2021, 5:07 p.m., https://x.com/Puglaas /status/1443683917131751424?.

"Trudeau Visits First Nation to Apologise after Holiday Snub," BBC News, October 18, 2021.

Aaron Wherry, "Trudeau Strikes a Triumphant Tone after an Election That Was His to Lose," CBC News, September 28, 2021.

Steve Scherer, "Canada's Trudeau Exploits Rival's Split on Vaccines as Parliament Reconvenes," Reuters, November 16, 2021.

Public Order Emergency Commission hearing, November 1, 2022 (testimony of Brigitte Belton), https://publicorderemergencycommission.ca/files/documents /Transcripts/POEC-Public-Hearings-Volume-14-November-1-2022.pdf.

John G. Smith, "Belton Describes Journey from TikTok Video to Freedom Convoy Avatar," Trucknews.com, November 1, 2022.

Rachel Gilmore, " 'Fringe Minority' in Truck Convoy with 'Unacceptable Views' Don't Represent Canadians: Trudeau," Global News, January 26, 2022.

Public Order Emergency Commission hearing, October 14, 2022 (testimony of Zexi Li), https://publicorderemergencycommission.ca/files/documents/Transcripts /POEC-Public-Hearings-Volume-2-October-14-2022.pdf.

Jonathan Kay, "Canada's Truck Convoy Is Just a Stunt in a Country Where Populism Is Still Taboo," *Washington Post*, February 7, 2022.

Edward Riche, "Protest? Occupation? As the Diesel Fumes Dissipate in Ottawa, Words Fail Us," CBC News, February 26, 2022.

Richard Hofstadter, "The Paranoid Style in American Politics," *Harper's Magazine*, November 1964.

Canada Unity Memorandum of Understanding, Public Order Emergency Commission exhibits, no date.

David Ljunggren and Steve Scherer, "Canada's Trudeau 'Not Intimidated' by Truckers' COVID Protest," Reuters, January 31, 2022.

Shaamini Yogaretnam, "Ottawa Police Officer Charged after Racist Meme Circulates, Chief Addresses Criticisms of Police," *Ottawa Citizen*, June 2, 2020.

Michael Woods, "Ottawa Police Chief Has 'Lost the Room': Union President," CTV News (Ottawa), September 10, 2020.

Alistair Steele, "Ottawa Police Confirm Internal Investigation Involving Convoy Report Author," CBC News, November 9, 2022.

David Shield, "Mayor of Ottawa Demands Apology after Sask. Conservative MPs, Senator Take Picture at Convoy Protest," CBC News, February 3, 2022.

Alistair Steele, "Ottawa Wasn't Province's Top Priority during Convoy Protests, Ford told Trudeau," CBC News, November 8, 2022.

Ian Austen and Dan Bilefsky, "Trudeau Declares Rare Public Emergency to Quell Protests," *New York Times*, February 14, 2022.

Catharine Tunney, "Federal Government Invokes Emergencies Act for First Time Ever in Response to Protests, Blockades," CBC News, February 14, 2022.

"Liberal MP Joël Lightbound's Full Remarks: 'It's Time to Choose Positive, Not Coercive Methods,'" *National Post*, February 8, 2022.

Robert Fife, Marieke Walsh, Janice Dickson, and Erin Anderssen, "Police Move in to Clear Downtown Ottawa of Convoy Protesters after Weeks of Demonstrations," *Globe and Mail*, February 18, 2022.

Marieke Walsh, Marsha McLeod, and Bill Curry, "Trudeau Says He Made the 'Right Choice' to Use Emergencies Act to End Convoy Protests," *Globe and Mail*, November 25, 2022.

Nomi Claire Lazar, *States of Emergency in Liberal Democracies* (London, UK: Cambridge University Press, 2009).

Marsha McLeod and Marieke Walsh, "Trudeau's Use of Emergencies Act Was Appropriate, Inquiry Finds," *Globe and Mail*, February 17, 2023.

Marieke Walsh and Sean Fine, "Invoking Emergencies Act Wasn't Justified and Infringed on Charter Rights, Federal Court Rules," *Globe and Mail*, January 23, 2024.

Pierre Poilievre (@PierrePoilievre),"BREAKING: Judge rules Trudeau broke the highest law in the land with the Emergencies Act. He caused the crisis by dividing people. Then he violated Charter rights to illegally suppress citizens. As PM, I will unite our country for freedom," Twitter, January 24, 2024, 1:28 p.m., https://x.com/PierrePoilievre/status/1749861629607477294?s=20.

Tucker Carlson, "What's Happening to Truckers in Canada Reveals the Future of the United States," Fox News, February 21, 2022.

Melissa Fine, "Russell Brand Destroys Justin Trudeau in under Two Minutes Flat Using Russia-Ukraine Backdrop," *American Wire*, March 14, 2022.

Andy Blatchford, "With the World Watching Putin, Trump Targets Trudeau," *Politico*, February 27, 2022.

Brian Stelter, "This Infamous Steve Bannon Quote Is Key to Understanding America's Crazy Politics," CNN Business, November 16, 2021.

Stephen Maher, "Liberal and NDP Officials Mull Over a Potential Deal," *Maclean's*, October 29, 2021.

Ian Austen, "Trudeau Strikes Accord with Opponents to Secure Hold on Power," *New York Times*, March 22, 2022.

"Canada's NDP Agrees to Support Trudeau's Liberals until 2025," BBC, March 22, 2022.

CHAPTER 14

Stephen Maher, "Harper Apologizes, but His Attack Dog Keeps Barking," *Chronicle Herald*, June 14, 2008.

Stephen Maher, "The Word Is 'Espite'lsit': What a Residential Schools Survivor Tells Me about Pierre Poilievre's Worst Moment in Public Life," iPolitics, December 28, 2022.

Campbell Clark, "The Making of Pierre Poilievre, Conservative Proselytizer," *Globe and Mail*, September 16, 2022.

Bruce Cheadle, "Chief Electoral Officer Strikes Back at Government's Claim He Wears 'Team Jersey,' " Canadian Press, February 6, 2014.

"Quotes about Finance Minister Bill Morneau's Blind Trust Announcement," Canadian Press, October 19, 2017.

" 'Nobody Believes You': Poilievre Grills Trudeau as He Testifies over WE Charity Controversy," CTV News, July 31, 2020.

Alex Boutilier, "Pierre Poilievre's YouTube Channel Included Hidden Misogynistic Tag to Promote Videos," Global News, October 6, 2022.

Darren Major, "Pierre Poilievre Becomes First MP to Bid for Conservative Party Leadership," CBC News, February 5, 2022.

Frank Graves and Stephen Maher, "Pierre Poilievre: The Secret to His Success," *Walrus*, June 20, 2023.

"Poilievre Faces Off with Trudeau: 'Ground the Jet, Park the Hypocrisy, and Axe the Tax Hikes,'" Global News, September 22, 2022.

"Quotes about Pierre Poilievre's Conservative Leadership Victory," Canadian Press, September 10, 2022.

"2022 Fall Economic Statement," Department of Finance Canada, November 3, 2022.

Sarah Ritchie, "Freeland's Disney+ Comment Made Her a Villain, Records Show," Canadian Press, April 19, 2023.

Brian Kelly, "Poilievre Vows to Build Homes, Cut Tax," *Sault Star*, July 27, 2023.

CHAPTER 15

"Remarks by Director David Vigneault to the Centre for International Governance Innovation, Public Safety Canada," February 9, 2021.

Stephen Maher, "How to Prevent Foreign Interference in Elections," *Walrus*, May 15, 2023.

Walied Soliman (@waliedesq), "What's worse: our party was seeing clear signs of tampering in ridings with substantial Chinese diasporas. We made the conscious decision to work through the Task Force and appropriate security channels. Our concerns were never taken seriously," Twitter, February 17, 2023, 8:24 a.m.

John Paul Tasker, "As Conservatives Call for Crackdown, O'Toole Calls Chinese Influence a Grave 'Threat' to Canada," CBC News, November 17, 2020.

Helen Davidson, "China Ambassador Makes Veiled Threat to Hong Kong-Based Canadians," *Guardian*, October 16, 2020.

Han Dong speech, *As It Happens*, CBC Radio, March 23, 2023.

Robert Fife and Steven Chase, "Trudeau Government Decided CSIS Transcript of MP Han Dong Provided No 'Actionable Evidence,'" *Globe and Mail*, March 23, 2023.

Mickey Djuric, "'Fake Job': Poilievre Won't Meet Watchdog Investigating Foreign Interference," Canadian Press, May 18, 2023.

Leyland Cocco, "Canadian Special Rapporteur Rules Out Inquiry into Chinese Interference Claims," *Guardian*, May 23, 2023.

Christian Paas-Lang, "'Appearance of Bias' Undermines Special Rapporteur's Mission, Singh Says," CBC News, June 4, 2023.

Aaron Wherry, "Justin Trudeau and Sophie Grégoire Trudeau Announce Separation," CBC News, August 2, 2023.

Ian Brown, "The Challenge: In Search of the Real Justin Trudeau," *Globe and Mail*, October 2, 2015.

Justin Trudeau (@JustinTrudeau), "Happy birthday, Sophie. From this, to this, and everything in between, there's no one I'd rather have by my side . . . I love you, mon amour," Twitter, April 24, 2023, 8:12 a.m., https://x.com/JustinTrudeau/status/1650472882873462788?.

Claudia Aoraha, "Justin Trudeau's Wife Sophie Grégoire Was on Meghan Markle's Failed Archetypes Podcast and Exclaimed Women 'All Long to Be Free in Who We Are'—Months before Their Separation," *Daily Mail*, August 2, 2023.

Glen McGregor, "Sophie Grégoire Trudeau 'Re-partnered' with Ottawa Doctor, Ex-Wife Claims in Divorce Petition," *National Post*, October 25, 2023.

Catherine Zhu, "Sophie Grégoire Trudeau Publishing Two Books on the Importance of Personal and Collective Wellness," CBC Books, May 19, 2023.

Catherine Lévesque, "Poilievre's Speech to Conservatives Focuses on Message of 'Hope' for Canadians Who Have Lost Theirs," *National Post*, September 8, 2023.

Tom Mulcair, "Take a Closer Look at What Pierre Poilievre Is Peddling," CTV News, September 11, 2023.

Fred DeLorey, "Trudeau's Exit—A Cautionary Note for the Liberals," iPolitics, August 30, 2023.

Susan Delacourt, "Here's Why Justin Trudeau Went Public with an Explosive Allegation against India," *Toronto Star*, September 19, 2023.

Evan Dyer and Alexander Panetta, "Canada Has Indian Diplomats' Communications in Bombshell Murder Probe: Sources," CBC News, September 21, 2023.

"At G20, PM Modi Points Out 'Anti-India Activities' in Canada to Justin Trudeau," *India Today*, September 10, 2023.

Dylan Robertson, "Saskatchewan Government Accuses Trudeau of Keeping Provinces in the Dark about Trade Talks with India," Canadian Press, September 12, 2023.

John Paul Tasker, "Trudeau Accuses India's Government of Involvement in Killing of Canadian Sikh Leader," CBC News, September 18, 2023.

Sadanand Dhume, "Why Indians Can't Stand Justin Trudeau," *Wall Street Journal*, September 27, 2023.

Kyle Duggan, "Nazi-Linked Veteran Received Ovation during Zelenskyy's Canada Visit," *Politico*, September 24, 2023.

"Trudeau's Plane Had Cocaine During G20, Claims Former Indian Diplomat," *Toronto Sun*, September 26, 2023.

CHAPTER 16

Guy Lawson, "Trudeau's Canada, Again," *New York Times*, December 8, 2015.

Pierre Elliott Trudeau, *The Essential Trudeau*, ed. Ron Graham (Toronto: McClelland & Stewart, 1998).

Charles Foran, "The Canada Experiment: Is This the World's First 'Post-National' Country?" *Guardian*, January 4, 2017.

Livio Di Matteo, "Canada Must Grow Denser and More Populated," Fraser Institute, September 1, 2018.

Walkom, Thomas, "Justin Trudeau Is Acting as 'Head Waiter to the Provinces': His Father Would Be Horrified," *Toronto Star*, June 2, 2021.

Stephen Maher, "It Was Chrétien's Night, but It's Trudeau's Party," iPolitics, May 7, 2023.

Don Martin, "The Fall of Justin Trudeau Has Begun," CTV News, June 14, 2022.

Toronto Star. "PM Justin Trudeau's Year-End Interview with Terry Di Monte," YouTube video.

Chris Hannay, "Obama Says 'NATO Needs More Canada,' and Trudeau Obliges," *Globe and Mail*, June 30, 2016.

Alexander Panetta, "U.S. Report Claims Trudeau Told NATO Canada Will Never Meet Its Military Spending Target," CBC News, April 19, 2023.

Sarah Katherine Gibson, "Dreams of a 'Fireproof House,'" *Kingston Whig-Standard*, September 16, 2013.

Stephen Maher, "The RCMP Keep Failing, People Keep Dying. After Portapique, They Shouldn't Get Another Chance," *Toronto Star*, April 8, 2023.

Stephen Maher, "The RCMP Is Broken," *Maclean's*, July 9, 2020.

BEING JUSTIN

Darren Major and Rosemary Barton, "PM Trudeau Gives Poilievre Credit for Tapping into Canadians' Concerns about Affordability," CBC News, December 19, 2023.

"Trudeau Family to Jet to Jamaica for Post-Christmas Sun Vacation," Canadian Press, December 22, 2023.

Glen McGregor, "Trudeau Given Free Stay at $9,300-a-Night Luxury Jamaican Villa over Christmas Holidays," *National Post*, January 4, 2024.

Stephanie Levitz, "Pierre Poilievre's Conservatives Ask Why Justin Trudeau Was Allowed to Accept $80,000 'Gift,'" *Toronto Star*, January 10, 2024.

INDEX